This collection of essays seeks to answer the following question: when Christians speak of the death of Christ as a sacrifice what have they meant and does it make sense today? The political and psychological connotations of sacrificial language have in modern times given rise to great unease. The book contains studies of these difficult and controversial matters at the formative moments in history, from Old Testament times to contemporary theology. The variety of points of view expressed reflects the diversity of modern approaches to this topic.

SACRIFICE AND REDEMPTION

DURHAM ESSAYS IN THEOLOGY

SACRIFICE AND REDEMPTION

DURHAM ESSAYS IN THEOLOGY

EDITED BY

S. W. SYKES
Bishop of Ely

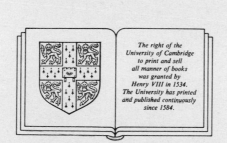

The right of the
University of Cambridge
to print and sell
all manner of books
was granted by
Henry VIII in 1534.
The University has printed
and published continuously
since 1584.

CAMBRIDGE UNIVERSITY PRESS

Cambridge
New York   Port Chester
Melbourne   Sydney

Published by the Press Syndicate of the University of Cambridge
The Pitt Building, Trumpington Street, Cambridge CB2 1RP
40 West 20th Street, New York, NY 10011, USA
10 Stamford Road, Oakleigh, Melbourne 3166, Australia

First published 1991

Printed in Great Britain at the University Press, Cambridge

British Library cataloguing in publication data

Sykes, S. W. (Stephen Whitefield) 1939–
Sacrifice and redemption
1. Jesus Christ. Sacrifice
1. Title
232'.4

Library of Congress cataloguing in publication data

Sacrifice and redemption: Durham essays in theology / edited by S. W. Sykes.
p.   cm.
Includes index.
ISBN 0-521-34033-0
1. Sacrifice–Christianity–History of doctrines. 2. Sacrifice–Biblical teaching. 3.
SAcrifice–Comparative studies. 4. Lord's Supper–Sacrifice–History of doctrines. 5.
Atonement–History of doctrines. 1. Sykes, Stephen.
BT263.S23   1990
232'.4–dc20   89-35779

ISBN 0 521 34033 0 hardback

CONTENTS

vii

viii CONTENTS

CONTRIBUTORS

Mr Gerald Bonner: Emeritus Reader in Theology, University of Durham

Dr A. N. Chester: Lecturer in Divinity, University of Cambridge

Professor I. U. Dalferth: Stellvertretender Ephorus, Evangelisches Stift, Tübingen

Dr George Dion Dragas: Senior Lecturer in Theology, University of Durham

Professor J. D. G. Dunn: Professor of Divinity, University of Durham

Dr P. J. FitzPatrick: Reader in Philosophy, University of Durham

Dr A. Gelston: Reader in Theology, University of Durham

Dr S. W. Gilley: Senior Lecturer in Theology, University of Durham

Dr S. Hardman Moore: John Laing Lecturer in the History and Theology of the Reformation, University of Edinburgh

Dr R. Hayward: Lecturer in Theology, University of Durham

Professor Edward Hulmes: Spalding Professorial Fellow in World Religions, Department of Theology, University of Durham

Professor D. R. Jones: Emeritus Professor of Divinity, University of Durham

Dr A. L. Loades: Senior Lecturer in Theology, University of Durham

Dr J. F. McHugh: formerly Senior Lecturer in Theology, University of Durham

Dr George Pattison: Rector, Badwell Ash, Suffolk

Dr Alan M. Suggate: Lecturer in Theology, University of Durham

The Right Reverend S. W. Sykes: Bishop of Ely

PREFATORY NOTE

All the authors represented in this collection teach or have taught in Durham's Department of Theology, except Dr FitPatrick who is Reader in the Department of Philosophy, and Dr George Pattison who was a research student working under Dr Loades. The editor wishes to express his deep gratitude to his former colleagues and members of the department for their friendship over eleven exceptionally happy years, and to thank them for their forbearance during the protracted period of this book's production.

INTRODUCTION

S.W. SYKES

It is a characteristic of contemporary ecumenical theology to refer to the 'sacrifice of Christ' without further elaboration. Doubtless the wholly understandable reason for this is the need to find a commonly agreed point of reference from which to tackle the hotly disputed question of the eucharistic sacrifice. All the major Christian traditions have affirmed that Christ's death is sacrificial in character; a typical ecumenical statement can accordingly be framed in the following terms:

The eucharist is the sacrament of the unique sacrifice of Christ, who ever lives to make intercession for us. (From the Lima Document of the World Council of Churches, *Baptism, Eucharist and Ministry*, Faith and Order Paper 111, p. 11)

But the truth of the matter is that in modern times there has been no agreement about the nature of sacrifice, and thus no agreement about the sense in which the interpretation of Christ's 'sacrificial' death is to be understood. The statements constitute, in effect, a consensus that this language should remain in circulation. But as a point of departure for further terminological qualification, for example in the phrase 'sacrament of a sacrifice', they are necessarily unstable.

The controversial and wide-ranging work of René Girard, much of which has been appearing during the period of the gestation of this book, will ensure the continued currency of sacrifice as a theological issue in the next decades. Although biblical study and theology have been in fruitful conversation for a century with social anthropology, there is some evidence that its revival will catch theology unprepared (McKenna 1985). The reason for this seems to be that while contemporary Protestant theology has been growing progressively disenchanted with sacrificial language, it has apparently not been a vibrant part of those theological traditions with a continuing investment in it. The theology of the atonement has not recently been a lively aspect of the discipline.

The essays in this volume, which represent explorations of the theme of sacrifice from a number of contributors, most but not all of whom are

I

members of one British Department of Theology, suggest that there is a good deal here yet to resolve. One could not attribute this discovery to any remarkable degree of internal theological disagreement. Indeed Durham has been singularly fortunate in the recent past in combining a coherent programme of theological study of the Christian tradition with a remarkable variety of denominational allegiance. The essays, which were commissioned in 1981, and which have been gathered together in batches since that time, are not the product of a prolonged process of discussion. The circumstances of departmental life, and not least the acute trials of British universities in recent years, have precluded the pursuit of any self-conscious programme of synthesis. And yet, at the same time, what is remarkable about this exceedingly diverse collection of essays on a common theme is the fruitfulness and coherence of the outcome.

First, a word must be said about the fate of sacrifice in recent theology. As Professor Dalferth, whom the Department welcomed for two all-too-brief terms from the University of Tübingen, explains, Anglican theologians have been conspicuous in their emphasis upon the importance, and even centrality, of the sacrificial understanding of the death of Christ (see below, pp. 299–325). As long ago as 1930 the cause of inter-Anglican ecumenism was being championed by a theologian who sought to make fruitful for eucharistic theology some newer ideas, deriving from anthropology, on cultic sacrifice in the Old Testament (see Hicks 1930).

The sacrificial interpretation of the eucharist, controversial but sustainable in Anglicanism from the seventeenth century, has remained largely foreign to Lutherans and Calvinists into our own century. For Anglicans it became an almost untouchably sensitive point of contention. An earlier and remarkable focussing of spiritual and theological writing upon the high priesthood of Jesus broke apart on the offence of a sacerdotal interpretation of Christian priesthood popular in the later nineteenth-century ritualist phase of Anglo-Catholicism. At the same time the high christological 'orthodoxy' of the Epistle to the Hebrews yielded ground to the quest of the historical Jesus, and atonement theology registered a sharp reaction away from substitutionary theologies, especially those of a penal character (see Hancock 1985).

The final blow to the assumed acceptability and currency of sacrificial language was the discovery of its secular potential when enlisted in the cause of European nationalisms. In this collection the essays of Dr Gilley and Dr Suggate both illustrate the twentieth-century misuse, or rather the equivocal use, of the slogan of sacrifice in the rhetoric of Irish nationalism and the British First World War effort. But precisely the same language was subsequently deployed by Adolf Hitler in his persuasion of the German people to accept economic deprivation and loss of civil liberties as the cost of national revival (Stern 1975). It is openly acknowledged by contemporary

German theologians that the rhetoric of sacrifice has been defiled to the point where it is unusable in normal Christian preaching; and it cannot be an accident that opposition to the idea of its centrality as a theme of Christian theology is commonest amongst German Protestants.

Given the fact that such painful experience is not the common property of the whole Christian Church, the questions which are posed are nevertheless radical enough, not least in this collection. Conservatism is also well represented. Some authors assume, upon the basis of long-standing Christian tradition, that not merely is the death of Christ properly spoken of as 'the atoning sacrifice', but the ritual commemoration of that death in the eucharist must constitute one of the ways in which Christian theology construes the place which sacrifice occupies in the Christian world of meaning. Sacrifice, in other words, is in some sense a *datum* of Christian theology: doubtless a *datum* in the sense of a problem to be wrestled with, and elucidated in connection with contemporary aids, but on no account to be given up or despaired of.

Not so, say some of the more radical authors of this collection. There is even, from the pen of a New Testament scholar, Dr Chester, a serious argument against the assumption that the Epistle to the Hebrews can be enlisted as evidence for understanding Christ's death as a sacrifice. The document is rather, he urges, a means whereby, for essentially practical purposes, a lesson could be taught to certain early Christian groups who were not persuaded that the whole Jewish cultus had been made redundant. Admittedly, says Chester, this provokes a question about the status of the Old Testament in Christian thought. The two chapters on the patristic tradition, by Dr Dragas and Mr Bonner, show the classic solution to this dilemma. For the great fourth-century Greek theologian, Athanasius, the Old Testament sacrificial tradition, though right for its time, has been utterly replaced. The shadow and the type have yielded to the spirit and the truth. This standard argument enabled patristic theology as a whole to redeploy sacrificial language, making the sacrifice of the cross the central norm. By the third century, Latin theology had restored explicitly cultic language to Christian theology, and Bonner shows how, with Augustine, the unbreakable connection was made between the sacrifice on the cross and the 'daily sacrifice' of the Church.

But why should we hesitate to subject this venerable tradition also to critical scrutiny? So demands the challenging essay from Dr FitzPatrick. Although writing in highly original vein upon the eucharistic sacrifice in the middle ages, he treats his subject against the wider background of atonement theology and developments in the understanding of eucharistic presence. The fundamental problem, according to FitPatrick, lies in the notion of satisfaction which, from whatever ultimate source, became inseparably linked with that of sacrifice after the creative but flawed work of

St Anselm. FitzPatrick's contribution to ecumenism consists not in reconciling Luther and the Council of Trent, but in undermining both to take a sharper and more critical look at the premisses which both took for granted, especially those concerning the equity of God's dealings with humanity and the transmission of inherited guilt.

Radical, but in a gentler if more insidious vein, are the group of contributions gathered in Part III from the history and thought of the modern Church. The very success and popularity of certain uses of the concept of sacrifice raise fundamental questions about that tradition. It is one thing to demonstrate the impeccable pedigree of the sacrificial understanding of the death of Christ; it is quite another matter to observe, with Gilley, the disastrous ease with which the violence of the Gaelic inheritance was grandiloquently idealized as Christian chivalry, and the bloodshed of violent revolution identified as cleansing and sanctifying on the pattern of Christ. It is sobering, with Suggate, to acknowledge the popularity of vacuous chatter about 'corporate self-sacrifice', and to wrestle realistically with the tension between love and the demands of justice in human affairs. Or again in the cases of Kierkegaard, as expounded by Dr Pattison, and Simone Weil, by Dr Loades, there are profound objections to the impact which the tradition of the sacrifice of the cross may have upon certain persons in certain circumstances. It emerges that there is a very narrow ridge between optimistic waffle about sacrifice being the 'law of the universe', and a deeply Manichaean alternative which hates and despises the demands of the body and human sociality. As Suggage, Pattison and Loades all show, a theology of sacrifice cannot be isolated from other elements in a theological system, especially not from those of creation, incarnation and eschatology.

What, then, is the unity of this collection of essays? It is the discovery of the complexity and plurality of themes concealed in this metaphor of sacrifice: its ambiguity. Professor Jones in the opening essay reminds us of the fact that there is no one word, in Hebrew or in Greek, to correspond to the English word 'sacrifice'. To discuss the nature of sacrifice, as he does, is a synthetic and constructive task. Jones, much as FitzPatrick, sees it as dealing with the fundamental human situation of the perceived gulf between desire and achievement, in the sense of separation, exclusion or defilement. The strength of such a view is the explanation it provides not merely for the durability of the concept of sacrifice long after sacrificial cultus has any overt currency, but also for the hospitality of both rites and concept to different degrees and intensities of rationalization. The shift from the external perspective to the disposition of the heart is a common theme in many of the essays, and Professor Hulmes shows how this movement can be seen in Hindu, Buddhist and Muslim theologies as well as in Christianity.

It clearly emerges from these essays that there has never been within

Christianity one rational explanation of sacrifice. Dr Hayward's suggestive interpretation of ben Sira's view of sacrifice demonstrates the plasticity of the ritual to conceptual reformulation, in his case to the belief that the cultic order is part of the divine order of the universe, and revelatory of divine wisdom. Hence it is open for St Paul to argue that the Wisdom of God has been made plain in the sacrificial death of Jesus, whose offering embraces and redeems the whole created order (see pp. 35–43, below). Dr Gelston, likewise, in expounding the sacrificial language of one of the earliest eucharistic liturgies, points to the lack of precision in the thought of the text. This lack, as the investigations of FitzPatrick and Dr McHugh demonstrate, was abundantly exploited in the era of theology which demanded articulation and precision. Thus FitzPatrick warmly commends St Thomas Aquinas' good sense, moderation and lack of desire to evacuate belief of its elusiveness, and his sensitive treatment of the eucharistic sacrifice (though not the eucharistic presence) in explicit relation to its *ritual* commemoration of the death of Christ. So, too, McHugh can commend the openness of the decisions taken at Trent to further theological explanation and exploration.

The continuing constructive potential of the theme of sacrifice is exemplified in many essays. In Professor Dunn's treatment of St Paul's theology of the atonement a two-fold polemic is mounted against fellow New Testament scholars, who either with Käsemann and some of his successors seek (perhaps for reasons already mentioned) to downgrade or eliminate the cultic references, or, with Leon Morris, link them exclusively to substitutionary patterns of thought. Although here, of course, we are dealing with differences of historical interpretation, we have every ground for observing the openness of the Pauline material to differing interpretations.

In two overtly constructive essays Dalferth and I take alternative but by no means contradictory courses in the construing of the available evidence. I urge that a theology which takes the theme of sacrifice as one central concept is a possibility; Dalferth, with justice and not a little *ad hominem* argumentation, contends that such a course is by no means a necessity. Both essays are evidence for the justice of FitzPatrick's strictures against what he calls 'the scenario of tit-for-tat', and the need not to disguise disbelief as deeper understanding.

One final introductory remark suggests itself. Study of these essays will leave the reader in no doubt that there are still living representatives of the traditional Reformation divisions to be found in Durham's Theological Department, those who believe, despite the efforts of contemporary ecumenism, that there is continuing substance in either Luther's position on the eucharistic sacrifice, or in Trent's reply. It is also the case that this collection contains genuinely traditional Anglican counterclaims. The essay which contains the most unequivocal descriptions of Protestantism's non-eucharistic spirituality, Dr Hardman Moore's painstaking research into the sacrificial rhetoric of Puritanism, also makes abundantly clear that Protestantism, too, had a problem of formalism to overcome. The protest of Luther against the turning of the eucharist into a good work, had to be made later against the turning of the *language* of sacrifice into a formula. St Augustine would have understood the point. The fact that what God desires is the invisible sacrifice, the offering of a broken heart, makes redundant neither the visible sacrifices of the Church, nor the words of the Christian. The cult of the heart, she shows, could acquire its own rationalizations as fantastic as anything that the medieval period could produce in relation to ritual practices. But the hallmark of Christian insight into sacrifice at every period and in every tradition appears to be the realization of the contemporaneity of the crucified and risen Christ.

REFERENCES

Hancock, C. D. (1985). *The Priesthood of Christ in Anglican Doctrine and Devotion, 1827–1900*. Unpublished Ph.D. Thesis, University of Durham
Hicks, F. C. N. (1930). *The Fullness of Sacrifice. An Essay in Reconciliation*. London: Macmillan
McKenna, A. J. (ed.) (1985). *Semeia* 33. Decatur, Georgia: Scholars Press
Stern, J. P. (1975). *Hitler. The Führer and the People*. London: Collins

I

I

SACRIFICE AND HOLINESS

D. R. JONES

When in English we speak of the institution of sacrifice, we commonly refer to the system of worship which has its most characteristic and effective action in the slaughter of a victim. Sacrifice is pre-eminently bloody sacrifice. But the word has a wider connotation and comprehends the surrender to the deity of some object or possession which may be other than a beast or a bird, for the purpose of propitiation or homage. 'Sacrifice' may also denote the victim itself or anything else that is offered. A derivative usage is its application to human self-giving. A man may sacrifice comfort or income for the sake of some higher goal, or in war may, as we say, pay the supreme sacrifice.

The picture however becomes progressively less clear as we examine the use of the word 'sacrifice' in the English Versions of the Bible, the Vulgate, the Septuagint, the Greek New Testament and the Hebrew of the Old Testament. Neither in the Old Testament nor in the New is there any word for the institution as a whole. Yet in the Authorized Version and the English Versions dependent upon it the noun is used up to two hundred times. In the majority of cases in the Old Testament, 'sacrifice' renders the Hebrew word *zebah*. Although the verb means 'to kill', this is the term for a particular sacrifice to be distinguished from the *'olāh* or holocaust. When the two terms occur together, the English Versions, including the New English Bible and Revised English Bible (which for example in Leviticus, carefully distinguishes the *zebah* as 'shared-offering') render them as 'sacrifice and burnt-offering', or, in the case of the NEB 'sacrifice and whole-offering'. This is confusing. The whole-offering is as much, generally, a sacrifice as the shared-offering. S. R. Driver (in Sanday 1901, 14) concluded not only that the definition of sacrifice is difficult, but also that 'it is doubtful whether the Hebrews have any term exactly co-extensive with our sacrifice'.

None of the translators of the versions has distinguished the particular character of the *zebah* in such passages. But the Vulgate, with apparently better resources than English, most frequently translates it as either *hostia* (an animal sacrificed, a victim) or *victima* (a beast for sacrifice, also a

sacrificial term and often synonymous with *hostia*). *Sacrificium* on the other
hand is used, in the Latin authors, principally of the whole rite. They refer
frequently to the public and private sacrifices. The victims are supplied for
the sacrifice ('hostias ad sacrificium praebere'). Sacrifice is offered (*facere*) or
prepared (*parare*). There is, however, little sign that the Vulgate consistently
makes a nice or precise distinction. There are cases where it is not clear why
sacrificium, *hostia* or *victima* is preferred, all rendering the Hebrew *zebaḥ*. For
example, 1 Sam. 15:22 ('to obey is better than sacrifice') is rendered
'meliora est obedientia quam victimae'. One would suppose that *sacrificium*
would be more appropriate to state the general principle. The often repeated
combination of 'shared-offerings and holocausts' is 'hostias et holocausta'.
At the same time one sees a certain appropriateness in 'in domum sacrificii'
in 2 Chron. 7:12 for 'they have chosen this for a house of sacrifice'. In
general the use of *sacrificium* in the Vulgate is comparatively rare. Ps. 4:5
has 'sacrificate sacrificium iustitiae', splendid, one would think, in poetry.
In Ps. 50:5, 8 the covenant made by sacrifice is 'in sacrificio'. But 'sacrifice
and offering' in Ps. 40:6, a context which shows the whole system is in
mind, is 'victima et oblatione'. Again Proverbs, referring to sacrifice in
principle (15:8; 21:3) has *victimae*. Hos. 3:4 sounds right: 'sine sacrificio et
sine altari'. The translator of this book seems to prefer the word (compare
6:6; 9:4; though *hostia* in 8:13). In Jer. 7:26 *sacrificium* is listed with
holocausta and *victima*. In several cases *sacrificium* is the rendering of the
Hebrew *minḥāh* (gift-offering) which, in the pre-exilic period, was the
nearest equivalent for sacrifice in general (Isa. 1:11; Hos. 10:6). It also
translated the evening sacrifice in 1 Kgs. 18:29, 36; Ps. 141:2 and Ezra
9:4, 5.

A not dissimilar picture emerges from examination of the translation of
the verb *zābaḥ*. *Sacrificare* is used rarely. 'To sacrifice to the LORD' is
'sacrificemus' in Exod. 5:3 (cf. 8:8). But much more frequently it is
immolare. Sometimes one sees a special suitability in this word (as for
example in Zech. 14:21 or Ps. 106:37), but often not.

In the LXX *thusia* is used indiscriminately for *zebaḥ* and the corresponding
verb accordingly. The LXX does not anticipate the distinctions of the
Vulgate.

The requirements of the Hebrew text can be approached more satis-
factorily from the more comprehensive view of context. A number of
passages, employing the word *zebaḥ* and in the first instance referring to the
shared-offering, nevertheless refer to it in such a way as to show that the
principle of sacrifice is in mind – *pars pro toto*. Some of these have been
quoted above (1 Sam. 15:22; 2 Chron. 7:12; Ps. 40:6 and 50:5, 8; Prov.
15:8 and 21:3, 27; Isa. 1:11; Hos. 6:6; Ps. 4:5). These include the most
important passages in which the Vulgate employs *sacrificium*. But it has to
be admitted that the most characteristic Vulgate equivalent of 'to offer

sacrifice' is 'immolare victimas'. We can however conclude that the
Hebrew, having no obvious word for the institution as a whole, made its
meaning clear by the context. The 'shared-offering and the holocaust',
when, as so often, they occurred together in pre-exilic passages, comprehended sacrifice as a whole. There are also passages where the *zebaḥ* is
referred to typically of sacrifice as a whole. When therefore, in such a
context, the English translators rendered *zebaḥ* by 'sacrifice', they were not
wholly untrue to the intention of the author, confusing as their lack of
finesse may be.

In the New Testament the English translators' use of the word 'sacrifice'
has a similar background. In the Greek it is universally *thusia*. In the
Vulgate *sacrificium* is rare, occurring in those quotations from the Old
Testament where it already stands (such as Matt. 9: 13 and 12: 7, and in
Heb. 5: 1, 'dona et sacrificia'). The preferred word is *hostia* (Heb. 7: 26; 8: 3;
9: 9, 23, 26; 10: 1, 5; 8: 11, 12, 26; 11: 4; 13: 15, 16). 'A living sacrifice' in
Rom. 12: 1 is 'hostiam viventem'. 'A sacrifice to God' in Eph. 5: 2 is
'hostiam Deo'. 'An acceptable sacrifice' in Phil. 4: 18 is 'hostiam acceptam'.
'Spiritual sacrifice' in 1 Peter 2: 5 is 'spirituales hostias'. 'Christ our
passover is sacrificed for us' in 1 Cor. 5: 7 is 'etenim Pascha nostra
immolatus est, Christus'.

All this shows beyond a doubt that the *use* of the word 'sacrifice' in the
English versions was not based on *the use of* its Latin equivalent *sacrificium*.
Only occasionally is 'sacrifice' the best rendering of the Hebrew *zebaḥ* and
the Greek *thusia*, though clearly there is more to be said for it in the New
Testament than in the Old. Its importance lies in its intrinsic capacity to
indicate a many-sided concept, in the light of its empirical usage in the
English language.

Intrinsic capacity is best tested by a study of usage. But there are two
considerations which make the word 'sacrifice' specially significant. The
first is etymology. *Sacrificium* is *sacrum-facere* – to make sacred. Sacrifice
involves consecration. Because the word has in English developed such a
cluster of meanings and because its use in the English Bible is so much wider
than its restricted use in the Vulgate, it is not possible to argue that
etymology is therefore a powerful pointer to the meaning of sacrifice as
indicated in either the Latin or the English tradition. But the second
consideration happens to confirm the first, perhaps to show that the
etymology is thus significant, perhaps not, but certainly to reaffirm it. The
second consideration is the nature of sacrifice as elucidated by the
examination of the pattern or structure of sacrifice generally.

Here we encounter a problem of methodology. When sacrifice is so
widespread in time and space, and the documentary evidence rarely
answers our questions directly, how is it possible to speak of the nature of
sacrifice? Is there some sort of unity behind the diversity? In attending to

this diversity in the Judaeo-Christian tradition, is it necessary to go beyond this tradition? When there is clear evidence in the Biblical tradition that the institution of sacrifice radically changes both in form and meaning, at what point in history shall the movie-camera be stopped? Does the evidence permit such a photograph to be taken?

First, the vital importance of going outside the Judaeo-Christian tradition must be reaffirmed. Sacrifice is a factor in the religious evolution of mankind, not merely of the Hebrews. It may be possible to maintain, as does Young (1979), that sacrifice is a strictly universal religious phenomenon. On the other hand the fact that some hunting societies did not have sacrificial rituals (see James Woodburn, quoted in Sykes 1980, 61, 82), does not do more than provide the exception to a virtually universal practice. Nor must it be forgotten that much of the institution of sacrifice was learnt by the Hebrews from their Canaanite environment. The language of the cult is Canaanite; the architectural structure of the temple was on Canaanite models; the old Feasts were Canaanite. One of the most fascinating exercises of Old Testament study is the attempt to distinguish what was Canaanite and legitimately baptized into the biblical system (like the *zebaḥ* and the temple), what was Canaanite and repudiated (like sacred prostitution) and what was original to the Hebrews (like the historicization of Feasts). The prophet Amos seemed to be aware of a tradition that sacrifice, as practised by his contemporaries, was not a feature of the wilderness traditions, that much evil was a result of what we would call syncretism and that a period of exile at the hands of a foreign enemy was needed to drive them to their senses and teach them to do without the ritual that allures and defiles:

Did you bring me sacrifices and gifts, you people of Israel, those forty years in the wilderness? No! but now you shall take up the shrine or your idol king and the pedestals of your images, which you have made for yourselves, and I will drive you into exile beyond Damascus.[1] (5:26–7; see Jones 1963)

Whatever the uncertainties, there is enough evidence to show that the institution of sacrifice, as presented in the Old Testament, owes much to Israel's environment and itself bears witness to a human and not simply a Hebraic phenomenon.

Second, it is clear that the very habit of giving the name 'sacrifice' to rituals which are widespread in time and space shows that there is a common factor which requires identification. It is therefore proper to look to evidence as far apart as the Sanskrit texts of the Hindu religion as well as those of the Hebrew scriptures. These are of special significance because they are substantial. For Greek and Roman sacrifices the evidence is more scattered and sporadic. The attempt to discover a common scheme of sacrifice in these fields was precisely the task undertaken by Henri Hubert and Marcel Mauss ([1898] 1964). What these authors did was to examine the complexity of the rituals as set forth in the texts and to look for 'thoroughly typical facts', to try 'to dis-entangle the simple and elementary forms'. This is in the first instance a structuralist technique, using the material synchronically.[2] They are open to the criticism that they have ignored the historical dimension revealed by the critical study of the Old Testament. But the fault is apparent only. Allowing for a long history of a thousand years, substantial developments, inter-cultural influences, reactions and purifications; allowing also for resultant uncertainties and the difficulty of knowing *exactly* what was done at any given time; allowing also for gaps in our knowledge (much is necessarily assumed), it is still possible to put the question to the texts as they have come down to us and to ask what are the common features that survive through all the changes. A scheme or structure is discernible. And in general, the scheme or structure discerned by Hubert and Mauss has stood the test of time. They themselves insisted that they were presenting no more than a provisional hypothesis.

The diachronic aspect of sacrifice will in fact be seen to be of crucial importance, particularly in relation to its interpretation and rationale. The changing attitude to an institution in which a fundamental structure may be perceived is the subject of this volume. Within the Old Testament there are signs of profound change. The sacrificial cult operating in the post-exilic period is different in detail and completeness from that operating under the kings. In particular we shall find a change in the attitude to piacular sacrifices, a deepening of the idea of the holy and the appearance of an equivocal approach to the institution as a whole. Finally the Christian 'fulfilment' of sacrifice in Christ implies, with the repudiation of animal sacrifices, the reaffirmation of sacrifice at a deeper level. The question is: what is the deeper principle or pattern or scheme which remains when otherwise everything changes?

Hubert and Mauss ([1898] 1964) believed rightly that there was a continuity in the form of sacrifice. They found the following 'scheme' to be exemplified in such evidence as there is:

(a) *The entry.* The person to be benefited, whoever performs the rite, the place and the instruments all have to be prepared with varying degrees of detail. From this beginning everything must proceed in right order and without interruption. The worshipper 'enters cautiously step by step, into the sacred world' (pp. 19–28).

(b) *The victim.* Precisely chosen, the victim was destroyed and thus separated from the profane world. 'It was *consecrated*, it was *sacrified* [*sic*] in the etymological sense of the word.' The method varied and the treatment of the remains varied, but always there is a definite continuity. This continuity Hubert and Mauss thought 'one of the most remarkable characteristics of sacrifice' (p. 44). By consecration forces are aroused and allowed to escape 'some to the beings of the sacred world, some to the beings of the profane world'. There is a curve of religiosity, reaching a climax and then diminishing (pp. 28–45).

(c) *The exit.* The worshipper himself passes through the same curve of rising and diminishing holiness. His return is therefore carefully prescribed (pp. 45–9).

It is clear that sacrifice involves both sacralization and desacralization. Hubert and Mauss summed up the unity that exists at the heart of the diversity of sacrifice as follows: its unity lies in the fact that

beneath the diverse forms it takes, it always consists in one same procedure, which may be used for the most widely differing purposes. *This procedure consists in establishing a means of communication between the sacred and the profane worlds through the mediation of a victim, that is, of a thing that in the course of the ceremony is destroyed.* (p. 97)

This analysis seems to me to be correct and unaffected by the historical and critical problems inherent in the study of Hebrew sacrifice. It means that the very idea of sacrifice is dependent upon the prior notion of the holy and of the two worlds. The word 'holy' is a direct equivalent of the Hebrew *qōdesh*. The argument over etymology has proved indecisive. The word is found in Accadian (meaning 'pure', 'consecrated'), Ugaritic, Phoenician, Aramaic, Syriac and Arabic. In Ugaritic it is already an epithet for 'god'. The conclusion, however, that the Hebrews learned it from their Canaanite environment is hardly tenable when one bears in mind the important wilderness traditions of Qadesh-barnea (also Qadesh on the Orontes, capital of the Hittites). Once again our only safe guide to the meaning of the word is context. This, in the Old Testament, is clear enough. The unifying factor behind the frequent use of *qōdesh* and its cognates is separation, that is, separation from profane use to God's. Indeed the opposite of the holy is the profane (*ḥōl*) or common, a distinction which is nicely brought out in 1 Sam. 21.4: 'I have no ordinary bread available. There is only the sacred bread.' The two worlds are presupposed. The moral and spiritual sense of 'holy' is derivative and secondary. The idea of the numinous, the *mysterium tremendum* which evokes both awe and fascination, as defined by Rudolf Otto in his *Idea of the Holy* ([1917] 1923) is plainly present in the story of Jacob's dream (Gen. 28: 10–22) and the inaugural vision of Isaiah (chapter 6). The appropriate response is awe (the fear of the LORD). But equally a feature of older usage is the dynamistic idea of mana, conspicuously in the story of Uzzah and the ark (2 Sam. 6: 1–11). The use of the word 'holy', as much as anything in the Old Testament, illustrates the power of Israel's faith, under prophetic guidance, to deepen, purify and transform. The phrase 'the Holy One of Israel' as used in every part of the Isaiah corpus, comprehends all that Israel came to understand of the mystery of God. And yet *at the same time* the dynamistic ideas were maintained in the post-exilic cult, and Ezekiel's vision of the temple rebuilt in Jerusalem is of the Holy One at the centre of concentric circles of decreasing holiness. The holy in the Old Testament thus moves through the whole gamut from notions which are crude to those which are sublime, and several conceptions may co-exist. But even the most refined idea of holiness means that there is a distance, a separation between God and man which sinful man cannot bridge on his own terms. There are two worlds, even within our world. No sentimental or facile confidence is appropriate. Even when the sacrificial cult is not available and not required by God himself (Ps. 51:16), the requirement of the holy God is total self-awareness and confession (verses 3, 4, 6), a desire for cleansing (verses 2, 7), indeed such a profound recognition of the impediments inherent in the divine–human encounter as to amount to the sacrifice of a broken spirit (verse 17). Where the relationship between God and man is broken, nothing short of a new creative act of God will mend it (verse 10, cf. Ezek. 16:62; 34:11–16; 36:22–32; 37:1–14). Such is the seriousness of the human condition, because such is the holiness of God. The spatial and cultic imagery of sacrifice becomes the pattern of insights psychologically true and profoundly personal. The *theological* pattern thus to be discerned in sacrifice within the Old Testament is therefore something like this:

(1) *Holiness means distance, separation.* The holiness of God is such that there is a distance between himself and sinful man. This holiness which separates him from man is not identical with His 'wrath' (Balentine 1982), though holiness comprehends the wrath properly understood. The holiness of God is that which leads sinful man to feel and exemplify a sense of alienation, of exclusion. The sense of cultic impurity, of moral imperfection, of alienation (today sometimes expressed in denying God's existence) are all different ways of expressing the pattern.

(2) *The divine initiative.* This distance can be bridged only by the initiative of God himself. When the sacrificial cult was operative, it was effective because it was regarded as God's provision to bridge the sacred and profane worlds. God has so commanded through Moses in Exodus, Leviticus and Numbers. In Deuteronomy Moses commanded in God's name. The essential human response was obedience. Obedience was understood to be paramount (1 Sam. 15:22; Hos. 6:6; Ps. 40:6–8), so that to offer sacrifice otherwise than as God provides was as though to murder a human being or cut off a dog's neck or offer swine's blood or bless an idol (Isa. 66:3). In the period of the Old Testament, Israel came to see, under the influence of the prophets, that there were occasions when God withdrew the institution of sacrifice. Such occasions were exile or the destruction of the temple. Then it became clear that the primary requirement was a right disposition of the heart, born of chastisement (Hos. 3:4; Amos 5:25–6; Ps. 40:6–7 and

51:16–17, cf. 18–19). Ezekiel represents the Old Testament as a whole when he insists that, if the covenant relationship between God and man is broken by moral obliquity, no rites (even those of sacrifice) will avail to mend it. A creative initiative of the divine spirit is necessary (Ezek. 36:23–7; 37). Only *then* may the temple be rebuilt and the rites become effective again to maintain the relationship thus restored (cf. chapters 40–8) (Jones 1963). Underlying this insistence on the divine initiative is the presupposition that the alienation of man from God is of so serious a character that nothing man can do will overcome it. Sometimes the blood of sacrifice, according to the divine prescription, is adequate but from time to time the vicissitudes of history and the blood of defeat are necessary to bring God's people to a total dependence on God. Always the cost of redemption is death, the death of the victim, the 'death' of the temple, the 'death' of the people (Ezek: 37:1–14).

(3) *Sacrifice is normally the indispensable means* of overcoming the alienation, but also some sort of sacrifice remains necessary to *maintain* the relationship between God and man. Sacrificial rites express this in ways that change and develop according to deepening understanding of both the character of God and the nature of sin. They express that total self-giving which is owed by man to God, the very purpose of his existence and ultimately his highest joy. Sacrifice whether by means of rites or by self-giving corresponds to the seriousness with which the distance (separation, alienation) between God and man is taken. Restoration is costly. The symbol of this cost is blood. When sacrificial rites as practised are exploited as *ex opere operato* escape-mechanisms, then God himself points to the priorities (1 Sam. 15:22; Hos. 6:6) and provides alternatives, also holding out the hope of an ultimate reconciliation (the messianic hope). The Old Testament never abandons the principle but ends in uncertainty and ambivalence as to the exact expression which sacrifice should take. This uncertainty is the last word of the Old Testament.

The question now arises whether this analysis is correct for the New Testament. What difference did the ministry of Jesus make? The Old Testament ideas of holiness are clearly present. Peter, after the miraculous haul of fish, fell at Jesus' knees and cried: 'Depart from me for I am a sinful man, O Lord.' The disciples felt awe (fear) when Jesus stilled the storm. The transfiguration is presented as a numinous experience. It was 'shuddering awe' that Jesus himself felt in Gethsemane. If Mark 16:8 is the end of the gospel, the last words, 'for they were afraid', must surely indicate awe at the news of the resurrection rather than servile terror.

It is sometimes argued that these elements of the gospels are residual traces of an idea of holiness which has been stood on its head by the known teaching and person of Jesus (Davies 1973). He explicitly taught that God was not to be feared. He called God 'abba' ('father') implying the easy familiarity of a child at home with his parent. Everywhere he obliterated the distinction between the sacred and the profane, finding the holy in the common. Jesus is himself the model of holiness for Christians and therefore the passages above should be regarded as the inevitable failure of discarded, outmoded Old Testament presuppositions. The holy, Christianly understood, is to be discerned *in* the common and worldly. We are not to seek to draw apart from the world and enter a sacred realm. The very idea of the two realms is to be surrendered. The distance no longer exists. There is no such thing as an *other-worldly* reality.

I believe this argument, which underlies the modern theological movements for holy-worldliness and the death of God, to be profoundly erroneous. It posits a degree of revolution in the thought of Jesus which belongs essentially to the nineteenth and twentieth centuries. It fails to take any serious account of the degree of reinterpretation which had already taken place within the Old Testament and in Judaism in the understanding of the sacred and profane. Jesus drew on elements which were part of the complex of the Old Testament and of Judaism as a whole. Moreover to claim that this distinction, which Mircea Eliade maintains is fundamental to all religions (Eliade [1956] 1968), is not to be found in the New Testament, is to overlook the place of presupposition. This presupposition is rarely explicit, like all presuppositions. It is never explicitly repudiated and there are ubiquitous signs of its presence in the language of the New Testament which is fundamentally that of the Old. We should thus be liberated to take seriously the central message of the Epistle to the Hebrews, which otherwise runs the risk of being dismissed as an example of 'early catholicism' reverting to outmoded sacrificial concepts.

Here it is not difficult to discern both the anthropological and the theological patterns of sacrifice and the prior notion of the holy. The word pattern (*hupodeigma*) is used of the things on earth (Heb. 9: 23) as pointing to the deeper heavenly mysteries. The word shadow (*skia*) is also employed with the same intention (10: 1; 8: 5). There is a true form (*eikon*) of these realities. 'It was therefore necessary', wrote the Author, 'that the patterns of things in heaven should be purified with these rites [i.e. sacrifices involving the shedding of blood]; but the heavenly things with better sacrifices than these' (9: 23). Communication between the sacred and profane worlds is established by means of a victim who is also a priest. The concept of sacred and profane is no longer *cultically* understood; but the separation is as real. It is the difference between our earth-bound existence and the freedom of heaven: Jesus is 'a great high-priest who has passed into the heavens' (4: 14). 'We have such a high-priest who sat down at the right hand of the throne of the Majesty in the heavens' (8: 1) and so overcame the separation. As such he is 'the minister of the sanctuary and of the true tabernacle which the Lord pitched not man' (8: 2). And the argument proceeds: 'Christ, having come an high-priest of the good things to come, by a greater and more perfect tabernacle, not made with hands, neither by the blood of goats and calves, but by his own blood he entered once and for all into the holy place' (9: 11–12). That is to say, by means of his sacrifice he overcame the separation. And this is in order that we may through him have *our* access to God: 'Christ is entered into heaven itself, now to appear in the presence of God for us' (9: 24). Hence our 'boldness to enter into the holiest by the blood of Jesus, by a new and living way' (10: 19–20). The analogical character of this language is emphasized by the use of a different analogy to express the same truth: 'you have come to Mount Zion', he writes, 'to the heavenly Jerusalem, the city of the living God' (12:22).

This is the sense in which communication is established between the sacred and profane worlds. Both sacred and profane are reinterpreted but not so as to obliterate the distinction. There are two worlds and Jesus Christ is both victim and priest who enables us to pass from one to the other here and now: (1) The entry is achieved by Christ who takes us with him (4: 14; 8: 1, 2; 9: 24; 9: 19–20; 12: 22, quoted above). (2) The victim and 'sacrifier' [*sic*][3] is Christ himself: 'He has appeared once for all at the end of the ages to do away with sin by the sacrifice of himself' (9: 26, 28). (3) As to the exit, 'he has passed into the heavens' (4: 14; 8: 1; 10: 11–12; 9: 24). This is that we should also share his holiness: 'We have been made holy by the sacrifice of the body of Jesus Christ once for all' (10: 10). It is also that we may be fitted for the service of the living God in holiness (9: 14).

The theological pattern is also pronounced: (1) *The distance or separation of alienation* is everywhere presupposed. The analogy of the wilderness wandering is used to suggest the notion of a journey to the promised land considered a Sabbath-rest for the people of God. But there are those (the alienated) who 'shall never enter my rest' (chapter 4). The sacrificial system was inadequate to achieve the reconciliation and restoration of the sinful: 'The way into the Most Holy Place had not hitherto been disclosed' (9: 8). Already Jeremiah had predicted a new covenant, showing that the first was obsolete (chapter 8). The sacrifices of Israel function as 'an annual reminder of sins because it is impossible for the blood of bulls and goats to take away sins' (10: 3–4). The analogical language to which we have drawn attention reinforces this emphasis upon the notion of distance. Because God is holy, there is a holiness without which no one can see him (12: 14): 'Our God is a consuming fire' (12: 29). What we have called the seriousness of the human condition implied by the very word 'sacrifice' is expressed in 10: 31: 'It is a dreadful thing to fall into the hands of the living God.' St Paul also pointed to the human predicament in the very passage in which he spoke of Christ's work as a sacrifice: 'All have sinned and fall short of the glory of God' (Rom. 3: 23). What *is* needed is a way back, an access, and this is exactly what is offered through the sacrifice of Christ. The language is the analogical language of sacrifice and Christ is the High Priest who sacrificed for sins once for all, moving into the sacred realm of heaven.

(2) *The divine initiative is paramount.* In the Epistle to the Hebrews every human response is dependent upon the prior sacrifice of Christ. God provides a new order (covenant) through Christ, just as the Holy Spirit showed it in advance through the prophecy of Jeremiah (chapter 8). And St Paul preceded and followed the passage quoted above (Rom. 3:23) with the same emphasis: 'But now a righteousness from God, apart from law, has been made known, to which the Law and Prophets testify. This righteousness from God comes through faith in Jesus Christ . . . God presented him as a sacrifice of atonement, through faith in his blood' (Rom. 3:21, 22, 25).

(3) But equally the *indispensability of sacrifice* is stressed. If the victims of the sacrificial cult are impotent to cleanse from sin and open the way to God, they nevertheless foreshadow the one effective sacrifice: 'The law requires that nearly everything be cleansed with blood, and without the shedding of blood there is no forgiveness' (Heb. 9:22). That is to say, though the sacrificial system is ineffective, it yet bears witness to the principle that without the deeper notion of sacrifice the relation between God and man cannot be mended. 'Christ came as high priest . . . he went through the greater and more perfect tabernacle . . . he entered the Most Holy Place once for all by his own blood' (9:11–12). 'The blood of Christ, who through the eternal spirit offered himself unblemished to God, will cleanse our consciences' (9:14). 'Christ was sacrificed once for all to take away the sins of many people' (9:28). While 'it is impossible for the blood of bulls and goats to take away sins' (10:4), and the daily priestly performance in the Temple is useless (10:11), Christ's sacrifice and Christ's priesthood is effective and indispensable. 'By one sacrifice he has made perfect for ever those who are being made holy' (10:14). Here, it is claimed, is not the shadow, but the reality: not the ineffective precursor but the all-embracing divine provision for mankind. It is possible for us to ask how this claim would be affected if Christ had not died. It is possible to answer that the human condition would have received no remedy, just because the broken relationship between God and man cannot be restored simply by turning a blind eye. Sacrifice is the total self-giving required, the utter final and absolute act which avails when nothing less can, the way through death to life. It answers to the seriousness of the human predicament. It also answers to a profound intuition which belongs to human nature and has not changed with the ages. Only its expression has changed. Is it not the danger of the modern age to lose the reality as it observes the transformation of its expression?

This examination of the term 'sacrifice' and the prior notion of 'the holy' suggests therefore that the category of sacrifice is not to be dispensed with as outmoded. It has itself been subject to change and become a complex idea corresponding in fact to the many-sided English word 'sacrifice'. Its comparative rarity in the teaching of Jesus is irrelevant. At a certain point in the life of the Church it was necessary to assess the whole phenomenon of Jesus Christ, crucified and risen. It is significant and appropriate that the author of the Epistle to the Hebrews, one of the theologians of the New Testament, should function in a way not dissimilar to a systematic theologian of the Christian tradition: 'He tries to catch up what Christ(ianity) is basically all about in a single, synoptic, imaginative judgment' (Kelsey 1975, 159). This does not exclude other metaphorical or symbolic judgements as in the theology of St Paul and St John. Such a 'discrimen', as Kelsey calls this judgement, involves 'a configuration of criteria that are in some way organically related to one another as reciprocal co-efficients'. This is precisely what the related concepts of sacrifice and priesthood provide. Complex, as we have seen, in themselves, they relate to other biblical concepts in ways that constitute the unity of the New Testament. This study of the idea of sacrifice and the prior notion of the holy may be regarded as a test case in the search for the unity of both the Old and the New Testament. It is also an attempt to distinguish the permanent from the culturally relative. If the argument pursued here is correct, that unity is substantial and profound. Sacrifice is part of the *preparatio evangelica* of the Christ.

NOTES

1 The translation of Amos 5:26 is from the NEB and is a conjectural emendation. But even if a more traditional translation is preferred, the point remains.
2 A procedure criticized by Rogerson (1980, 45).
3 The word in this form was minted by Hubert and Mauss ([1898] 1964).

REFERENCES

Balentine, S. E. (1982). *The Hidden God: The Hiding of the Face of God in the Old Testament*. Oxford: Oxford University Press
Bourdillon, M. F. C. and M. Fortes (eds.) (1980). *Sacrifice*. London: Academic Press
Davies, J. G. (1973). *Every Day God: Encountering the Holy in World and Worship*. London: SCM Press
Eliade, Mircea ([1956] 1968). *The Sacred and the Profane*. New York: Harcourt, Brace and World [a translation of *Le Sacré et le profane*, 1956]
Hubert, H. and M. Mauss ([1898] 1964). *Sacrifice, its Nature and Function*. London: Cohen and West [a translation of *Essai sur la nature et la fonction du sacrifice*, 1898]
Jones, D. R. (1963). Cessation of Sacrifice after 586 B.C. *Journal of Theological Studies* 14: 1, 12–31
Kelsey, D. H. (1975). *The Uses of Scripture in Recent Theology*. London: SCM Press
Otto, Rudolf ([1917] 1923). *The Idea of the Holy*. London: Oxford University Press [a translation of *Das Heilige*, 1917; 2nd edn, 1950]

Rogerson, J. (1980). Sacrifice in the Old Testament: Problems of Method and Approach. In Bourdillon and Fortes (1980), pp. 45–9

Sanday, W. (ed.) (1901). *Different Conceptions of Priesthood and Sacrifice*. London: Longmans, Green & Co.

Sykes, S. W. (1980). Sacrifice in the New Testament and Christian Theology. In Bourdillon and Fortes (1980), pp. 61–83

Young, F. (1979). *The Use of Sacrificial Ideas in Greek Christian Writers from the New Testament to John Chrysostom*. Cambridge, Mass.: Philadelphia Patristic Foundation

2

SACRIFICE AND WORLD ORDER: SOME OBSERVATIONS ON BEN SIRA'S ATTITUDE TO THE TEMPLE SERVICE

R. HAYWARD

The rich and complex traditions which we find about sacrifice in the Hebrew Bible were passed on and cherished by priests and scribes of Second Temple times (520 BC–AD 70), and the ancient rituals prescribed by the scriptures were, for the most part, faithfully carried out day by day. But what might sacrifice mean? Once the Torah had been acknowledged by the Jews as the Word of God, the unfailing and unfaltering guide to the pious individual in his journey through life and the state constitution of the Chosen People (see Neh. 8–9), such a question would inevitably arouse interest. At least one profound thinker of Second Temple times, Jesus ben Sira, was concerned with our topic, and his theological insights are not without significance for Jewish sacrificial ideology in general and for one particular aspect of New Testament theology.

The Wisdom of Jesus ben Sira is of outstanding importance for the study of pre-rabbinic Judaism. Indeed, it has been justifiably described as 'the most crucial source that we possess of the period preceding the Hasmonean revolt' (Rivkin 1963, 322). It is to be dated to the first decades of the second century BC (Stadelmann 1980, 1–4, Eissfeldt 1966, 597). As such, it gives us a precious glimpse of Jewish social, economic, political and religious life in the land of Israel before the Hellenistic crisis came to a head and shattered the old way of life as it had been lived under the Zadokite high priests. The book was highly esteemed by very different groups of Jews. For the Egyptian Diaspora, ben Sira's grandson translated it into Greek (Hengel 1974, 131); the Qumran sectarians and the defenders of Masada possessed copies of it (Milik 1959, 33–4; Yadin 1965); the Mishnah quotes it; some Talmudic sages cite it with approval (m. Aboth 4:4 cites ben Sira 7:17: see also b. Sanhedrin 100b, b. Ḥagigah 13a, and Smend 1906, xlvi–lvi); and Christians drew on its teachings from the earliest days of the Church (Box and Oesterley, in Charles 1913, 294–6).

It is hardly surprising, then, that ben Sira's view of sacrifice has been

22

often studied (Smend 1906, xxiv–xxv; Schmitz 1910, 59–69; Wenschkewitz 1932, 78–82; Stadelmann 1980, 40–138; Marböck 1971, 65–8,
74–6). Unlike other biblical 'wisdom writers', ben Sira has a good deal to say
about the priesthood, sacrificial service and cultic regulations of his own
day. His work even reaches its climax in the grand description of the high
priest Simon as he offers sacrifice in the temple liturgy (50: 5–21). Yet his
apparent interest in and affection for the cultus goes hand-in-hand with a
kind of piety which many scholars regard as essentially non-cultic: he has a
strongly personal, almost individualistic interior spirituality, characterized
by moral and ethical values which at times seem to overshadow, or even to
take the place of, such external things as sacrifice and priestly dues:

> He who repays a favour offers fine flour,
> And he who gives alms sacrifices a thank-offering . . .
> And expiation is to depart from wrong. (35: 2–3 LXX)

How best to explain this apparent dichotomy in ben Sira's attitude to
sacrifice is a constant problem for commentators. Does he 'spiritualize' the
demands of the cult, as the passage quoted above may imply? (See Wright
1966, 13–17, 131–8; Crenshaw 1981, 151.) Or does he indulge in a
'making cultic' (*Kultisierung*) of ethical commandments, as has recently
been suggested by Helge Stadelmann? (See Stadelmann 1980, 96–112;
compare Klinzing 1971 for the Qumran sect's attitude to sacrifice.) Is his
interest in cult strictly secondary to his ethical concern, sacrifice being
offered simply because the Torah commands it, and for no other reason?
(See Smend 1906, xxiv; Pfeiffer 1949, 375; Duesberg and Fransen 1966,
712–15.) Or is the cult a source from which his ethical thinking derives
some of its most profound and distinctive ideas? (See Stadelmann 1980,
52–4.)

Clearly, such complex questions cannot adequately be discussed in the
course of a short chapter. It would, moreover, serve no useful purpose to
repeat here what can readily be found elsewhere. We shall, therefore,
confine ourselves to an investigation of ben Sira's account of the ritual
performed by the Zadokite high priest Simon (50: 5–21). What, we may
ask, did ben Sira understand this ritual to mean? A brief answer may be
given at once, and it is possible that it may shed some light on the questions
posed above. In the mind of ben Sira, the high priest and his colleagues, as
they carry out the sacrificial service, perfectly embody that Wisdom which
elsewhere he identifies with the Torah (ben Sira 24: 23; for this observation,
compare very closely Perdue 1977, 189–90, and Crenshaw 1981, 153).
Sacrifice, it would seem, openly displays before men that very Wisdom
whose devoted servant ben Sira wishes to be. How is this so?

In the first place, a comparison of the description of Simon the high priest
with ben Sira's picture of Wisdom reveals important similarities which have

not, perhaps, been sufficiently appreciated hitherto. (But see Marböck
1971, 74–5.) Most striking is the use of imagery derived from fruit and trees
to describe both Wisdom and Simon, as the following quotations show. (The
Hebrew text of ben Sira 24 is lost. The oldest available text is therefore the
Greek translation of the book made by ben Sira's grandson, now preserved
in the Septuagint, and from this we shall work for the moment. See my note
on the editions used on p. 33.)

WISDOM	SIMON
I was exalted like a cedar in Lebanon	[Simon] like a sprout (*blastos*) of Lebanon in the days of harvest (50:8);[1] [Aaronide priests] like sprouts (*blastēma*) of cedars in Lebanon (50:12).[2]
and like a cypress on the mountains of Aermon (24:13).[3]	[Simon] like a cypress exalted in the clouds (50:10)[4]
Like a palm tree I was exalted in Engaddi,	[Aaronide priests] like the stock of palm trees (50:12)[5]
and like a rose plant in Jericho[6]	[Simon] like flower of roses[7] in the days of the new moon (50:8)
and like a comely olive in the plain (24:14).	like an olive[8] shooting forth fruits (50:10)
Wisdom is compared with cinnamon, aspalathus[9] and choice myrrh,	[Aspalathus is a *hapax legomenon* in LXX, but cinnamon and myrrh are ingredients of the holy oil with which priests were anointed (Exod. 30:23–4, 30).
galbanum, onyx, stacte and with the fume of incense (*libanos*) in the tent (24:15).[10] These are ingredients of incense: see Exod. 30:34–5, where it is termed *thumiama* (cf. Marböck 1971, 34).	Simon is like fire and incense (*libanos*) (50:9).[11]]

With the exception of incense (*libanos*) and roses, which are spoken of in
39:13–14, none of these words – cedar, cypress and so forth – occur in ben
Sira outside the verses which we have quoted. So many of the points of
comparison between Wisdom and Simon are identical; we are bound,
therefore, to enquire what the relationship between the two figures may be.

The imagery itself yields some valuable information. Incense figures
prominently: this substance, which was offered on the golden altar

immediately in front of the Holy of Holies, was from a very early period held to symbolize those who labour in Torah by studying it. This is clear from ben Sira's own words, as when he exhorts his pupils:

> Give heed to me, holy children, and send out shoots like a rose
>   growing by a water-stream;
> And like incense give a sweet odour,
> And put forth flowers like a lily. (ben Sira 39:13–14 Greek)

This use of incense imagery was fairly widespread. As an example of its use outside ben Sira, we may note the following lines from the Qumran Florilegium:

[God] has commanded that a Sanctuary of men be built for himself, that there they may send up, like the smoke of incense, the works of the Law. (4QFlor 1:6–7; translated Vermes 1975, 246)

Furthermore, Targum Yerushalmi 1 to Exodus 40:5 explains that the golden altar was set up

on account of the wise, who labour in the Torah, and their smell is spread abroad like sweet incense.

The actual effects of Torah-study, then, are compared with the incense smoke, which falls into the category of a 'most holy thing', and rises up at the very place in the sanctuary where God is present to meet his people (Exod. 30:36). As he offers sacrifice, Simon is compared with this incense which is so close to the Divine Presence. But let us also notice that ben Sira's 'holy children', who may not have been priests, are compared with incense; they are students of Wisdom–Torah and as such draw near to the Presence of God. Acquisition of Wisdom–Torah and priestly service are, by this comparison, placed on the same level (see below, p. 28, and compare Schürer 1979, 323).

Incense is offered in the sanctuary where, according to ben Sira, Wisdom herself takes up residence at God's express command (24:8–12). In this connection, the Lebanon imagery takes on great significance. As Geza Vermes has shown, an ancient exegetical tradition of Palestinian Judaism understood the geographical term 'Lebanon' symbolically to mean the Jerusalem Temple (Vermes 1961, 26–39); once again, by comparing with Lebanon both Wisdom and the high priest as he sacrifices, ben Sira links both to the sanctuary and indicates the intimate bond between them. Sanctuary imagery appears again in 50:12, where Simon, taking the sacrificial portions from his fellow priests, is compared with a young cedar in Lebanon, and his fellows with stocks of palm trees. This comparison, as Vermes (1961, 37) has shown, depends on Ps. 92:13–14:

> The righteous shall shoot forth like a palm tree,
> Like a cedar in Lebanon he shall grow great.

Those planted in the house of the Lord
Shall shoot forth in the courts of our God.

Here, palms and cedars are in the sanctuary. Ezekiel reports that, in the
restored sanctuary, palm trees shall be carved on the walls of the courts and
on the doors (Ezek. 40: 16, 22, 26; 41: 18, 19, 20, 25). Cypress will be used
for the building of the renewed temple; and the Psalmist who trusts in God
speaks of himself as a green olive tree in the house of his God (Isa. 60: 13; Ps.
52: 10; cf. Jer. 11: 16).

The use of tree imagery in this way is comprehensible when we recall
that, according to ben Sira, both Wisdom and the priests perform priestly
service (leitourgein) before the Lord on Mount Zion. Of herself, Wisdom
declares:

In the holy tent I served as priest (eleitourgēsa) before him,
And thus was I fixed on Zion. (24: 10).

The sacrifices offered by Simon and the priests in the temple on Mount Zion
are likewise a priestly service (leitourgia) before God:

[And Simon,] finishing the priestly service (sunteleian leitourgōn) at
   the altars,
To adorn the offering of the Most High, the Almighty,
Stretched out his hand to the libation cup. (50: 14–15)

And the people besought the Lord Most High
In prayer before the Merciful One
Until the adornment of the Lord was finished;
And they completed his priestly service [tēn leitourgian autou]. (50: 19)

In LXX leitourgein often translates the Hebrew root šrt (to render priestly
service): the root is used, for example, in Hebrew ben Sira 50:14, 19.
Sacrifice, it seems, is intimately bound up with Wisdom. Both of them are
part of the service of God on Zion. It is possible, however, that we can be
even more explicit about the nature of this service. Imagery involving trees
which are, as it were, present in the temple is extended by ben Sira to
include references to the Garden of Eden. This is especially evident in his
description of Wisdom, resident in the temple. For ben Sira tells how God
makes Wisdom abound like Pishon, Tigris, Euphrates and Gihon, the four
rivers which issued from the Garden of Eden (Gen. 2: 10–14). He also
remarks that the first man did not know her perfectly (ben Sira 24: 25–8;
reference to the Jordan in verse 26 does not destroy the Paradise imagery,
but ties the four Paradise rivers close to the land of Israel). His language is, in
all probability, an extension of that imagery which the prophet Ezekiel uses
in his picture of the Paradise river which flows from the right side of the
temple, its banks lined with trees (Ezek. 47: 1–12; cf. Zech. 14: 8; Ps. 46: 5;
Rev. 22: 1–2; see also Eichrodt 1970, 580–7, and Wevers 1969, 333–6). It

would appear, therefore, that ben Sira has portrayed the temple as an earthly Eden which sends out the Paradise waters of Wisdom.

The temple is identified with Paradise in other literature of the period. Most explicit is the book of Jubilees, whose traditions are very nearly contemporary with ben Sira. The most recent study of Jubilees (van der Kam 1977, 287) dates the work 'almost certainly between 161 and 140 BC and probably between 161 and 152', although most scholars date its final compilation to around 100 BC (for example, Eissfeldt 1966, 607–8). Jubilees tells us that Noah

knew that the Garden of Eden is the Holy of Holies, and the dwelling of the Lord, and Mount Sinai the centre of the desert, and Mount Zion – the centre of the navel of the earth: these three were created as holy places facing each other. (8: 19, translated Charles 1913, 26)

The Qumran sect, which was organized not long after ben Sira's time, looked upon itself as a sanctuary of men: see above, p. 25, and compare the Community Rule (1QS) 8:4–16 (Gärtner 1965). Not surprisingly, this sanctuary is depicted as an Eden-Paradise. Thus the community is described as a plantation of cypress, pine and box trees, Hebrew *brwš*, *tdhr*, and *t'ššwr* (Thanksgiving Hymn [1QH] 8: 5). These very same trees are found in the same order in the Hebrew Bible at Isa. 60: 13, where the prophet tells how they are destined to glorify the place of the Lord's sanctuary. The Qumran poet goes on to tell how his own community is hedged in by the flame of fire which turns this way and that, just as the Garden of Eden was (1QH 8: 12; Gen. 3: 24); and the plantation itself is to be an Eden of glory with well-watered trees (1QH 8: 16–20; see Mansoor 1961, 154). And the Psalms of Solomon, composed in the first century BC, echo the kind of thinking which we have already encountered when they speak of the Paradise of the Lord, the trees of life, as 'His holy ones' (Ps. Sol. 14: 2).

The position of the high priest in all this is not hard to determine. Here the Hebrew text of ben Sira is particularly helpful, in that it indicates that Simon's role in the temple cult is in some ways analogous to the place of the first man in the Garden of Eden. We are told that Adam's splendour, *tp'rt*, is above that of every living being: in the very next breath, ben Sira calls Simon the high priest the 'splendour' (*tp'rt*) of his people (cf. Marböck 1981, 128):

Shem and Seth and Enosh were visited,
And above every living being is the splendour of Adam [*tp'rt 'dm*].
The greatest of his brothers and the splendour of his people [*tp'rt 'mw*],
Was Simon the son of Johanan the priest. (49: 16–50: 1, Geniza MS B supported by Syriac. Like Smend (1906, 476–9), we accept this as the original reading.)

When Simon offers sacrifice, he does so in garments of splendour, *bgdy tp'rt* (50: 11), like Aaron, the ancestor of all priests. The high priest's vestments were symbols of Simon's religious and political authority (Schmitz 1910, 62–3), and his political power was very considerable (Stadelmann 1980, 157–63). According to later Rabbinic tradition, the vestments were none other than the garments which God had made for Adam, according to Gen. 3: 21 (see Numbers Rabbah 4: 8). Now Adam's splendour, *tp'rt*, relates most probably to his *rulership* over the created order. He is above every living creature, as ben Sira explains elsewhere:

> [God] set the fear of him over all creation,
> And gave him the rulership [*katakurieuein*] over
>   wild beasts and birds. (ben Sira 17: 4 Greek)

The reference could be to humanity's control over creation; but it was specifically to Adam that God gave this power, together with Adam's wife (Gen. 3: 21). Simon's splendour, *tp'rt*, also relates to his rulership. In his garments of splendour, in his priestly office, he exercises rulership over Israel which is the Lord's portion chosen out of all the nations of the earth. The chapter which begins with an account of man's creation and his rulership over the created world leads ben Sira to an acknowledgement of the unique status of Israel (17: 1–17). Adam is over all creation, Simon is over Israel, especially so over the temple, where Wisdom takes up residence.

It is important to notice, however, that, although Simon is the splendour of his people, others, who are not priests, may possess splendour, *tp'rt*. Thus ben Sira encourages his pupils, some of whom may not have been priests, to put on Wisdom like garments of glory and like a crown of splendour, *'trt tp'rt* (6: 31); the splendour of the stranger, the foreigner and the poor man is their fear of God, that is, their fidelity to God's commandments (10: 22); and the Fathers of Israel whom ben Sira singles out for praise as examples of those who possess Wisdom have their own splendour (44: 7).

Why all this should be so is clear, when it is remembered that ben Sira has identified divine Wisdom, resident in the temple, with the Torah, God's gift of ethical and ritual commandments to his people Israel (24: 13). The whole of his writing is planned so as to instil into his pupils a love for Wisdom–Torah and the upright following of her commandments. Wisdom is the highest of all gifts, reserved for those who love the Lord (1: 4–10); but she is granted only to those who keep her commandments (1: 26; 21: 11). Sacrifice is, in fact, specifically singled out as a mark of one who observes the commands of Wisdom–Torah:

> He who keeps the Law makes many offerings;
> He who devotes himself to the commandments sacrifices
>   a peace-offering. (35: 1)

All sacrificial activity is to be carried out *charin entolēs* (35:4), for the sake of the commandment, a phrase also used in connection with almsgiving, but on no other occasion in ben Sira's work:

> For the sake of the commandment help a poor man
> And according to his need do not send him away empty. (29:9)

Now it is in the highest degree unlikely that ben Sira counsels almsgiving simply because of the written commandment, and for no other reason. By the same token it seems unlikely that he regards sacrifice as desirable only because of the written commands to do it. In an illuminating and penetrating discussion of ben Sira 35:1ff., Stadelmann (1980, 88) is surely right in saying

für den Siraziden ist der Kultus göttliche Setzung und Gabe, nicht aber blosse dem Gebot korrespondierende Pflichtübung.

The precise meaning of ben Sira's encouragement of his pupils to act for the sake of the commandment can only be properly appreciated when it is recalled that he gives to Torah, identified with Wisdom, a cosmic role to play. Gerhard von Rad expresses most accurately and succinctly what many scholars have observed when he comments on ben Sira, chapter 24 as follows:

The question is not, 'Where does Torah come from?', but 'To what extent is Torah a source of Wisdom?' The answer is, *'Because Torah is a self-presentation of primeval order*, it is able to help men towards wisdom.' In the final section (vv. 25–34), the poem returns once again to the praise of wisdom and of its fullness. If one approaches this from the direction of the traditional presentation in the saving history ... one cannot marvel enough at how differently Sirach regards the prehistory of the Mosaic Torah. *It is the primeval order inherent in the whole world* ... In this provenance lies its worth. (von Rad 1972, 246; italics mine)

A little later, von Rad (247ff.) firmly dismisses any notion of 'nomism' from ben Sira's thinking, and in this assessment he is followed by Stadelmann (1980, 65–8).

Enough has been said to allow us to conclude. In the picture of Simon offering sacrifice, ben Sira draws a parallel with Wisdom's residence and priestly service on Mount Zion. In short, Simon, as he offers sacrifice, openly displays Wisdom. This is so, whether the service which ben Sira is describing is the ritual of the Day of Atonement or the daily ritual lamb sacrifice and incense offering ('Ó Fearghail 1978, 301–16). In the cultus, we find at least one aspect of that Wisdom which, to use von Rad's words, is a 'self-presentation of primeval order' and 'the primeval order inherent in the whole world'. Sacrifice, duly offered by the legitimate priests in the sanctuary chosen by God, is thus to some extent an earthly reflection of that divine order which permeates the universe and on which the creation stands. It is certainly a reflection of *primeval* order because, as we have seen, the sacrificing high priest in the sanctuary robed in his vestments is analogous to Wisdom ministering in the sanctuary and to the first man who worked in the Garden of Eden. It is interesting here to record a rabbinic tradition preserved in Targum Yerushalmi 1 to Gen. 2:7 that Adam was created of dust from the temple mount. That same Targum, Targum Neofiti 1, and the Fragment Targum to Gen. 2:15 agree that Adam was put into Eden to work in the Torah and to keep its commandments.

But Torah consists of more than commands to offer sacrifice. Ethical and moral commands are included, and it contains the deep and hidden mysteries of the divine plan (ben Sira 4:11–18; 14:20–7; 43:32–3; Hengel 1974, 144–56, 159–60). Torah study gives Wisdom (ben Sira 39:1–11; Stadelmann 1980, 232–46). If we have understood ben Sira correctly, the wise man, priest or layman, sends forth incense like Wisdom herself, and like the high priest (literally and metaphorically) as he offers sacrifice. The wise man, also, has a splendour, *tp'rt*, of his own (see above, p. 28).

The opposite of the wise man is the fool: such a man does not observe the commands of the Torah. He is wicked, unrighteous and lawless. A sacrifice offered by the wicked man, by the man who does not keep the commandments of the Torah, cannot reflect Wisdom, the primeval order of the universe. Indeed, ben Sira goes out of his way to say that God has not *commanded* anyone to sin (15:20). Hence we may account for his justly famous attack on those who offer sacrifices wrongfully gotten, in the wrong spirit and in a state of 'sin':

> He that sacrificeth of a thing wrongfully gotten, his offering is
>   made in mockery;
> And the mockeries of wicked men are not well-pleasing.
> The Most High hath no pleasure in the offerings of the ungodly;
> Neither is he pacified for sins by the multitude of sacrifices.
> (34:18–19, Revised Version translation)

It is possible that our observations may throw some light on the questions which are commonly asked about ben Sira's cultic piety and its relationship to his personal, apparently non-cultic spirituality and religious practice. For him, the Torah is the divine order inherent in the universe. It has been granted to men, but in a very special way: Torah is resident, at God's command, in the temple at Jerusalem and, as a result of this, the Jewish people have a special, indeed unique relationship with it. Sacrifice is part of Torah: that is to say, it is part of the divine order of the universe, and it is openly displayed on Mount Zion when the high priest, as political and religious head of the Jewish people, performs his sacrificial functions. But

Torah includes also the ethical and moral commands which ben Sira so heavily emphasizes. Right conduct, too, is a part of the divine order of the universe. As far as ben Sira is concerned, there can be no question of a dichotomy between ritual and moral commandments. Both kinds of commandment derive from Wisdom–Torah, and the wise man, the righteous, pious and learned man, is the one who, in tune with the divine order of the universe, observes all the commandments – ritual and ethical (compare Perdue 1977, 199, 211).

That the temple cult manifests an aspect of the primeval order of the universe is a notion which is based in part on biblical data. According to the Pentateuch, the pattern of the sanctuary was revealed to Moses directly from heaven (Exod. 25:9, 40). The Chronicler took up this idea, and considerably elaborated it (1 Chron. 28:11–19; Myers 1965, lxvii–lxxiii). In ben Sira's writing, the whole cultic order is linked to Wisdom, the Torah which is from heaven and from of old. Thus ben Sira is the earliest datable witness to a belief which was destined to become fairly widespread in Judaism. The book of Jubilees, for example, some of whose traditions may be as old as the time of ben Sira, expresses the idea that sacrifice and temple service are part of the order of the cosmos by stating that they are inscribed on the heavenly tablets. These contain Torah (Jub. 3:10; 4:32; 18:19) and records of men's deeds (30:19). Two originally separate traditions about their contents may have been combined by Jubilees (Davenport 1971, 10), but as containing Torah, they witness to a heavenly order and reality which is to be reflected on earth, especially in the sacrificial service. This service is, in fact, carried on by the angels in heaven in unison with the Israelite priests on earth. Thus the angel who reveals Jubilees to Moses tells him:

And the seed of Levi was chosen for the priesthood, and to be Levites, that they might minister before the Lord, *as we*, continually . . . (Jub. 30:18, trans. Charles 1913, 59)

Chapter 32 of Jubilees tells how the institution of Levi as a priest, and the ordering of cultic dues, tithes and so on and the celebration of the Feast of Tabernacles take place according to what had been indicated before in the heavenly tablets. The heavenly origin of the cultus and the choice of Levi is set in the context of God's covenant with Jacob at Bethel, when Jacob's name is changed to Israel (Jub. 32:17–19), and it is even possible that the recently published Temple Scroll from Qumran similarly regards the cultus as an earthly expression of the heavenly order (Maier 1978, 89–90, commenting on column 29, lines 8–10). Finally, it is perhaps not without significance that the Mishnah attributes to Simeon the Righteous – in all probability the Simon of whom ben Sira is writing (Moore 1927; Schürer 1979, 359–60) – the famous saying:

Upon three things the universe stands: upon the Torah, and upon the Temple service, and upon deeds of loving-kindness. (m. Aboth 1:2; see also Hengel 1974, 161)

It would be difficult to find a more appropriate summary of ben Sira's attitude to sacrifice and non-cultic piety than this.

For the earliest Christians it was, of course, Jesus who embodied the fullness of sacrifice and who represented its universal and cosmic significance: the Epistle to the Hebrews makes this much very plain. But in certain Pauline writings we find Christ crucified, that is to say, Christ as sacrifice, described precisely in the terms of Wisdom:

But we preach Christ crucified, unto Jews a stumbling-block, and unto Gentiles foolishness; but unto them that are called, both Jews and Greeks, Christ the power of God, and the Wisdom of God. (1 Cor. 1:23-4, Revised Version)

A few verses later in the same chapter, the writer speaks of Christ as having been made by God into Wisdom, righteousness and sanctification and redemption (1:30). The Wisdom of God is made manifest, for St Paul, in the sacrificial death of Jesus, whose offering embraces and redeems the whole created order, thus restoring to it its former perfection (Col. 2:8-23; 2 Cor. 5:14-19).

NOTES

1 Lat.: 'quasi tus redolens'. This reading probably derives from a pun on Hebrew *lbnwn* (Lebanon), *lbwnh* (incense), and Greek *libanos* (incense). The Hebrew (Geniza MS B) reads 'like the flower of Lebanon in the days of summer fruits, and like the fire of incense upon the offering'. On this, see further above, p. 25 and n. 11, below.

2 Syr. omits.

3 Syr.: 'like an oil tree in Senir, The Mount of Snow'; Lat.: 'quasi cypressus in monte Sion'.

4 Syr.: 'like an oil tree...'; see above, n. 3. Syr. agrees that Wisdom and Simon share the same point of comparison.

5 Syr. omits; Hebrew (Geniza MS B): 'like poplars of the wadi', *k'rby nhl*, an entirely different image. The Hebrew phrase occurs in Lev. 23:40, where it is associated with palm branches in the composition of the *lulab* for the Feast of Tabernacles, and in Job 40:22. But see Smend 1906, 485-6.

6 Syr.: *w'yk 'rbt wrd'*.

7 Hebrew (Geniza MS B) is corrupt; Smend (1906, 482) restores *nẓny 'npym* ('blossoms of branches'). Syr.: 'blades of corn', which Lévi (1901, 209) rightly regards as a 'fantaisie' deriving from a mistaken reading of Hebrew *qsyr* (harvest, crop), instead of *qyṣ* (summer fruits).

8 Hebrew (Geniza MS B): 'like a green olive tree full of berries'.

9 Syr.: 'like fumes of incense'.

10 Lat.: 'et quasi storax et galbanus et ungula et gutta et quasi libanus non incisus vaporavi habitationem meam, et quasi balsamum non mixtum odor meus',

with which compare Syr.: 'and like incense and galbanum and onychos and balsam, and like good oil I gave my smell'.

11 Hebrew (Geniza MS B) 'and like the fire of incense upon the offering, '*l hmnḥh*'. This could mean the incense offered as a memorial portion of the meal offering upon the outer altar of burnt offering (Lev. 6:8); so I. Lévi (1901, 209). But Greek and Syr. read 'incense upon the fire-pan', reading Hebrew *mḥth* for *mnḥh*. Lévi argues that both readings can equally be defended. The Greek and Syr. are, however, to be preferred, since it is generally agreed that ben Sira is describing either the Yom Kippur ritual or the Tamid ceremonies: see above, p. 29. In either ritual, incense figures prominently. On Yom Kippur it was taken into the Holy of Holies, and it would be surprising if ben Sira did not allude to it. If, however, our author is describing the Tamid, he would surely refer to the offering of incense on the golden altar, a ceremony whose performance the priests coveted (*Babylonian Talmud Yoma* 26a). In both these rituals, a fire pan or thurible was necessary. The incense of the meal offering, however, was a very minor ritual, and is hardly likely to have merited ben Sira's attention here. For the importance of the incense-offering on the inner golden altar, see Philo, *De Specialibus Legibus* I. 275–6 (Loeb Classical Library edition of *Philo*, vol. VII, translated by F. H. Colson [Cambridge, Mass.: Heinemann, 1968]).

REFERENCES

For the Hebrew Text of ben Sira, I have used *The Book of Ben Sira* (The Academy of the Hebrew Language and the Shrine of the Book. Jerusalem: Keter Press, 1973): for the Septuagint (LXX), A. Rahlfs, *Septuaginta*, vol. II (Stuttgart, 1935); and for the Latin and Syriac, F. Vattoni, *Ecclesiastico, Testo Ebraico con apparato critico e versioni greca, latina, e siriaca* (Naples: Instituto Orientale di Napoli, Pubblicazioni del Seminario di Semitistica, 1968).

Charles, R. H. (1913). The Book of Jubilees. In *Apocrypha and Pseudepigrapha of the Old Testament*, ed. R. H. Charles, vol. I, pp. 1–82. Oxford: Oxford University Press
Crenshaw, J. L. (1981). *Old Testament Wisdom. An Introduction*. London: SCM Press
Davenport, G. L. (1971). *The Eschatology of the Book of Jubilees*. Leiden: E. J. Brill
Duesberg, H. and I. Fransen (1966). *Les Scribes inspirés*. Paris: Maredsous
Eichrodt, W. (1970). *Ezekiel*. London: SCM Press
Eissfeldt, O. (1966). *The Old Testament. An Introduction*. Oxford: Blackwell
Gärtner, B. (1965). *The Temple and the Community in Qumran and the New Testament*. Cambridge: Cambridge University Press
Hengel, M. (1974). *Judaism and Hellenism*, vol. I. London: SCM Press
Klinzing, G. (1971). *Die Umdeutung des Kultus in der Qumrangemeinde und im Neuen Testament*. Göttingen: Vandenhoeck & Ruprecht
Lévi, I. (1901). *L'Ecclésiastique; ou, La Sagesse de Jésus, fils de Sirach*. Paris: Leroux
Maier, J. (1978). *Die Tempelrolle vom Toten Meer*. Munich: E. Reinhardt
Mansoor, M. (1961). *The Thanksgiving Hymns*. Leiden: E. J. Brill
Marböck, J. (1971). *Weisheit im Wandel: Untersuchungen zur Weisheitstheologie bei ben Sira*. Bonn: P. Hanstein
(1981). Henoch – Adam – der Thronwagen. *Biblische Zeitschrift* 25, 103–11

Milik, J. T. (1959). *Ten Years of Discovery in the Wilderness of Judaea*. London: SCM Press

Moore, G. F. (1927). Simeon the Righteous. In *Jewish Studies in Memory of Israel Abrahams*, pp. 348–64. New York: Jewish Institute of Religion

Myers, J. M. (1965). *I Chronicles*. New York: Doubleday

Ó Fearghail, F. (1978). Sir. 50, 5–21: Yom Kippur or The Daily Whole Offering? *Biblica* 59, 301–16

Perdue, L. G. (1977). *Wisdom and Cult*. Missoula: Scholars Press

Pfeiffer, R. H. (1949). *A History of New Testament Times with an Introduction to the Apocrypha*. New York: Harper and Row

Rivkin, E. (1963). Ben Sira and the Non-Existence of the Synagogue. A study in Historical Method. In *In the Time of Harvest. Essays in Honour of Abba Hillel Silver*, ed. D. J. Silver, pp. 321–54. New York: Macmillan

Schmitz, O. (1910). *Die Opferanschauung des späteren Judentums und die Opferaussagen des Neuen Testaments*. Tübingen: Mohr

Schürer, E. (1979). *The History of the Jewish People in the Age of Jesus Christ*, vol. II (revised edn by G. Vermes, F. Millar and M. Black). Edinburgh: T. & T. Clark

Smend, R. (1906). *Die Weisheit des Jesus Sirach erklärt*. Berlin: Reimer

Stadelmann, H. (1980). *Ben Sira als Schriftgelehrter*. Tübingen: Mohr

van der Kam, J. C. (1977). *Textual and Historical Studies in the Book of Jubilees*. Missoula: Scholars Press

Vermes, G. (1961). Lebanon. In *Scripture and Tradition in Judaism*, pp. 26–39. Leiden: E. J. Brill

(1975). *The Dead Sea Scrolls in English* (2nd edn). Harmondsworth: Penguin Books

von Rad, G. (1972). *Wisdom in Israel*. London: SCM Press

Wenschkewitz, H. (1932). Die Spiritualisierung der Kultusbegriffe Tempel, Priester, und Opfer im Neuen Testament. *Angelos* 4, 78–82

Wevers, J. W. (1969). *Ezekiel*. London: Nelson

Wright, R. B. (1966). Sacrifice in the Intertestamental Period. Unpublished Ph.D. thesis: Hartford Seminar Foundation

Yadin, Y. (1965). *The ben Sira Scroll from Masada*. Jerusalem: Israel Exploration Society and the Shrine of the Book

3

PAUL'S UNDERSTANDING OF THE
DEATH OF JESUS AS SACRIFICE

J. D. G. DUNN

The thesis put forward in what follows is that Paul's understanding of Jesus' life as having representative significance is the key which opens up to us his understanding of the significance of Jesus' death. Or to put the point in more technical shorthand: Paul's Adam christology is integral to his theology of Jesus' death as atoning sacrifice. The claim in essence is hardly a new one. It has been familiar in systematic theology in one form or another, as we might say, from Irenaeus ('theory of recapitulation' – Kelly 1960, 170–4) to Pannenberg (1968, 260–9). But it has been largely ignored or overshadowed in recent decades in New Testament scholarship, with the principal exception of M. D. Hooker (1971, 1978, 1981), and deserves more attention than it has received. Independently of Hooker I had developed my own version of the thesis (Dunn 1974) and now re-present it in an updated version.

JESUS AS REPRESENTATIVE MAN

The fact that Paul tells us next to nothing about the historical Jesus has always been at the heart of one of the most intractable problems in New Testament theology and Christian origins – the relation between the gospel of Jesus and the theology of Paul. The discontinuity between the two had been stressed by Liberal Protestantism and by the history-of-religions school, particularly W. Heitmüller (1912) and W. Bousset ([1921] 1970). And although R. Bultmann (1929, [1936] 1960) shared many of their conclusions, he did attempt to demonstrate a significant element of continuity between Jesus and Paul. More recently the probable influence of particular sayings of Jesus on Paul have been highlighted (Stanley 1961; Riesenfeld 1970; Dungan 1971; Barrett 1972; Allison 1982; Wenham 1985), and a link is still possible along the lines of *imitatio Christi* (1 Cor. 11: 1; Eph. 4: 20; Col. 2: 6; 1 Thess. 1: 6). Perhaps we should also mention that at the other end of the spectrum Paul's apparent lack of knowledge of

35

the historical Jesus has been made the main justification for a further attempt to revive the nevertheless thoroughly dead thesis that the Jesus of the gospels was a mythical figure (Wells 1971).

What does not seem to have been adequately appreciated is that for Paul the Jesus of history is integral to his soteriology; it is of vital significance for Paul that Jesus actually lived and died in history. Paul calls men not to take up some timeless ideal, not merely to believe in a divine being contemporary with him, but to believe in the Jesus who lived and died and now lives again. The contemporary Christ is one and the same as the Jesus of history. If it is not the same Jesus, then his gospel falls in ruins. It is the Jesus of history now exalted who challenges presumptuous and self-indulgent man; it is the presence here and now of the Jesus who lived and died which brings men to the crisis of decision. Paul's soteriology therefore hangs on the wholeness of his christology (cf. Rawlinson 1926, chapter 5; Davies 1948, 41–2, 49–57; Black 1954; Whiteley 1957; Scroggs 1966, 92–112; Hultgren 1987); separation of the Jesus of history from the Christ of faith does not characterize Paul's soteriology, it destroys it.

Why is this so? Because for Paul the earthly Jesus was not significant primarily for what he *said* or *did* during his life, but for what he *was*. And what he *did* by his death and resurrection gains its significance for salvation primarily from what he *was*. The key idea which runs through Paul's christology and binds it to his soteriology is that of solidarity or *represent-ation*. To adapt the words of Irenaeus, *Jesus became one with man in order to put an end to sinful man in order that a new man might come into being. He became what man is in order that by his death and resurrection man might become what he is.*

The most sustained expositions of Jesus' representative significance come in Rom. 5:12–21 and 1 Cor. 15:20ff., 45–9. In both instances Jesus is compared and contrasted with Adam. The point of the comparison and contrast lies in the representative significance of the two men. 'Adam' means 'man', 'humankind'. Paul speaks about Adam as a way of speaking about mankind. Adam represents what man might have been and what man now is. Adam is man, made for fellowship with God, become slave of selfishness and pride. Adam is sinful man. Jesus too is representative man. He represents a new kind of man – man who not only dies but lives again. The first Adam represents physical man (*psuchē zōsa, sōma psuchikon*) – man given over to death; the last Adam represents pneumatic man (*pneuma zōopoioun, sōma pneumatikon*) – man alive from the dead.

Now it is clear from the 1 Corinthians passage that Jesus only takes up his distinctively last Adam/man role as from the resurrection; Christ is eschatological Adam/man, 'the firstfruits of those who have fallen asleep'; only in and through resurrection does he become life-giving Spirit (Dunn 1973b, 1980).[1] How then can we characterize his representative function in his life and death? The answer seems to be that for Paul the earthly Jesus represents *fallen* man, man who though he lives again is first subject to death. Adam represents what man might have been and by his sin what man is. Jesus represents what man now is and by his obedience what man might become. This is most clearly expressed in four passages:

(a) Rom. 8: 3: 'What the law could not do, because it was weakened by the flesh, God has done – by sending his own Son in the very likeness of sinful flesh ('en homoiōmati sarkos hamartias')...' *Homoiōma* here as elsewhere in Paul means a very close likeness, a mirror image. In Rom. 1:23 its use with *eikōn* must signify an intensifying of the idea of likeness/image, otherwise the phrase *en homoiōmati eikonos* is merely tautologous – perhaps, indeed, an example of the semitic tendency to give added force to an idea by repeating it (compare Moulton and Howard 1929, 419–20). Thus: 'changed the glory of the incorruptible God into what was *nothing more than* the image of corruptible man...'. In Rom. 5: 14: 'death reigned from Adam to Moses even over those who did not sin *in just the same way* as Adam' ('epi tō homoiōmati tēs parabaseōs Adam'). In Rom. 6: 5 the 'likeness of Christ's death' does not mean baptism nor the death of Christ itself but the convert's experience of death to sin and life to God beginning to work out in himself, which Paul characterizes as a sharing in Christ's death and so as an experience which is the mirror image and actual outworking of Christ's own death to sin within the present age (6:10; Dunn 1970, 142–3). So in Rom. 8: 3 'en homoiōmati sarkos hamartias' must mean 'in the very form of sinful flesh' (see further Dunn 1988, on Rom. 6: 5 and 8: 3).

But is Paul saying then that Jesus became guilty of sin? No! As is generally recognized, *sarx* in Paul is not evil, otherwise he could not use it in a neutral sense, or speak of it being cleansed (2 Cor. 7: 1; Robinson 1926, 114–15; Stacey 1956, 162; Schweizer 1971, 135). Flesh is not evil, it is simply weak and corruptible. It signifies man in his weakness and corruptibility, his belonging to the world. In particular it is that dimension of the human personality through which sin attacks, which sin uses as its instrument (Rom. 7: 5, 14, 18, 25) – thus *sarx hamartias*. That is to say, *sarx hamartias* does not signify *guilty* man, but man in his *fallenness* – man subject to temptation, to human appetites and desires, to corruption and death. The 'sinful flesh' is nothing other than the 'sinful body' (Rom. 6: 6), the 'body doomed to death' (Rom. 7: 24).

Thus in Rom. 8: 3 Paul is saying simply that God sent his Son in the very form of fallen man, that is, as representative of fallen men. *Homoiōma* in other words does not distinguish Jesus from sinful flesh or distance him from fallen man, as is often suggested; rather it is Paul's way of expressing Jesus' *complete identity* with the flesh of sin, with man in his fallenness (cf. Althaus 1966; Barrett 1957; Kuss 1959; Jewett 1971, 150ff.). So far as Paul was concerned, Jesus had to share fallen humanity, sinful flesh, otherwise he could not deal with sin in the flesh. It was only because he shared man's sinful flesh that his death was 'a sacrifice for sin' and so served as God's act of judgement on sin in the flesh (see further below, pp. 42–7).

(b) Gal. 4: 4–5: 'When the fullness of time had come, God sent forth his Son, born of woman, born under the law ...'. The point is the same here. 'Born of woman' was a familiar phrase in Jewish ears and denoted simply 'man' (Job 14: 1, 15: 14 and 25: 4; 1QS 11: 20–1; 1QH 13: 14 and 18: 12–13, 16; Matt. 11: 11). 'Born under the law' likewise denotes the human condition, specifically that of the Jew (cf. 1 Cor. 9: 20; Gal. 4: 21), but of the Jew in a state of tutelage and bondage which is typical of mankind generally in its fallen enslavement under the 'elemental spirits' (Gal. 4: 3, 9). It was only by virtue of his identity with the human condition in its enslavement that Jesus could (by his death and resurrection) 'redeem those under the law' and enable them to share his sonship by adoption (Gal. 4: 5–7; cf. Rom. 8: 15–17) (see further Dunn 1980, 40–2).

(c) Phil. 2: 7–8. It is very likely that the Christ-hymn of Phil. 2: 6–11 uses an Adam christology, patterning the description of Christ on the well-established strand of Jewish reflection on Adam and his fall, but in such a way as to show how Jesus corrected the pattern. Adam, made in the image of God, sought equality with God and became man as he has been ever since, enslaved to corruption (cf. Rom. 8: 18–21) and the elemental spirits (cf. Gal. 4: 3), subject to death by virtue of his disobedience (cf. Rom. 5: 15–19). Christ, likewise in the form of God, refused to grasp at equality with God, but chose nevertheless to embrace the lot of man, accepting his condition of enslavement (Phil. 2: 7), and submitting himself to death as an act of obedience rather than the consequence of disobedience (Phil. 2: 8) (see further Dunn 1980/1989, xvii–xix, 114–19).

In particular we might simply note the two lines:

> en homoiōmati anthrōpōn genomenos
> kai schēmati heuretheis hōs anthrōpos.

This is the only other occurrence of *homoiōma* in Paul: he became the very likeness of men; he became just what men are. Indeed, he came 'hōs anthrōpos', that is, not just as one man among many, but *as man*, as representative man (cf. Martin 1967, 109–10 – man, who, be it noted, is immediately described as subject, obedient to death.

(d) 1 Cor. 15: 27: Paul explicitly quotes Ps. 8: 6 – 'He has put all things in subjection under his feet' – and refers it to the exalted Christ. Since Ps. 8: 4–6 was widely used in the early churches as a testimonium to Christ (Mark 12: 36 pars.; Eph. 1: 22; Phil. 3: 21; Heb. 2: 6–9; 1 Pet. 3: 22), it is probable that Paul had the whole passage in mind (cf. Dodd 1952, 32ff., 120ff., 126; Lindars 1961, 50ff., 168). That is to say, it is probable that Paul understood Ps. 8:4–6 with reference to Jesus in the same way as did the writer of the Epistle to the Hebrews. Jesus was the man who fulfilled the destiny God had originally intended for man (Barrett 1968; Bruce 1971; Dunn 1980, 108–11). Man had been made 'lower than the angels', but had not yet been crowned with glory and honour and granted Lordship over all things. But in contrast, Jesus *had* fulfilled that destiny. He too was man 'for a short while lower than the angels', but had now been crowned with glory and honour 'because he suffered death' (Heb. 2:9). That this train of thought is in Paul's mind in 1 Cor. 15:27 is likely in view of the explicit Adam christology in the immediate context of the quotation. In other words, Jesus entered his role as New Man only after living and suffering as Man. Adam had missed his destiny because of sin and his destiny had become death (1 Cor. 15:21–2). Only after Jesus lived out that destiny (death) and through it created a new destiny (resurrection) could the original destiny be fulfilled. Only by his living out the destiny of Adam could the destiny of the Last Adam become a reality.

Space prohibits an elaboration of this aspect of Paul's theology – that *for Paul Jesus in his life and death is representative man, representative of fallen man – by living out that fallenness to the death and overcoming it in resurrection he becomes representative of new life, of new man.* It must suffice to refer briefly to other passages where the same christology is reflected: Rom. 1:3 – as man he lives, like man, *kata sarka* – through flesh, and to some extent anyway, in terms of flesh (Dunn 1973a); Rom. 6:9–10 – as man of flesh, like men, he is subject to death. In short, as representative man he shares the weakness and corruptibility of man's flesh; as representative man he knows the power of the powers, law, sin and death, which enslave men. 'Christ dies the death of the disobedient, of sinners' (Rom. 5:6, 8; 2 Cor. 5:21) (Delling 1964).

We might mention also Paul's use of the title *Christos*. It is frequently assumed that Paul uses the title quite conventionally and adds nothing to it (for example, Bultmann 1952; Cullmann 1959; Fuller 1965). This is not, however, true. And the way in which Paul does use it is of special interest for us. For, on the one hand, he links it firmly to Jesus in his death: the Christ is the Crucified One (1 Cor. 1:23 and 2:2; Gal. 3:1). And, on the other, it becomes the chief vehicle for Paul's expression of Christ's representative capacity, the solidarity of believers with the risen Christ: he is baptized in the Spirit *into* Christ (Rom. 6:3; 1 Cor. 12:13; 2 Cor. 1:21; Gal. 3:27); he has died *with* Christ, is crucified *with* Christ, his life is hid *with* Christ in God, and so on (Rom. 6:3–4, 8; 8:17; Gal. 2:19–20; Eph. 2:5; Phil. 1:23; Col. 2:20; 3:1, 3; 1 Thess. 5:10); his present life in all its aspects is lived *in* Christ (for example, Rom. 6:11 and 8:39; 1 Cor. 15:22; 2 Cor. 5:17, 19; Gal. 2:4; Phil. 2:1; Col. 1:28; 1 Thess. 2:14); he is member of the *body* of Christ (Rom. 12:5; 1 Cor. 12:12, 27 etc.); Christ is the offspring of Abraham to whom the promise has been made, and all who identify themselves with Christ are counted as Abraham's children (Gal. 3:16, 26–9). The two distinctively Pauline emphases in Paul's use of *Christos* cannot be unrelated. *Christ is representative man precisely as the Crucified One* (see further Dunn 1975, 324–38; and for further material where Adam christology provides the basic structure of the thought see also Black 1954 and Scroggs 1966).

2 Cor. 5:14 now becomes clearer as one of the most explicit expressions of Paul's understanding of Jesus as representative man – 'one man died for all; therefore all mankind [*hoi pantes*] has died'. When we talk of Christ as representative man we mean that what is true of him in particular is true of men in general. When we say Adam is representative man in his fallenness, we mean that *all men* are fallen. So when Paul says Christ died as representative man he means that there is no other end possible for men – all mankind dies, as he died, as flesh, as the end of sinful flesh, as the destruction of sin. Had there been a way for fallen man to overcome his fallenness and subjection to the powers, Christ would not have died – Christ as representative man would have shown men how to overcome sinful flesh. His death is an acknowledgement that there is no way out for fallen men except through death – no answer to sinful flesh except its destruction in death. 'Man could not be helped other than through his annihilation' (Barth, cited in Berkouwer 1956, 135). Only through death does the New Man emerge in risen life. In other words, if we may follow the train of thought a little further, Christ's identification with fallen men is up to and into death. But there it ends, for death is the end of fallen men, the destruction of man as flesh – Christ died, all died. Beyond death he no longer represents all men, fallen man. In his risen life he represents only those who identify themselves with him, with his death (through baptism), only those who acknowledge the Risen One as Lord (2 Cor. 5:15). Only those who identify themselves with him in his death are identified with him in his life from death. Hence it is a mistake to confine the 'all' of 5:14 to believers (*pace* Martin 1986). The 'all' of 4:14–15 are not identical with 'the living' of 5:15. Jesus' representative capacity before resurrection (sinful flesh – Rom. 8:3) is different from his representative capacity after resurrection (spiritual body – 1 Cor. 15:44–5). All die. But only those 'in Christ' experience the new creation (2 Cor. 5:17) (cf. Hooker 1978, 479; 1981, 71). In short, as Last Adam Jesus represents only those who experience life-giving Spirit (1 Cor. 15:45).

JESUS' DEATH AS A SACRIFICE

We must now attempt to view Jesus' death through Paul's eyes from another angle and then bring the two viewpoints together to give us a fuller picture of Paul's thinking about the cross. I refer to Paul's understanding of

Jesus' death in terms of cultic sacrifice. The idea of blood sacrifices and of divine–human relationships being somehow dependent on them is so repellent to post-Enlightenment man that many commentators have instinctively played down or ignored this side of Paul's theology. E. Käsemann, for example, reacts against undue emphasis being given to the idea of sacrificial death by firmly denying that Paul ever definitely called Jesus' death a sacrifice, and sums up: 'The idea of the sacrificial death is, if anything, pushed into the background' (1971, 42–5; cf. Hengel 1981, 45–6). Similarly G. Friedrich, in one of the most recent studies of the topic, goes out of his way to play down any sacrificial significance in the passages we are about to cite (1982, 47, 66, 70–1, 75, 77). An examination of Paul, however, makes it difficult to escape the conclusion that Käsemann and Friedrich have fallen into the trap of making Paul's language less foreign and less distasteful and so have missed both the offence of Paul's thought and its point (see particularly Stuhlmacher's critique of Friedrich, 1983, especially 297–304).

In Rom. 3:25 *hilastērion* cannot have any other than a sacrificial reference. Since the word is used so often in LXX for the lid of the ark, the 'mercy-seat', the only real debate has been whether it should be understood as *place* or *means* of expiation/propitiation – the latter ('means') being probably the more appropriate (cf. 4 Macc. 17:22; Josephus, *Antiquities*, 16:182; Gen. 6:16 Sym.) (see Morris 1955–6; Kertelge 1967, 55–7; Schlier 1977; otherwise Janowski 1982, 350–4; Hultgren 1985, 55–60). And even if the verse is a quotation (see e.g., Stuhlmacher 1981; Williams 1975, 5–19; Meyer 1983), Paul gives it such a central place in a key passage of his exposition that it must be very expressive of his own thinking; indeed in such a case one quotes from an earlier text or source because it puts the point as well as or better than one can oneself.

The attempt has sometimes been made to see as the immediate background of Rom. 3:25 the martyr theology which finds its clearest expression in 4 Macc. 17:21–2, where *hilastērion* is used to describe the atoning significance of the Maccabean martyrs' deaths (Lohse 1963, 152 n.4; Hill 1967, 41–5; Williams 1975, 248). This is certainly possible. But two qualifications are necessary. First, martyr theology is itself an application of sacrificial metaphor; the reason why the death of the martyrs can be thought to carry such weight of atonement is because their death can be seen as a kind of sacrifice. Indeed in Diaspora Judaism martyr theology is sacrificial precisely because it served as one of the substitutes for the sacrificial cult in faraway Jerusalem (Lohse 1963, 71). Second, in Rom. 3:25 the *hilastērion* is presented by God himself. This thought is not present in Jewish martyr theology but is quite common in connection with the sacrificial cult in the Old Testament (cf. Kertelge 1967, 57–8; 1976). Thus, whether or not Paul was consciously alluding to martyr theology here, it is most likely that the primary reference to his metaphor was to Christ's death as cult sacrifice (cf. Kuss 1959, 165–6).

Rom. 8: 3: 'God sent his Son in the very likeness of sinful flesh and for sin' ('peri hamartias'); the New English Bible translates the last phrase 'as a sacrifice for sin'. And this is wholly justified since *peri hamartias* is regularly used in LXX to translate the Hebrew *hatta'th* (sin offering – e.g. Lev. 5: 6–7, 11 and 16: 3, 5, 9; Num. 6: 16 and 7: 16; 2 Chron. 29: 23–4; Neh. 10: 33; Ezek. 42: 13 and 43: 19; in Isa. 53: 10 it translates the Hebrew *'asham*, guilt-offering) (see particularly Wright 1980 and Wilckens 1980; O. Michel changed his mind in favour of this view in the fifth edition of his *Der Brief an die Römer* (1977), 251). It is likely that Paul drew the words from this background as a deliberate allusion, since otherwise the phrase is unnecessarily vague.[2] Some commentators object that such a reference confuses Paul's thought at this point (for example, Schlatter 1935, 257; Lohse 1963, 152 n. 6; Friedrich 1982, 68–71), although Paul is well known for his mixed metaphors (see, for example, Rom. 7: 1–6; Gal. 4: 1–6, 19). But is the charge just? The logic of Paul's thought is, in fact, quite straightforward: the sin-offering was just what the law provided to cover the unwilling sins which Paul has been lamenting in chapter 7 (Wright 1980). And when Paul says that God sent his Son 'peri hamartias' ('in order that the just requirement of the law might be fulfilled in us . . .'), does he not include the law of the sin-offering as part of 'the just requirement of the law'?

1 Cor. 5: 7: Paul explicitly states, 'Christ, our paschal lamb, has been *sacrificed*.' It is frequently remarked that 'the Paschal victim was not a sin-offering or regarded as a means of expiating or removing sins' (Gray 1925, 397). However, the Passover is already associated with atonement in Ezek. 45: 18–22, and this link was probably already firmly forged in the double association of the Last Supper with the Passover and with Jesus' 'blood poured out [*ekchunnomenon*] for many', which we find in the Synoptic traditions (Mark 14: 24 pars), where the language is unavoidably sacrificial and signifies atonement (Jeremias 1966, 222ff.). The same tendency to run together different metaphors and descriptions of Jesus' death so that old distinctions are blurred and lost is clearly evident elsewhere in the early churches (1 Pet. 1: 18–19; John 1: 29), and Paul's language in 1 Cor. 5: 7 and elsewhere hardly suggests that it was otherwise with him.

2 Cor. 5: 21: 'God made him into sin, him who knew no sin.' The antithesis 'made into sin' / 'sinless', makes it difficult to doubt that Paul had in mind the cult's insistence on clean and unblemished animals for the sacrifices (Daly 1978, 237, 239). A more specific allusion to the Day of Atonement's scapegoat is probable (Windisch 1924). Perhaps there is also an allusion to the suffering servant of Isa. 53 (Cullmann 1959, 76; Jeremias 1965a, 97 n. 441; Bruce 1971; Furnish 1984; Martin 1986); but this

should not be seen as a way of lessening the sacrificial allusion, since Isa. 53 itself is studded with sacrificial terminology and imagery, and the role of the Servant cannot fully be understood apart from the sacrificial background of his death (Taylor 1958, 190; Barth 1961, 9–10).

Similarly the several passages in which Paul uses the phrase 'in or through his blood' cannot be understood except as a reference to Christ's death as a sacrifice (Rom. 3:25 and 5:9; Eph. 1:7 and 2:13; Col. 1:20). Again attempts have been made to avoid the full offensiveness of the allusion (e.g. those cited in Davies 1948, 232ff.). But the emphasis on blood can hardly have come from the tradition of Jesus' death since it was not particularly bloody (Schweizer 1962, 74) and must be drawn from the understanding of Jesus' death in terms of cult sacrifice (for example, Taylor 1958, 63–4; Davies 1948, 236; Lohse 1963, 138–9; Barth 1961, 7). Likewise Paul's talk of Jesus' death as 'for sins' (Rom. 4:25 and 8:3; 1 Cor. 15:3; Gal. 1:4) or 'for us', and so on (Rom. 5:6–8 and 8:32; 2 Cor. 5:14–15, 21; Gal. 2:20 and 3:13; Eph. 5:2, 25; 1 Thess. 5:9–10) probably reflects the same influence, even if, in the latter case, it is mediated through martyr theology (Riesenfeld 1972; cf. Delling 1964, 87).

PAUL'S THEOLOGY OF ATONING SACRIFICE

Granted then that Paul sees Jesus' death as a sacrifice, what light does this throw on Paul's understanding of Jesus' death? The obvious way to answer the question is to enquire into the Old Testament or Jewish theology of sacrifice. But here we run into a considerable problem. For, as is well known, there is no clear rationale in Judaism concerning sacrifice. No doubt the sacrifices were very meaningful to the pious and penitent worshipper in Israel (Rowley 1967, chapter 4). But just what the essence of atonement was for the Jew remains an unsolved riddle. 'It seems necessary to admit that we do not know or understand what the Old Testament and "Judaism" really believed and taught about the mystery of expiating sacrifice' (Barth 1961, 13).

On the other hand, in view of the passages cited above, particularly Rom. 3:25 and 8:3 and 2 Cor. 5:21, it seems likely that Paul himself had a fairly well-defined theory of sacrifice. Moreover, whereas rabbinic thought may already have begun to play down the importance of sacrifice and to recognize other means of expiation (Davies 1948, 253–9; Lohse 1963, 21ff.), Paul seems to retain an important place for the category of sacrifice in describing the effect of Jesus' death (cf. Barth 1961, 33). This too suggests that, however obscure Jewish theology was, or at least now appears to our perception, Paul himself could give a fairly clear exposition of atoning sacrifice. One possible way forward, therefore, is to read back Paul's understanding of sacrifice by correlating the two conclusions we have already reached – that Paul thinks of Jesus dying both as representative man and in terms of cultic sacrifice – and by examining the sacrificial ritual in their light. The exercise is necessarily speculative, but it may help to illuminate Paul's understanding of Jesus' death.

(a) First, we note that the *sin*-offering, like Jesus' death in Rom. 8: 3, was intended to deal with sin. In some sense or other, the ritual of killing the sacrifice removed the sin from the unclean offerer. Now it is true that the sin-offering dealt only with inadvertent or unwilling sins – according to Old Testament ritual there was no sacrifice possible for deliberate sins. But at the same time the fact that a death was necessary to compensate for even an inadvertent sin signifies the seriousness of even these sins in the cult. The others were too serious for any compensation to be made. In such cases the sinner's *own* life was forfeit – no other life could expiate his sin (de Vaux 1964, 94–5).

(b) Second, as Jesus in his death represented man in his fallenness, so presumably Paul saw the sin-offering as in some way *representing* the sinner in his sin. This would probably be the significance for Paul of that part of the ritual where the offerer laid his hand on the beast's head. Thereby the sinner identified himself with the beast, or at least indicated that the beast in some sense represented him (Nagel 1958, 379; Rowley 1967, 133; Gese 1981, 105–6; Daly 1978, 100–6; Janowski 1982, 199–221; Hofius 1983, 35–6): that is, represented him *as sinner*, so that his sin was somehow identified with it, and its life became forfeit as a result – just as Christ, taking the initiative from the other side, identified himself with men in their fallenness (Rom. 8: 3), and was made sin (2 Cor. 5: 21).

It is by no means universally held that this was the generally understood meaning of the act. The laying of a hand on the head of the beast is sometimes given a far less significant role – simply indicating ownership, or signifying the readiness of the offerer to surrender that which belonged to him (see particularly Eichrodt 1961, 165–6; de Vaux 1964, 28, 63; cf. Schillebeeckx 1980, 487). But this hardly seems an adequate explanation of the importance attached to this action in the detailed instructions of Lev. 4. And if that was all the action meant we would have expected it to be repeated in all sacrifices, non-bloody ones as well, whereas, in fact, it only occurs in the case of sacrifices involving blood. Again, where the same action is used outside the sacrificial ritual, *identification seems to be the chief rationale*. Thus, in Num. 27: 18, 23 and Deut. 34: 9, Moses lays hands on Joshua, thereby imparting some of Moses' authority to him, that is, conveying some of himself in his role as leader to Joshua, so that Joshua becomes in a sense another Moses. In Num. 8: 10, the people lay their hands on the Levites so that the Levites become their representatives before the Lord, in particular taking the place of their first-born. Finally, in Lev. 24: 14, hands are laid on a blasphemer prior to his execution by stoning.

The whole people performs the execution, but only those who witnessed the blasphemy lay their hands on his head. This suggests that they do so to identify themselves with the blasphemer insofar as by hearing the blasphemy they have been caught up in his sin (cf. Daube 1956, 226–7).

The only place where the significance of laying hands on an animal in cultic ritual is explained is Lev. 16:21, where the high priest lays both his hands on the second goat in the Day of Atonement ceremony – thereby explicitly laying the sins of the people on the head of the goat. Of course, it was the first goat which was sacrificed as a sin-offering, whereas the second goat was not ritually killed, only driven into the desert (and left to die). But were the two layings-on of hands seen as quite distinct and different in significance? In the most recent full-scale treatment B. Janowski (1982, 219–20) would so argue, against those who have understood them to bear the same significance (Janowski disputes with P. Volz, R. Rendtorff and K. Koch). But is the transfer of sin and identification with the animal *as sinner* as different as Janowski suggests? Is it not more likely that the two goats were seen as part of the one ritual, representing more fully and pictorially what one goat could not? Perhaps, indeed, part of the significance of the Day of Atonement ritual was that the physical removal of the sins of the people out of the camp by the second goat demonstrated what the sin-offering normally did with their sins anyway – sin-offering and scapegoat being taken as two pictures of the one reality (Wilckens 1978, 237). This is certainly the implication of Mishnah, *Shebuoth* 1:7:

R. Simeon says: As the blood of the goat that is sprinkled within (the Holy of Holies) makes atonement for the Israelites, so does the blood of the bullock make atonement for the priests; and as the confession of sin recited over the scapegoat makes atonement for the Israelites, so does the confession of sin recited over the bullock make atonement for the priests.

And a similar merging is already implied in the Temple Scroll from Qumran, where the same formula is used for both sin-offering and scapegoat (cols. 26–7). Rom. 8:3 and 2 Cor. 5:21 strongly suggest that Paul too had in mind such a composite picture of Jesus' death as sacrifice.

Against this view, that the sin-offering was thought to represent the offerer, it has been argued that if the beast became laden with the offerer's sin it would be counted as unclean and so could not be used in sacrifice (Eichrodt 1961, 165 n. 2; Nagel 1958, 378). But does not this objection miss the point? The animal must be holy, wholly clean, precisely so that priest and sinner may be certain that its death is *not its own*, that it does not die for any uncleanness of its own. Only a perfect beast can represent sinful man; only the death of a perfect animal can make atonement for imperfect man.

Alternatively the argument has been put that the sin-offering could not embody sin since the priests ate the meat left over from some of the sin-offerings. Since they could not eat contaminated flesh, the sacrifice could not have been contaminated by sin (Eichrodt 1961, 165 n. 2; de Vaux 1964, 94). But again this seems to miss a key point – namely that the life of the animal was regarded as its blood (Lev. 17: 10–12; Deut. 12: 23). The priests did not, of course, eat the blood. On the contrary, the blood was wholly used up in the ritual. Indeed, the blood played a more important role in the sin-offering than in any other sacrifice (de Vaux 1961, 418; 1964, 92; Daly 1978, 108). And the sprinkling of the blood 'was regarded as the essential and decisive act of the offering up' (Büchler 1928, 418–19); 'it is the blood, that is the life, that makes expiation' (Lev. 17: 11). Thus, since the life *is* the blood, so the *life* of the sacrifice was wholly used up in the ritual. The equivalence between the life of the man and the life of the beast lay in the *blood* of the victim, not in the whole victim. And, since the blood was wholly used up, the use made of the carcase did not affect its role as sin-offering; that role was completed in the blood ritual.

(c) Third, if we extend the line of reasoning in the light of Rom. 8: 3 and 2 Cor. 5: 14, 21, the conclusion follows that Paul saw the death of the sacrificial animal as the death of the sinner *qua* sinner, that is, the destruction of his sin. The manner in which the sin-offering dealt with sin was by its death. The sacrificial animal, identified with the offerer in his sin, had to be destroyed in order to destroy the sin which it embodied. The sprinkling, smearing and pouring away of the sacrificial blood in the sight of God indicated that the life was wholly destroyed, and with it the sin of the sinner.

One can hardly fail to recognize what we may call the sacrificial chiasmus or 'interchange' (see Hooker 1971, 1978, 1981):

By the sacrifice the *sinner* was made *pure* and *lived free of that sin*;
By the sacrifice the *pure* animal *died*.

And we can hardly fail to fill out the rest of the second line by adding:

By the sacrifice the *pure* animal was made *impure* and *died for that sin* –

by its death destroying the sin. That this is wholly in accordance with Paul's thought is made clear by 2 Cor. 5: 21, the clearest expression of the sacrificial chiasmus/interchange:

For our sake God made the *sinless one* into *sin*
so that in him *we* might become the *righteousness* of God.

So too Rom. 8: 3:

[God] condemned *sin* in the flesh [of *Jesus*]
in order that the *just requirement of the law* might be fulfilled in *us*.

So too Gal. 4:4–5:

God sent forth his *Son*,
A   born of woman,
B   born *under the law*,
B   in order that he might redeem those *under the law*,
A   in order that we might receive the *adoption*.

So too Gal. 3:13, although here the metaphor is not directly sacrificial:

Christ redeemed us from the *curse* of the law
having become a *curse* for *us*.

In short, *to say that Jesus died as representative of fallen man and to say that Jesus died as sacrifice for the sins of men is for Paul to say the same thing.* His death was the end of fallen man, the destruction of man as sinner. But only those who, like the offerer of old, identify themselves with the sacrifice may know the other half of the chiasmus and interchange, the life of Christ beyond the death of sin, the righteousness of God in Christ.

PAUL'S *THEOLOGIA CRUCIS*

We cannot go further into Paul's soteriology in this essay. But since his understanding of the *process* of salvation also falls under the heading of a 'theology of the cross', we should simply note the extent to which the above exposition is confirmed thereby. I have developed the point elsewhere (Dunn 1975, 326–38) and need only summarize it here.

For Paul, union with Christ in his death is not a once-for-all event of initiation now past and gone for the believer. Despite the aorist tenses of Rom. 6:3–4, Paul also uses perfect tenses (Rom. 6:5; Gal. 2:19–20; 6:14): identification with Christ in his death is a *process* as well as an *event*. The event is more precisely to be defined as the event which sets the process in motion. The believer has been nailed to the cross of Christ, and is still hanging there! This is simply a vivid way of saying that the death of 'the old nature', of 'the body of sin' is not accomplished in an instant. Rather it is a lifelong process, only completed in the resurrection of the body (Rom. 8:17–23; 2 Cor. 4:7–5:5). Only then will the union with Christ in his resurrection be complete (Rom. 6:5–8). In the between-time of the present, the process of salvation is the outworking of Christ's death as well as of his life, a sharing in his sufferings as well as in the power of his resurrection (Rom. 8:10–11; 2 Cor. 4:10; Phil. 3:10–11). Unless this two-sidedness of Paul's soteriology is appreciated Paul's soteriology is bound to be misunderstood (see further Dunn 1987, 2858–64; 1988, 301–3).

It is this soteriology which we can now see to be wholly consistent with and indeed consequential upon Paul's understanding of Jesus' death as a representative and sacrificial death of sinful humankind. One side of the process of salvation is the *destruction* of the sinner *qua* sinner, of man in his belongingness to this age, as determined by the desires and values of this age, 'the old man'. And this, if we are correct, is what the sin-offering accomplished ritually or sacramentally. It is precisely by identification with Christ in his death as a *sacrifice* that the process of the dying away of the believer in his dependence on this age can be accomplished; only so can the *destruction* of the sinful flesh, the body of death, be accomplished without destroying the believer at the same time. In short, the rationale of sacrifice as expounded above is integral to Paul's whole gospel.[3]

CONCLUSIONS AND COROLLARIES

This recognition of the representative and sacrificial character of Jesus' death confirms the central importance of the death of Jesus in Paul's understanding of how God's saving purpose actually works. Jesus' death as sacrifice is not an incidental throwback to Paul's pre-Christian faith which can be discarded without affecting his theology as a whole. Sacrifice is not merely one metaphor among many which can be set aside without loss in favour of more pleasing metaphors, such as 'reconciliation'. It *is*, of course, a metaphor, but one which goes so much to the heart of Paul's understanding of the death of Jesus and sheds so much light on Paul's understanding of the process of salvation that to set it aside would be to close an important window into Paul's theology.

Since Jesus' death as sacrifice is such an important category for Paul's thought we should take special care to ensure that the key words used to describe it reflect Paul's emphases as closely as possible. Otherwise there is a real danger that Paul's theology as a whole will be skewed and the concerns which the very metaphor was intended to express will be misunderstood. This seems to me still to be a danger in the continued insistence on the part of some scholars that the words 'propitiation' and 'substitution' are fundamental terms in any restatement of Paul's theology (e.g. Ladd 1975, 427–33).

(a) *Propitiation.* Should we translate *hilastērion* in Rom. 3.25 as 'propitiation' or 'expiation'? The debate was re-initiated by C. H. Dodd more than fifty years ago by his rejection of all propitiatory significance for the *hilaskesthai* word group in LXX (Dodd 1935). The most effective response came from L. Morris and made unavoidable some retreat at least from Dodd's overstatement (Morris 1950–1; 1955, chapters 4–5; see also Nicole 1955; Hill 1967, 23–36). Particularly important was Morris' reminder that context as well as individual usage must always be considered.

Nevertheless, in view of the larger understanding of Jesus' death which we have gained above, and without neglecting the context, 'expiation' does seem to be the better translation for Rom. 3:25. The fact is that for Paul *God is the subject of the action*; it is God who provided Jesus as a *hilastērion*. And if God is the subject, then the obvious object is sin or the sinner. To argue that God provided Jesus as a means of propitiating *God* is certainly possible, but less likely. For one thing, regularly in the Old Testament the immediate object of the action denoted by the Hebrew *kipper* is the removal of *sin* – either by purifying the person or object, or by wiping out the sin; the act of atonement 'cancels', 'purges away', sin. It is not God who is the object of this atonement, nor the wrath of God, but the sin which calls forth the wrath of God (Dodd 1935; Schlatter 1935, 145; Büchsel 1965, 314ff., 320ff.). So, for example, 2 Kgs 5:18: Naaman prays, 'May *Yahweh* expiate [*hilasetai*] your *servant*'; Ps. 24:11; 'For the honour of thy name, O Lord, expiate [*hilasē*] my *wickedness*'; Ecclus. 5:5–6:

> Do not be so confident of pardon [*exilasmou*]
>> that you sin again and again.
> Do not say, 'His mercy is so great,
>> he will pardon my sins, however great [*exilasetai*].'

And for another, if we have indeed gained an insight into Paul's understanding of the rationale of sacrifice, then it follows that for Paul the way in which Christ's death cancels out man's sin is *by destroying it* – the death of the representative sacrifice as the destruction of the sin of those represented, because it is the destruction of man's sinful flesh, of man as sinner. The New English Bible therefore correctly translates Rom. 3:25: 'God designed him to be the means of expiating sin by his sacrificial death.'

On the other hand, we must go on to recognize that a secondary and consequential result of the destruction of a man's sin in the sin-offering is that he no longer experiences the wrath of God which his sin called forth. At this point we must give weight to Morris' reminder that this section of Romans follows immediately upon the exposition of God's wrath 'against all ungodliness and wickedness of men' (Rom. 1:18). Almost inevitably, therefore, the action of God which makes righteousness possible for men does involve the thought that wrath need no longer apply to them. As C. K. Barrett notes: 'It would be wrong to neglect the fact that expiation has, as it were, the effect of propitiation: the sin that might have excited God's wrath is expiated (at God's will) and therefore no longer does so' (1957, 78).

But we must be clear what we mean by this. As Rom. 1:18–32 shows, God's wrath means a process willed by God – the outworking of the destructive consequences of sin, destructive for the wholeness of man in his relationships (see particularly Travis 1970; also Morris 1955, 161–6; Whiteley 1964, 61–72). Jesus' death therefore does not propitiate God's wrath in the sense that it turns an angry God into one who forgives; all are agreed on that point of exegesis. But, in addition, it is not possible to say, as some do, that Jesus' death propitiates God's wrath in the sense of turning it away. The destructive consequences of sin do not suddenly evaporate. On the contrary, they are focussed in fuller intensity on the sin – that is, on fallen humanity in Jesus. In Jesus on the cross was focussed not only man's sin, but the wrath which follows upon that sin. The destructive consequences of sin are such that if they were allowed to work themselves out fully in man himself they would destroy him as a spiritual being. This process of destruction is speeded up in the case of Jesus, the representative man, the *hilastērion*, and destroys him. The wrath of God destroys the sin by letting the full destructive consequences of sin work themselves out and exhaust themselves in Jesus. Such at any rate seems to be the logic of Paul's theology of sacrifice.

This means also that we must be careful in describing Jesus' death as penal, as a suffering the penalty for sin. If we have understood Paul's theology of sacrifice aright, the primary thought is the *destruction* of the malignant, poisonous organism of sin. Any thought of *punishment* is secondary. The wrath of God in the case of Jesus' death is not so much retributive as preventative (cf., for example, Farmer 1943; Moule 1968). A closer parallel may perhaps be found in vaccination. In vaccination germs are introduced into a healthy body in order that by destroying these germs the body will build up its strength. So we might say the germ of sin was introduced into Jesus, the only one 'healthy'/whole enough to let that sin run its full course. The 'vaccination' seemed to fail, because Jesus died. But it did not fail, for he rose again; and his new humanity is 'germ-resistant', sin-resistant (Rom. 6: 7, 9). It is this new humanity in the power of the Spirit which he offers to share with men.

(b) *Substitution.* As we have to seek for a sharper definition of *hilastērion* than 'propitiation' affords, so that of the two words 'expiation' seems more able to bear that fuller meaning, so we must examine 'substitution' to check whether it is the best word to describe Paul's theology of the death of Christ. For many, 'substitution' is perhaps the key word in any attempt to sum up Paul's thought at this point. It is significant that D. E. H. Whiteley's whole discussion of the death of Christ in Paul's theology is framed with reference to this question (with chiefly negative conclusions) (1964, 130–48). Both Morris and D. Hill argue from 4 Macc. 6: 29 and 17: 21 that the idea of 'substitution' is involved in the thought of Rom. 3: 24–5 – that for Paul Jesus' death was substitutionary (Morris 1955, 173; Hill 1967, 75–6; cf. Jeremias 1965b, 36). And Pannenberg gives the word 'substitution' a central role in his exposition of the meaning of Jesus' death, though he does take care to speak of 'inclusive substitution' (1968, 263–4). So too for Morris, 2 Cor. 5: 14, 21 can hardly be understood except in substitutionary terms – 'the death of the One took the place of the death of the many' (1965, 220). This is a very arguable case, and it certainly gains strength from the theology of sacrifice outlined above – for there it would be quite appropriate to speak of the death of the sacrifice as a substitutionary death.

Nevertheless, although 'substitution' expresses an important aspect of Paul's theology of the atonement, I am not sure that Paul would have been happy with it or that it is the best single word to serve as the key definition of that theology. The trouble is that 'substitution' has two failings as a definition: it is too one-sided a concept, and it is too narrow in its connotation.

'Substitution' is too *one-sided* because it depicts Jesus as substituting for man in the face of God's wrath. But we do no justice to Paul's view of Jesus' death unless we emphasize *with equal or greater weight* that in his death Jesus also substituted *for God* in the face of man's sin – 'God was in Christ reconciling the world to himself' (2 Cor. 5:19). In other words, 'substitution' shares the defects of 'propitiation' as a description of Jesus' death. It still tends to conjure up pagan ideas of Jesus' standing in man's place and pleading with an angry God. 'Substitution' does not give sufficient prominence to the point of primary significance – that God was the subject: God provided Jesus as the *hilastērion*; God sent his Son as a sin-offering; God passed judgement on sin in the flesh; God was in Christ reconciling the world to himself – '*God in Christ*. No thought is more fundamental than this to St Paul's thinking' (Taylor 1958, 75; the point is strongly reiterated by Wilckens 1978, 236–7 and Hofius 1983). Our earlier exposition of Paul's theology of Jesus as Man suggests that a much more appropriate word is *representation*: in his death Jesus represented not just man to God but also God to man. And while 'substitution' is an appropriate description of Paul's theology of sacrifice, it is perhaps more definite than our knowledge of Paul's thought, and of the sacrificial ritual, permits; whereas, in discussing Paul's view of sacrifice, 'representation', the identification of the offerer with his sacrifice, was a word we could hardly avoid. So here, 'representation' gives all the positive sense of 'substitution' (a positive sense I by no means deny) which the context requires, while at the same time bringing in the other side of the equation which 'substitution' tends to exclude.

'Substitution' is also too *narrow* a word. It smacks too much of individualism to represent Paul's thought adequately. It is true, of course, that Paul can and does say Christ 'loved me and gave himself for me' (Gal. 2:20). But his more typical thought is wider. For as we have seen, in Paul's theology Jesus represents *man*, not just a man, on the cross. Christ died as man, representative man. As Adam represents man so that his fallenness is theirs, so Jesus represents fallen man so that his death is theirs. The point is that he died not *instead of* men, but *as* man; 'he died for all, therefore all have died' (2 Cor. 5:14). That is to say, fallen men do not escape death – any more than they escape wrath; *they die!* Either they die their own death without identifying themselves with Christ; or else they identify themselves with Christ so that they die his death – his death works out in their flesh. And only insofar as it does so do they live (Rom. 7: 24–5; 8: 10–13, 17; 2 Cor. 4: 10–12; Phil. 3: 10–11; Col. 1: 24) (see further Dunn 1975, 326–38; cf. Delling 1964, 91–2; Tannehill 1966). Either way *fallen humanity cannot escape death*; resurrection life, the life of the Spirit, lies on the other side of death, his death. Jesus' death was the death of the old humanity, in order that his resurrection might be the beginning of a new humanity, no longer contaminated by sin and no longer subject to death (Rom. 6: 7–10). In short, Jesus dies not so much as substitute in place of men, but as man, representative man (so also Hooker 1971, 358; 1981, 77).

As I implied at the beginning of the second section, an emphasis on Paul's theology of Jesus as representative man and of his death as sacrifice for sin increases the strangeness of Paul's gospel to twentieth-century man. But if we can only do justice to Paul's theology by highlighting these aspects of it, then this is unavoidable. Indeed it is necessary to face up squarely to this strangeness and not baulk at it, for only by tracing out the warp and woof of Paul's thought will we begin to understand its overall pattern; and only by thinking through his mind, so far as we can, will we be able to reinterpret his thought to modern man without distorting its character and central emphases (for examples of such an attempt, see Knox 1959, chapter 6; Moule 1968). I do not suggest that that reinterpretation is easy, and to undertake it requires a much fuller investigation of the other side of Jesus' death – the life of the Spirit (Rom. 8: 1ff.), the life-giving Spirit (1 Cor. 15: 45). But that is another story.

NOTES

1 R. P. Martin has recently (1984) contested this interpretation by arguing that the passage alludes to 'Christ's pretemporal existence' rather than to his eschatological state, an interpretation I find very odd. The whole topic is the resurrection body, and the logic is that Christ, the first resurrected man, sets the pattern for the rest, just as Adam set the pattern for man in this age (cf. Rom. 8: 29; Phil. 3: 21). Martin's rejoinder to me in 1983 (p. xxi) falls under the same critique.

2 Among others Barrett (1957) thinks that Paul means nothing more precise than Gal. 1: 4 – Jesus Christ gave himself 'for our sins' ('huper tōn hamartiōn'). But LXX in Ezekiel usually uses *huper* instead of *peri* in reference to the sin-offering, and Paul may well regard *peri hamartias* and *huper tōn hamartiōn* as equivalent phrases. In the mind of a Jewish Christian could 'for our sins' have any other reference than to the cult? The NEB has, quite rightly, 'Jesus Christ, who sacrificed himself for our sins'.

3 N. T. Wright criticizes my treatment of Adam christology (Dunn 1980, 111–13) as 'a bare exemplarist view: Jesus is the pattern to show people how to attain to the new sort of humanity'. 'It is not clear, from this account, why the cross should

have been necessary at all' (Wright 1983, 388). I find this caricature astonishing since it has completely ignored the references made in the passage criticized to an earlier version of this chapter (Dunn 1974). I do not expound the wholeness of Paul's theology in every treatment of a Pauline theme. The coherence of my exposition of Paul's understanding of Jesus' death and resurrection as saving events should be clear to anyone who has read my *Jesus and the Spirit* (1975, 326–38).

REFERENCES

Allison, D. C. (1982). The Pauline Epistles and the Synoptic Gospels: The Pattern of Parallels. *New Testament Studies* 28, 1–32.

Althaus, A. W. H. P. (1966). *Der Brief an die Romer* (10th edn), Das Neue Testament Deutsch, 6. Göttingen: Vandenhoeck

Barrett, C. K. (1957). *The Epistle to the Romans*. London: Black
(1968). *The First Epistle to the Corinthians*. London: Black
(1972). I am not ashamed of the Gospel. In *New Testament Essays*, pp. 116–43. London: SPCK

Barth, M. (1961). *Was Christ's Death a Sacrifice?* Edinburgh: Oliver & Boyd

Berkouwer, G. C. (1956). *The Triumph of Grace in the Theology of Karl Barth*. Grand Rapids: Eerdmans

Black, M. (1954). The Pauline Doctrine of the Second Adam. *Scottish Journal of Theology* 7, 170–9

Bousset, W. ([1921] 1970). *Kyrios Christos*, English translation (2nd edn). Nashville: Abingdon

Bruce, F. F. (1971). *1 & 2 Corinthians*. London: Oliphants

Büchler, A. (1928). *Studies in Sin and Atonement*, Jews' College Publications, 11. London: Humphrey Milford

Büchsel, F. (1965). Hilasterion. In *Theological Dictionary of the New Testament*, vol. III, pp. 318–23. Grand Rapids: Eerdmans

Bultmann, R. (1952). *Theology of the New Testament*, vol. I. London: SCM Press
([1936] 1960). Jesus and Paul. In *Existence and Faith*. London: Fontana, 217–39
([1929] 1969). The Significance of the Historical Jesus for the Theology of Paul. In *Faith and Understanding: Collected Essays*, London: SCM Press, 220–46

Cullmann, O. (1959). *The Christology of the New Testament*. London: SCM Press

Daly, R. J. (1978). *Christian Sacrifice*. Washington: Catholic University of America

Daube, D. (1956). *The New Testament and Rabbinic Judaism*. London: Athlone

Davies, W. D. (1948). *Paul and Rabbinic Judaism*. London: SPCK

de Vaux, R. *See* Vaux, R. de

Delling, G. (1964). Der Tod Jesu in der Verkündigung des Paulus. In *Apophoreta, E. Haenchen Festschrift*. Berlin: Topelmann

Dodd, C. H. (1935). Atonement. In *The Bible and the Greeks*. London: Hodder and Stoughton
(1952). *According to the Scriptures*. London: Nisbet

Dungan, D. L. (1971). *The Sayings of Jesus in the Churches of Paul*. Oxford: Blackwell

Dunn, J. D. G. (1970). *Baptism in the Holy Spirit*. London: SCM Press

54 J. D. G. DUNN

(1973a). Jesus – Flesh and Spirit: an Exposition of Romans 1: 3–4. *Journal of Theological Studies* n.s. 24, 40–68

(1973b). 1 Corinthians 15:45 – Last Adam, Life-giving Spirit. In *Christ and Spirit in the New Testament*, C. F. D. Moule Festschrift, ed. B. Lindars and S. S. Smalley, pp. 127–41. Cambridge: Cambridge University Press

(1974). Paul's Understanding of the Death of Jesus. In *Reconciliation and Hope*, L. L. Morris Festschrift, ed. R. J. Banks, pp. 125–41. Exeter: Paternoster

(1975). *Jesus and the Spirit*. London: SCM Press

(1980). *Christology in the Making*. London: SCM Press [2nd edn 1989]

(1987). Paul's Epistle to the Romans, An Analysis of Structure and Argument. *Aufstieg und Niedergang der Römischen Welt* II. 25:4, 2842–90

(1988). *Romans*. World Biblical Commentary. Dallas, Texas: Word

Eichrodt, W. (1961). *Theology of the Old Testament*, vol. 1. London: SCM.

Farmer, H. H. (1943). The Notion of Desert Bad and Good. *Historisches Jahrbuch* 41, 347–54

Friedrich, G. (1982). *Die Verkündigung des Todes Jesu im Neuen Testament*. Neukirchen-Vluyn: Neukirchener

Fuller, R. H. (1965). *The Foundations of New Testament Christology*. London: Lutterworth

Furnish, V. P. (1984). *II Corinthians*, Anchor Bible, 32A. New York: Doubleday

Gese, H. (1981). *Essays on Biblical Theology*. Minneapolis: Augsburg

Gray, G. B. (1925). *Sacrifice in the Old Testament*. Oxford: Oxford University Press

Heitmüller, W. (1912). Zum Problem Paulus und Jesus. *Zeitschrift für die Neutestamentliche Wissenschaft* 13, 320–37

Hengel, M. (1981). *The Atonement*. London: SCM Press

Hill, D. (1967). *Greek Words and Hebrew Meanings*. Cambridge: Cambridge University Press

Hofius, O. (1983). Sühne und Versöhnung. Zum paulinischen Verständnis des Kreuzestodes Jesu. In *Versuche, das Leiden und Sterben Jesu zu verstehen*, ed. W. Maas, pp. 25–46. Munich: Schnell & Steiner

Hooker, M. D. (1971). Interchange in Christ. *Journal of Theological Studies* n.s. 22, 349–61

(1978). Interchange and Atonement. *Bulletin of the John Rylands Library* 60, 462–81

(1981). Interchange and Suffering. In *Suffering and Martyrdom in the New Testament*, ed. W. Horbury and B. McNeil, pp. 70–83. Cambridge: Cambridge University Press

Hübner, H. (1983). Sühne und Versöhnung. *Kerygma und Dogma* 29, 284–305

Hultgren, A. J. (1985). *Paul's Gospel and Mission*. Philadelphia: Fortress

(1987). *Christ and his Benefits: Christology and Redemption in the New Testament*. Philadelphia: Fortress

Janowski, B. (1982). *Sühne als Heilsgeschehen*. Neukirchen-Vluyn: Neukirchener

Jeremias, J. (1965a). *The Servant of God* (revised edn). London: SCM Press

(1965b). *The Central Message of the New Testament*. London: SCM Press

(1966). *The Eucharistic Words of Jesus* (revised edn). London: SCM Press

Jewett, R. (1971). *Paul's Anthropological Terms*. Leiden: Brill

Käsemann, E. (1971). *Perspectives on Paul*. London: SCM Press

Kelly, J. N. D. (1960). *Early Christian Doctrines* (2nd edn). London: Black

Kertelge, K. (1967). 'Rechtfertigung' bei Paulus. Münster: Aschendorff
    (1976). Das Verständnis des Todes Jesu bei Paulus. In Der Tod Jesu: Deutungen im
    Neuen Testament, ed. K. Kertelge, pp. 114–36. Freiburg: Herder
Knox, J. (1959). The Death of Christ. London: Collins
Kuss, O. (1959). Der Römerbrief, vol. II. Regensburg: Pustet
Ladd, G. E. (1975). A Theology of the New Testament. London: Lutterworth
Lindars, B. (1961). New Testament Apologetic. London: SCM Press
Lohse, E. (1963). Martyrer und Gottesknecht (2nd edn). Göttingen: Vandenhoeck
Martin, R. P. (1967). Carmen Christi. Cambridge: Cambridge University Press
    (1983). Carmen Christi (2nd edn). Grand Rapids: Eerdmans
    (1984). The Spirit and the Congregation: Studies in 1 Corinthians 12–15. Grand
    Rapids: Eerdmans
    (1986). 2 Corinthians, Word Biblical Commentary 40. Waco, Texas: Word
Meyer, B. F. (1983). The Pre-Pauline Formula in Rom. 3, 25–26a. New Testament
    Studies 29, 198–208
Michel, O. (1977). Der Brief an die Römer (5th edn). Göttingen: Vandenhoeck
Morris, L. (1950–1). The Use of hilaskesthai etc. in Biblical Greek. The Expository
    Times 62, 227–33
    (1955). The Apostolic Preaching of the Cross. London: Tyndale
    (1955–6). The Meaning of hilasterion in Romans 3, 25. New Testament Studies 2,
    33–43
    (1965). The Cross in the New Testament. Exeter: Paternoster
Moule, C. F. D. (1968). The Christian Understanding of Forgiveness. Theology 71,
    435–43
Moulton, J. H. and W. F. Howard (1929). A Grammar of New Testament Greek.
    Edinburgh: T. & T. Clark
Nagel, G. (1958). Sacrifices. In Vocabulary of the Bible, ed. J. J. von Allmen,
    pp. 275–80. London: Lutterworth
Nicole, R. R. (1955). C. H. Dodd and the Doctrine of Propitiation. Westminster
    Theological Journal 17, 117–57
Pannenberg, W. (1968). Jesus: God and Man. London: SCM Press
Rawlinson, A. E. J. (1926). The New Testament Doctrine of the Christ. London:
    Longmans
Riesenfeld, H. (1970). Parabolic Language in the Pauline Epistles. In The Gospel
    Tradition, pp. 187–204. Oxford: Blackwell
    (1972). Huper. In Theological Dictionary of the New Testament, vol. VIII,
    pp. 507–16. Grand Rapids: Eerdmans
Robinson, H. W. (1926). The Christian Doctrine of Man (3rd edn). Edinburgh: T. & T.
    Clark
Rowley, H. H. (1967). Worship in Ancient Israel. London: SPCK
Schillebeeckx, E. (1980). Christ. London: SCM Press
Schlatter, A. (1935). Gottes Gerechtigkeit. Stuttgart: Calwer
Schlier, H. (1977). Der Römerbrief. Freiburg: Herder
Schweizer, E. (1962). Erniedrigung und Erhöhung bei Jesu und seinen Nachfolgern.
    Zürich: Zwingli
    (1971). Sarx. In Theological Dictionary of the New Testament, vol. VII, pp. 98–151.
    Grand Rapids: Eerdmans
Scroggs, R. (1966). The Last Adam. Oxford: Blackwell

Stacey, W. D. (1956). *The Pauline View of Man.* London: Macmillan

Stanley, D. M. (1961). Pauline Allusions to the Sayings of Jesus. *Catholic Biblical Quarterly* 23, 26–39

Stuhlmacher, P. (1981). Zur neueren Exegese von Röm. 3, 24–26. In *Versöhnung, Gesetz und Gerechtigkeit*, pp. 117–35. Göttingen: Vandenhoeck

 (1983). Sühne oder Versöhnung. In *Die Mitte des Neuen Testaments, E. Schweizer Festschrift*, ed. U. Luz and H. Weder, pp. 291–316. Göttingen: Vandenhoeck

Tannehill, R. C. (1966). *Dying and Rising with Christ.* Berlin: Topelmann

Taylor, V. (1958). *The Atonement in New Testament Teaching* (3rd edn). London: Epworth

Travis, S. H. (1970). Divine Retribution in the Thought of Paul. Unpublished Ph.D. thesis, Cambridge University

Vaux, R. de (1961). *Ancient Israel.* London: Darton

 (1964). *Studies in Old Testament Sacrifice.* Cardiff: University of Wales Press

Wells, G. A. (1971). *The Jesus of the Early Christians.* London: Pemberton

Wenham, D. (1985). Paul's Use of the Jesus Tradition. Three Samples. In *The Jesus Tradition Outside the Gospels. Gospel Perspective*, 5, pp. 7–37. Sheffield, JSOT Press

Whiteley, D. E. H. (1957). St. Paul's Thought on the Atonement. *Journal of Theological Studies* n.s. 8, 242–6

 (1964). *The Theology of St. Paul.* Oxford: Blackwell

Wilckens, U. (1978). *Der Brief an die Römer*, vol. I (Rom. 1–5). Evangelisch-katholischer Kommentar zum Neuen Testament, 6. Zürich: Benziger

 (1980). *Der Brief an die Römer*, vol. II (Rom. 6–11). Evangelisch-katholischer Kommentar zum Neuen Testament, 6. Zürich: Benziger

Williams, S. K. (1975). *Jesus' Death as Saving Event.* Missoula: Scholars

Windisch, H. (1924). *Der zweite Korintherbrief.* Göttingen: Vandenhoeck

Wright, N. T. (1980). The Meaning of *peri hamartias* in Romans 8.3. In *Studia Biblica 1978* III, *Journal for the Society of the New Testament* supp. 3, pp. 453–9. Sheffield: JSOT Press

 (1983). Adam in Pauline Christology. In *Society of Biblical Literature Papers*, ed. K. H. Richards. Chico: Scholars

4

HEBREWS: THE FINAL SACRIFICE

A. N. CHESTER

Hebrews is of obvious importance for any consideration of sacrifice in Christian theology. The Epistle as a whole is concerned, more fully and intensively than any other book in the New Testament, with the themes of priesthood and cult, and it sets these closely in relation to its interpretation of the death of Christ. Indeed, the main argument of Hebrews seems clear and simple enough: Jesus as high priest has made the perfect offering of himself, atoning for sin once and for all, and thus rendering obsolete the endless, ineffective sacrifice of the cult.

Yet on closer inspection we find a more complex picture. We are confronted not only with much cultic detail, but also with talk of a heavenly sanctuary, a throne in heaven and a heavenly altar; there is also a great deal said of angels, a long discourse about Melchizedek and other apparently strange material. Clearly it is important in the first place to do justice to what Hebrews actually says. This obvious point has to be made over against recent studies (above all Daly 1978a; 1978b) which impose an alien perspective upon the Epistle. Thus Daly uses Origen's three categories (the sacrifice of Christ, the sacrifice of the Christian, the Christian as the New Temple) as the norm by which to evaluate the evidence of Hebrews. Hence he reckons the unique and extensive treatment of sacrifice in Hebrews to be unsafe as the basis for a New Testament theology of sacrifice, for which Paul provides a more reliable starting-point (*sic*). On this basis, Daly is content to assert that there is nothing in Hebrews that does not or cannot harmonize with Paul's teaching on sacrifice. This whole approach simply begs questions; if the writer of Hebrews cannot be allowed to speak for himself, it would be better to leave him alone.

We must, then, examine Hebrews on its own terms. First, then, it should be emphasized that the argument of the book is not abstract, but is a 'word of consolation' (13:22, Revised Standard Version, here and below) addressed to a specific situation. It is not enough, however, simply to recognize that the emphasis of Hebrews is above all paraenetic. Thus, for example, Laub (1980) stresses this theme but, equally, constantly reiterates his view that the cultic christological and soteriological emphasis should be determinative for interpreting Hebrews, and the history-of-religions' background at best secondary. Hence, ironically, he fails to do justice to (*inter alia*) Hebrews' distinctive presentation of Jesus' high-priesthood and sacrifice (thus, for instance, he posits a false dichotomy between Jesus' death on the cross and his entry into the heavenly world). It is obvious enough that Hebrews says much that is of christological and soteriological importance, and uses cultic language to this end; but Laub's method of approach does not allow him to do justice to the significance of this.

Secondly, therefore, we have to stress that Hebrews is not simply exhortatory, but is dealing with urgent and threatening issues which have arisen within the particular situation that it addresses. The proper perspective for understanding Hebrews, therefore, is to specify (as far as possible) what these questions are, how and why they arose and the resources the writer draws on to deal with them. It is of course notoriously difficult to say with any certainty what is the date, provenance and purpose of Hebrews; it is correspondingly difficult to be sure of its precise 'history-of-religions' and conceptual context. Possibly, indeed, it is the complexity of these questions, and the unconvincing nature of the various solutions proposed, that have led Laub and others to abandon the approach of setting Hebrews in context. Thus, for example, the influential argument advanced by Käsemann (1939), positing links between Hebrews and Gnosticism, has been properly criticized by, among others, Hofius (1970, 1972). Again, the apparently impressive case that can be made for dependence on Philo (above all Spicq 1952–3; cf. Dey 1975, Strobel 1975, Thompson 1977, 1979) is in fact untenable (Williamson 1970); equally, the close connections with the Qumran texts (see especially Kosmala 1959) do not in themselves provide an adequate explanation for Hebrews.

These and similar arguments thus fail to do justice to Hebrews. The mistake, at least as far as the links with Philo and Qumran are concerned, is to make traditions and usages which Hebrews draws on from what is commonly available within first-century Judaism the basis for limiting Hebrews exclusively to a particular sphere where such usage is prominent. This point is especially well made by Horbury (1983); he himself argues cogently for the main determinative influence upon the writer of Hebrews to be the hierocratic-theocratic outlook widespread within first-century Judaism. As Horbury shows, the same basic attitude goes back to pre-Maccabean times and continues well beyond 70 AD; it is strongly evidenced for the first century by Philo and Josephus. What especially characterizes this attitude is a distinctive understanding of the importance of the levitical, but above all Aaronic, priesthood, developed from the Pentateuchal basis but diverging in a number of significant respects. The Aaronic priesthood (and high priest) assume an important role especially because they mediate

God's rule over his people; this pervasive influence also has considerable political, social and economic implications. In short, it is a developed view of the priesthood which potentially impinges upon the whole way of life of Judaism in the first century, not only in Palestine but also beyond.

For the most part, Horbury's argument is extremely plausible; it also has the obvious advantage of explaining the overriding emphasis in Hebrews on sacrifice and priesthood. If the community addressed in Hebrews had known the temple cult as providing the sole means of atonement for sin, and the Aaronic priesthood as directly mediating the divine rule, it would be surprising if these did not continue to offer an attraction, particularly in view of the delay of the Parousia. Undoubtedly the status of the temple posed a pressing problem for Jewish-Christians from early on: the question, that is, of whether atonement was now 'located' in the temple or in the death of Christ, and whether these two were mutually exclusive. Clearly this dilemma was most acute for Jewish-Christians living in Palestine and especially in Jerusalem; it led to some compromise and continued particip-ation in the temple worship (Hengel 1981, 54–6). As Horbury argues, a pre-70 Palestinian setting for Hebrews is at least possible; it would account especially well for the urgency of the author's argument, directed especially against priesthood and sacrifice. Since, however, as Horbury has indicated, the basic view involved extended into the Diaspora and well beyond 70, it is not necessary here to discuss further the particular setting.

One obvious point that emerges from all this is that the categories of priesthood and cult are forced upon the writer of Hebrews; it is not that he chooses them, from a number of possibilities, because they seem especially suitable. It is the fact that these categories have formed the central focus and frame of reference for the community the writer is addressing, and that this community is in danger of lapsing from its faith in Christ, that compels the writer to use these categories to explain the significance of Christ. Yet although this may account for the main themes of the long central section (4:14–10:39) and other material, in a sense it raises rather than resolves important questions of interpretation. Above all, what has to be explained is *how* the writer shows that Christ transcends and renders invalid these cultic categories. It is, of course, clear that the writer makes skilful, positive use of the themes that he is constrained to employ, so that priesthood and cult are made to appear to be the best possible categories for expressing the significance of Christ. Equally, it is evident that he uses a rich variety of resources available to him from developed Jewish tradition (for example, the Melchizedek figure and the Aqedah motif). Again, however, simply to indicate what were the constraints and resources determinative for the writer, in the historical situation, still begs the question of the way in which he developed his own distinctive interpretation.

What, then, are the distinctive and controlling perspectives of the writer's approach? First, we must note the eschatological emphasis of Hebrews, the importance of which has been demonstrated above all by Barrett (1956). It is central to the understanding of the Epistle to recognize that for the writer the final eschatological event has already taken place, once-for-all, and that the messianic age is set in motion. Hebrews in this sense, of course, belongs to and reflects the early Christian messianic-eschatological tradition. Equally, however, it is these emphases amongst others that appear to provide close links with the Qumran community; certainly the Christian messianic claim is distinctive, but nevertheless we need to probe further to discern important aspects of Hebrews' approach.

Thus, secondly, as Barrett already hints and as others have subsequently argued more fully, it is the distinctive categories of the developed Jewish apocalyptic tradition that must be invoked in order to explain the distinctive terminology and conceptual framework of the Epistle. The importance of this approach has been indicated by various scholars (thus, for example, Hofius 1970; 1972; 1976; Schenke 1973; Williamson 1976; cf. Hengel 1976; Rowland 1982). Indeed the argument has at times been set in exaggerated terms or rather loose terminology (thus especially Schenke 1973); the same criticism would also apply, to an extent, to the pioneering work of Scholem ([1960] 1965), and this may partly explain its rejection by a number of scholars (e.g. Laub 1980). It appears that similar overstatements of this position may have also given rise to the objections of Horbury (1983); while he notes sympathetically some general similarities between Hebrews and *merkabah* mysticism, he doubts that Hebrews can be seen as a first-century visionary work, since it lacks reference to the chariot, the various heavens and the esoteric practice (amongst other things) characteristic of the mystic and especially *hekhaloth* texts. With all this I fully agree; it neither can nor should be claimed that the writer of Hebrews is a visionary or that Hebrews itself is a visionary work (as Revelation, for example, within the New Testament, is). Hence, since the concern of Hebrews is not with the revelation of divine secrets, we should not expect any reference to esoteric practice, chariot ascent, elaborate description of the heavenly world or other technical detail. In arguing for the relevance of apocalyptic-mystical categories, I do not imply that Hebrews is an esoteric speculative work; all I wish to claim is that Hebrews reflects, and indeed the author makes active use of, the spatial dualism and general cosmological framework of the apocalyptic-mystical tradition. Certainly there are implicit here difficult questions, especially concerning the relation between the earlier apocalyptic traditions and the developed *hekhaloth* material, and the dating and interpretation of the material as a whole, which must be clearly recognized. Yet is it clear that the author is drawing upon an apocalyptic cosmology widely familiar within first-century Judaism; it provides simply the framework of thought for, and not the dominant theme of, the Epistle, and the author clearly expects it to be intelligible. Further, it is very plausible that cultic and priestly background is important for the development of the apocalyptic-mystical tradition (compare, for example, Maier 1964; Kuhn 1964; Aune 1972; Gruenwald 1980); it would then suit the author's purpose especially well to use this tradition in order to interpret the cultic themes with which he has to deal. There is, therefore, no suggestion that the author of Hebrews belongs to an exclusive or esoteric movement; instead he is simply drawing upon a tradition itself widely intelligible and influential within first-century Judaism. It is this that enables him to offer his own distinctive interpretation of the central cultic categories: that is, it is the spatial dualism of this tradition that allows the author to set aside the claims and centrality of the earthly cult and priesthood in favour of the heavenly priesthood and its unique sacrifice.

The point of all this, therefore, is that it is the apocalyptic-mystic cosmology in general, and the spatial dualism in particular, that provides an important conceptual framework without which it is impossible to explain adequately what the Epistle says about sacrifice. It is the whole argument, and not simply passages such as 9: 24 and 12: 18–24, to which this applies. What is vital for the author's argument, then, is the unique eschatological relationship between the earthly and the heavenly worlds; the journey that Christ has made into the innermost sanctuary of heaven; the fact that Christ's death achieves its full saving power in the heavenly sanctuary itself, not just on an altar or in a sanctuary set on earth; that Christ is now set at the right hand of God and affords direct access to the divine presence; that even in their earthly worship the community can reflect the heavenly angelic worship of God and of Christ. It is the use of this framework of thought and this nexus of themes that allows the author to argue for the certainty of the community's salvation through Christ and their means of direct access to God in the heavenly sanctuary, in complete contrast to the limited, repeated earthly ritual of the Jerusalem temple.

In fact it is not simply in relation to the cult that the writer employs this framework; he uses it also in the first three chapters, in arguing for the superiority of Christ over the angels and Moses. Thus the argument in chapters 1 and 2 is intelligible only when it is set against the background of the developed cosmology and angelology of first-century Judaism. The author is here concerned to demonstrate the superiority of Christ in face of the exalted position and status ascribed to (at least the highest) angels, who are set alongside God and provide the means of access and mediation both to God and also to the heavenly world; Jesus alone is given the title Son, the name above the angels, so that they worship him just as they worship God. Thus the author uses the categories of angelology (especially that of the name) precisely in order to show that Christ is altogether different from the angels; so also we find the remarkable phenomenon of Old Testament hymns and the divine titles *theos* and *kyrios* (1:8–9, 10–12, 13; cf. Hengel 1978) being taken over and applied directly to Jesus. Thus the writer is concerned to argue that Jesus uniquely shares the nature of God, and his place in the heavenly world (1:3), and is alone able to mediate this (1:2; 2:10, 18). Paradoxically, however, what most sets Christ apart from the angels is the lowly status and the kind of death that he takes upon himself (1:3; 2:6–18); this also provides an important link with the author's treatment of the cult.

Again in 3:1–6, in the comparison between Moses and Jesus, the main point is that Moses, as a servant, belongs on the side of man, whereas Jesus, as Son, belongs on the side of God (Barrett 1956). For the writer, of course, Christ belongs fully with both man and God, and thus alone can mediate between them; because he belongs fully with God, he alone can give access to God and the heavenly world where the believer really belongs (cf. 3:1). 3:7ff. show the tenor of the argument, and the context, to be strongly eschatological. As in chapters 1 and 2 the author may well be countering the attractions of a developed angelology, so here he is probably opposing the strong appeal for the community of the exalted figure of Moses, familiar from developed Jewish tradition (cf. d'Angelo 1981). At any rate, he finds urgent cause to call them to give their allegiance to Jesus rather than Moses, in order to gain their true inheritance in heaven. What we find in the comparison with both angels and Moses, then, is that Jesus is shown to share what is important in both categories, but without their limitations; above all, however, in comparison with them, Jesus is shown to exist on a different level and to stand in a different relationship to God.

The argument in these first three chapters may then help us understand what the writer is saying in his much longer discussion of Jesus in relation to the cult. Thus in the first place he is concerned to show that Jesus incorporates all that is important about both priesthood and cult. He does so primarily by taking up relevant categories and descriptions deriving from the biblical material or the developed hierocratic tradition; this aspect of Hebrews' handling of the theme has been excellently demonstrated by Horbury (1983). Thus where the writer speaks of Jesus as a merciful and faithful high priest (2:17; cf. 3:1), holy and guileless (7:28), made like his brethren and tempted in every respect (2:17; 4:15), able to sympathize with human weakness (4:15; 5:2), he is not portraying Jesus as completely different from the contemporary high priests; he is using the terminology and categories applied to those high priests within the first century. Similarly, where he presents Jesus as making purification (1:3; cf. 2:17) and offering gifts and sacrifices for sins (5:1; 8:3), he is deliberately setting him in the same role as the high priest of his time. The implication, then, is that the important characteristics of the high priest are to be found fully in Christ as well. Those the writer is addressing do not therefore need to go back to the Jewish cultus; in Christ they still possess a high priest who has precisely these attributes (8: 1). Indeed, even in this respect the writer may wish to take his argument further: in 5: 7–10 he moves on from speaking in the same terms of both Jesus and the high priests to describing the intense prayer and suffering of Jesus. It is quite plausible that he has Gethsemane and the passion in mind; the main point, however, seems to be that the qualities shown by Jesus exceed those expected of the high priest himself. Certainly it is significant that it is precisely in this context that Jesus is spoken of as Son, and his priesthood as according to that of Melchizedek.

This brings us to the second main aspect of the writer's presentation: the strong emphasis he lays on the marked differences between Christ and the cult. The recurring theme of these contrasts is clear: the cultic priests and sacrifices are many (7: 23), repeatedly the same, tainted by sin (7: 27; cf. 5: 3 and 9: 7), impermanent, limited to this earth, and unable to deal with sin or offer access to God. Jesus, as High Priest, is alone sinless, unique, eternal and in heaven (4.15; 7.23–8); his sacrifice is once-for-all, effective for all sin for ever, for others not himself, and opening up heaven and full access to God (7: 27; 9: 6–14). This underlying theme is clearly central to the other distinctive ideas the author uses in this section: thus the Melchizedek analogy is used to argue that Jesus is eternal, having no beginning or end (7: 3). He is a priest of God himself and, as the first priest mentioned in scripture (Horton 1976), he has unique status, belonging to an order different and superior to that of the Levites (7: 4–10); probably the author also draws on the tradition (familiar otherwise from 11Q Melch.) of Melchizedek as an exalted being set alongside God in heaven. Again, the new covenant initiated by Jesus' sacrifice is perfect and implicitly eternal, in contrast to the old covenant which is weak and fading (6: 13–18; 7: 18–22; 8: 6–13; 9: 15–22). Further, in contrast to the tabernacle of the cult, which is fashioned by man and belongs to this world, Jesus enters the true tabernacle, both greater and more perfect, which is neither made with hands nor belongs to this creation (8: 1–5; 9: 23–4).

There are, then, several key ideas that characterize the author's argument: Jesus, his priesthood and his sacrifice, can variously be spoken of as eternal, perfect, sinless, unchangeable, once-for-all, fully effective for salvation and access to God. Equally, however, it is clear that these themes, which form the constant refrain of the argument, are inextricably bound up with the language which speaks of Jesus as having entered heaven itself and being set at the right hand of God. Thus in 1: 3, in the exordium to the Epistle, the statement about Jesus' supreme salvific sacrifice is juxtaposed with a reference to his assuming his place alongside God in heaven. Again in 4: 14, in the introduction that is set over the whole treatment of sacrifice that follows, Jesus is designated as high priest specifically as he who has passed through the heavens. It is this that shows Jesus' saving work to have final effect, and Jesus as high priest to afford direct access to the presence of God. So also in 8:1ff. the writer says that the point of his argument about Jesus as high priest is that he is seated at the right hand of the throne of majesty in heaven. What is important about Jesus is that he is neither on earth nor a priest according to the law; hence, viewed from this perspective, his covenant, ministry and promises are all better.

It is in fact precisely because the author argues from this perspective that he is able to pass final judgement on the cultic system, while at the same time taking over and appropriating for Jesus all that is important about it. Thus by speaking in 7:11 ('If perfection had been attainable through the levitical priesthood...') and 8:7 ('For if the first covenant had been faultless...') as though perfection had never been available through the Jewish cultus, he contradicts what both he and his community would have accepted in their earlier adherence to Judaism. The argument is clearly retrospective: it is because the writer has appropriated for Jesus what is essentially claimed for the cult that he is able to devalue it in this way. Equally, it is because he sees Jesus, the full and final revelation of God (1:2ff.), as having offered the final sacrifice and being set at God's right hand in heaven, that he has to affirm that he supersedes the whole priestly and sacrificial system. What forces the writer into this mode of argument is the practical issue, that the atoning effect claimed for the temple cult on the one hand and the death of Christ on the other results in a mutual incompatibility (Hengel 1981). There cannot be two rival modes of atoning for sin or providing mediation and access to God; therefore that which is recognized within the Jewish framework of reference must now be radically disallowed. The argument here is similar, *mutatis mutandis*, to that used by Paul in connection with the Law in Gal. 2:21; 3:21 (cf. Sanders 1977); the view that Paul rejects, that the Law could ever have had an effective role, is one which as a Pharisee he would have held. Both Paul and the writer to the Hebrews are dealing with problems that immediately threaten the communities that they are addressing; the absoluteness and vehemence of their assertions are called forth by the urgent need to prevent members of the community abandoning or compromising their acceptance of Christ.

Hence we find in Hebrews nothing less than a radical rejection of the whole Jewish cultus; the writer deliberately polarizes the positions and drives a wedge between the nascent Christian and Jewish movements. Yet at the same time he insists on the Jewish cultic conditions and means of atonement being met in full. The point of this paradox, as we have argued, is his need to counter the strong attraction of the cult, to show that every important aspect of priesthood and sacrifice is now to be found in Jesus. Just as he takes up an elevated view of priesthood, and shows how Jesus is fully adequate to meet the requirements and expectations of this, so also he stresses the intrinsic importance of the Tamid and Yom Kippur offerings, and the fact that Jesus satisfies their demands as well – 'without the shedding of blood, there is no forgiveness of sins' (9:22): Jesus has met not only the general requirement of the cultic law that a sacrifice must be offered to make atonement for sin, but also the more specific demand that blood should be shed. It is very probable that the writer draws on the developed Aqedah theme (Swetnam 1981) in order to show the unique nature of Christ's sacrifice in this respect. Thus over against the developed tradition that Isaac voluntarily offered himself but did not actually die, and that this was a human meritorious act, the writer presents Jesus as both offering himself and actually being put to death, shedding his own blood. Yet this act makes no claim upon God, but shows God himself providing the sacrifice and effecting universal forgiveness for sin. Thus 9:22 would take on a still sharper edge.

Hence it is that the writer lays so much stress on the sheer mechanics of sacrifice. The intricate detail and operation of this system has been of immense importance for those he is addressing; it has to be demonstrated, therefore, that Jesus has achieved all that this whole ritual claimed to effect. The writer wrestles deeply with the question of how Jesus stands in relation to the whole cult; he does so precisely in order to disallow the strong claims of the Jerusalem temple to provide the sole means of atonement for sin and access to God. Thus, he argues, the sacrificial system can never remove sin, because it is limited by the present imperfect sanctuary and world, and operated by priests who are tainted with sin. There can therefore be no guarantee of forgiveness; when the high priest each year enters the holy of holies, he gains no direct access to God and can offer the people no final expiation for their sins. The perpetual re-enactment of the whole mechanism demonstrates its weakness; it operates in the wrong way and on the wrong level.

The writer resolves the issue by removing it to the true, perfect, heavenly world and sanctuary. This is where Christ has entered, penetrating behind the veil (6:19–20) into the presence of God, as the perfect high priest who has offered the perfect sacrifice that atones for all sin for all time; hence the sacrificial system of the Jewish cult is defunct. Once again it must be emphasized that this is not an abstract argument, but an urgent exhortation addressed to a community torn in its allegiance and in danger of abandoning its faith; thus the stark warning set at both start and end of this whole section on sacrifice (5:11–6:12; 10:19–32; cf. chapters 11–12) shows why the writer needs to draw an absolute contrast between what Christ has done and what the Jewish sacrificial system cannot do.

There is a clear tension inherent within this argument, since the writer is working at the same time with both a positive appraisal of the cultic traditions and also the need to pass a radically negative judgement upon them. Indeed, he presents what on one level is a parody of the Jewish model he is using, in the portrayal of the high priest making the sacrifice of himself, and presenting his own blood to God within the heavenly realm. Yet this, of course, is precisely the point of the argument: the final, once-for-all death of Christ on the cross, to which he voluntarily submits, compels this radical reinterpretation of the Jewish means of atonement for sin and access to God. Just as in the demonstration of Christ's superiority to the angels it is, paradoxically, the insistence on Christ's humble acceptance of human nature, suffering and death that is the vital point of the argument, so also here it is this that provides forgiveness of sin and means of access to the heavenly realm and to God himself; and what allows this argument to be effective is the framework of cosmic dualism.

The argument of Hebrews is, then, remarkable. To his Jewish-Christian community, for whom the temple and its cult still hold enormous religious significance, the writer declares that this sacrificial system has been brought to an absolute end. The radical nature of this assertion can be understood only by seeing Hebrews within the context of contemporary attitudes to sacrifice within Judaism. Thus we have already noted that Hebrews itself reflects the influence of one important development within Judaism, namely the hierocratic view. It is especially in light of this that Hebrews' absolute rejection of the cult seems so startling. Yet absolute rejection was not the only way within the first century to resolve the tension between attachment to the hierocratic tradition and unease about the operation of the cult. We have seen that Philo, for example, also reflects this influence; but in Alexandria he is clearly faced with, and indeed shares, the sophisticated philosophical abhorrence of the blood-sacrifices offered to a deity. He does not reject the sacrificial system as such; in fact he defends the temple against attack, and actually goes to offer sacrifice. Yet he is concerned especially to interpret the true meaning of sacrifice in terms of prayer and thanksgiving, and above all of adopting a proper attitude and living a virtuous life. Thus he allegorizes and spiritualizes the temple and the sacrificial rites themselves.

At first sight it is the Qumran community that appears to stand closest to Hebrews in its attitude to temple and sacrifice. It is misleading to speak of a single Qumranic view in this respect (Lichtenberger 1980); yet it can be said that what the texts as a whole evince is not a spiritualizing of the sacrificial system, but a complete rejection of the system as practised in the Jerusalem temple, and the priesthood in charge. Yet the main complaint is against the wicked priesthood at Jerusalem who have corrupted the system entirely; hence they have removed themselves physically from Jerusalem, and constitute, in themselves as a community, a new temple and priesthood in the wilderness. The fulfilment of their hope will be to take over the Jerusalem temple and conduct the cult in proper manner. This, then, is a relative not absolute rejection of the sacrificial system; nor is it a spiritualization of the cult. The Temple Scroll provides further evidence of the strong, continued interest within the Qumran community in the detail of cultic practice.

In fact in many ways the most interesting point of comparison for Hebrews is the evidence provided by the Pharisaic and early rabbinic traditions. The primary sources are extremely difficult to evaluate; but it appears that the main attitude evinced by the Pharisees in the pre-70 AD period was both simple and radical. They revered the temple as the place where atonement for sin was effected; their criticism was not of the cult as such, but of the priests (Neusner 1980). The extraordinary development they brought about was to make the levitical purity laws apply outside the temple, so that the Pharisees, and potentially the whole people, took on the status of temple priests; at the very least, then, the importance and unique standing of the temple were circumscribed. Yet even so, they did not look for an end to the temple; Joshua ben Hananiah's cry of woe at the destruction of the temple, as the place where atonement for Israel's sin was made, is fully consonant with the attitude outlined above.

Even more remarkable, however, are the developments in the post-70 period; faced with the destruction of the temple, it would seem that for nascent rabbinic Judaism the reply of Johanan ben Zakkai to Joshua ben Hananiah provided the best answer: a way of life lived fully according to Torah is a better sacrifice than anything offered in the temple. Yet that same Rabbinic community that Johanan founded at Yavneh reached its climax in the code of the Mishnah. It is not simply that Torah-Judaism took over, although the Torah is of course of central importance for the whole of the Mishnah. The real point is that in an almost incredible and superbly sustained theological enterprise the cultic requirements are not set aside but are reaffirmed and reinforced by the detailed discussion of the purification and sacrificial ritual. Thus a massive code of legislation is produced for a cultic system that cannot be, and (at least in the post-Bar Kochba period) apparently never will be, realized in practice. It is an apparent nonsense; on one level, of course, it represents an appropriation of the control of the cult by those who already have control of Torah. But it goes deeper: it represents a deliberate act of defiance, eschewing the obviously easier option of diverting attention away from the cult, and instead emphasizing its importance. We have already seen that the Piyyutim, Targumin and other post-70 sources show a positive appraisal of the cult (Horbury 1983); there is no lack of such emphasis in the Talmuds, Midrashim and other rabbinic literature as well. The instance of the Mishnah is the most striking, but the emphasis itself is not unique. Thus post-70 Judaism, in many of its facets, shows a reluctance to play down the importance of sacrifice for regulating the relationship between man and God, despite the desuetude of the cult.

What assessment, then, are we to make of Hebrews within its first-century context? In the first place, there is the obvious and expected overlap with attitudes within contemporary Judaism; thus we have already noted the importance of the developed hierocratic tradition in this respect. There is also, superficially at least, common ground with the treatment of the cult reflected in the Qumran and Pharisaic-Rabbinic literature; so, for instance, it may be said that Hebrews removes from the priesthood control of the presence of God, while similarly the sanctuary loses its supreme position.

Secondly, however, the precise problems that the cult poses are of course different for Hebrews, and so also therefore is the response that it makes to them. Thus it does not make the new community constitute a new temple; nor does it relativize the significance of the cult by extending the sphere of holiness to the whole people. Nor again does it merely offer a spiritualizing of the sacrificial system; in using the Old Testament proof-texts (10: 15ff.), the writer is simply taking over the negative emphasis on the inadequacy of sacrifices in themselves, not the positive reinterpretation. What supersedes sacrifice is Christ doing the will of God (10: 9–10), and this, precisely, by offering himself as the supreme sacrifice.

This indeed brings us to the writer's radically disjunctive solution. Working, as of necessity he must, within the constraints of sacrificial terminology, with priesthood and sacrifice as his controlling categories, his simple message is that the cult is no longer of any effect. What it represents, and continually demands, has been fully realized and satisfied by the one final sacrifice of Christ. More precisely, he emphasizes the death of Jesus the Messiah as God's final decisive act; he insists, that is, that this shameful death is central and constitutive for what God has done in relation to the cult. In setting this apparently absurd and embarrassing fact at the heart of its argument, and juxtaposing with it emphasis on the exalted nature of Christ and the sphere to which he belongs, Hebrews does not of course stand alone within the New Testament; above all, Phil. 2: 6–11 provides at least a partial parallel (Hofius 1976; Hengel 1976). Hebrews is, however, unique in the detail of its argument and in setting Christ within the cultic sphere of reference in order that he may be shown to supersede it. It is in keeping with this that while Hebrews has to speak of Jesus as a high priest, because of the cultic constraints of his argument, the writer uses the designation 'Son' (cf. Loader 1981) as the decisive term for his distinctive understanding of the way Jesus fulfils the cult's demands and God's will in a different way and on a different level.

The writer's constant refrain, then, is that the death of Christ has brought the sacrificial system to an end once and for all. It seems obvious enough to us in retrospect that he should interpret the Jewish cult in this way. Yet within its first-century Jewish context it represents a remarkable and extreme position, deriving from an extreme and urgent historical situation, and basing itself on an embarrassing historical event. It may be worth noting here the suggestive remark of Neusner (1980) that the Mishnah's detailed provision for the cult, in defiance of the facts, might well be intended as an answer to Hebrews, even though there is no direct evidence for this. In face of Hebrews' uncompromising assertion that the sacrificial system, and along with it a large part of Torah, is irrevocably brought to an end, the Mishnah's uncompromising reaffirmation that the system still stands and that nothing has changed, in spite of all appearances, would clearly be intelligible.

Thus faced with an urgent situation, the writer of Hebrews provides a profound and radical solution to the acute problem of where the true locus of atonement and presence of God himself is to be found, in terms of the death of Christ set within cultic categories and the framework of cosmic dualism. The conclusion for the Jewish-Christian community is unambiguous. Cult and sacrifice are at an end; what God has done in Christ alone has final validity. Thus Hebrews stands as a watershed in the emergence of the nascent Christian movement from its Jewish origins. Over against its Jewish context it insists on the cultic conditions being fully met, while removing these to a different sphere. For a Jewish-Christian community it uses above all cultic categories to interpret the impact and significance of Christ; yet in doing so, as we have seen, it renders this cultic model redundant.

In fact, therefore, it becomes apparent that the validity of the central argument of Hebrews is independent of the cultic model that it has to use. Setting aside the sacrificial terminology, what the writer wants to say is that Christ provides the sole means of atonement and access to God, and that he does so directly, finally, once-for-all. The writer does of course lay great stress on the death of Christ within terms of the sacrificial model, and indeed, as we have seen, specifically interprets it as the supreme sacrifice. But this death itself is something brought about by God for man, and as such involves a change in the understanding of the nature of God and the relationship between God and man, in a way that could not be envisaged within the cult. Further, the writer does not use the sacrificial model for the whole way of life of the Christian community; nor does he interpret Christ's sacrifice in a sacramental, eucharistic way (even if chapter 13 is an original part of the letter, 13:10 can scarcely be interpreted thus, while 13:15 refers to the community's response on earth to the praise of God in heaven).

Within his constrained and pressing situation, the writer does not work out the full logic or implications of his argument; indeed, in the context within which he is writing it would be impossible for him to do so. Yet Hebrews, seen in perspective, has very clear implications for the use of sacrifice to interpret the death of Christ, or more generally within Christian theology. The point implicit in Hebrews is already evident elsewhere in the

New Testament; thus Paul, engaged in the Gentile mission where sacrificial language would scarcely be relevant or intelligible, abandons the cultic model (except for a few instances taken over from traditional usage) for interpreting the death of Jesus (Hengel 1981). Certainly Paul does at times quite casually use cultic terms of reference, but the point is that these are not integral to his argument. Thus at an early stage of the Christian proclamation it is clear that cultic terminology is not indispensable, and that it is not necessary to understand the death of Christ as a sacrifice. Within the Jewish-Christian context of Hebrews, of course, the issue is different; it is not that the cultic model is unintelligible, but that, according to the author, it has been brought to an end. Yet once the issue of the status of sacrifice has been resolved, and the lines of division clearly drawn, as happens in Hebrews, then the question is clearly raised: if the death of Christ is the final sacrifice, then what further place has sacrifice within a Christian world of meaning? If a model is rendered redundant, then it is best to abandon it. And if that is so even within Hebrews, with all the constraints of its own particular situation, it is all the more the case once the peculiar and pressing circumstances of the Epistle are left behind. It is of course still possible to use sacrifice to interpret the death of Christ, the eucharist, or the Christian life; but it would be misleading to use Hebrews to support such a position, as even Daly (1978a; 1978b) almost admits. Indeed, we have already seen that Hebrews, in its reworking of the sacrifice theme, raises fundamental questions about the way in which God is to be understood, in his relation to Christ and his dealings with man, which cannot be contained within cultic categories. Once we have moved on from the context of Hebrews, then, we may certainly ask what are the appropriate ways of interpreting the death of Christ, and what part, if any, sacrificial terminology has to play within a developed Christian theology.

This may seem a negative conclusion; certainly this understanding of Hebrews raises questions not only about sacrifice but also about the status of the Old Testament. On the one hand the author uses scripture as an eloquent and decisive witness for his argument; thus what God has brought about in Christ can be seen as the fulfilment of what is already in the Old Testament. In the specifically Jewish context of his discussion, it is important that he can use both scriptural text and developed traditions in this way. Indeed, as we have seen, he has to use the Old Testament as an integral part of his argument, in dealing with the cult, since it is understood by his community as that which undergirds the sacrificial system. Yet in disallowing a central part of the scriptural provision, the writer implicitly raises the question of the status and validity of the Old Testament as a whole. If we take the radical nature of the argument of Hebrews on its own terms, then we have to reckon seriously with its consequences. If the death of Christ is the final sacrifice, then it has to be asked what exactly has been brought to an end. This need not be merely negative; I have already argued that Hebrews causes us to question, within its own context, the precise understanding of God and his saving activity. If we see Hebrews in this way, then it is a central task for Christian theology to find the framework, model and terminology appropriate for working out the implications of what the Epistle has to say.

REFERENCES

Aune, D. E. (1972). *The Cultic Setting of Realized Eschatology in Early Christianity.* Leiden: Brill

Barrett, C. K. (1956). The Eschatology of the Epistle to the Hebrews. In *The Background of the New Testament and its Eschatology,* ed. W. D. Davies and D. Daube. Cambridge: Cambridge University Press, pp. 363–93

Baumbach, G. (1979). 'Volk Gottes' im Frühjudentum: eine Untersuchung der 'ekklesiologischen ' Typen des Frühjudentums. *Kairos* n.f. 21, 30–47

Buchanan, G. W. (1972). *To the Hebrews,* Anchor Bible. New York: Doubleday

Daly, R. J. (1978a). *The Origins of the Christian Doctrine of Sacrifice.* London: Dartman, Longman and Todd

   (1978b). *Christian Sacrifice: The Judaeo-Christian Background before Origen,* The Catholic University of America Studies in Christian Antiquity, 18. Washington: Catholic University of America Press

d'Angelo, M. R. (1981). *Moses in the Letter to the Hebrews.* Missoula: Scholars Press

Dey, L. K. K. (1975). *The Intermediary World and Patterns of Perfection in Philo and Hebrews.* Missoula: Scholars Press

Gereboff, J. (1979). *Rabbi Tarfon: The Tradition, The Man and Early Rabbinic Judaism.* Missoula: Scholars Press

Gruenwald, I. (1980). *Apocalyptic and Merkavah Mysticism.* Leiden/Cologne: Brill

Hengel, M. (1976). *The Son of God.* London: SCM Press

   (1978). Hymn and Christology. In *Studia Biblica III: Papers on Paul and other New Testament Authors,* ed. E. A. Livingstone. Sheffield: *JSOT* Press

   (1981). *The Atonement.* London: SCM Press

Hofius, O. (1970). *Katapausis.* Tübingen: JCB Mohr (Paul Siebeck)

   (1972). *Der Vorhang vor dem Thron Gottes.* Tübingen: JCB Mohr (Paul Siebeck)

   (1976). *Der Christushymnus Philipper 2. 5–11.* Tübingen: JCB Mohr (Paul Siebeck)

Horbury, W. (1983). The Aaronic Priesthood in the Epistle to the Hebrews. *Journal for the Study of the New Testament* 19, 43–71

Horton, F. L. (1976). *The Melchizedek Tradition.* London: Cambridge University Press

Käsemann, E. (1939). *Das wandernde Gottesvolk: eine Untersuchung Zum Hebräerbrief,* FRLANT n.s. 37. Göttingen: Vandenhoeck & Ruprecht

Kosmala, H. (1959). *Hebräer. Essener-Christen.* Leiden: Brill

Kuhn, H. W. (1964). *Enderwartung und gegenwärtiges Heil.* Göttingen: Vandenhoeck & Ruprecht

Laub, F. (1980). *Bekenntnis und Auslegung.* Regensburg: Verlag Friedrich Pustet

Lichtenberger, H. (1980). Atonement and Sacrifice in the Qumran Community. In *Approaches to Ancient Judaism,* ed. W. S. Green, vol. II. Chico: Scholars Press

Loader, W. R. G. (1981). *Sohn und Hohepriester*. Neukirchen: Neukirchener Verlag

Maier, J. (1964). *Vom Kultus zur Gnosis*. Salzburg: Otto Müller Verlag

Michel, O. (1966). *Der Brief an die Hebräer* (6th edn). Göttingen: Vandenhoeck

Moule, C. F. D. (1982). *Essays in New Testament Interpretation*. Cambridge: Cambridge University Press.

Neusner, J. (1970). *A Life of Rabban Johanan b. Zakkai ca. 1–80 C.E.* 2nd edn. Leiden: Brill

(1975). *Early Rabbinic Judaism*. Leiden: Brill

(1980). *A History of the Mishnaic Law of Holy Things*, vol. vi. Leiden: Brill

Rowland, C. (1982). *The Open Heaven*. London: SPCK

Sanders, E. P. (1977). *Paul and Palestinian Judaism*. London: SCM Press

Schenke, H.-M. (1973). Erwägungen zum Rätsel des Hebräerbriefes. In *Neues Testament und christliche Existenz*, ed. H. D. Betz and L. Schottroff, pp. 421–37. Tübingen: JCB Mohr (Paul Siebeck)

Scholem, G. ([1960] 1965). *Jewish Gnosticism, Merkabah Mysticism and Talmudic Tradition* (2nd edn). New York: Schocken Books

Spicq, C. (1952–3). *L'Epître aux Hébreux* (2 vols.). Paris

Strobel, A. (1975). *Die Briefe an Timotheus und Titus; Der Brief an die Hebräer*, trans. and expl. J. Jeremias and A. Strobel, NTD 9. Göttingen: Vandenhoeck and Ruprecht

Strugnell, J. (1960). The Angelic Liturgy at Qumran – 4Q Serek Šîrôt 'Ôlat Haššabāt. In *Supplements to Vetus Testamentum VII*. Leiden: Brill

Swetnam, J. (1981). *Jesus and Isaac*. Rome: Biblical Institute Press

Thompson, J. W. (1977). The Conceptual Background and Purpose of the Midrash in Hebrews VII. *Novum Testamentum* 19, 209–23

(1979). Hebrews 9 and Hellenistic Concepts of Sacrifice. *JBL* 98, 567–78

Thurén, J. (1973). *Das Lobopfer der Hebräer*. Äbo: Äbo Akademi

Wenschkewitz, H. (1932). *Die Spiritualisierung der Kultusbegriffe Tempel, Priester und Opfer im Neuen Testament*. Leipzig: Eduard Pfeiffer

Williamson, R. (1970). *Philo and the Epistle to the Hebrews*. Leiden: Brill

(1976). The Background of the Epistle to the Hebrews. *Expository Times* 87, 232–7

Young, F. M. (1975). *Sacrifice and the Death of Christ*. London: SPCK

Zimmermann, H. (1977). *Das Bekenntnis der Hoffnung*. Cologne, Bonn: Peter Hanstein Verlag

5

ST ATHANASIUS ON CHRIST'S SACRIFICE

GEORGE DION DRAGAS

Though St Athanasius did not write a special treatise on Christ's sacrifice, the theme is central to his thought, especially to his teaching concerning the saving work of Christ. This is apparent in his early apologetic work *De Incarnatione*,[1] but it also appears in his other writings wherever he deals with the salvation which has been granted by God in Christ, particularly through Christ's death and resurrection.[2]

This fact has not escaped the attention of modern patristic scholars who have dealt with Athanasius' soteriology. Many have commented on it,[3] though their conclusions to a certain extent have varied, especially with regard to particular aspects of this doctrine. Such have been the aspects which relate to the rationale of Christ's sacrifice (God's justice, law, character, love, etc.), the nature of it (substitutionary, vicarious, representative, etc.), the precise identity of the recipient of it (death, the Father, evil powers), the connection of it with such traditional notions as those of a 'debt' or a 'ransom' which have to be paid so that mankind's redemption might be secured, and so on. I shall refrain from saying anything about these conclusions, until we have conducted a fresh examination of the relevant Athanasian texts.

The close study of the Athanasian texts reveals that, broadly speaking, there are three kinds of sacrifices which Athanasius discusses: the pagan, the Jewish and the Christian. For Athanasius, as for all the theologians of the Church who preceded him, the Christian sacrifice, which, in his thought, is primarily connected with Christ's death upon the cross, is clearly distinguished from pagan and Jewish sacrifices, from the former in a more radical and from the latter in a more moderate way. This differential distinction is due to the fact that ontologically there is a radical discontinuity between the false gods of the pagans – fictional constructions of fallen humanity, or demonic deceit, in Athanasius' perception – and the God of the Christians, who stands in continuity with the God of the saints of ancient Israel. Though Athanasius did not elaborate very much on this theme, his thought is quite clear when one gathers together his actual statements and expounds their meaning and significance on a sound exegetical basis which is rooted in a thorough study of the texts to which they belong. In view of this I shall divide my treatment of the subject matter of this essay into three parts, dealing respectively with pagan, Jewish and Christian conceptions of sacrifice.

Athanasius does not say as much about pagan sacrifices as he says about paganism. The latter is actually the general context for the former and a lot of what is said about it is implicitly applicable to the former. Thus, inasmuch as paganism rests on a false conception of God which was invented by fallen humanity, pagan sacrifices are inevitably stamped with the mark of falsehood and artificiality. This is explicitly stated in Athanasius' early treatise *Contra Gentes*, where he traces the course of the development of idolatry.[4] It is in his exposition of the deification of dead ancestors[5] that Athanasius makes the remark that 'even sacrifices were invented (reconstructed) for them [*kai thysias anaplasantes*] as the honour due to the true God was ascribed to them ... and thus the human beings came to suffer what is not according to nature [*pragma paschontes ou kata physin*]'.[6] The obvious implication is that pagan religion and pagan sacrifices are unnatural inventions or reconstructions and, therefore, should be regarded as arbitrary, artificial and false.

Later in the same treatise Athanasius comes to argue that they are also expressions of irreligion (*atheotēs, asebeia*), irrationality (*paraphrosynē, aphrones*), shamefulness (*apotropiasmata*), pollution and demonism. Thus he points out that 'those who are regarded as gods by some are offered as sacrifices and libations [*thysiai kai spondai*] to the so-called gods of others'.[7] Worse still is 'the slaughtering and offering as sacrifice to false gods of human beings', which, as Athanasius reports, was practised by various ancient peoples, Scythians, Egyptians, Phoenicians, Cretans and Romans.[8] 'This deed', remarks Athanasius, 'which was peculiar to the evil of idols and demons', resulted in the fact that 'simply everyone without exception committed and incurred pollution: they incurred it by committing the murders and committed it to their own temples by raising the smoke of such sacrifices'. 'Thus it was from such sacrifices that numerous evils befell the human race.'[9] In the sequel to the above treatise, the *De Incarnatione*, Athanasius summarizes his views as follows: 'Such indeed was their impiety that they came to worship demons, proclaiming them to be gods and fulfilling their lusts. For they made sacrifices of irrational animals and slaughterings of human beings, as their due, all the more binding themselves down by their passions ... and thus everything they did was full of impiety and lawlessness ...'[10]

Furthermore Athanasius explains the uselessness and powerlessness of paganism and pagan sacrifices for effecting a change in the fallen human character or amending broken human relationships. 'Though they worshipped the idols and offered sacrifices to demons', he remarks, 'they were in no way able to re-educate themselves concerning their ways of thinking and acting, through the superstition of the idols.'[11] A real change, he claims, could only be and had actually been effected by Christ, who, 'through the ministry of his disciples persuaded the nations to turn away from their unnatural superstition about false gods and from their savage dealings with one another', and 'to develop peace and friendship among themselves'. 'Even now', writes Athanasius,

those barbarians who possessed an innate savagery of manners, as long as they still sacrifice to the idols of their country, are enraged with madness against one another and cannot endure to be a single hour without weapons; but as soon as they hear the teaching of Christ, they immediately turn to the cultivation of the land instead of fighting, stretch their hands to prayer instead of arming them with swords and, generally speaking, arm themselves against the devil and the demons, fighting them with soberness and virtue of soul, instead of fighting among themselves.[12]

It is, then, not only by revealing their false theological basis, but also by describing what they do and do not do that Athanasius exposes and rejects paganism and pagan sacrifices. Not only do they have nothing in common with Christianity but also they stand in opposition to it and as such they are totally unacceptable.

There is, furthermore, another set of texts in Athanasius' writings which shows how unacceptable to and unworthy of Christians were for him the pagan sacrifices and generally the pagan religion, which ought to be mentioned here. These texts relate to those Christians who at the time of persecution became lapsed and offered sacrifice to the false gods of the pagan Roman state. Such a deed was treated as a crime and was punishable in a number of ways, including the loss of the right to ordination for the lapsed person. Thus he mentions the accusation that 'Eusebius of Caesarea had offered [pagan] sacrifice which some of the confessors who resided in Alexandria had brought against him';[13] or the Arian atrocities against the Christian virgins who 'had been threatened with altars and sacrifice';[14] or that 'Peter of Alexandria had deposed the so-called bishop Melitius from Egypt who had been accused of unlawful deeds and of offering [pagan] sacrifice.'[15] Particularly interesting in this connection is the case of Asterius, 'who had offered [pagan] sacrifice [*ho thysas*]', as Athanasius disparagingly calls him whenever he refers to him,[16] because his sinful deed of offering sacrifice is made equal to his heretical teaching which denied the true divinity of Christ, thereby revealing the complete incompatibility between paganism and Christianity. Thus in his *De Synodis* Athanasius writes of 'Asterius from Cappadocia, a many-headed Sophist, one of the followers of Eusebius, whom they could not advance into the Clergy, as having offered sacrifice in the former persecution in the time of Constantius' grandfather' and who 'writes, with the agreement of Eusebius and his fellows, a small treatise, which was what they wanted and also an equal token of the audacity of his [pagan] sacrifice [*ison de tō tēs thysias autou tolmēmati*]'.[17] Further on in the same Epistle Athanasius returns to the same point, having supplied some extracts from Asterius' treatise (the *Syntagmation*) in order to illustrate the latter's heretical teaching on Christ. 'This is why', he points out,

they [the Arianizers] put forward Asterius as an advocate of their impiety [*asebeias*], who had sacrificed and was a Sophist, so that he might not shrink from pronouncing against the Lord or from misleading the steadfast Christians by his probability talk [*pithanologia*]. But those unlearned men were ignorant that by doing this they were working against themselves, since the stink of the sacrifice offered to the idols by their advocate showed even more plainly that the heresy is in opposition to Christ [*hē dysōdia tēs eis ta eidōla thysias tou synēgorou eti pleon tēn hairesin Christomachon edeiknye*].[18]

The important point that emerges from this group of texts is that offering pagan sacrifice is as bad a crime as, if not equal to, heresy, especially the heresy which denies the true Godhead of Christ. This is why the unacceptability of those who offered pagan sacrifices for entering the ranks of the Christian priesthood is perfectly matched with the unacceptability of those heretics who denied the Godhead of Christ for entering the same service.

Finally the Christian disapproval of pagan sacrifices is shown not only in that Christians are in no way allowed to offer such, but also in that pagans are, in their turn, not allowed to offer gifts to Christian sanctuaries and altars. This can be shown from several texts of Athanasius, which are of particular historical interest. The first text is connected with Pope Liberius of Rome and the Arianizing policy of the Emperor Constantius. In his attempt to impose Arianism Constantius had sent a certain eunuch Eusebius with a letter and 'gifts' [bribes] to Liberius to ask for the latter's cooperation in subscribing to the condemnation of Athanasius and holding communion with the Arians. When Liberius refused to comply with the imperial wish and asked instead for an ecclesiastical council which would be unbiased by state interference, Eusebius

went away with the gifts and proceeded to perpetrate an offence which is foreign to a Christian ... He went to the Martyrion [place of martyrdom] of Apostle Peter and then presented the gifts to it! ... Liberius on his part ... was very angry with the person who kept the Martyrion, in that he had not prevented him and cast out the gifts as an *unlawful sacrifice* [*ta dōra tou eunouchou ... hōs athyton thysian aperripse*].[19]

The other texts refer to pagan sacrifices which were offered by Arians and pagans on Christian altars and which Athanasius regards as blasphemous and sacrilegious. Thus he writes about the Arians who 'attempted to sacrifice a young calf and who would have done it had that not been a female one';[20] or he writes about 'the sacrifice and blasphemy against Christ which Arians and Greeks [pagans] offered in the great church of the Caesarium at the command of Costyllius';[21] or he recalls 'the great impiety and lawlessness which was committed on the Holy Table' by Jews and pagans at the invitation of the prefect Philagrius (a compatriot and supporter of the Arian Cappadocian Gregory and also a usurper of Athanasius' throne) 'in sacrificing birds and turtle doves, honouring with them the idols and defaming in the very churches our Lord and Saviour Jesus Christ, the Son of the living God . . .'[22] Here too we should mention the 'prophesy of Anthony', as Athanasius calls it, concerning 'the sacrilege against the altar of God which the Arians committed [*bdelychthēsetai to thysiastērion mau*]'.[23]

All the above texts make it quite obvious that for Athanasius and the Church of his time pagan sacrifice was a mark of irreligion and as such was completely unacceptable to Christians. These were considered to have committed a punishable crime if they had offered such a sacrifice while pagans were thought to have committed sacrilege if they offered sacrifices on Christian premises. Christians who lapsed were regarded as opponents of Christ, on a par not only with heretics but also with non-Christian Jews. It is to the latter, or rather to what Athanasius says about their sacrifices, that we shall now turn.

Athanasius' texts clearly reveal that Jewish sacrifices were equally as unacceptable to Christians as the pagan ones, though the reasons connected with these two cases were different. On the whole Jewish sacrifices were thought by Athanasius to have been fulfilled through Christ's sacrifice and, therefore, to have subsequently ceased to be necessary – a fact which, as Athanasius argues on several occasions, was actually confirmed by the historical events – and even to be as unlawful as the pagan ones. Athanasius' statement in his early apologetic treatise *De Incarnatione*, according to which 'there is nothing which the Lord did not fulfil . . . hence we see now that there is no king, no prophet in Jerusalem, *no sacrifice*, nor any vision among them [the Jews]',[24] is typical of his own and of the general Christian thinking on this matter.

In his trilogy *Contra Arianos* we do find some sort of general elaborations of this thinking of Athanasius on Jewish sacrifices, all of which are occasioned by his anti-Arian exegesis of verses from the Epistle to the Hebrews, but it is really in his *Epistolae Festales* (*Festal Letters*), the subject matter of which is the meaning of the feast and date of the Christian Easter, the 'true Passover', as Athanasius calls it, that we find his richest and most suggestive teaching on this topic. We shall examine first the former and then the latter.

In the final section of his first discourse *Contra Arianos*, where Athanasius explains the orthodox understanding of Heb. 1 : 9 in opposition to the Arian view,[25] that is to say that Christ 'was made better [*kreitton*]' than the angels, not as having been inferior to the latter, but as having been responsible for an economy or new covenant which was 'better' than the old one, administered by them, we come across Athanasius' claim of the superiority of Christ's sacrifice over the sacrifices of the Jews and of the real reason for it, which is directly connected with the divine person of Christ. Citing Heb. 7: 2 [*kreittonos diathēkēs*], 8: 6 [*kreittonos diathēkēs*], 7: 19 [*epeisagōge kreittonos*] and 29: 3 [*kreittosi thysiais*], Athanasius adds:

Both then, now and through all he [the Apostle] ascribes the word 'better' [*to kreitton*] to the Lord, who happens to be 'better' and other than originated things. Because *better is the sacrifice through him*, better the hope in him; and also the promises through him, not merely as great compared with small, but the former differing from the latter in nature, because he who made this economy is 'better' than originated things.[26]

Clearly Christ's sacrifice is superior to those of the old covenant, because as God he is superior in nature to those who administered the old covenant who, as originated (created) beings, must be inferior to him.

Athanasius' claim concerning the superiority of Christ's sacrifice over the Jewish ones of the old covenant becomes much clearer in his second discourse in *Contra Arianos*, where he produces more absolute statements as he elaborates his views on the absolute high-priesthood of Christ in contrast to the relative one of Aaron by expounding the orthodox meaning of Heb. 3: 2.[27] In this connection Athanasius says that

Christ offers a sacrifice which is trustworthy [*pisten thysian*], of lasting effect [*menousan*], and of unfailing status [*mē diapiptousan*]; for, whereas the sacrifices offered according to the Law were not trustworthy [*ouk eichon to piston*], since they had to be offered every day, and were again in need of cleansing [*deomenai palin katharsion*], the Saviour's sacrifice, having been offered once, has accomplished the whole and has become trustworthy as lasting for ever [*hapax genomenē teteleiōke to pan kai pistē gegone menousa diapantos*].[28]

But Athanasius goes further still. Not only the sacrifice of Christ but also his high-priesthood is superior to that of Aaron, inasmuch as the latter 'had had those who succeeded him [*tous diadechomenous*], and the whole priesthood of the Law through time and death passed over the previous ministers', whereas Christ has a 'high-priesthood which is untransitional and unsuccessional [*aparabaton kai adiadekton echōn tēn apchierōsynēn*]'. It is because of this that Christ 'has become a trustworthy high priest, lasting for ever, and trustworthy according to the promise, that he may listen to, and not mislead, those who come to him'.[29]

We may conclude, then, on the basis of the above texts, that for Athanasius Jewish sacrifices have been fulfilled and, consequently, replaced by the once and for all sacrifice of Christ, which rests upon his unique and incommunicable high-priesthood. Jewish sacrifices were insufficient, untrustworthy, ineffective and time-conditioned, whereas Christ's sacrifice is trustworthy, effective and everlasting.

These fundamental points are stated and elaborated in several texts of Athanasius, contained in his *Festal Letters*, which deal with the sacrifice of the Jewish Passover and other Old Testament sacrifices in the light of the sacrifice of Christ – *our passover*, as Athanasius calls it in every Letter, citing I Cor. 5: 7 – and show the typological and provisional character of the former as compared and related to the latter. To these we shall now turn.[30]

In his very first *Festal Letter* (for AD 329) Athanasius writes about 'the foolish Jews, who, receiving indeed this divine food' (which is, as far as we can gather from the context, the Word of God, or the revelation [vision] of God, or the virtues which issue out of the conversation of God with man, or Jesus Christ himself)

typically, and eating a lamb in the Passover but not understanding the type, even to this day eat the lamb being in error; the more so in that they are without a city and the truth. As long as Judaea and the city existed, there were a type, and a lamb, and a shadow, since the Law thus commanded: 'These things shall not be in another city, but in the land of Judaea – but without [the land of Judaea] in no place whatever' [Deut. 12: 11, 13f.]. And besides this, the Law commanded them to offer whole burnt-offerings and sacrifices, when there was no other altar and temple built, and they were commanded to carry out these rites in that city only, to the end that when that city should come to an end, then also those things which were figurative might receive their end. Now observe that that city, since the coming of the Saviour, has had an end, and all the land of Judaea has been laid waste; so that from the testimony of these things (and we need no external proof, being assured by our own eyes of the fact) there must, of necessity, be an end of the shadow.[31]

Having said this Athanasius goes on to cite a relevant text from the prophet Nahum (1: 15–2: 1),[32] which he understands as referring to Christ, and then adds:

Look to our Saviour who went up, and breathed upon the face, and said to his disciples, Receive ye the Holy Spirit [John 20: 22]. For as soon as these things were done, everything then came to an end, for the altar was broken and the veil of the Temple was rent; and although the city was not yet laid waste, yet the abomination was ready to sit in the midst of the Temple, and the city, and those ancient

ordinances, to receive their final consummation. Since then we have passed the time
of the shadow, and no longer perform rites under it, but have turned, as it were, unto
the Lord, 'For the Lord is a Spirit and where the Spirit of the Lord is, there is liberty' [2
Cor. 3: 17], as we hear from the priestly trumpet; no longer slaying a material lamb,
but that true Lamb that was slain, even our Lord Jesus Christ, 'Who was led as a
sheep to the slaughter, and was dumb, as a lamb before its shearers' [Isa. 53: 7];
being purified by the precious blood which speaks of better things than that of
Abel...[33]

Obviously these texts witness to the deeper religious meaning of the
Jewish Passover and indeed of the entire Jewish sacrificial rite which was
thought by Christians to have been fulfilled in and replaced by the sacrifice
of Christ. With the coming of Christ the time of shadow and type, which
includes the Jewish sacrificial system with its figurative ordinances, has
passed, and the whole reality of Christ has emerged as the true foundation of
everything, of the old rite which looked forward to its fulfilment and of the
new rite which is established as an eternal presence. By rejecting the
revelation and fulfilment which was brought about by Christ and insisting
on the celebration of the rites of the shadow the Jews, according to
Athanasius' argument, 'stood in error'. Later on Athanasius will be more
severe in his judgement concerning the Jewish rejection of Christ, which
was allegedly made in the name of the old Law. In his *Fourth Letter to
Serapion* and in discussing the critical attitude of the Pharisees to the Lord,
Athanasius will write, 'But the Pharisees, who were thought to be mature
with respect to the Law, who broadened the lower ends of their garments
and boasted as knowing something more than others, were not ashamed at
this' (claiming that Jesus had an impure and demonic spirit);

and according to what is written [Deut. 32: 17] the wretched ones *sacrificed to a
demon and not to God by saying that the Lord is demon possessed* and that God's works
were performed by demons. They suffered this for no other reason, but in order that
they may deny that he who did such things was God and Son of God. For if his eating
and the countenance of his body showed him to be a man, why could they not see
him from his works to be in the Father and the Father to be in him?

Indeed Athanasius goes on to argue that such a rejection comes from the
devil 'who enters into those who adopt it and leads them to acknowledge
him as God instead of Christ and to become sharers with him in the eternal
punishment by fire'.[34] Clearly, then, for Athanasius Jewish sacrifices are
both false and demonic – false, as rejecting the truth (reality) of Christ's
sacrifice in the name of its type and shadow, and demonic, in rejecting
Christ's Godhood and attributing his miraculous works to the devil or a
demon.

In his *Festal Letter IV* (for AD 332) Athanasius first speaks about the
character and the significance of religious feasts and then turns to the feast

of Easter comparing it to the Jewish Passover. The Jewish Passover, he says, commemorated the death of Pharaoh and the deliverance of the Israelites from bondage. The Christian Passover commemorates the 'slaying of the devil, that tyrant against the whole world, and the abolition of death and the devil's dominion'.[35] In other words, the former was a temporal, earthly and limited feast but the latter is eternal, heavenly and universal. The former was in the shadows, but the latter is in the truth. Athanasius makes several such contrasts, amongst which the overarching one seems to be that of the 'shadow' and the 'truth', which is connected with all the rest, including that of the sacrifice of the Jewish Passover and the sacrifice of Christ. Here is the most pertinent Athanasian text for our present investigation:

Israel of old ... as in a figure, came to the feast [of the Passover]. Such things were then set forth as in the shadows. But we, my beloved, the shadow having received its fulfilment, and the types being accomplished, should no longer consider the feast as a figurative one; neither should we go up to Jerusalem which is beneath, to sacrifice the Passover, according to the unseasonable observance of the Jews, lest, while the season passes away, we should be regarded as acting unseasonably; but in accordance with the injunction of the Apostle, let us go beyond the types, and sing the new song of praise; For this they also observed; ... for no longer were these things done in Jerusalem which is beneath, neither was it considered that the feast should be celebrated there alone; but wherever God willed it to be. Now he willed it to be in every place, so that 'in every place incense and a sacrifice might be offered to him' [Mal. 1:11] ... Our Saviour also, since he was changing the typical for the spiritual, promised them that they should no longer eat the flesh of a lamb, but his own, saying, Take eat and drink, this is my Body and my Blood. When we are then nourished by these things we shall also, my beloved, properly keep the feast of the Passover.[36]

This fascinating text, so rich in nuances, contrasts not only the ancient deliverance of the Israelites from Egypt to the deliverance of the human race from death and the bondage of evil,[37] regarding the former as a temporal, earthly, limited and partial shadow and type of the latter, and the latter as the eternal, heavenly, unlimited and universal truth and spirit of the former, but also, the celebrations of both events, focussed on the sacrifice and eating of the Jewish Passover lamb and the eucharistic sacrifice of Christ and eating of his flesh and drinking of his blood, regarding the former as unseasonable and parochial and the latter as timely and universal (ecumenical). Particularly interesting to note here is Athanasius' under-standing of the 'sacrifice' mentioned in Malachi's prophecy in eucharistic terms, which is, of course, in line with the whole patristic tradition. The real import of this is that the celebration of the eucharist, involving the partaking of or communion in the humanity of Christ – which is called 'spiritual' [i.e., true or inner] in contrast to 'typical' [i.e., figurative or outer]

– is now the only way to celebrate *properly* the Passover, which is now completely renewed, inasmuch as it is no longer related to the deliverance of the ancient Israelites from a human bondage and an entry into an earthly land, but to the salvation of all humanity from death and the devil, and entry into heaven. As a consequence Jewish sacrifice and celebration of the Passover is now impossible. It should be noted here that the fulfilment of the Jewish Passover by the eucharist does not imply that the eucharistic meal which Jesus ate with his disciples was for Athanasius a Passover meal. If that was the case then the shadow would determine the reality of the truth. For Athanasius, however, as for the unanimous tradition of the Fathers, the eucharistic meal acquired its meaning from the new and unique event of the sacrifice of Christ which was effected through his acceptance of the cross. This view is derived from the crucial Pauline statement 'our passover, Christ, is sacrificed' (1 Cor. 5:7) which is central to Athanasius' teaching concerning the Christian sacrifice in his *Festal Letters*.

In view of the above we can understand why, in making a similar point about 'shadow' and 'type' in his *Festal Letter V*, Athanasius radically contrasts the Church's celebration of the Passover – which he calls 'the blessed Passover in which our Lord was crucified'[38] – to the Passover celebration of the Jews, which he conjoins with the religious celebrations of the heathen, the heretics and the schismatics ... 'Let us not', he writes,

be like the heathen, or the ignorant Jews, or as the heretics and schismatics of the present time. For the heathen think the accomplishment of the feast is in abundance of food; the Jews, erring in the *type and shadow*, think it still such ... But let us, my brethren, be superior to the heathen, in keeping the feast with sincerity of soul and purity of body; to the Jews in no longer receiving the *type and the shadow*, but as having been gloriously illumined with the light of truth, and as looking upon the Sun of righteousness; to the schismatics in not rending the coat of Christ, but in one house, even in the catholic Church, eating the Passover of the Lord ...[39]

Particularly interesting here are the phrases 'looking upon the Sun of righteousness', 'not rending the coat of Christ', 'the catholic Church' and 'the Passover of the Lord' because they reveal Athanasius' catholic perspectives which have a Christ-centred and Church-centred orientation. It is precisely their errors in christology and ecclesiology (christology in the wider sense) that respectively deprive Jews, as well as heretics and schismatics, of the right of participation in the celebration of Easter and convict them of committing falsehood, in their sacrificial celebrations, and even of becoming identical with the pagans.

In his *Festal Letter VI* (for AD 334) Athanasius becomes even more explicit:

To the Jews forsooth when they thought they celebrated the Passover, because they persecuted the Lord, the feast was useless, since it no longer bore the name of the

Lord, even according to their own testimony. It was not the Passover of the Lord, but that of the Jews. The Passover was named after the Jews, my brethren, because they denied the Lord of the Passover.[40]

And further on,

For the whole service of the Law has been removed from them, and henceforth and for ever they remain without a feast. And they observe not the Passover; for how can they? They have no abiding place, but they wander everywhere. And they eat unleavened bread without fulfilling the Law, since they are unable first to sacrifice the lamb, as they were commanded to do when eating unleavened bread. But in every place they transgress the Law and judgements are inflicted on them by God ... now the cause of this to them was their slaying of the Lord, and their non-reverencing the Only-begotten.[41]

Particularly notable at this point is the way in which Athanasius once again conjoins the heretics and the schismatics with the Jews and argues that the latter, like the former, are excluded from the Feast of Easter for similar reasons: their opposition to Christ. Here are his words:

At this time also, the altogether wicked heretics and ignorant schismatics are in the same case [as the Jews]; the one in that they slay the Word, the other in that they rent the Robe. They also remain expelled from the feast, because they live without godliness and knowledge and emulate the conduct shown in the manner of Bar Abbas, the robber, whom the Jews desired instead of the Saviour. Therefore the Lord cursed them under the figure of the fig-tree.[42]

In saying this and in stating it quite bluntly and in all sincerity, Athanasius shows that he is not anti-Jewish, but that he simply condemns all opposition to Christ, whether Jewish or gentile. In fact he demonstrates this particular point in this same Letter by recalling the Pauline teaching about the good olive tree of the ancient Fathers and Saints of Israel and the wild olive tree of the nations, found in the Epistle to the Romans (chapter 11) and, thereby, clarifies the position of the early Church in her full acceptance of the Old Testament and her rejection of the later Jews who stood in opposition to Christ. In any case it is crystal clear that for Athanasius a sacrifice based on Jewish, or heretical or schismatical premises is unlawful and unacceptable because it does not rest on a sound christological faith.

For Athanasius, however, the Old Testament was proper for its time, especially because it pointed to Christ; but the coming of Christ brought about its fulfilment and the replacement of its shadowy provisions. This point is subtly made by stressing that Christ did not curse the 'root' of the fig-tree but its fruit. 'He brought the shadow to nought', says Athanasius, 'causing it to wither; but preserving the root, so that we might be grafted upon it.'[43] Actually by the 'root' Athanasius means the 'Israel of God', who is to be seen not in the Israelite nation as such but in the faithful patriarchs and saints of ancient Israel, for it is to the first of them, Abraham, the father of the faith, that he turns. Thus, pointing out that the Jews, 'cursed because of their negligence, were removed from the new moons, the true lamb and that which is truly the Passover', he argues that this true Passover 'came to us [Christians] ... as our own festival, and that we are bound to celebrate it not to ourselves, but to the Lord who bore our afflictions...' And then he adds:

The pagans and those who are destitute of our faith [presumably the non-Christian or anti-Christian Jews, together with the heretics and schismatics, who are often called 'Jews' by Athanasius] keep feasts according to their own will and have no peace since they sin against God; but the saints [of the Old Testament, the righteous in the Lord], like those who live to the Lord [i.e. the Christians] also keep the feast to him so that they also may be gathered together to sing that common and festal Psalm, 'Come let us rejoice', not in ourselves, but in the Lord.[44]

To illustrate this last point Athanasius produces a fascinating Christian exposition of Abraham's sacrifice of Isaac, which is obviously based on New Testament exegetical premises.

'The Patriarch Abraham', he writes, 'saw not his own day but that of the Lord, ... "he saw it and was glad" [John 8: 56]'. It was

by faith that he sacrificed Isaac and offered up his only begotten son, he who had received the promise; and in offering his son, he worshipped the Son of God, and being restrained from sacrificing Isaac, he saw the Messiah in the ram [lamb?] which was offered up instead as a sacrifice to God. The Patriarch was tried then, through Isaac; not, however, in that he [Isaac] was crucified, but He who was pointed out in Isaiah; 'He shall be led as a lamb to the slaughter ...' [Isa. 53: 7]; who took away the sin of the world.[45]

It is obvious at this point that Athanasius explains diachronically the story of the sacrifice of Isaac, drawing not only from prophesy but also from the actual event of the sacrifice of Christ as understood and expounded in the tradition of the early Church against its Old Testament background. This is stated even more explicitly in what he goes on to say about Abraham's understanding of Christ's sacrifice through his offering of Isaac.

It was on account of this understanding, he says, that

Abraham was restrained from laying his hands on the lad, lest the Jews, taking occasion from the sacrifice of Isaac, should reject the prophetic declarations concerning the Saviour, even all of them, but more especially those uttered by the Psalmist – 'Sacrifice and offering Thou wouldest not'; 'a body Thou has prepared for me' [Ps. 40: 6] – and should refer all such things as these to the son of Abraham.

And Athanasius proceeds to explain it further:

For the sacrifice was not properly the establishment of Isaac, but of Abraham, who also offered, and by that he was tried. Thus God accepted the will of the offerer, but prevented that which was offered from being sacrificed. For the death of Isaac did not procure freedom to the world, but that of our Saviour alone, by whose stripes we all are healed. For he raised up the fallen, healed the sick, satisfied those who were hungry, and filled the poor; and what is more wonderful, raised us all from the dead; having abolished death, he has brought us from affliction and sighing to the rest and gladness of this feast, a joy which reaches even to heaven.[46]

The most important point in this christocentric exposition is its diachronic character which is demanded by the eternal event of the sacrifice of Christ – the critical hermeneutical key for the Christian understanding of the Jewish sacrifices which are recorded in the Old Testament. It is on this basis that Athanasius can claim his experience as a Christian of seeing and rejoicing in the saving sacrifice of Christ as perfectly matching the experience of Abraham and, indeed, of all the Fathers and Saints of Israel! This ultimately means that in the Athanasian, and for that matter in the patristic – for the same approach is adopted by the Church Fathers – theological tradition Christ is the criterion of the history of salvation seen in its Old Testament and New Testament settings and, consequently, of all history.[47] To reverse this perspective, that is, to subject Christ to history, seeing him only as a merely historical entity, in line with the many others, is to revert to the errors of Judaism, heresy, schism and, even, paganism. All-important in this exposition is the comment that in Abraham's case God 'accepted the will of the offerer' because it implies a deeper theological rationale of sacrifice, namely the self-offering of human life to God, which is clarified in several of the following *Festal Letters*, as we shall see. Here we should simply note that the case of Abraham's sacrifice is treated once more in *Festal Letter XXIX* (for AD 357), where Athanasius, being in exile, speaks of the primacy of keeping the faith over keeping a religious place[48] and of the unavoidability of tribulations and sufferings for those who decide to follow Christ;[49] but whereas in *Festal Letter VI* he emphasized the christological scope of the 'sacrifice' of Isaac and the importance of Abraham's offering of his 'will' to God, here he explains that it was Abraham's offering of his 'love' to the Lord, above all else, including his only son, that made his sacrifice so acceptable. Here too Athanasius supplies further examples from the lives of other Old Testament saints in order to stress the link between love and sacrifice and to demonstrate the deeper spiritual meaning of sacrifice which is fully and perfectly revealed in the sacrifice of Christ.

In his *Festal Letter VII* (for AD 335) Athanasius repeats his distinctive Christian view concerning the Passover, focussing attention upon the person of Christ: 'For the Passover is not of the Gentiles, nor of those who are Jews in the flesh; but of those who acknowledge the truth in Christ according to the declaration of him who was sent to proclaim such a feast; "our Passover, Christ, is sacrificed" [1 Cor. 5: 7].'[50] In his *Festal Letter X* (for AD 338) Athanasius makes Christ the basis for the old and the new sacrifices

of the Passover, which is, therefore, identical with him. 'This is the Lord ...',
he writes,

who, being truly the Son of the Father, at last became incarnate for our sakes, that
he might offer himself to the Father in our stead, and redeem us through his offering
and sacrifice. This is he who once, in old time, brought the people out of Egypt; but
who afterwards redeemed all of us, or rather the whole race of men from death, and
brought them up from the grave. This is he who, in old time, was sacrificed as lamb,
having being typified in the lamb; but who afterwards was slain for us, for 'Christ,
our Passover, is sacrificed' [1 Cor. 5: 7].[51]

  The same applies to *Festal Letter XI* (for AD 339) where Athanasius
continues to stress the understanding of the Passover in terms of Christ's
sacrifice, offered through his death upon the cross, but here he also draws
out some aspects of the typological relation of the Old Testament celebration
of it through the sacrifice of the Passover lamb by the Israelites to the New
Testament celebration of it through the eucharist by the Christians. Thus he
says that 'as the Israelites could not sacrifice the Passover to the Lord their
God while they were in Egypt' (Exod. 8: 26), so 'he who is defiled with the
pollutions of the wicked is not able to sacrifice Passover to the Lord our God',
because, as he explains, 'a man should depart from wickedness and deeds of
iniquity, that he may be able properly to celebrate the feast',[52] that is, to
offer or participate in the eucharistic sacrifice of Easter. Athanasius also
stresses this point further on in the same Letter when he says that 'because
he [Christ our Passover] was sacrificed [1 Cor. 5: 7], let each of us feed upon
him and with alacrity and diligence partake of his sustenance',[53] and
thereby shows that proper human contact or human responsibility are
critical prerequisites for a Christian's worthy participation in the eucharist.
In line with this Athanasius recalls the 'pure sacrifice' of Mal. 1: 11[54] to
stress the superiority of the Christian Passover, accomplished by the
sacrifice of Christ, over the Jewish one, focussing on the former's inner
validity and universal range.

  In his *Festal Letter XIII* (for AD 341) the distinction between the Jewish
sacrifice for the Passover and the sacrifice of Christ, who is again said to be
the true Passover, is drawn out in the most direct way: 'Let us be mindful of
him who was sacrificed in the days of the Passover; for we celebrate this,
because Christ, the Passover, was sacrificed.'[55] It is crystal clear here that
for Athanasius Christ's sacrifice has replaced the Old Testament Jewish
sacrifices performed for the Passover celebrations and that he now
constitutes in himself the essence or truth of the Passover Feast. It is in his
following Letter, however, *Festal Letter XIV* (for AD 342), that we see more
plainly what Athanasius means by his central and unequivocal statement
that Christ himself is the Passover. Here Athanasius once more emphasizes
Christ and his sacrifice as the present truth which was typified by the
shadows and types of the old dispensation. 'The children of Israel', he says,

'were counted worthy to receive the type. For the type had respect to this feast [the Christian Easter, Christ the Passover], nor was the feast now introduced on account of the type ... these things took place before, as it were, in shadows, and were typical, but now, the truth is nigh unto us, the Image of the invisible God, our Lord Jesus Christ...'[56] Indeed, 'it is Jesus who calls us to the feast, who is all things for us and was laiden in ten thousand ways for our salvation'.[57] 'Therefore let us also, when we come to the feast, no longer come as to old shadows, for they are accomplished; neither as to common feasts; but let us hasten as to the Lord, who is himself the feast.'[58]

This theme of Christ himself, or rather Christ's sacrifice, as the truth of the Passover, as contrasted to its shadow or type, the Jewish Passover sacrifice, is again discussed in *Festal Letter XIX* (for AD 347), but here Athanasius proceeds to show that the replacement of the latter by the former does not imply that the latter had been unacceptable all along since the time of its introduction. He does this as he attempts to answer the seeming contradiction between the apparently unequivocal prophetic condemnation of the Old Testament sacrificial system and the apparently divine institution of this system as witnessed to by the Old Testament Law. He begins by pointing out that 'The feast is no longer proclaimed to us by trumpets, but made known and brought near to us by the Saviour, who suffered on our behalf and rose again; even as Paul preached, saying, *Our Passover, Christ, is sacrificed* [1 Cor. 5: 7].' And he goes on,

The feast of the Passover, then, is ours, not that of a stranger, nor of the Jews any longer. For the time of shadows is abolished, and these old things have ceased; and now the month of the new things is at hand, in which every man should keep the feast, in obedience to him who said, *Observe the month of the new things, and keep the Passover to the Lord thy God* [Deut. 16: 1].[59]

This means that since Christ's sacrifice was accomplished the festivals of pagans have been fully reproved and those of the Jews exposed as hypocritical – something which had already been pronounced in Old Testament times (cf. Ps. 102: 10 and Isa. 1: 14).

To stress this last point Athanasius also cites Jer. 6: 20 which declares Israel's sacrifices to be unacceptable to God and several other verses from Jeremiah and Isaiah[60] making the point that it was Israel's lack of faith and disobedience to God's commandments that rendered its sacrificial practice unacceptable. But then he raises the inevitable question of how such prophetic condemnations of Jewish sacrifices are to be reconciled with the fact that 'by Moses God gave commandment respecting sacrifices, and all the book of Leviticus is entirely taken up with the arrangement of these matters, so that he [God] might accept the offerer?'[61] Although he immediately rejects any suggestion that either the scriptures contradict themselves or God is false, Athanasius does not find it easy to supply an answer to this apparent dilemma, for he prays to God that 'the remarks he presumes to make may not be far from the truth'.

Athanasius' claim is that 'not at first were the commandment and the law concerning sacrifices, neither did the mind of God, who gave the Law, regard whole burnt-offerings, but those things which were pointed out and prefigured by them' and bases this claim on Heb. 10: 1 and 9: 10 which he cites.[62] Thus he goes on to argue that initially the Law did not treat of sacrifices, though, after the Exodus and after the Israelites' attempt to return to their Egyptian customs, a commandment about sacrifices to be offered to God was actually added in order to free them from the idols and teach them to pay all their attention to God himself and to what he commanded. This means that the Old Testament sacrifices were introduced only as prefigurations or shadows of the reality which was to come, since the Israelites were unable to see it at that time:

They attained to know what time the shadow should last, and not to forget the time that was at hand, in which no longer should the bullock of the herd be a sacrifice to God, nor the ram of the flock, nor the he-goat, but all these things should be fulfilled *in a purely spiritual manner*, and by constant prayer, and upright conversation, with godly words.[63]

What Athanasius actually means by this *spiritual manner of offering a sacrifice*, which constitutes for him the reality to which the 'typical or shadowy' sacrifice of animals actually pointed, should be understood in terms of both 'prayer' and 'righteous life'. This is obvious from his citing of such verses as Ps. 104: 34, 141: 2, 50: 14, 23 and 4: 5; 1 Sam. 15: 32; and Hos. 6: 6, which speak of offering both 'meditation and prayer' or 'sacrifice of praise', and of 'sacrifice of righteousness and of mercy'. Ultimately, however, both of these concepts of prayer and life are connected with the Lord himself and the necessity for the Israelites to be dedicated and to be faithful to him – something which they totally failed to perceive, since, as Athanasius puts it, 'had they known they would not have crucified the Lord of glory' (1 Cor. 2: 8).

Athanasius' point about the Christian sacrifice being characterized by a *spiritual manner*, as distinct from the Jewish sacrifice which is fleshly and material, far from introducing any docetic or dualistic connotation, should be understood in a human realistic perspective, that is, in terms of a human life-offering which entails right praise and right conduct – orthodoxy and orthopraxy – as contrasted to a symbolic (figurative) perspective which is tied to an animal-offering and enjoys only a 'typical' (external or conventional) and shadowy status. What we have here is an appeal to what we would call today Christian spirituality which is practical, as much liturgical as it is human-ethical.[64] It is precisely because of their failure to perceive this human spiritual dimension as the reality that lies behind, or rather ahead of, the 'typical' ordinances of the Law, especially those that are concerned with animal sacrifice, that the Jews are accused by Athanasius as hypocrites. That his charge is much more serious and deeper than it sounds at first hearing is clearly revealed in the fact that the rest of *Festal Letter XIX*, apart from the last chapter, is entirely given to an exposition of the real foolishness and error of the Jews concerning their human ethical conduct which is exposed as being both sinful and erroneous. It seems that with this *Festal Letter* one has arrived at the heart of the problem of Jewish sacrificial practice, as Athanasius understands it on the basis of the New Testament christocentric teaching, but also at the beginning of getting to grips with the broader meaning of the Christian notion of sacrifice – the offering of a spiritual life, the life of faith, the life in the Spirit, which is centred on the eucharistic offering and communion. As Athanasius puts it, 'what is there more consonant with the feast, as turning from wickedness, and a pure conversation, and prayer offered without ceasing to God, with thanksgiving?'[65] In *Festal Letter XX* (for AD 348) Athanasius will put it like this: 'But the Saints, having their senses exercised by reason of practice, and being strong in faith and in understanding the word, and ... passing through water and fire, to a place where they can breathe freely, they duly keep the feast, offering up prayers with thanksgiving to God who has redeemed them.'[66] And further on, he will add, 'For such is the love of the saints at all times, that they never once leave off, but offer the uninterrupted, *constant sacrifice* to the Lord, and continually thirst and ask of him to drink.'[67] This last text perfectly illustrates the Athanasian, and for that matter, the patristic understanding of the Christian sacrifice, namely the offering of ourselves to God and our partaking of the eternal drink of his grace, which is principally focussed on the eucharist and its presupposition, the sacrifice of Christ.

Similar points are made in *Festal Letter XXIV* (for AD 352) which survives in a fragmentary form in a Coptic version.[68] Here Athanasius expounds the tension between faithlessness and faith in the life of ancient Israel, focussing his argument upon the saints of old, who, through faith, foresaw in Christ the fulfilment of the Law, and were justified. In contrast to these saints 'the Jews ... have adopted a superficial approach to the Law which has made them to celebrate Easter in a fleshy manner, eating the flesh of an irrational animal and never arriving at the rational nurture of the true Lamb, our Saviour Jesus Christ, who is the true Bread, come down from heaven and giving life to the world.'[69] In effect, Athanasius goes on to say, the Jews are irrationally nourished by shadows and types and are thus unable to see the reality which was prefigured by them and which is identical with our Lord Jesus Christ, upon whom the Christians feed. Clearly Athanasius refers here to Christ's sacrifice as the fulfilment of the Old Testament sacrifices of the

Law, which he links with the life of sanctity and the eucharist in both of which the Christians are called and obliged to participate.

The need for Christians to link a life of sanctity with the eucharist, that is, ethics with liturgy, in order to celebrate worthily and effectively the sacrifice of Christ – the Christian or true Passover, as Athanasius likes to call it – is again expounded in *Festal Letter XXV*, for the following year (AD 353), which is also preserved in a fragmentary form in a Coptic version.[70] Here Athanasius uses Rom. 12: 1 and stresses that only 'if we [Christians] obey the Apostle at all times and especially at the time of the feast, that is, if we present our bodies as a living sacrifice, pure and acceptable to God, which is our rational worship, can we sit at the table with the Lord, like the apostles in participating at the spiritual nurture which he administers to us; but, when we eat, we must remain close to him with perseverance and never betray the truth through Jewish thoughts and fables, like the wretched Judas; for whoever arrives at the point that he does not eat the Easter with a suitable respect but is immersed in such thoughts, he pays attention to the devil who bewitches him.'[71] Athanasius goes on to explain that what he has in mind at this point is the life of sanctity which, he says, 'should be especially proclaimed at Easter, since on our Easter, Christ was sacrificed for us [1 Cor. 5: 7]'.[72]

Similar points are made in *Festal Letter XXVI* (for AD 354)[73] and especially in *Festal Letter XXVII* (for AD 355) in which Athanasius exposes the deceit of the Jews concerning the feast of Easter, which is due to their attachment, in celebrating it, to 'themselves' and to 'earthly pleasures', as opposed to 'the Lord' and 'the heavenly vocation'.[74] In another fragment from *Festal Letter XXVIII* (for AD 356), which is preserved both in Coptic and in a Greek citation in Cosmas Indicopleustes, the link between Christ's offering of himself as a sacrifice for all and the obligation of human beings 'to adhere to his words' and 'to participate in his living teaching', so that they may receive the heavenly joy with the saints, is explicitly emphasized. Access to heaven as the result of Christ's sacrifice is presented in a way that invites Christians to a life of both imitation and participation.[75] In the last analysis what he is actually saying is that only those who are prepared in this way are invited by the Lord to the eucharist.

This particular point is especially emphasized in a fragment from *Festal Letter XL* (for AD 368) which reads as follows:

Ye are they that have continued with me in my temptations; and I appointed you a kingdom, as my Father has appointed unto me, that ye may eat and drink at my Table in my kingdom [Luke 22: 28–30]. Being called to the great and heavenly Supper, in that upper room which has been swept, let us cleanse ourselves, as the Apostle exhorted, from all filthiness of the flesh and spirit, *perfecting holiness* in the fear of God [2 Cor. 7: 1]; so that, being spotless within and without – without, clothing ourselves with temperance and justice; within, by the Spirit rightly dividing the word of truth – we may hear, 'Enter into the joy of Thy Lord' [Matt. 25:21].[76]

The same applies to another fragment from *Festal Letter XLII* (for AD 370),

For we have been called, brethren, and are now called together, by Wisdom, and according to the Evangelical parable, to that great and heavenly Supper, and sufficient for every creature; I mean, to the Passover, – to Christ, who is sacrificed; for 'Christ our Passover is sacrificed.' They, therefore that are thus prepared shall hear, Enter into the joy of the Lord.[77]

Finally in Athanasius' last *Festal Letter* (*XLV*, for AD 373, the year of his falling-asleep) we come across two of the points that we encountered in earlier Letters, namely, that the Christian notion of sacrifice is connected with a life of sanctity and that it has a heavenly setting which was typified by Solomon's Jerusalem and by the Tabernacle ordered through Moses. 'Let us take up our sacrifices', he writes

observing distribution to the poor, and enter into the holy place, as it is written: whither also our forerunner Jesus is entered for us having obtained eternal redemption [Heb. 6:20, 9:12]... And this is a great proof, that whereas we were strangers, we are called friends; from being formerly aliens, we are become fellow-citizens with the Saints, and are called children of the Jerusalem which is above, whereof that which Solomon built was a type. For if Moses made all things according to the pattern which he saw in the mount, it is clear that the service performed in the Tabernacle was a type of the heavenly mysteries, whereto the Lord, desirous that we should enter, prepared for us the new and abiding way. And as all the old things were a type, so the festival that now is, is a type of the joy which is above, to which coming with psalms and spiritual songs, let us begin the fasts.[78]

We may conclude, then, that in Athanasius' mind Jewish sacrifices were equally as unacceptable as the pagan ones, when measured by the standard of the Christian sacrifice which is rooted in the sacrifice of Christ and celebrated in the eucharist. The reason for this is that they were only provisional types and shadows of the Christian sacrifice, and as such they became unseasonable when they were fulfilled and replaced by the latter. Indeed as types and shadows they were symbolic, temporal, earthly, limited and even parochial, in contrast to the Christian sacrifice which is real and spiritual (true), eternal and heavenly, unlimited and universal. Whereas originally they were godly and acceptable because they were directed to God, when God appeared in Christ and both he and his sacrifice were rejected in their name, they ceased to be godly, were falsified and were even rendered demonic. Such a problem had already appeared in Old Testament times and was properly exposed by the holy prophets, inasmuch as the types and shadows became ends in themselves and were divorced from the Lord to whom they were meant to point and from his commandments. But the true understanding and use of the Old Testament sacrifices was demonstrated by

the saints, inasmuch as they looked to Christ through the types and
shadows and lived a godly life in faith and sanctity, praising and
communicating with God. It is clear that in developing the contrast and the
connections between the Jewish sacrifices and the Christian sacrifice
Athanasius reveals the main lines of his understanding of the latter.
Christian sacrifice is primarily connected with Christ's sacrifice, accomplished through his death upon the cross, and also with the eucharist
through which the Christians appropriate or communicate in the grace
which was procured by the sacrifice of Christ. What this actually means is
explained by Athanasius in another set of texts most of which are found in
his early apologetic treatise *De Incarnatione*. It is to these that we shall now
turn before we draw our general conclusions concerning this investigation.

In his work *De Incarnatione*, where he explains the dynamics of salvation as
they issue out of the life and activity of the Inhominated Son/Logos of God,
Athanasius provides an extensive and coherent account of his understanding of the sacrifice of Christ. The event of the Divine Inhomination had had
two basic soteriological causes for humanity: the abolition of corruption
and death which had irreversibly seized the human nature and the
restoration of mankind in the image and likeness of God. Since the two
human needs which lie behind these two causes had emerged as a result of
humanity's sin against and turning away from its Creator, the Logos of God,
and since their character was such that they could not be overcome by
humanity *per se*, it was the Logos' intervention through his Inhomination
that provided the solution. The Inhomination is absolutely crucial for
understanding the logic of Christ's saving work. To be sure, for Athanasius
it is God the Creator who saves,[79] but as Saviour he is not merely God, but
God incarnate or inhominated, who uses his humanity in order to justify,
redeem, save the whole of mankind.[80] The humanity which the Creator
Lagos assumed from the all-holy Virgin Mary at the Incarnation[81] is seen by
Athanasius as a 'temple' [*naos*] wherein the Logos dwelt and as an
'instrument' [*organon*][82] which is offered as a sacrifice [*thysia*][83] in order to
effect his redemptive and saving work, the destruction of death and the
beginning of the resurrection. There are several aspects to this sacrifice
or offering which emerge from a close examination of Athanasius' texts and
which are important to note here.

First of all it is a vicarious sacrifice which is offered 'instead of all' [*anti
pantōn*] and 'for all' [*huper pantōn*].[84] This is understood in realistic rather
than legal/forensic terms, as it is revealed in several Athanasian statements,
as, for example, in the statement that 'when Christ died all human beings
died in him'[85] or that 'in offering himself to the Father Christ actually offered
all of us to him', and so forth.[86] Neither is this a sort of 'Platonic'
(universalist) realism as it has been claimed by some modern scholars[87]

given that Christ's humanity is for Athanasius an individual one.[88] Rather it is the divine person of Christ and especially the fact that his humanity, which is identical with that of other human beings, excepting sin, exists and subsists in the person of the Creator/Logos, that makes it a real substitute [*antipsychon*][89] for all human beings. Thus the inner logic, as it were, of this substitutionary act is not to be traced to an abstract principle of forensic sacrificial transaction but to the headship of the Divine Logos in creation whereby he is related to all human beings and as such can act on their behalf as their true representative. Thus the substitutionary offering of one single body (humanity) for all rests on the fact that it is the 'Dominical body' [*to Kyriakon sōma*],[90] that is to say, the body of him who is 'above all' [*ho epi pantōn*] and 'for all' [*ho epi pantas*] and, therefore, the one who can also be 'instead of all' [*ho anti pantōn*], as the representative of all.[91]

As regards the recipient of Christ's sacrifice and offering, though in his work *On the Inhomination* and elsewhere Athanasius explicitly states that this is 'death',[92] in the last analysis he identifies the recipient with the Father.[93] There is no contradiction here if one takes into account the point he makes that the dominion of death is derived from the law of the Father[94] according to which mankind would incur death for itself if it sinned against his commandment. Thus the offering of Christ's humanity to death is in fact an offering in fulfilment of God's law concerning death – a fact which makes it possible to speak of Christ's sacrifice as having been offered both to death (to God's just judgement) and to God. But there is another seeming contradiction here, inasmuch as one could also assume that the sacrifice was actually offered to the devil – something which Athanasius does not explicitly say but actually implies,[95] inasmuch as he clearly sees the devil as the one 'through whose envy death entered into the world'[96] and who 'has the dominion of death' [*ton echonta to kratos tou thanatou*].[97] The importance of raising this point is further supported by Athanasius' use of the 'ransom' [*lutron*] language which is directly linked with the 'sacrifice' or 'offering' of Christ's body to death and which also envisages the devil.[98] Here too our answer to this question should be an unequivocal 'No', namely, that there is no contradiction, because the devil's dominion over mankind through death does *not naturally* belong to him, but is derived from his appeal to the law of God, which sentenced mankind to death and which the devil avenges as mankind's deceiver and accuser. This aspect of the sacrifice of Christ is part of the wider soteriological theme of Christ's fighting with the devil which is as typical of Athanasius as it is of the New Testament authors.[99] Thus, a careful examination of the textual data shows that there is no problem concerning the recipient of Christ's sacrifice, because the identification of him with all three, death, the devil and God, witnesses to different nuances of meaning, all of which are determined by their connection with the divine law concerning death.[100] Ultimately, however, it is to God that the sacrifice is offered and the ransom is paid, not in the sense that he requires it for himself, but in the sense that it is required for the mending of the relation between the Creator and the creature which secures the creature's life and well-being. This in no way means that in the sacrifice of Christ 'God paid the debt to his integrity', or that 'this sacrifice had to be offered by God himself in a process of self-reconciliation, and, if we may invent the term, self-propitiation', as a contemporary patristic scholar has put it![101] This is the case not only because for Athanasius Christ offered his humanity (not his Godhead) as a sacrifice, acting as an Inhominated God or Lordly man (not as God) on behalf of and for mankind, but also because he was not himself the executor of himself – that is, he did not commit some sort of suicide – but accepted the death from others.[102] It is plainly wrong to claim that 'Athanasius was the first to express the notion of divine self-reconciliation', and to go on to conclude on this basis 'that Athanasius's account of Atonement is a rationalisation of the elements of conflicting Christian Traditions' and that 'Athanasius does not basically use sacrifice to understand Atonement', because 'sacrifice language appears merely as a metaphor for the payment of the debt to death'.[103] Indeed Athanasius explicitly states that the Son of God 'did not come to die his own death, but to bring to an end the death of human beings [*ou ton heautou thanaton, alla ton tōn anthrōpōn ēlthe teleiōsai*]',[104] and that 'the Logos who redeemed the sin of others did not himself sin . . . so that . . . he might offer himself for himself as a sacrifice in order to redeem himself!'[105]

The effects of Christ's sacrifice, as Athanasius outlines them, are both universal and far-reaching. They include automatic benefits to all humanity but without cancelling any of mankind's obligations towards God which were initially embedded in the order of creation. Death and the dominion of the devil are destroyed, human sins are forgiven, and humanity has access to heaven and to God. In Christ humanity is redeemed, glorified and exalted, in short, deified. Human beings are called to a new life of imitation and participation which ensures the appropriation of this deification. The means for achieving this are union with Christ through baptism and abiding in Christ through the life of holiness and the celebration of the holy eucharist, all of which have sacrificial status. These means constitute what might be called the Christian sacrifice which, in the last analysis, is but an imitation and participation in the unique sacrifice of the Inhominated Son/Logos of God. It seems that Athanasius' profound expositions of this sacrifice, in contrast to those of the pagans, the Jews, the heretics and the schismatics, is rooted in his experience of it, which to him seems to have been quite overwhelming, as his *Letter to Adelphius*, which deals with the Worship of the Inhominated, crucified and exalted Lord, indicates. Here is one of his most comprehensive statements:

But this is our orthodox faith, starting both from the teaching of the apostles and the tradition of the Fathers, being confirmed both by the New and the Old Testament; for the prophets say, Send out Thy Word and Thy Truth (Ps. 42: 3), and, Behold the Virgin shall conceive and bear a Son, and they shall call his name Emmanuel, which is being interpreted God with us (Isa. 7: 14, Matt. 1: 23). But what is this, if not that God has come in the flesh? While the Apostolic Tradition teaches, in the words of blessed Peter, Forasmuch then as Christ suffered for us in the flesh (1 Pet. 4: 1); and in what Paul writes, Looking for the blessed hope and appearing of our Great God and Saviour Jesus Christ, who gave himself for us that he might redeem us from all iniquity, and purify unto himself a people for his own possession, and zealous of good works (Tit. 2: 13). How then has he given himself for us, if he had not put on flesh? For *having offered it, he gave himself for us*, in order that taking death upon him in it, he might bring to nought the devil who had the power of death. Hence we always offer the eucharist in the name of Jesus Christ and we do not disregard the grace which came to us through him. For the Saviour's incarnate presence has been ransom for death [*thanatou lutron*] and salvation for all Creation.[106]

NOTES

1 *De Incarnatione*, chs. 10[bis], 16, 20, 21, 25, 31 (*PG* 25: 113B10, 113C3, 124D2, 132A3, 133B15, 140C14, 149D3).

2 *De Decretis*, ch. 14 (*PG* 25: 440B10); *Contra Arianos I*, ch. 59 (*PG* 26: 137A15); *Contra Arianos II*, ch. 9[bis] (*PG* 26: 165B4, 165B7); *Ad Epictetum*, chs. 4, 4[bis], 6 (*PG* 26: 1057B5, 1057C6, 1057B13, 1061A2), *Epistolae Festalis XXVIII* (*PG* 26: 1433B6); to these we may add several more if we take into consideration the equivalent term *prosphora*. It should be noted that all translations are the author's with the exception of those from the Syriac original. Those from Coptic originals are the author's from the French translation as noted.

3 P. G. Alves de Sousa, El concepto de *Sōtēria* en el *De Incarnatione Verbi* de San Atanasio (*Scripta Theologica* (Pamplona), 10 (1978)), pp. 9–32; J. F. Bethune-Baker, *An Introduction to the Early History of Christian Doctrine to the Time of the Council of Chalcedon* (London, 1903), pp. 345–9; J. Coman, Apopseis tines tēs sōtēriologikēs didaskalias tou M. Athanasiou, *Klēronomia*, 5 (1973), 331–46; R. S. Franks, *A History of the Doctrine of the Work of Christ in its Ecclesiastical Development*, vol. 1 (London 1918), pp. 63ff.; J. Kalogerou, Christologia kai Sōtēriologia en tō syndesmō tōn kata ton M. Athanasion, in *Tomos Eortios 1600 ēs Epeteiou M. Athanasiou 373–1973*, ed. G. I. Mantzarides (Thessalonica, 1974); J. N. D. Kelly, *Early Christian Doctrines* (5th edn, London, 1977), pp. 377ff.; M. Scott, *Athanasius on the Atonement* (Stafford, 1914); R. C. Moberly, *Atonement and Personality* (London, 1901), pp. 349–67; H. Rashdall, *The Idea of Atonement in Christian Theology* (London, 1920), pp. 294–300; D. Unger, A special aspect of Athanasian Soteriology (*Franciscan Studies*, 6 (1946)), pp. 30–53, 171–94.

4 *Contra Gentes*, chs. 7ff.

5 *Ibid.*, ch. 10 (*PG* 25: 21).

6 *Ibid.*, ch. 10 (*PG* 25: 21D).

7 *Ibid.*, ch. 24 (*PG* 25:48BCD, 49A).

8 *Ibid.*, ch. 25 (*PG* 25:49BC).

9 *Ibid.*, ch. 25.

10 *De Incarnatione*, ch. 11 (*PG* 25: 116C).

11 *Ibid.*, ch. 51 (*PG* 25: 199B).

12 *Ibid.*, ch. 52.

13 *Apologia contra Arianos*, ch. 8 (*PG* 25: 261C).

14 *Ibid.*, ch. 15 (*PG* 25: 273AB).

15 *Ibid.*, ch. 59 (*PG* 25: 356B).

16 *Contra Arianos II*, ch. 24 (*PG* 26: 200A13); *De Decretis*, ch. 8 (*PG* 25: 429A7); *De Synodis*, ch. 18 (*PG* 26: 713B2); *ibid.* ch. 20 (*PG* 26: 716C).

17 *De Synodis*, ch. 18 (*PG* 26: 713B).

18 *Ibid.*, ch. 20 (*PG* 26: 713BC).

19 *Historia Arianorum*, ch. 37 (*PG* 25: 736CD).

20 *Ibid.*, ch. 56 (*PG* 25: 761A).

21 *Ibid.*, ch. 74 (*PG* 25: 781D).

22 *Epistola Encyclica*, ch. 3 (*PG* 25: 229A).

23 *Vita Antoni*, ch. 82 (*PG* 25: 960A).

24 *De Incarnatione*, ch. 40 (*PG* 25: 168B3).

25 *Contra Arianos I*, chs. 54ff.

26 *Ibid.*, ch. 59 (*PG* 26: 137A).

27 *Contra Arianos II*, chs. 6–11a.

28 *Ibid.*, ch. 9 (*PG* 26: 165B). It should also be noted here that, according to what Athanasius says in *Contra Arianos II*, ch. 6, in this case *to piston* = *to axiopiston*, i.e., what is trustworthy.

29 *Ibid.*, ch. 9.

30 Only a few Greek fragments from some of these Letters have actually come down to us (i.e., Letters xxii, xxiv, xxviii, xxix, xxxix, xl, xlii, xliii and xlv), thanks to Cosmas Indicopleustes. The following Letters are extant in a Syriac version (British Museum Add. 14.569) in their entirety apart from the last five which are fragmentary: i–viii, x–xiv, xvii–xx, xxvii, xxix, xxxix and xliv. This Syriac text was first edited by W. Cureton in his *The Festal Letters of Athanasius* (London, 1848). The first English translation was made by H. Burgess and published in the series 'A Library of Fathers of the Holy Catholic Church anterior to the division of the East and West', vol. xxxviii (Oxford, 1854) (henceforth cited as LFHCC). A revised English translation with some additions was published in the 'Select Library of Nicene and post Nicene Fathers of the Christian Church', vol. iv (London, 1891, reprinted by Eerdmans, Grand Rapids, Michigan, 1971) (henceforth cited as SLNPNF). F. Larsow published a German translation of the Syriac version in his *Festbriefe d. h. Athanasius* (Leipzig, 1852). A Latin translation, with the Greek Fragments included, was published by A. Maius in his *Nova Bibliotheca Patrum*, vol. iv: 2 (Rome, 1853), apparently based on an Italian translation of the Syriac original. This is the edition reproduced by J. P. Migne in his *Patrologia Graeca*, vol. 26: 1360–1444. Finally a Coptic collection of large fragments of some of these Letters (i.e., I, II, VI, XXIV–XXIX, XXXVI–XLIII) with a French translation was published by L.-Th. Lefort in his *S. Athanase Lettres Festales et Pastorales en Copte, Scriptores Coptici*,

vol. XIX (edited) and vol. XX (translated) in the series *Corpus Scriptorum Christianorum Orientalium*, vols. CL and CLI (Louvain, 1955) (henceforth cited as Lefort).

31 LFHCC, p. 10, and SLNPNF, ch. 7, pp. 508–9.

32 The LXX text which Athanasius cites here reads as follows: 'keep thy feasts O Judah; pay to the Lord thy vows; For they shall no more go to that which is old; it is finished; it is taken away; he is gone up who breathed upon the face and delivered thee from affliction'.

33 LFHCC, p. 11, and SLNPNF, chs. 8–9, esp. p. 509.

34 *Epistola ad Serapionem IV*, ch. 18 (*PG* 26: 665AB).

35 LFHCC, p. 33, and SLNPNF, ch. 3, p. 516.

36 LFHCC, p. 38, and SLNPNF, ch. 4, pp. 516–17.

37 This particular point is most clearly stated in *Festal Letter X*, where we read: 'This is he who once, in old time, brought the people out of Egypt; but who afterwards redeemed all of us, or rather the whole race of men, from death ...'; LFHCC, p. 79, and SLNPNF, ch. 10, p. 531.

38 LFHCC, p. 41, and SLNPNF, ch. 4, p. 517.

39 LFHCC, p. 41, and SLNPNF, ch. 4, pp. 518–19.

40 LFHCC, pp. 45–6, and SLNPNF, ch. 2, p. 520.

41 LFHCC, pp. 48–9, and SLNPNF, ch. 6, p. 521.

42 LFHCC, p. 49, and SLNPNF, ch. 6, p. 521. Cf. also *Festal Letter XXXIX* (for AD 367) in Lefort XX, p. 34, where Athanasius speaks of those who approach Easter hypocritically and with human vanity and identifies them with Jews, Arians and Meletians.

43 Here Athanasius has obviously in mind Rom. 11, which refers to 'the holy root and the branches' (verse 16), since he actually cites verse 24 in order to show that the Jews, who were cut off because of their rejection of Christ, could certainly be regrafted on it, considering it as their own, provided that they turned away from their unbelief.

44 LFHCC, pp. 49–50, and SLNPNF, ch. 7, p. 521.

45 LFHCC, p. 50, and SLNPNF, ch. 8, p. 552.

46 LFHCC, p. 51, and SLNPNF, chs. 8–9, esp. p. 522.

47 Cf. Jean Daniélou's *The Lord of History* (London, 1953).

48 SLNPNF, pp. 550–1.

49 Lefort XX, p. 25.

50 LFHCC, p. 58, and SLNPNF, ch. 3, p. 524.

51 LFHCC, P. 79, and SLNPNF, ch. 10, p. 531.

52 LFHCC, p. 93, and SLNPNF, ch. 9, p. 536.

53 LFHCC, p. 97, and SLNPNF, ch. 14, p. 538.

54 LFHCC, p. 94, and SLNPNF, ch. 11, p. 537.

55 LFHCC, p. 110, and SLNPNF, ch. 7, p. 541.

56 LFHCC, p. 113, and SLNPNF, ch. 3, p. 542.

57 LFHCC, p. 114, and SLNPNF, ch. 4, p. 543.

58 LFHCC, p. 115, and SLNPNF, ch. 5, p. 543.

59 LFHCC, p. 121, and SLNPNF, ch. 1, pp. 544–5.

60 Jer. 7: 21, 22, 18, 34; Isa. 1: 11, 12 and 66: 3.

61 LFHCC, p. 124, and SLNPNF, ch. 3, p. 545.

62 *Ibid.*

63 LFHCC, p. 125 and SLNPNF, ch. 4, p. 546. Italics mine.

64 Cf. here Francis Young's thesis, *The Use of Sacrificial Ideas in Greek Christian Writers from the New Testament to John Chrysostom* (Patristic Monograph Series, 5; The Philadelphia Patristic Foundation Ltd, 1979), which stresses the 'spiritual' character of the Christian sacrifice in a non-human manner which implicitly, at least, suggests docetism or dualism.

65 LFHCC, p. 129, and SLNPNF, ch. 8, p.547.

66 LFHCC, p. 128, and SLNPNF, ch. 7, p. 547.

67 LFHCC, p. 132, and SLNPNF, ch. 1, p.548. Italics mine.

68 See Lefort xx, pp. 8ff.

69 Lefort xx, p. 19.

70 Lefort xx, pp. 14–16.

71 Lefort xx, pp. 15, 3–13.

72 Lefort xx, pp. 15, 18–26.

73 Lefort xx, pp. 16f.

74 Lefort xx, pp. 18–20.

75 Lefort xx, p. 21, and SLNPNF, p. 550; cf. also *PG* 26: 1433B6–C8.

76 SLNPNF, p. 552, and *PG* 26: 1440AB. Italics mine.

77 SLNPNF, p. 552, *PG* 26: 1440B and Lefort xx, p. 45.

78 SLNPNF, p. 553.

79 Cf. *De Incarnatione*, ch. 1 (*PG* 25: 97C5–12).

80 Cf. my book *Athanasiana* (London, 1982), pp. 143–55.

81 Athanasius usually employs the term '*soma*' when he deals with the Incarnation and, especially, with Christ's sacrifice, most probably because of biblical precedent and of his anti-docetic stance, but apart from the fact that he uses the term '*kata synekdōchen*' to denote the totality of human nature, he also employs a variety of other terms which clearly indicate that as far as the humanity of Christ is concerned he is 'anti-Apollinarian', accepting both the integrity of the humanity of Christ and its individual nature, without, however, falling into the opposite error of 'Antiochian' Christological dualism. On this see ch. 7, 'The Christology', in my book, *St Athanasius Contra Apollinarem* (Church and Theology, 6; Athens, 1985), pp. 400–546. As for the question concerning the 'soul' of Christ in Athanasius' thought, which was first raised by certain liberal German critics in the second half of the nineteenth century and was defended by M. Richard and A. Grillmeier in this century, see ch. 6 of the above book, pp. 289–399.

82 Cf. *De Incarnatione*, ch. 8 (*PG* 25: 109C9–10).

83 He uses the term '*thysia*' in *De Incarnatione*, chs. 10, 16, 20, 21 (*PG* 25: 113B10, 113C3, 124D2, 132A3, 133B15); *De Decretis*, ch. 14 (*PG* 25: 440B10); *Contra Arianos I*, ch. 59 (*PG* 26: 137A15); *Contra Arianos II*, ch. 9 (*PG* 26: 165B4, 165B7); *Ad Epictetum*, chs. 4, 6 (*PG* 26; 1057B5, 1061A2); *Epistolae Festales XXVIII* (*PG* 26: 1433B6); etc., and the term '*prosphora*' in *De Incarnatione*, chs. 9, 10 (*PG* 25: 112A13, 112D5); *Apologia Contra Arianos*, chs. 29, 83 (*PG* 25: 296C3, 296C6, 396D3).

84 *De Incarnatione*, chs. 6, 9, 20, 25, 31 (*PG* 25: 112A7, 124D3, 140C14, 149D3); *De Decretis*, ch. 14 (*PG* 25: 440B10); *Contra Arianos II*, chs. 7, 14, 69 (*PG* 26:

161B5, 176B10, 293B2); *Ad Epictetum*, ch. 5 (*PG* 26: 1057B13); *Ad Serapionem II*, ch. 20 (*PG* 26: 669A13); etc.

85 Cf. for example *De Incarnatione*, ch. 9 (*PG* 25: 112ABC); *Contra Arianos I*, ch. 41 (*PG* 26: 97A3); *Contra Arianos II*, ch. 69 (*PG* 26: 293B).

86 '*hēmeis ēmen hoi chrēzontes ous anepheren autos dia tou idiou sōmatos autou*', *De Incarnatione*, ch. 25 (*PG* 25: 140C); cf. also *Contra Arianos II*, ch. 53 (*PG* 26: 260B).

87 See J. N. D. Kelly, *Early Christian Doctrines* (London, 1960), p. 378; contrast my book *St Athanasius Contra Apollinarem*, p. 387.

88 Cf. P. Galtier, 'St Athanase et l' âme humaine du Christ' (*Gregorianum*, 30–36 (1956)), pp. 533–89; A. van Haarlem, *Incarnatie en verlossing bij Athanasius* (Wageningen, 1961); L. Bouyer, *L' Incarnation: l' église corps du Christ dans la théologie de S. Athanase* (Paris, 1943); see also my book *St Athanasius Contra Apollinarem*, pp. 372ff.

89 *De Incarnatione*, chs. 9, 37 (*PG* 25: 112B1, 161A13).

90 *De Incarnatione*, chs. 8, 20, 22, 26, 30 (*PG* 25: 109D2, 132B7, 136A13, 141B15, 148B12, 149C11); *Expositio Fidei*, ch. 3 (*PG* 25: 205B9); *Ad Epictetum*, ch. 2 (*PG* 26: 1053A13).

91 Cf. the statement, '*hina tou epi pantōn Logou metalabōn anti pantōn hikanon genētai tō thanatō* in *De Incarnatione*, ch. 9 (*PG* 25: 112A6–7) and see my book *St Athanasius Contra Apollinarem*, pp. 235f.

92 *De Incarnatione*, ch. 8 (*PG* 25: 109C13–14; ibid., ch. 9 (112A11–12); ibid., ch. 16 (124D2); ibid., ch. 20 (132A3); ibid., ch. 25 (140C14); ibid., ch. 31 (149D2–3); *Contra Arianos II*, ch. 69 (*PG* 26: 293B2); etc.

93 *Contra Arianos I*, ch. 41 (*PG* 26: 96D2, '*hina houtōs heauton huper hēmoñ dia tou thanatou prosenenkē tō Patri*').

94 *De Incarnatione*, chs. 3, 4, 5, 6, 7, 10, 20, 21 (*PG* 25: 101C, 104B, 105A, 105D–108A, 108C, 113C, 132ABC, 132CD, etc.).

95 *Contra Arianos II*, ch. 55 (*PG* 26: 261C13–264AB); see also the little treatise *In Illud* (*PG* 26: 209ff.).

96 Cf. *De Incarnatione*, chs. 4–5 (*PG* 25: 104, 105), and Wisdom of Solomon 2: 21–22.

97 Cf. Heb. 2: 14; *De Incarnatione*, chs. 10, 20, 24 (*PG* 25: 113B, 132C2–5, 137C8; *Contra Arianos II*, ch. 8 (*PG* 26: 164BC); *Ad Adelphium*, ch. 6 (*PG* 26: 1080C4–5).

98 For death and *lutron*, see *De Incarnatione* 21, 25 (*PG* 25: 133C11–12, 140A6–7, 140B1); *Contra Arianos I*, ch. 45 (*PG* 26: 105A3–5); *Contra Arianos II*, ch. 7 (*PG* 26: 162B11); *Ad Adelphium*, ch. 6 (*PG* 26: 1080C8–9); *Contra Apollinarem I*, chs. 17, 18 (*PG* 26: 1125A6ff., 1125D1–2); for death, sin and ransom see *De Incarnatione*, chs. 37, 40 (*PG* 25: 161A1–13, 165A15); *Contra Arianos I*, chs. 16, 43, 50 (*PG* 26: 45C16–17, 101B12, 117A10ff.); *Contra Arianos II*, ch. 7 (*PG* 26: 161A); *Contra Arianos III*, chs. 23, 31 (*PG* 26: 372C5–6, 389BC); *Contra Apollinarem I*, ch. 15 (*PG* 26: 1120CD, 1121A).

99 Cf. Acts 26: 18; Col. 1: 13; John 12: 31, 14: 30; 1 John 3: 8.

100 I would argue that it is in this sense that some of Origen's or Gregory of Nyssa's statements can be explained, but cf. the following essays on this issue: Theodorou, 'The Theory concerning the Rights of Satan in the Soteriology of

the Ancient Eastern Church', (in Greek) *Theologia* (Athens), 28 (1957), pp. 103–14, 225–37, 412–19; also, D. G. Tsamis, 'The Teaching of the Fathers of the Church on the Recipient of the "ransom"', (in Greek) *Kleronomia* (1970), 88–111.

101 See Young, *Use of Sacrificial Ideas*, p. 207.

102 *De Incarnatione*, chs. 20, 24 (*PG* 25: 133B14–15, 137C).

103 Young, *Use of Sacrificial Ideas*, pp. 207 and 209.

104 *De Incarnatione*, ch. 22 (*PG* 25: 136A).

105 *Ad Epictetum*, ch. 4 (*PG* 26: 1057B2–5).

106 *Ad Adelphium*, ch. 6 (*PG* 26: 1080ABC). Italics mine.

6

THE DOCTRINE OF SACRIFICE: AUGUSTINE AND THE LATIN PATRISTIC TRADITION

GERALD BONNER

Thus the true sacrifice is offered in every act which is designed to unite us to God in a holy fellowship, every act, that is, which is directed to that Final Good which makes possible our true felicity.[1]

This familiar, and comprehensive, definition of sacrifice is typical of Augustine's thought: he sees it as an action directed to union with God, which alone makes us truly happy. The eudaemonistic element in this definition is characteristically Augustinian: although Augustine has generally little concern for the transitory happiness of the present age ('in huius vitae infelicitate'), in his desire for eternal beatitude he is a thorough hedonist. 'Nulla est homini causa philosophandi nisi ut beatus sit' – the only purpose man has in philosophizing is the attainment of happiness. Yet Augustine is clear that happiness without God is impossible: 'that which makes man happy is the Supreme Good itself'.[2] Furthermore, the only way to attain to the Supreme Good is through the mediation of the God-man, Jesus Christ.[3] From this it follows inevitably that Augustine's approach to sacrifice will be determined by his christocentricity and that he will, without hesitation, accept the earlier tradition which understood the eucharist, the great action of Christian unity, in sacrificial terms. Not every sacrifice, in Augustine's theology, is the eucharist; but every eucharist is a sacrifice.

It is very easy, when dealing with Augustine or with any great thinker, to overestimate his originality and to neglect his debt to the past; but Augustine would have been the first to reject any suggestion that he sought to introduce new doctrine, like some theological Paracelsus burning the books of his predecessors and making a fresh start. Augustine's originality is not iconoclastic. Rather, he amplifies and enriches the thought and feeling of earlier generations. No Christian thinker is more aware of, and more concerned to follow, the tradition of the Catholic Church.

This consideration governs Augustine's attitude to his sources and their possible influence upon him. Of the place of the Bible in his thought there can be no doubt but there remains the question of non-Christian influences, and especially that of pagan philosophy, whether read in translations of the Neoplatonists or mediated by Cicero.[4] To these should be added the actuality of pagan sacrificial worship in Augustine's own day. Although banned by the laws of Christian emperors, paganism remained a force in Roman Africa, and it was possible to find Christians who held that pagan sacrifices, no less than Jewish, had been legitimate in their time and had only become otiose – and illegal – with the rise of Christianity.[5] Such a view forced Augustine to distinguish between Jewish and pagan sacrifice and to maintain the validity of the former before the coming of Christ, while asserting that the latter had always been illegitimate, being directed not to the one true God but to the demons, who had fraudulently appropriated what was due to God alone. A large part of *De Civitate Dei* is devoted to precisely this sort of refutation. Nevertheless, Augustine could not fail to take account of pagan philosophical argument, particularly when he found it in a thinker like Porphyry, whose good qualities he was very ready to recognize. It is, however, unwise to ascribe an Augustinian idea to a pagan source when the Bible provides a likely inspiration. To give an example, in *De Civitate Dei* Augustine writes:

There are some who suppose that these visible [pagan] sacrifices are suitable for other gods, but that for the One God, as He is invisible, greatest and best, only the invisible, the greatest and the best sacrifices are proper; and such sacrifices are the services of a pure mind and a good will. But such people evidently do not realize that the visible sacrifices are the symbols of the invisible offerings, just as spoken words are the symbols of things. Therefore in our prayers and praises we address significant sounds to Him, as we render to Him in our hearts the realities thus signified. In the same way, in offering our [Christian] sacrifices we shall be more aware that visible sacrifice must be offered only to Him, to whom we ourselves ought to be an invisible sacrifice in our hearts.[6]

The most obvious subject of these remarks is Porphyry who, in his treatise *De Abstinentia*, rejected any sort of sacrifice to the supreme gods and declared that the intelligible gods should only be worshipped by hymns and that to the gods of the world and to the astral gods – the planets and the fixed stars – there should be no bloody sacrifices, but only offerings of corn, honey, fruits and flowers.[7] In similar fashion a saying ascribed to Apollonius of Tyana, preserved by Eusebius of Caesarea, asserts that the highest god has no need of sacrifices at all, and that the only fitting offering is man's reason (*logos*), not the word that comes out of his mouth: 'We men should ask the best of beings through the best thing in us for what is good – I mean by means of the mind, for mind needs no material things to make its prayer.'[8] It is very likely that Augustine was familiar with sentiments like those of Porphyry and Apollonius from his reading; but it is improbable that they exercised much influence on his thinking, if only because the whole point of the polemic against the Neoplatonists in Book x of *De Civitate Dei* is that sacrifice may only be offered to the One God and that *any* offering to an inferior being is idolatry. The horror of pagan sacrifices lies precisely in the fact that they have been usurped by the demons from the One True God.

Accordingly, in his maintaining that God has no need of sacrifice, even though He desires it of men, it is more likely that Augustine's inspiration came from biblical texts like Ps. 15[16]: 2: 'Thou art my God, my goods are nothing unto thee', which he quotes repeatedly,[9] than from any Neoplatonic author. 'The sacrifice of God is a troubled spirit: a broken and contrite heart, O God, shalt thou not despise' (Ps. 50: 19[51: 17]).[10]

Again, it is possible that Augustine's doctrine of the mediation of Christ by his sufferings and death, shown forth in the sacrifice of the altar,[11] could have been influenced by Neoplatonic ideas. There is a passage in the curious handbook of pagan doctrine, *De Diis et Mundo*, by the fourth-century Neoplatonist theologian Salutius (Sallustius), relating to sacrifice. In the best Neoplatonic tradition Salutius declares that the divine has no need of anything and that human worship is offered for man's advantage, and not for the benefit of the gods. Divine Providence is everywhere, and it requires only worthiness, by imitation (*mimesis*) and likeness (*homoiotēs*), to receive its benefits. Hence the apparatus of religious worship imitates its archetypes: temples copy heaven, altars the earth, and statues represent life, which is why they are made in the image of living beings.[12] This leads Salutius to a discussion of how sacrifices unite men with the gods. The primordial and highest life, he declares, is that of the gods. Human life is life of some sort, and in order for communion to exist between these two lives, there must be a mediator (*mesotēs*) to join them. But the mediator must be like the two natures which are to communicate. It therefore follows that life is needed to mediate between divine and human life and hence the need for a mediating victim.[13]

There is here a certain resemblance to Augustine's teaching with regard to the mediation of Christ, and there is no reason to reject the supposition that this particular aspect of Neoplatonic thinking (though not necessarily this particular text) might have been familiar to him. However, similar doctrine was available to Augustine in the Epistle to the Hebrews (especially 2: 14) which, in default of positive evidence to the contrary, would seem a more obviously immediate source of inspiration.

More generally, it may safely be assumed that the Platonic conception of the relation between existing things and the archetypes which they resemble – the more nearly an image approaches its archetype, the more closely it resembles it – played its part in Augustine's theology: 'Everything', says Salutius, 'rejoices in what it resembles and turns away from unlikeness'.[14] The efficacity of any image depends upon its relation to its original. Such a philosophy would harmonize with Augustine's understanding of the relation between Old Testament sacrifices, Christ's final and definitive sacrificial offering and the efficacious signs of bread and wine by which that offering is now shown forth in the Christian eucharist. Yet Augustine could equally well, and actually did, point to the words of St Paul: 'figurae nostrae fuerunt' – 'these things were our types or images' (1 Cor. 10:6) – to explain their significance:

With all this, you dare to denounce the sacrifices of the Old Testament [he tells Faustus the Manichee] and to call them idolatry, and to attribute to us the same impious notion. To answer for ourselves: in the first place, while we no longer consider it a duty to offer sacrifice, we recognise sacrifices as part of the mysteries of Revelation, by which the things prophesied were foreshadowed. For *they were our images* [*figurae*], and in many and various ways they all pointed to the One Sacrifice which we now commemorate.[15]

And again:

As regards animal sacrifices, every Christian knows that they were enjoined as suitable to a perverse people, and not because God had any pleasure in them. Still, even in these sacrifices *there were types* [*figurae*] of what we enjoy, for we cannot obtain purification or the propitiation of God without blood. The fulfilment of these types [*figurarum*] is Christ, who is the Truth, by whose blood we are purified and redeemed.[16]

The conclusion which may reasonably be drawn from the foregoing is, then, that while Augustine was unquestionably influenced by Neoplatonic thought – an influence which he never denied – it is not necessary, and may indeed be positively misleading, to emphasize that influence at the expense of the more obviously immediate influence of the Bible, on which his mature theology is fundamentally based.

In his understanding of the idea of sacrifice, Augustine had to take account of three particular connotations of the word in his own day: the physical sacrifices of the pagans, now illegal, and of the Jews, now discontinued; the self-offering of Christ on Calvary, the great sacrifice, which had fulfilled and rendered redundant the Jewish sacrifices;[17] and the Christian eucharist, which had long been regarded as re-presenting or re-actualising the sacrifice of the cross.[18] In his consideration of this third aspect Augustine followed a tradition to which Tertullian, Cyprian and Ambrose had borne witness, and one moreover which was sustained by popular practice. The principle that the law of prayer is the law of belief was never more strikingly illustrated than by the attitude of the early Church to the commemoration of the departed at the offering of the eucharist: 'sacrificium pretii nostri' ('the sacrifice of our redemption'), as Augustine was to call it, when describing the burial of his mother.[19] Furthermore, popular devotion to the dead, as exemplified in the feasts at the tombs of the martyrs, had a superstitious element inherited from paganism, which caused bishops like Ambrose and Augustine to seek to transfer it to orthodox public worship, in which the sacrifice of the altar would replace unregulated devotion, and the enthusiasm of the worshipper be more surely directed from the martyr to the One True God.[20]

It was the actuality of animal sacrifice in a dying but still tenacious paganism – Augustine had, in his youth, refused the offer of a sorcerer to offer victims to ensure his success in a rhetorical competition[21] – and the fact that it had been practised by the saints of the Old Testament, to whom the Christian Church looked for example, that brought an element into the patristic treatment of sacrifice which is not easily intelligible to later ages, for whom animal sacrifice is a matter for the anthropologist and the student of primitive religion. This was not the case in the fourth and fifth centuries. A hostile critic of Catholic Christianity, like the Manichaean bishop Faustus, could accuse the Catholics of being the heirs of both paganism and Judaism;[22] yet there was a very real pastoral problem confronting the Catholic episcopate: to what extent was it permissible to identify Christian practice with the ideas derived from pagan society and from the Judaism described in the Bible, of which the Church claimed to be the only legitimate heir? Here, the crucial decision, made in the second Christian century, to regard the Old Testament as authoritative, played a vital role. If the Catholic Church had decided, like the Gnostics, to reject the Old Testament, many of the problems which arose from the Christian polemic against paganism would never have existed.

The theological key for understanding Augustine's doctrine of sacrifice is his conception of Christ the Mediator, the God-man, who is the great high priest after the order of Melchizedek.[23] In this approach Augustine was not original. Such an attitude was common to his predecessors, such as Cyprian[24] and Ambrose of Milan.[25] What was original in Augustine was his ability to bring together different elements in traditional theology and to weave them into a coherent whole. This is especially apparent in the tenth book of De Civitate Dei, a wonderful tour de force in which dogmatic and speculative theology is applied to anti-pagan polemic to produce one of the most profound discussions of the nature of sacrifice in Christian literature.

It may be said at the outset that for Augustine the one, true, perfect and sufficient sacrifice, oblation and satisfaction, upon which all others depend, is that offered on Calvary:

By his death, which is indeed the one and most true sacrifice offered for us, he purged, abolished and extinguished whatever guilt there was by which the *principalities and powers* lawfully detained us to pay the penalty; and by his resurrection he called us, *whom he had predestined*, to new life, *justified those whom he had called, and glorified those whom he had justified* [Rom. 8: 30].[26]

It is upon this act of self-oblation that Augustine bases Christ's priesthood. He offered himself, the one sinless victim, for humanity, of whom he had become one:

Who then is so righteous and holy a priest as the only Son of God, who had no need of sacrifice to purge his own sins, either Original or the sins which are added in the course of human life? And what could he take more fittingly from men to offer on their behalf than human flesh? And what was more suitable for such sacrificial offering than mortal flesh? And what was so pure for purifying the vices of mortals than the flesh born without any infection of fleshly lust within and from the womb of the Virgin? And what could more acceptably be offered and received than the flesh of our Sacrifice, made the Body of our Priest? Since there are four things to be considered in any sacrifice: to whom it is offered, by whom it is offered, what it is that is offered, and for whom it is offered, so the One True Mediator, who reconciles us to God by the sacrifice of peace, remained one with him to whom he offered; made one in himself those for whom he offered; and was himself both the offerer and the thing which was offered.[27]

It is in the tenth book of *De Civitate Dei* that Augustine gives his definition of sacrifice as 'every act which is designed to unite us to God in holy fellowship', which, combined with his earlier statement that 'The visible sacrifice is the sacrament, the sacred sign, of the invisible sacrifice',[28] may be said to epitomize Augustine's understanding. One may note here the comprehensive character of the definition: a sacrifice is 'omne opus' – every act – and not simply the visible sacrifice of the eucharist.[29] Here Augustine is in accord with African tradition, for the word 'sacrifice' had early been applied in Africa to the oblations of the faithful, and St Cyprian can rebuke a rich woman who comes to church 'sine sacrificio' – 'without an offering' – and who therefore communicates from the offerings of the poor.[30] Nevertheless, the notion of sacrifice had simultaneously a more technical sense, being applied to the eucharist, in which Christ's self-offering on Calvary is shown forth. Thus Tertullian can urge those who are observing a fast not to fear that it will be broken by attendance at the Sacrifice and the reception of the body of the Lord.[31] By the time of Cyprian, *sacrificium* is the regular word for the eucharist, instituted by Christ,[32] celebrated by the bishops, 'who daily as priests solemnize the sacrifices of God',[33] and offered for the departed.[34] The same language is found in Optatus of Mileve, Augustine's predecessor as a Catholic apologist against the Donatists,[35] and in Ambrose of Milan.[36]

Nevertheless, the eucharist is a sacrifice only because of its relation to Christ's self-offering as a propitiation for human sin.[37] Foreshadowing this great and supreme sacrifice[38] were the sin-offerings of the Jews, offered by the high priest, both for himself as a sinner and for his sinful people. Christ's sacrifice differs from, and completes, the earlier sacrifices, because here the priest and the offering are one and the same, and the priest, no less than the victim, is pure:

... by the grace of God he was in a marvellous and ineffable manner conjoined and interknit in unity of person with the Father's only-begotten Word, who is not by grace but by nature the Son, and therefore himself committed no sin. Yet because of the *likeness of sinful flesh* [Rom. 8: 3] in which he came, he was himself described as sin [2 Cor. 5: 21], seeing he was to be sacrificed for the washing away of sins. In fact in the old Law, sacrifices for sins were called by the name of sins [Lev. 6: 25; Num. 8: 8; Hos. 4: 8]; and he became that in truth of which those sacrifices were shadows.[39]

Christ was not, however, only the victim, but the priest as well. Augustine was helped here by the fact that in the Old Latin Bible which he used the word 'propitiation' (*hilasmos*) of 1 John 4: 10: 'and sent his Son as the propitiation for our sins', was translated by *litator*, 'an offerer of sacrifices'.

And he sent his Son to be the propitiator for our sins – propitiator, that is, offerer of sacrifice. He offered sacrifice for our sins. Where did he find the offering, the pure victim that he would offer? Because he could find no other, he offered himself.[40]

It is this sort of understanding of the character of Christ's sacrifice which underlies the famous passage in Book x of *De Civitate Dei* which is, perhaps, the finest short statement of Augustine's thought in the whole of his writings:[41]

Hence it is that the true Mediator, insofar as he *took the form of a servant* and was thus made the *mediator between God and mankind, the man Christ Jesus* [1 Tim. 2: 5], receives the sacrifice *in the form of God* [Phil. 2: 6, 7], in union with the Father, with whom he is one God. And yet *in the form of a servant* he preferred to be himself the sacrifice than to receive it, to prevent anyone from supposing that sacrifice, even in this circumstance, should be offered to any created being. Thus he is both the priest, himself making the offering, and the oblation. This is the reality, and he intended the daily sacrifice of the Church to be the sacramental symbol of this; for the Church, being the Body of which he is the Head, learns to offer herself through him. This is the true sacrifice, and the sacrifices of the saints in earlier times were many different symbols of it. This one sacrifice was prefigured by many rites, just as many words are used to refer to one thing, to emphasize a point without inducing boredom. This was the supreme sacrifice and all the false sacrifices yielded place to it.[42]

Given the patristic view that the Old Testament writings are prophetic, not only in the specifically prophetic books but as a whole, it was desirable to find in them a figure who would foreshadow the coming of Christ and anticipate the ending of animal sacrifices and their replacement by the offering of bread and wine, instituted by Christ at the Last Supper. Such a figure was found in the person of Melchizedek, king and priest, from the letter to the Hebrews. Here again, Augustine was by no means the first Latin Christian author to dwell on his significance. The relation between him and Christ, 'the pontifex of the uncircumcised priesthood', had already been urged by Tertullian:[43] but it was to be richly developed by St Cyprian in his sixty-third letter, the earliest extended study of the eucharist, cited by Augustine.[44] Cyprian was concerned to denounce the practice of some bishops who used water in the eucharist instead of the traditional mixed chalice. His argument turns upon his conception of Christ as the true priest of which Melchizedek was a type.[45]

The influence of the figure of Melchizedek as a type of Christ in relation to the understanding of the eucharist in African theology was immense.[46] In the first place, by seeing Melchizedek as a prophetic image of Christ, it was possible to explain why the Aaronic sacrifices of the Old Testament had ceased, superseded by the unbloody rites of the Christians – a useful argument in controversy with the Jews. So Augustine could write:

[Abraham] received at that time a public blessing from Melchizedek, who was the priest of the Most High God. Many important things are written about Melchizedek in the epistle entitled *To the Hebrews* . . . Here we certainly see the first manifestation of the sacrifice which is now offered to God by Christians in the whole world, in which is fulfilled what is said in prophecy, long after the event, to Christ who was yet to come in the flesh: *Thou art a priest for ever after the order of Melchizedek.* Not, it is to be observed, in the line of Aaron, for that line was to be abolished when the events prefigured by these shadows came to the light of day.[47]

Again, in a sermon, he could declare:

There was formerly, as you know, animal sacrifice among the Jews after the order of Aaron, and this was allegorical, for there was not, as yet, the sacrifice of the Body and Blood of the Lord, which the Faithful and those who read the Gospel know – a sacrifice now spread over the whole world. Therefore set before your eyes two sacrifices, the one after the order of Aaron, the other *after the order of Melchizedek*, for it is written: *The Lord sware and will not repent: thou art a priest for ever after the order of Melchizedek.* About whom is it said: *Thou art a priest for ever after the order of Melchizedek?* About our Lord Jesus Christ. Who was Melchizedek? The king of Salem. Salem was a city of former times which afterwards, as learned men have shown, was called Jerusalem. Therefore before the Jews ruled there, there was that priest Melchizedek, who is described in Genesis as *the priest of the Most High God.* He met Abraham when he had freed Lot from the hand of those who pursued him, and had laid low those by whom Lot was held; after the liberation of his kinsman, Melchizedek met him. And Melchizedek, by whom Abraham was blessed, was very great. *He brought forth bread and wine* and blessed Abraham, and Abraham gave him tithes. You see what he brought forth and whom he blessed; and afterwards it was said: *Thou art a priest for ever after the order of Melchizedek.* David said this in the spirit long after Abraham, for Melchizedek was contemporary with Abraham. About whom else does he say: *Thou art a priest for ever after the order of Melchizedek* except about Him whose sacrifice you know? So the sacrifice of Aaron has been taken away and the sacrifice *after the order of Melchizedek* has begun.[48]

Augustine, however, owed more to Cyprian than the conception of the prophetic character of Melchizedek fulfilled in the person of Christ, whose passion and resurrection are shown forth in the eucharist, which is now the universal and only valid sacrifice. In Cyprian Augustine also found the conception, which he was to develop in his arguments with the Donatists with regard to the validity of baptism administered by sinners, of Christ being the true priest at the eucharist, with the ordained minister being only his representative:

For if Christ Jesus, our Lord and God, is himself the great High Priest of God the Father, and if he offered himself as a sacrifice to the Father and directed that this should be done in remembrance of him, then without doubt that priest truly serves in Christ's place [*vice Christi*] who imitates what Christ did; and he offers up a true and complete sacrifice to God the Father in the Church when he proceeds to offer it just as he sees Christ himself to have offered it.[49]

In a similar spirit Augustine can write to the Donatists in 409:

Why then do we not speak the truth and rightly understand that, while the grace is of God and the sacrament of God, the ministry is always of a man who, if he is good, cleaves to God and works with God; but if he is bad, God works the visible form of the sacrament through him, but himself gives the invisible grace? Let us all understand this and let there be no schism among us.[50]

Yet Christ is not only the true priest, himself offering the sacrifice of the Faithful; he has also associated the Faithful with himself, offered in the bread and wine. So Augustine, preaching to the newly baptised on Easter Day, explaining to them the character of the sacrament, describes the action of the eucharist up to the consecration, and continues:

Then, after the sanctification of the sacrifice of God, because He has willed that we ourselves should offer sacrifice, as was clearly indicated at the first institution of that sacrifice of God which we are – or, rather, of which we are the sign – well then, when the sanctification has taken place, we say the Lord's Prayer.[51]

This passage, expressed by Augustine in rather disjointed phraseology, is clarified by *De Civitate Dei* 10, 6:

So then, the true sacrifices are acts of compassion, whether towards ourselves or towards our neighbours, when they are directed towards God; and acts of compassion are intended to free us from misery and thus to bring us to happiness – which is only attained by the Good of which it has been said: *As for me, my true good is to cling to God* [Ps. 72 [73]: 28]. This being so, it immediately follows that the whole redeemed community, that is to say the congregation and fellowship of the saints, is offered to God as a universal sacrifice, through the great Priest who offered himself in his suffering for us – so that we might be the Body of so great a head – under *the form of a servant* [Phil. 2: 7]. For it was this form he offered, and in this form he was offered, because it is under this form that he is the Mediator, in this form he is the Priest, in this form he is the Sacrifice.[52]

The complexity of construction of the argument of this passage is remarkable, even by Augustine's standards. Starting from his premiss that a sacrament is every act which is designed to unite us to God in holy fellowship, he argues that acts of compassion are sacrifices, and immediately applies this conception to the eucharist, in which Christ, the priest, offers his Body, which is at one and the same time the human body which suffered on Calvary; the bread and wine on the altar, which are offered by the Faithful; and the Faithful themselves. The result is an astonishing piece of theological exposition. Yet the thought underlying it had been formulated by Cyprian in his Letter 63 long before Augustine:

And this bonding and union between water and wine in the Lord's cup is achieved in such a way that nothing can therefore separate the union between Christ and the Church, that is, the people who are established within the Church and who steadfastly and faithfully persevere in their beliefs. Christ and his Church must remain ever attached and joined to each other by indissoluble love ... And just as the Lord's cup consists neither of water alone nor of wine alone but requires both to be intermingled together, so, too, the Lord's body can neither be flour alone nor water alone but requires that both be united and fused together so as to form the structure of one loaf of bread. And under this same sacred image our people are represented as having been made one, for just as numerous grains are gathered, ground, and mixed all together to make into one loaf of bread, so in Christ, who is the bread of heaven, we know there is but one Body, and that every one of us has been fused together and made one with It.[53]

The Cyprianic image of bread and wine as representing the unity of a multiplicity of individuals may well have been in Augustine's mind when he delivered his Sermon 227 to the newly baptised:

This bread which you see on the altar, sanctified by the word of God, is the Body of Christ. This cup – or, rather, what this cup contains – being sanctified by the word of God, is the Blood of Christ. Through these our Lord Jesus Christ willed to entrust to us his Body and Blood, which he poured out for us for the remission of sins. If you have received them in good faith, you are what you have received. Now the Apostle has said: *We, being many, are one bread, one body* [I Cor. 10: 17]. Thus he has explained the sacrament of the Lord's table: *We, being many, are one bread, one body*. He has shown you in this bread how you ought to love unity. Was this bread made from one grain? Were there not rather many grains of wheat? But before they came to be one loaf they were separate; they have been conjoined after a sort of crushing, for unless the wheat is ground and sprinkled with water, it will by no means come to that form which is called bread. Such was your condition before being, as it were, ground by the humiliation of fasting and the sacrament of exorcism. Then came baptism and you were, so to say, moistened by the water so that you might come to the form of bread ... The Holy Spirit came, fire after water [of baptism] and you became the bread which is the Body of Christ.[54]

This notion of unity with and in Christ in the eucharist, illustrated by the images of bread and wine made into his own Body and Blood by the high priest, who offers his people who make up his Body, had its effect upon Augustine's ecclesiology and, in particular, on the relation between the Church Militant and the City of God with regard to the faithful departed. Of the significance of the eucharist offered for the dead in the early Church, and in Roman Africa in particular, there is no question. Monica, on her death-bed, desired her sons, wherever they might be, to remember her at God's altar,[55] and when Augustine's own time came, 'the holy Sacrifice was offered up, commending his body to the earth, and he was buried'.[56] Augustine repeatedly declares that the departed receive much benefit from it, provided that they have been baptized and that their earthly lives have been such as to justify our intercession.[57] Deprivation of the help of the Sacrifice after death was a terrible penalty, to be imposed only for grave offences, such as making one of the clergy an executor or guardian (an appointment which could not legally be refused), 'for he does not deserve to be named at the altar of God in the prayers of the priests who would call the priests and ministers away from the altar'.[58] Indeed, so great was African confidence in the efficacy of funerary celebration that it became necessary to forbid the practice of placing the eucharist in the mouth of the corpse at burial, 'for it was said by the Lord: *Take and eat*; but corpses are not able either to take or to eat'.[59]

There was, clearly, a very considerable element of superstition in the popular attitude to the cult of the dead, of which Augustine disapproved. Of the propriety of the practice of eucharistic commemoration of the dead, however, he had no doubt:

Accordingly, funerary ostentation, huge congregations, lavish expenditure on the burial, expensive construction of tombs – these are some sort of consolation to the living, but no help to the dead. But there is no doubt that the dead *are* helped by the prayers of Holy Church, by the saving Sacrifice, and by alms which are expended for their spirits, so that they may be more mercifully treated by God than their sins have deserved. The universal Church observes this custom, handed down by the Fathers, that prayer should be made for those who have died in the communion of the Body and Blood of Christ, when they are commemorated at the appropriate place in the Sacrifice, and also that it should be proclaimed that It is offered for them.[60]

It was this sense of the unity of all faithful Christians, the living and the departed alike, in the offering of the eucharist, which enabled Augustine to find a theological understanding to replace the old literal belief in a Thousand Year Reign of Christ with his saints before the Last Judgement, as described in Revelation 20:4. The passage of the centuries had made a literal interpretation of the Apocalypse less and less attractive; but this apart, it was not congenial to Augustine's mind to seek to define times and seasons:

We are now in the Sixth Epoch [of the world], but that cannot be measured by the number of generations, because it is said: *It is not for you to know the dates: the Father has decided those by his own authority* [Acts 1:7].[61]

For this reason Augustine, although constrained by controversy with the Donatists to maintain that the Church Militant must, at the present time, be a mixed body, containing both good and bad Christians, is nevertheless prepared to identify her with the Kingdom of Christ:

For the souls of the pious dead are not separated from the Church, which is even now the Kingdom of Christ. Otherwise they would not be commemorated at the altar of God at the time of the partaking of the Body of Christ, nor would it be of any avail to have recourse to the Church's baptism in time of peril, for fear that this life should end without baptism, nor to have recourse to reconciliation at such time, if it happens that one is separated from this Body under penance or through one's own bad conscience. Why are such steps taken, unless it is because the Faithful are still members of this Body, even when they have departed this life? And therefore their souls, even though not yet with their bodies, already reign with Him while those thousand years are running their course. That is why we read, in another place in the same book: *Blessed are the dead who die in the Lord. Yes indeed, says the Spirit, from henceforth they may rest from their toils, for their deeds go with them* [Rev. 14:13]. And so the Church now begins to reign with Christ among the living and the dead.[62]

It would be going too far to assert that this rejection of millenarianism and Augustine's unhesitating declaration that both the living and those who die in the peace of the Church are equally members of the Church Militant are directly derived from Augustine's doctrine of eucharistic sacrifice. What cannot reasonably be disputed is that they are in harmony with the whole tenor of his thought on the eucharistic sacrifice as revealed in his writings. The eucharist proclaims the self-offering of Christ on Calvary. It is not, however, a mere commemoration, but an active re-presentation by Christ himself, the true Minister who is in his own person both Priest and Victim. Hence, in the action of the eucharist, time impinges on eternity,

for sacrifice is a divine matter [*res divina*] in the phrase of the old Latin authors, even if it is performed or offered by a man...

and, significantly, Augustine adds:

Hence a man consecrated in the name of God, and vowed to God, is in himself a sacrifice, inasmuch as he *dies to the world* so that he may *live for God* [Rom. 6:11].[63]

– a reminder that death enters into the notion of sacrifice,[64] and most appropriately into the priesthood of Christ, who has died and is alive again.

Such a train of thought leads Augustine, by a kind of theological inevitability, to the triumphant declaration:

This is the sacrifice of Christians, who are *many, making up one body in Christ* [Rom. 12:5]. This is the sacrifice which the Church continually celebrates in the sacrament of the altar, a sacrament well-known to the faithful, where it is shown to the Church that she herself is offered in the offering which she presents to God.[65]

It has, in this essay, been argued that in his treatment of the notion of Christian sacrifice, Augustine is less original and more in harmony with earlier tradition than might have been expected, in view of his reputation as an innovator in Latin theology. In fact, comparison with his predecessors suggests that the character of Augustine's thought had already been determined by theologians of an earlier generation, with whom he was happy to agree. Nevertheless, it would be unreasonable and unfair not to recognize in Augustine's thinking a richness and an amplitude which justifies his peculiar reputation among the great theologians of the early Church. He draws out and amplifies what in his predecessors was only implicit or more briefly stated.

NOTES

Abbreviations

CCL	*Corpus Christianorum*. Series Latina, Turnhout
CSEL	*Corpus Scriptorum Ecclesiasticorum Latinorum*, Vienna
ep.	*epistola* (letter)
PL	*Patrologiae cursus completus*. Series Latina. Accurante J.-P. Migne, Paris
s.	*sermo* (sermon)
SC	*Sources chrétiennes*, Paris

1 *De Civitate Dei* (hereafter *Civ.*) 10, 6: 'Proinde verum sacrificium est omne opus, quo agitur, ut sancta societate inhaereamus Deo, relatum scilicet ad illum finem boni, quo veraciter beati esse possimus' (*CCL* XLVII, 278; trans., here and elsewhere, by Henry Bettenson (Penguin Classics, 1972); we gratefully acknowledge permission from Penguin Books to reprint these translations. Other translations below are mine, unless otherwise stated.) On sacrifice in the thought of Augustine see W. J. Sparrow-Simpson, *The Letters of St Augustine* (London, 1919), 276–300, Bonner (1978), Lécuyer (1954) and Cunningham (1886). This last contains *An Epistolary Dissertation Addressed to the Clergy of Middlesex wherein the Doctrine of St Austin concerning the Christian Sacrifice is set in a true Light. By Way of Reply to Dr Waterland's late Charge to them. By a Divine of the University of Cambridge*. This pamphlet, perhaps by the nonjuror George Smith (1693–1756), is a monument of erudition.

2 *Civ.* 19, 1, 3 (*CCL* XLVIII, 659).

3 *Expositio Epistulae ad Galatas* 24: 'Sic itaque unicus Filius Dei, mediator Dei et hominum factus est, cum Verbum Dei Deus apud Deum, et maiestatem suam usque ad humana deposuit, et humilitatem humanam usque ad divina subvexit, ut mediator esset inter Deum et homines, homo per Deum ultra homines' (*CSEL* LXXXIV, 87).

4 Note his reference (*Civ.* 19, 1, 1) to Cicero's treatise '*De finibus* enim *bonorum et malorum* multa et multipliciter inter se philosophi disputarunt' (*CCL* XLVIII, 657). It is all too easy to see Augustine as the pupil of Plotinus, and to neglect his continued and openly acknowledged debt to Cicero.

5 It was only in 399 that the temples at Carthage were finally closed; but paganism remained strong for years afterwards. See Charles-Picard 1965, 98–130; Hamman 1979, 170–93; and Bonner 1984, 347–50. On the attitude

of Christians who believed that pagan sacrifice had been valid before the coming of Christ, see *De Divinatione Daemonum* 2, 4: 'Contra hoc dictum est, iniusta quidem esse nunc ista, non tamen mala; et ideo iniusta, quia contra leges, quibus prohibentur, fiunt; ideo autem non mala, quia, si mala essent, numquam deo utique placuissent; porro si numquam placuissent, numquam et facta essent, illo non sinente, qui omnia potest, et qui talia non contemneret' (*CSEL* XLI, 601).

6 *Civ.* 10, 19 (*CCL* XLVII, 293).

7 Porphyry, *De Abstinentia* II, 34–7 (ed. J. Boffartigue and M. Patillon (Paris: Collection des Universités de France, Association Guillaume Budé, 1979), vol. II, pp. 100–4).

8 Eusebius, *Preparatio Evangelica* 4, 13 (*SC* CCLXII, 144; trans. G. R. S. Mead, *Apollonius of Tyana. The Philosopher-Reformer of the First Century A.D.* (New York, 1966), p. 154 (slightly modified).

9 *Civ.* 10, 5 (*CCL* XLVII, 276); 19, 23, 5 (*CCL* XLVIII, 694); *ep.* 102, 17 (*CSEL* XXXIV (2), 558–9); *ep.* 138, 1, 7 (*CSEL* XLIV, 132).

10 *Civ.* 10, 5 (*CCL* XLVII, 277). Note that Augustine quotes from the Old Latin version of the Psalms, made from the Greek version (the Septuagint), in which the numeration commonly differs from the Hebrew original, from which our English versions are made. I give both numbers here for ease of reference.

11 *Civ.* 10, 6: 'Hoc est sacrificium Christianorum: *multi unum corpus in Christo.* Quod etiam sacramento altaris fidelibus noto frequentat ecclesia, ubi ei demonstratur, quod in ea re, quam offert, ipsa offeratur' (*CCL* XLVII, 279).

12 *De Diis et Mundo*, 15, 1–3 (ed. G. Rochefort (Paris: Budé 1960), p. 20).

13 *Ibid.*, 16, 2; cf. 13, 5 (Rochefort edn, pp. 21; 19). Cf. Augustine, *De Trinitate* 8, 10, 14, providing an image of the Trinity: 'Quid est autem dilectio vel caritas quam tantopere scriptura divina laudat et praedicat nisi amor boni? Amor autem alicuius amantis est, et amore aliquid amatur. Ecce tria sunt, amans et quod amatur et amor. Quid est ergo amor nisi quaedam vita duo aliqua copulans vel copulari appetens, amantem scilicet et quod amatur?' ('What is the Love of Charity which Holy Scripture so greatly praises and preaches, except love of the good? But love supposes a lover and a beloved. So there are three things: the lover, the beloved, and love. And what is love *except a certain life, joining or seeking to join two beings*, the lover and the beloved?') (*CCL* L, 290–1). This would seem to be a clear instance of Neoplatonic thought affecting Augustine's imagery.

14 *De Diis et Mundo*, 3, 2 (Rochefort edn, p. 5). On the need for the image to be turned to the archetype, see Plotinus, *Enneads* V, 3, 7 (ed. A. H. Armstrong (Loeb Library; Cambridge, Mass.: Harvard University Press/London: William Heinemann, 1984), pp. 92–101).

15 *Contra Faustum Manicheum* 6, 5 (*CSEL* XXV (1), 290–1); trans. R. Stothert, *Augustine: Writings in Connection with the Manichacan Controversy* (Select Library of Nicene and Post-Nicene Fathers, 4; Buffalo (Christian Literature Company, 1887), p. 169), slightly modified). Here and below, italics in these quotations signify biblical quotations.

16 *Ibid.*, 18, 6 (*CSEL* XXV (1), 494–5).

17 *Enarrationes in Psalmos* 33, s. 1, 5 (*CCL* XXXVIII, 277), and *ibid.*, 39, 13: 'Det mihi modo gens iudaica sacerdotem. Ubi sunt sacrificia illorum? Certe perierunt,

certe ablata sunt nunc' (*CCL* xxxviii, 435; *ep.* 138, 1, 7: '... scriptura dicit: *Mutabis ea et mutabuntur, tu autem idem idem ipse es* (Ps. 101:27, 28 [102:26, 27])) insinuandum est eis mutationem istam sacramentorum testamenti veteris et novi etiam praedictam fuisse propheticibus vocibus' (*CSEL* xliv, 132); *Civ.* 17, 5, 2 (*CCL* xlviii, 562–3).

18 Cyprian, *ep.* 63, 9: 'quomodo autem, de creatura vitis novum vinum cum Christo in regno patris bibemus, si in sacrifico Dei patris et Christi vinum non offerimus nec calicem Domini dominica traditione miscemus?'; 17: 'Et quia passionis eius mentionem in sacrificiis omnibus facimus, passio est enim Domini sacrificium quod offerimus' (*CSEL* iii (2), 708; 714).

19 *Confessiones* 9, 12, 32 (*CCL* xxvii, 151).

20 On Ambrose, see Dassmann 1975, pp. 49–68, esp. pp. 54, 55. On Augustine, see his account of the ending of the *Laetitia* festival in *ep.* 29. For the attitude of a hostile critic, see the charge of Faustus: '... sacrificia vero eorum [paganorum] vertistis in agapes, idola in martyres, quos votis similibus colitis; defunctorum umbras vino placatis et dapibus, sollemnes gentium dies cum ipsis celebratis, ut Kalendas et solstitia. de vita certe mutastis nihil: estis sane schisma a matrice sua diversum nihil habens nisi conventum' (*Contra Faustum* 20, 4 (*CSEL* xxv (1), 538)).

21 *Confessiones* 4, 2, 3 (*CCL* xxvii, 41).

22 *Contra Faustum* 20, 4 (cited above, note 20); 6, 5 (*CSEL* xxv (1), 290–1).

23 *Enarrationes in Psalmos* 33, s. 1, 5, 6 (*CCL* xxxviii, 276–7); *Civ.* 16, 22; 17, 5, 5; 18, 35, 3 (*CCL* xlviii, 524–5; 565–6; 629–30).

24 Cyprian, *ep.* 63, 4 (*CSEL* iii (2), 703–4).

25 On the figure of Melchizedek in Ambrose, see Johanny 1968, 240–3.

26 *De Trinitate* 4, 13, 17: 'Morte sua quippe uno verissimo sacrificio pro nobis oblato quidquid culparum erat unde nos principatus et potestates ad luenda supplicia iure detinebant purgavit, abolevit, exstinxit, et sua resurrectione in novam vitam nos *praedestinatos vocavit, vocatos iustificavit, iustificatos glorificavit*' (*CCL* l, 183).

27 *De Trinitate* 4, 14, 19 (*CCL* l, 186–7).

28 *Civ.* 10, 5: 'Sacrificium ergo visibile invisibilis sacrificii sacramentum, id est sacrum signum est' (*CCL* xlvii, 277).

29 Cf. *Enarrationes in Psalmos* 49, 23: 'Videte autem quod sequitur, fratres mei. Iam enim nescio quis, quia dixerat illi Deus: *Immola Deo sacrifium laudis*, et hoc quodammodo vectigal indixerat, meditabatur sibi, et dicebat: Surgam quotidie, pergam ad ecclesiam, dicam unum hymnum matutinum, alium vespertinum, tertium aut quartum in domo mea; quotidie sacrificio sacrifium laudis, et immolo Deo meo. Bene facis quidem, si hoc facis; sed vide ne iam securus sis, quia iam hoc facis, et forte lingua tua Deum benedicat, et vita tua Deo maledicat' (*CCL* xxxviii, 593).

30 Cyprian, *De opere et eleemosynis* 15 (*CSEL* iii (1), 384).

31 Tertullian, *De Oratione* 19 (*CCL* i, 267–8).

32 Cyprian, *ep.* 63, 1: 'Iesus Christus Dominus et Deus noster sacrificii huius auctor et doctor fecit et docuit' (*CSEL* iii (2), 701).

33 Cyprian, *ep.* 57, 3: '... ut sacerdotes qui sacrificia Dei cotidie celebramus hostias Deo et victimas praeparemus' (*CSEL* iii (2), 652).

34 Cyprian *ep.* 1, 2 (*CSEL* III (2), 466).
35 Optatus, 2, 12; 3, 4; 4, 3; 7, 6 (*CSEL* XXVI, 47; 85; 104; 179).
36 Ambrose, *Expositio Evangelii secundum Lucam* 1, 28 (*CCL* XIV, 20).
37 *De Trinitate* 4, 13, 17, quoted above, note 26.
38 *Civ.* 10, 20 (*CCL* XLVII, 294).
39 *Enchiridion* 13, 41 (*CCL* XLVI, 72; trans. E. Evans, *Saint Augustine's Enchiridion* (London, 1953), p. 39).
40 *In epistulam Iohannis ad Parthos tractatus decem* 7, 9 (*PL* XXXV, 2033; trans. John Burnaby, *Augustine: Later Works* (Library of Christian Classics, 8; London, 1955), pp. 316–17).
41 But cf. *De Trinitate* 4, 14, 19, quoted above, p. 106.
42 *Civ.* 10, 20 (*CCL* XLVII, 294).
43 Tertullian, *Adversus Marcionem* 5, 9, 9 (*CCL* I, 690–1).
44 *De Doctrina Christiana* 4, 21, 45 (*CCL* XXXII, 151–2).
45 See Cyprian, *ep.* 63, 4 (*CSEL* III (2), 703; trans. G. W. Clarke. *The Letters of St Cyprian of Carthage*, vol. III (Ancient Christian Writers, 46; New York/Mahwah: Paulist Press, p. 99). All quotations from Cyprian's letters at any length are from this version; we gratefully acknowledge permission from the Paulist Press to reproduce these.
46 And in Italy, in the writings of Ambrose; see Johanny 1968.
47 *Civ.* 16, 22 (*CCL* XLVIII, 524–5).
48 *Enarrationes in Psalmos* 33, s. 1, 5, 6 (*CCL* XXXVIII, 276–7). Cf. *Civ.* 17, 5, 3; 18, 35, 3 (*CCL* XLVIII, 565–6; 629–30).
49 Cyprian, *ep.* 63, 14: 'nam si Christus Iesus Dominus et Deus noster ipse est summus sacerdos Dei patris et sacrificium patri se ipsum optulit et hoc fieri in sui commemorationem praecepit, utique ille sacerdos vice Christi vere fungitur qui id quod Christus fecit imitatur et sacrificium verum et plenum tunc offert in ecclesia Deo patri, si sic incipiat offerre secundum quod ipsum Christum videat optulisse' (*CSEL* III (2), 713).
50 *Ep.* 105, 3, 12: 'quare ergo non verum dicimus et recte sapimus, quia semper dei est illa gratia et dei sacramentum, hominis autem solum ministerium, qui si bonus est, adhaeret deo, et operatur cum deo; si autem malus est, operatur per illum deus visibilem sacramenti formam, ipse autem donat invisibilem gratiam? hoc sapiamus omnes et non sint in nobis schismata' (*CESL* XXXIV (2), 604).
51 *S.* 227: 'Deinde post sanctificationem sacrificii dei, quia nos ipsos voluit esse sacrificium suum, quod demonstratum est ubi impositum est primum illud sacrificium dei et nos – id est signum rei – quod sumus, ecce ubi est peracta sanctificatio dicimus orationem dominicam' (ed. S. Poque, *SC* 116, p. 240).
52 *Civ.* 10, 6 (*CCL* XLVII, 279).
53 Cyprian, *ep.* 63, 13 (*CSEL* III (2). 711–12).
54 *S.* 227 (ed. Poque, pp. 234–8).
55 *Confessiones* 9, 11, 27 (*CCL* XXVII, 148–9).
56 Possidius, *Vita Augustini* 31, 5 (ed. M. Pellegrino (Alba: Edizioni Paoline, 1955), p. 190; trans. F. R. Hoare, *The Western Fathers* (London: Sheed and Ward, 1954), p. 243).
57 *De anima et eius origine* 1, 11, 13; 2, 15, 21 (*CSEL* LX, 313; 356); *Enchiridion* 29, 110 (*CCL* XLVI, 108); s. 159, 1 (*PL* 38, 867–8); s. 172, 2 (*PL* 38, 936–7).

58 Cyprian *ep.* 1, 2 (*CSEL* III (2), 466).

59 *Brevarium Hipponense*, 4: 'Ut corporibus defunctis eucharistia non detur; dictum est enim a Domino: *Accipite et edite*; cadavera autem nec accipere possunt nec edere' (*CCL* CXLIX, 33–4).

60 *S.* 172, 2 (*PL* 38, 936–7). Cf. *Civ.* 1, 12: 'Proinde ista omnia [id est] curatio funeris, conditio sepulturae, pompa exequiarum, magis sunt vivorum solacia quam subsidia mortuorum' (*CCL* XLVII, 14).

61 *Civ.* 22, 30 (*CCL* XLVIII, 865–6).

62 *Civ.* 20, 9, 2 (*CCL* XLVIII, 717).

63 *Civ.* 10, 6: 'Etsi enim ab homine fit vel offertur, tamen sacrificium res divina est, ita ut hoc quoque vocabulo id Latini veteres appellaverint. Unde ipse homo Dei nomine consecratus et Deo votus, in quantum mundo moritur ut Deo vivat, sacrificium est' (*CCL* XLVII, 278).

64 A point noted by Rickaby (1925, p. 43 note 1).

65 *Civ.* 10, 6, quoted above, note 11.

REFERENCES

Bonner, G. (1978). The Church and the Eucharist in the Theology of St. Augustine. *Sobornost* ser. 7, no. 6, 448–61 [reprinted 1987 in *God's Decree and Man's Destiny* (London: Variorum Reprints, 6)]

(1984). The Extinction of Paganism and the Church Historian. *Journal of Ecclesiastical History* 35, 347–50

Charles-Picard, G. (1965). *La Carthage de Saint Augustine.* Paris: Fayard

Cunningham, W. (1886). *St. Austin and his Place in the History of Christian Thought.* London: Clay and Sons

Dassmann, E. (1975). Ambrosius und die Martyrer. *Jahrbuch fur Antike und Christentum* 18, 49–68

Hamman, A.-G. (1979). *La vie quotidienne en Afrique du Nord.* Paris: Hachette

Johanny, R. (1968). *L'eucharistie: centre de l'histoire de salut chez Saint Ambroise de Milan.* Paris: Beauchesne

Lécuyer, J. (1954). Le sacrifice selon Saint Augustin. In *Augustinus Magister (Congrès International Augustinien, Paris, 21–24 September 1954)*, vol. 2, pp. 905–14. Paris: Etudes Augustiniennes

Rickaby, J. (1925). *St. Augustine's City of God: A View of the Contents.* London: Burns & Oates

7

SACRIFICE IN THE EARLY EAST
SYRIAN EUCHARISTIC TRADITION

A. GELSTON

The question of the relation of the concept of sacrifice to the eucharist has, as is well known, proved a divisive one in the West since the Reformation period, though happily there have been in recent years signs of the growth of a new understanding and synthesis.[1] While the eucharist as such is not unambiguously termed a sacrifice within the New Testament, it is undeniable that this terminology appears early in the sub-apostolic age, though it is understood in a variety of ways by different patristic writers. A recent succinct but comprehensive review of patristic treatment of this subject to the early fourth century has been given by R. P. C. Hanson (1979).[2] The earliest ideas are those of the 'pure offering' of the Christians, thought to have been predicted in Mal. 1:11, consisting of the spiritual sacrifice of praise and thanksgiving and of the Christians' self-offering to God, and the offering to God of the elements of bread and wine in the eucharist. These ideas are already fused by the time of Justin. Irenaeus adds the idea that the bread and wine are offered as the firstfruits of God's creation. The concept of the eucharist as an offering of Christ by the celebrant first appears in Cyprian. This appears to be the basis of the whole medieval development of Western eucharistic theology. Hanson's survey closes with the much more judicious statements of the doctrine made by Eusebius of Caesarea.

Growing attention is being paid by liturgical scholars to the East Syrian tradition. There are several reasons for this. The Anaphora, or Eucharistic Prayer, of the Apostles Addai and Mari is one of the oldest extant liturgies, and almost certainly the oldest still in regular use. The significance of this liturgy is enhanced when we recall the innate conservatism of the East Syrian Church, now known officially as the Assyrian Church of the East, and its almost complete isolation from the rest of Christendom from at least the fifth century to the nineteenth (see Atiya 1968 and de Vries 1959). Furthermore the Edessene Syriac in which this liturgy is written is a dialect of the Aramaic language, another dialect of which was in all probability (for the debate, see Vermes 1973, 53–4) spoken by Jesus and the first disciples. It would then seem reasonable at first sight to look for the preservation within the East Syrian liturgical tradition of close links with the theology and practice of the primitive Church.

Unfortunately the matter is not so simple as this. For one thing it must be remembered that the detailed content of the Eucharistic Prayer was still largely at the discretion of the celebrant until at least the middle of the third century (Hanson 1961), though this may be partly offset by the evidence of Basil that certain usages in addition to the Institution Narrative were traditional.[3] Further caution is induced by the Syriac translations of the gospels, which seem at times to have lost touch with the original Aramaic tradition and to be simply a retroversion from the Greek.[4] A much more serious limitation is caused by the lack of manuscript texts of the Anaphora of Addai and Mari earlier than the tenth century. A succinct account of recent manuscript discoveries, of the publication of critical texts of Addai and Mari and of the Maronite Anaphora *Sharar* (whose relation to Addai and Mari is a matter of lively current debate) and of recent studies of these texts has recently been published by B. D. Spinks (1980) together with critical texts in English translation of the two anaphoras. Critical texts of the other two anaphoras in use in the East Syrian Church, those of Theodore of Mopsuestia and Nestorius, are currently being prepared by W. F. Macomber (see Spinks 1980, 3 n. 7; the theme of 'offering' in all three anaphoras is explored in Spinks 1984 and Stevenson 1986, both of which appeared after this chapter was first written). Further information may also be gleaned from the catechetical lectures of Narsai and of Theodore of Mopsuestia; the latter, though himself belonging to the Antiochene tradition, became influential in the East Syrian tradition.

The time is clearly not ripe for any complete or final assessment of the role of the sacrificial concept in the East Syrian eucharistic tradition. What is attempted here is a brief examination of the text of the Anaphora of Addai and Mari[5] with a view to assessing the use and meaning of sacrificial terminology in the oldest strata of the prayer. The working hypothesis is adopted that those parts of the Anaphora with direct parallels in *Sharar* are likely to belong to the oldest strata so far as can be determined at present.

The first striking passage occurs within the introductory dialogue. In place of the usual 'Let us give thanks to the Lord', attested as early as Hippolytus[6] and probably a survival from Jewish graces at meals,[7] the celebrant announces 'The offering is being offered to God the Lord of all' (line 19). This must surely be a modification of the usual formula, not least because the response is the usual 'It is meet and right' (line 20). The distinctive celebrant's formula recurs in expanded forms in the anaphoras of Theodore and Nestorius, and in the seventeenth homily of Narsai (Connolly 1909, 12). Theodore's own catechetical instruction however, quotes the usual formula, 'Let us give thanks to the Lord' (Mingana 1933,

99, 238). Precisely how and when the usual formula was modified within the East Syrian tradition must at present remain a matter for conjecture (Macomber 1971, 63–6, 83–4).

What is the significance of this modification of the usual formula? At first sight it seems to be an instance of the change of emphasis from the concept of thanksgiving which is dominant in Justin's account[8] to that of sacrifice which clearly emerges in Cyril of Jerusalem's exposition.[9] It is not clear, however, that the distinction should be drawn so sharply as this. The word translated 'offering' is *qurbana*, familiar from a gospel narrative (Mark 7:11), which incidentally indicates the wide semantic range of this word, extending far beyond the specifically cultic sphere. The basic meaning of the cognate verb, which is also used in the formula ('is being offered'), is to 'draw near', and in the intensive form it means to 'offer' or 'present', with such varied objects as 'supplication', 'remarks' and 'advice' as well as the cognate *qurbana* as in the present instance. This terminology then is general rather than specific, and of itself offers little insight into the East Syrian concept of the eucharist beyond the basic idea of an offering to God. A comment by Wigram (1929, 195) is pertinent:

In the Church services the Eucharist is naturally the central feature, being known as the 'Qurbana', a word of a singular wealth of import. Etymologically it is the same as the 'Korban' of the Gospels ... 'the thing dedicated to God,' but as used for the name of the Liturgy it unites the notions of approach to the Most High, of Offering made to Him, and of acceptance of such Offering by Him – a word of deep meaning indeed.

On the other hand the fact that the rite as a whole is called *Qurbana* does not necessarily mean that it is primarily conceived in terms of 'offering' any more than the use of the term 'eucharist' implies that those who use it think of the rite primarily in terms of 'thanksgiving'. In order to penetrate further into the meaning of *qurbana* in the East Syrian rite we must proceed to an examination of the Anaphora itself. The dialogue is followed by a statement by the celebrant to the effect that God is worthy of praise and confession (lines 22ff.) before the direct address to God, which begins only at line 27. The Semitic parallelism of this passage and the existence of some verbal parallels in *Sharar* suggest that it is ancient. The word translated 'worthy' is not the same as either of those used in the preceding congregational response, but those words could be used appropriately only in an abstract statement. The significant terms here for our purpose are 'praise' and 'confession', since it is reasonable to suppose that these are the essential content of the *qurbana* (Spinks 1980, 25). Of the two terms the second is the more interesting. The Syriac is *tawditha*, which, like the cognate Hebrew *todah*, has a fairly wide semantic range, including specifically 'thanksgiving' as well as 'profession' of faith. The term 'confession' is appropriate in translation because it leaves the precise nuance open. The context however suggests that 'thanksgiving' is the uppermost meaning in this passage, because it goes on to describe God as Creator and Redeemer and to emphasize his grace and mercy towards his creatures.

This conclusion is reinforced by the passage immediately following the Sanctus, which may not after all be an interpolation, *pace* Ratcliff ([1928] 1976, 86; cf. Spinks 1980, 26–7). Here the celebrant expresses the worship of the present congregation, using the verb cognate with *tawditha*, and going on immediately to relate what God has done for us (lines 33ff.). The meaning 'give thanks' is clearly the most appropriate: 'We also . . . give thee thanks, because thou hast dealt very graciously[10] with us.' After enumerating the saving acts of God in terms of the benefits which we have received, in another passage whose antiquity is suggested by the Semitic parallelism and confirmed by the parallels in *Sharar*, this part of the Anaphora ends with a doxology of which only the opening words 'And for all' are recorded in the oldest manuscript, printed by Macomber (1966) (line 40). The general sense, however, may be gained from the similar doxology at the close of the Anaphora: 'And for all thy wonderful dispensation which is towards us we give thee thanks and praise thee without ceasing . . .' (lines 69–70).

At the very least this evidence suggests that the primitive concept of the eucharistic sacrifice as consisting essentially of praise and thanksgiving is deeply rooted in the Anaphora of Addai and Mari, and has not as in some other ancient anaphoras been overlaid by other emphases. Nevertheless this by no means exhausts the meaning of *qurbana* in the Anaphora. A most significant passage in which the term occurs, and in which it is clearly used of the elements of bread and wine, is the Epiklesis: 'Let thy Holy Spirit come, O my Lord, and rest upon this offering [*qurbana*] . . . of thy servants, and bless it and sanctify it' (lines 64–6). The authenticity of this Epiklesis has been questioned by many (e.g. Ratcliff [1928] 1976), but is confirmed by its primitive nature (it asks not for a change in the elements but for the spiritual benefits of communion), its similarity to that in Hippolytus' model Anaphora (cf. Cuming 1976, 11) and the parallel in *Sharar*.

In the light of this we must now attempt to determine the meaning of lines 45–6: 'in the commemoration of the body and blood of thy Christ, which we offer to thee upon the pure and holy altar', another passage whose antiquity is confirmed by the parallel in *Sharar*. What is the antecedent of 'which'? Grammatically it is most likely to be 'the commemoration', the Syriac for which is *not* the same word as that used for *anamnesis* in Luke 22:19 (Old Syriac and Peshitta) and 1 Corinthians 11:24–5 (Peshitta), perhaps because this word (*dukrana*) has just been used in line 44 of the commemoration of the Fathers (see below, pp. 122–3). It is also possible that the antecedent of 'which' is more specifically 'the body and blood', and this might be suggested by the identification of the elements with the *qurbana* in line 64. The broader interpretation, however, seems more likely both on general syntactical grounds and in the light of the immediately following allusion to the dominical command: 'as thou hast taught us' (line 47).

These two passages clearly treat the eucharistic commemoration of the 'body and blood' of Christ in sacrificial terms. The Epiklesis makes it clear that this is a present offering of the worshippers. The ambiguity of the earlier passage in lines 45–6 prevents us from either affirming or denying that the East Syrian rite envisaged the eucharist as an actual offering of the 'body and blood' of Christ, though as we have seen the structure of the sentence suggests that what is offered is the 'commemoration', which may be held to consist on the one hand of the verbal thanksgiving for redemption and on the other of the eucharistic elements themselves. While the text is patient of an interpretation in which the sacrifice of the eucharist is identified with that of Christ on the cross, the most that can be affirmed positively of this ancient text is that the eucharistic elements are described as an offering, and that both they and the thanksgiving of which the eucharist essentially consists are brought into a close relation to the sacrifice of the cross. We may quote Wigram again: 'The whole rite is naturally spoken of habitually as an oblation or sacrifice, but there is no over-definition, happily, either of the rationale of that sacrifice, or of the method of the Presence, the reality of which all would affirm' (Wigram 1929, 197). This reticence from over-definition is further illustrated by the expression: 'and we celebrate this great and awesome mystery' (lines 61–2), where the word 'celebrate' – Spinks (1980) renders 'perform' – is the ordinary word to 'do' or 'make', cognate with the Hebrew *'abad*, which is also on occasion used of the offering of sacrifice (for example, Isa. 19:21). This passage however has no counterpart in *Sharar*, and may not belong to the oldest strata of the Anaphora.

There is, however, one further question which must be discussed, and that is the relation of the intercessions to the eucharistic offering. It is here that we are beset most seriously by questions of the antiquity of the text (cf. Engberding 1957). The passage which we have just been considering (lines 45–6) comes in the course of the first intercessory passage:

Do thou, O my Lord, in thine ineffable mercies make a good remembrance for all the upright and just fathers who were pleasing before thee, in the commemoration of the body and blood of thy Christ, which we offer to thee upon the pure and holy altar, as thou hast taught us; and make with us thy tranquillity and thy peace all the days of the age. (lines 43–8)

The next paragraph, despite the intervening 'Amen', is probably to be seen as a continuation of this prayer; it begins, 'that all the inhabitants of the world may know thee' (line 50). Despite some verbal parallels in *Sharar* with the latter part of this second paragraph, the only part of these two paragraphs with a direct counterpart in *Sharar* is the first sentence as far as 'thou hast taught us'. The only element in the intercession therefore of which we can be confident that it belongs to the oldest strata in the Anaphora is the commemoration of the fathers.

It is nonetheless significant that this commemoration of the fathers takes the form of a direct prayer that God will 'make a good remembrance for' them; it is therefore clearly an intercession and not merely a thanksgiving for departed saints. It is interesting in this connection to compare the rather more explicit intercession for the departed in the Eucharistic Prayer of Sarapion (Wordsworth 1923, 64) and the somewhat defensive justification of this practice given by Cyril in the *Mystagogical Catechesis* 5.9–10, suggesting that it was an innovation in the middle of the fourth century. If we are right in thinking that this is the only part of the intercession to belong to the oldest strata of this anaphora, it must be noted that the intercession is brought into only the loosest connection with the sacrifice either of the eucharist or of the cross, namely the preposition 'in' before 'the commemoration' of the eucharist. This need mean no more than that the eucharistic commemoration of the cross is seen as the appropriate occasion to ask God to remember for good the departed fathers. There is no attempt in this section to plead the sacrifice of either the eucharist or the cross as the ground for the intercession for the departed.

Our study of this ancient anaphora leads to the following conclusions. Even the oldest strata that we can trace are not necessarily original. The modification of the opening dialogue, so characteristic of the East Syrian tradition, must be secondary. There seems, however, to be ample evidence that the essential nature of the eucharistic offering is seen to consist in praise and thanksgiving, that the eucharistic elements themselves are seen as part of this thank-offering, and that the eucharistic offering is integrally related to the sacrifice of the cross because it is the commemoration which Christ ordered his disciples to make. Any attempt to define the eucharistic doctrine presupposed by the oldest elements in this anaphora more precisely can only be the result of reading later ideas into the text or attempting to define the precise nuance of its language beyond what can be established by analysis of the text itself. In particular it cannot be established that the oldest strata of this anaphora attest either the concept of an actual offering of Christ in the eucharist or that of the eucharistic offering as itself the basis for intercessory prayers. As such it seems to belong to a theologically pre-Cyrilline period. It may be added that there is nothing in this text to suggest that the celebrating priest has any more specific role in making the offering than the congregation as a whole whose spokesman he is. The prayers of offering are all expressed in the first person plural, and the subject of the verb 'celebrate' in line 61 is 'We ... thy servants ... who are gathered and stand before thee' (lines 58–9).

NOTES

1 See the documents assembled in *Modern Eucharistic Agreement* (London: SPCK, 1973).
2 The remainder of this paragraph is a very brief summary of Hanson's survey.
3 Basil, *De Spiritu Sancto* 27.66 (*Sources chrétiennes*, 17). Basil specifies the Epiklesis, but since he refers to things said before and after the Institution Narrative he must have more in mind than this.
4 See for example the reading of Mark 3: 17 in the Old Syriac and Peshitta versions.
5 I have used the Syriac text published by W. F. Macomber (1966), and references are to the lines of the Syriac text in that edition. The translation is my own. I am preparing a critical edition of the text with introduction and commentary, in which some of the matters treated here receive fuller attention.
6 *Apostolic Tradition*, chapter 4 (Cuming 1976, 10).
7 *Berakoth* 7.3 (Danby [1933] 1958, 8).
8 *1 Apology* 65.3, 67.5.
9 *Mystagogical Catechesis* 5.8–10 (*Sources chrétiennes*, 126). I accept the argument of Yarnold (1978) that the *Mystagogical Catecheses* are the work of Cyril, but belong to a later period than the pre-baptismal *Catecheses*.
10 This translation differs from those of Spinks and some others in its attempt to do justice to the Syriac idiom, which is similar to the Hebrew *'asah ḥesed 'im*. It is conceded that the translation offered here necessitates a paraphrase of the next two words of the Syriac: 'in a way which cannot be repaid'.

REFERENCES

Atiya, A. S. (1968). *A History of Eastern Christianity*. London: Methuen

Connolly, R. H. (ed.) (1909). *The Liturgical Homilies of Narsai*, Texts and Studies, 8. Cambridge: Cambridge University Press

Cuming, G. J. (ed.) (1976). *Hippolytus: A Text for Students*. Grove Liturgical Study no. 8. Bramcote: Grove Books

Danby, H. (ed. and trans.) ([1933] 1958). *The Mishnah* (repr. 1958 from corrected sheets of the 1933 first edition). Oxford: Clarendon Press

de Vries, G. (1959). La théologie sacramentaire chez les Nestoriens. *L'Orient Syrien* 4, 471–94

Engberding, H. (1957). Zym anaphorischen Fürbittgebet der ostsyrische Liturgie der Apostel Addaj und Mar(j). *Oriens Christianus* 41, 102–24

Hanson, R. P. C. (1961). The Liberty of the Bishop to improvise Prayer in the Eucharist. *Vigiliae Christianae* 15, 173–6

(1979). *Eucharistic Offering in the Early Church*, Grove Liturgical Study no. 19. Bramcote: Grove Books

Macomber, W. F. (ed.) (1966). The Oldest Known Text of the Anaphora of the Apostles Addai and Mari. *Orientalia Christiana Periodica* 32, 358–71

(1971). The Maronite and Chaldean Versions of the Anaphora of the Apostles. *Orientalia Christiana Periodica* 37, 55–84

Mingana, A. (ed.) (1933). *Commentary of Theodore of Mopsuestia on the Lord's Prayer and on the Sacraments of Baptism and the Eucharist.* Woodbrooke Studies, 6. Cambridge: Heffers

Ratcliff, E. C. ([1928] 1976). The Original Form of the Anaphora of Addai and Mari: A Suggestion. In his *Liturgical Studies* (first published in the *Journal of Theological Studies,* 1928 (o.s. 30)). London: SPCK

Spinks, B. D. (1980). *Addai and Mari – the Anaphora of the Apostles: a Text for Students,* Grove Liturgical Study no. 24. Bramcote: Grove Books

(1984). Eucharistic Offering in the East Syrian Anaphoras. *Orientalia Christiana Periodica* 50, 347–71

Stevenson, K. (1986). *Eucharist and Offering.* New York: Pueblo

Vermes, G. (1973). *Jesus the Jew.* London: Collins

Wigram, W. A. (1929). *The Assyrians and their Neighbours.* London: G. Bell and Sons

Wordsworth, J. (1923). *Bishop Sarapion's Prayerbook.* London: SPCK

Yarnold, E. J. (1978). The Authorship of the Mystagogic Catecheses attributed to Cyril of Jerusalem. *Heythrop Journal* 19, 143–61

II

8

ON EUCHARISTIC SACRIFICE IN THE
MIDDLE AGES

P. J. FITZPATRICK

Sir, this is sad stuff. (Dr Johnson, *passim*.)

'What will you make of the Articles?' That, Newman tells us in Part IV of his
Apologia, was the question put to him by friends when the *Tracts for the
Times* were calling the Church of England back to what was seen by the
authors of the *Tracts* as its neglected Catholic inheritance. That Church had
also inherited the Thirty-Nine Articles, and Article XXXI was one of those
that seemed to call for an explanation: 'The sacrifices of Masses in which it
was commonly said that the priests did offer Christ for the quick and the
dead, to have remission of pain or guilt, were blasphemous fables and
dangerous deceits.' Newman's exegesis of it in Tract XC amounted to
claiming that it did no more than attack superstitious and simoniacal
abuses condemned by Rome also ([Newman] 1842). It is notorious that
Tract XC aroused violent disagreement, but such views were already
regarded with abhorrence by those who opposed the Tractarians. Dr Arnold
wrote in 1841 of the primitive Christian notion of sacrifice as the offering of
ourselves, and described its corruption into the 'carnal and lying sacrifice of
the Mass' as exactly fulfilling 'the apostolical language concerning
Antichrist' (Stanley 1846, Letter 275). Here, one would think, is the
touchstone for distinguishing Catholic from Protestant. Given that, readers
may be as surprised as I was to learn that, while medieval theologians
agreed that the eucharist was a sacrifice, their agreement led to nothing
remotely comparable to the wealth in quantity of their reflections on the
presence of Christ in the eucharist, or on his atoning work in the sacrifice of
the cross. That the eucharist is a sacrifice was then a commonplace, but it
was a commonplace that seemed to call for little elaboration.

So my contribution to this volume might be very brief. That it is not brief
at all is a testimony, not to my own sympathy with the subject, but to the
patience of my editor and of my publisher. But there are limits even to their
patience, and what follows has been quarried from a much longer work. I

had intended to deal with my topic in three stages, letting accounts of
medieval theories of the atonement and of the eucharistic presence precede
what I have to say about theories of eucharistic sacrifice in those days; and
at each of the stages I meant to consider two sources – the writings of
Aquinas and a selection from earlier authors, so complementing his clarity
with their variety. This twofold investigation I shall still allot to the
medieval notion of eucharistic sacrifice itself, but the topics of atonement
and of eucharistic presence I shall deal with in what is, for me, a summary
fashion. Eucharistic sacrifice itself I shall then consider, first in earlier
authors and then in Aquinas. From Aquinas I move to sources of the later
middle ages, and so reach the point at which the tradition was attacked by
Luther. How the Council of Trent reacted to this will be considered by Canon
McHugh in his contribution to this volume. I will myself go on to reflect on a
tension that has run through what I have examined, and will draw some
morals. (I point out once for all that all references are to the References
section of this chapter, pp. 153–6, where my methods of citation are
explained.)

THE SETTING SURVEYED

And so in this first section to the summary account, and first of medieval
theories of the atonement. To palliate the impudence of attempting the
account, I limit myself to a glimpse, and to a glimpse of four writers earlier
than Aquinas: Gregory of Nyssa, Augustine, Anselm and Abelard. What I
have to say of Aquinas himself will, I hope, gain by the setting which they
provide.

The *Catechetical Oration* of Gregory of Nyssa (335–95) states one view
found in patristic sources: Christ's atoning work lay in paying a debt to the
devil, who had baited his hook with what only *seemed* good, and so had
deceived man. Man became thus the devil's legitimate slave, and could not
be freed by violence. Instead, the devil was got to over-reach himself in turn
by the bait of Christ's humanity, where the hook was his divinity (21–5; *PG*
45, 57–68). Augustine (354–430), whose works were to be of such
importance in the West, writes in this tradition in Book XIII of his *De
Trinitate*, and in another place even calls the cross a mouse-trap (Sermon
130; *PL* 38, 726). But he stresses the role of justice at the expense of
deception. The devil was to be overcome by justice rather than by force; in
his lust for power, he killed Christ, who (being sinless) was not in debt to
him; so we debtors, if we have faith in Christ, can be justly set free (*De
Trinitate* XIII, 12–18; *PL* 42, 1026–32). The abandonment of this idea of
bondage to the devil is associated with the *Cur Deus Homo* of Anselm
(1033–1109). Adam's failure to honour God calls in justice for a
recompense to him (Book I, 11 and 12); man cannot provide this in his

fallen state (I, 22); so satisfaction must be given by God made Man (II, 7); the sinless Christ in surrendering his life gave God something not already owed to him (II, 11); the recompense consequently owed by Father to Son is given to mankind (II, 19) (*PL* 158, 359–430).

With Abelard (1079–1142) is associated a rejection of many elements in all this. The devil has no rights over us, we cannot hand them over to him; but Christ's death was to give us an example of love, it was not pleasing to God (see the Second Book of his commentary on Romans, especially at *PL* 178, 834–6). I mention Abelard partly because the 'exemplary' role he gives to Christ's passion will recur in Aquinas, partly because I have a soft spot for the older 'devil's-due' theory of the atonement. Read it as a celestial war-game, and it is no more than funny, but its very naivety encourages us not to take it as more than suggesting picturesquely things worth suggesting – redemption reverses the power of evil in the world, Christ was exposed to its onslaught. Anselm's book-keeping is not naive, which is the trouble: he ends by replacing the dualism of the devil with a dualism of obligation – as Jove was subject to the Fates, so is God to Justice, and the Son has to cut the Gordian Knot by offering to make satisfaction. Anselm himself – it is one of his many merits – puts genuine objections into the mouth of his interlocutor (such as: why does not God live up to the Lord's Prayer? (I, 12)), but I can only express my distaste for the whole scenario of tit-for-tat so ingeniously elaborated by him.

Between Anselm and Aquinas (1227–74) had intervened the dissemination of the Aristotelian *corpus* of writings: the tensions in Aquinas between Aristotelian naturalism and the scriptural and patristic inheritance are not less real for being obscured by the etiquette of medieval commentary and speculation. Just as real is the growth in maturity shown in Aquinas between his early commentary on the Sentences of Peter the Lombard (a selection of patristic texts grouped by subject matter) and his mature *Summa Theologiae* (left unfinished some time before his death). In the earlier work – though accompanied by those qualifying phrases that so easily get overlooked by his readers – we find themes resembling what we found in Gregory and Augustine, such as cunning countered by cunning (habitually denied, but see 3 *S* 19.4.1 ad 3, 599/86, and recall that 'per contraria' means 'by the reversal', not 'by the opposite'). We also find a calculus of satisfaction reminiscent in its neatness of what Anselm wrote. The texts are at 4 *S* 15 (satisfaction in general, which calls for penal actions, not just for good ones), and 3 *S* 18-20 (Christ's redemptive work): satisfaction shows God's justice by involving punishment; it had to be by Christ; and by dying; and most suitably by a shameful death. But the *Summa* is different in tone and exhibits what I would call a relaxed good humour (e.g. why bring in justice, when mercy alone would have done? Well, nature gives us two eyes, not one, for better vision, *ST* 3.46.3 ad 1). Satisfaction is still there, but the whole setting is now concrete – the life of Christ – and the themes that dominate are our solidarity with him, and the fact that his manhood is an instrument of his godhead – a reflection of the 'bait' image without its oddity. And we have 'Abelardian' considerations, such that we are freed by Christ's passion through its inspiring us to love (*ST* 3.49.1).

Yet the good sense of Aquinas makes older talk in him stand out more awkwardly. Consider his treatment of original sin in the *Summa*. We inherit Adam's guilt as guilt, not as some physical defect, for which no punishment would be due; our disorder is willed by Adam, as our limbs obey our own will (*ST* 1/2.81.1). It is by seminal descent from Adam that we are moved by his power; so if a human being were miraculously made from flesh, it would not inherit original sin (Frankenstein would think otherwise!), and if Eve alone had sinned, original sin would not have been passed on (*ST* 1/2.81.4 and 5). All this is gratuitous enough, but what of us, who take the first chapters of Genesis as a myth or parable? What of the superstructure built by theologians like Aquinas on what we no longer believe to be true? Its very neatness of fit with the calculus of satisfaction demands that we say something. Offended honour calls for satisfaction (one thinks of duelling); satisfaction has to be got through Christ's death; no punishment of ours would do, for our plight is of itself irremediable; we are in this plight through seminal descent from Adam; it is more than an inherited defect, we are as it were one man in him. If this be not sad stuff, what is?

What answer I have to offer will have to be reached by our journey through the themes of this essay. So I turn to the second theme that provides the setting for eucharistic sacrifice – medieval theories of the eucharistic presence.

And here I can be even more summary, for I have already expressed my views (FitzPatrick 1972, 1973), and now, rather to my surprise, have three more items to do with it in print. One (FitzPatrick 1987c) is a slightly abbreviated reprint of what I published in 1972 and 1973. A second (FitzPatrick 1987a) analyses a debate on the topic between two scholastic theologians in the 1950s. The third (FitzPatrick 1987b) examines something of the disagreements over transubstantiation, when the scholastic tradition was under attack in the seventeenth century. Moreover, the publisher of this volume is to bring out a book of mine on the subject, *In Breaking of Bread*. It never rains but it pours. Given all that, it will be enough for me here to state and to illustrate my own position.

The Council of Trent used phraseology of Aquinas in its decree on the eucharistic presence, and declared the term 'transubstantiation' to be 'most fittingly' used (see the text in Denzinger and Schönmetzer 1963, at n. 1642; cf. n. 1652). As Aquinas used concepts like 'substance', 'accidents', 'matter' and 'form' derived from the Aristotelian tradition, theologians have argued over what degree of commitment to that tradition is involved in Trent's decree, and whether the commitment should be loosed. I simply deny that there is any commitment, because what Aquinas wrote is only a nonsensical abuse of Aristotelian terminology. The distinctions drawn by Aristotle must not (as he himself warns us) be treated as if they were between *things*, yet that is how they have to be treated in accounts of transubstantiation. The accidents and substance of the bread become *components*; the survival of the former, when the latter is replaced by the substance of Christ's body, becomes a matter of miracles, not of intelligibility. The perennial attention of transubstantiation lies in its pandering to perennial confusions. One, just mentioned, is taking distinctions as dissections; the other is identifying legitimate differences between appearance and reality with the notion that every conceivable appearance might be present but the reality be absent – a confusion that lies at the root of philosophical scepticism.

But it is not enough to say that the speculations of Aquinas are an abuse of philosophical distinctions drawn by Aristotle: not enough, because 'philosophical' has no one unchanging meaning over the centuries. An examination of the wider setting in which the terms were used shows that they were not simply 'philosophical' in our sense of the word, but part of what we should now call the obsolete science of their time. I have applied this thesis to seventeenth-century scholasticism (FitzPatrick 1987b), but confine myself now to asserting it with respect to medieval writers earlier than Aquinas, and to Aquinas himself. I gladly recommend here the excellent monograph of Jorissen (1965), which contains much material otherwise unprinted. Let the brief indications that follow suffice for my present purpose. Earlier writers draw parallels between the eucharist and material transformations, whether biblical (Lot's wife; the water at Cana), or natural (hay into glass, which *is* natural, whatever some modern writers cited by Jorissen think). They use similar analogies to explain how the eucharist (where there is no substance of bread or wine) can still nourish – do not Indian sages live off the smell of apples? The parallel becomes embarrassing in an anecdote (not in Jorissen) about some shepherds who recited the words of consecration over some bread in the fields – only to be struck down, while the bread was changed into flesh 'and perhaps even transubstantiated, if I may so speak, into the body of Christ' (John Belethus (d. *c.* 1165), *Rationale Divinorum Officiorum* 44; PL 202, 52). That is one of the earliest uses of the term, and gives it a setting we are liable to forget – a setting compounded for us of natural science and natural magic, not the setting of some timeless, philosophical abstraction. And the comments of Aquinas on his predecessors are of a piece with this. Abelard had suggested that the appearances of bread might be supported by the air, but Aquinas' objections are partly 'scientific': air cannot take such accidents, and moving a particle in fact drives the air away (*ST* 3.77.1). Just as 'scientific' is his

preferred verdict on the debate over what happens to the water mixed with
the wine at mass – it is first changed into wine, and then into the blood of
Christ (*ST* 3.74.8). If I have accused the theory of transubstantiation of
combining terms so as to yield no sense, I must now add that the terms
themselves mean what they do inside a setting that is not what we should
call simply philosophical. Those who wish to emancipate them from the
setting ought to, but do not, explain how the emancipation is to be effected.

As I turn from this survey of the setting to my specific topic of eucharistic
sacrifice, I give a last group of texts. These will, I hope, show that the
medieval setting was not propitious for a grasp of what the shape and
purpose of the eucharistic liturgy were. Aquinas asks whether the words
'Take and eat' are essential to the consecratory formula, and replies that
they are not, because the essence of the sacrament does not include
(ominous phrase!) 'the use of consecrated matter' (*ST* 3.78.1 ad 2). Dealing
elsewhere with the words of the mass, he writes that 'the mystery of faith'
refers to the *hiddenness* of Christ's presence (*ST* 3.78.3 ad 5). A further
question asked is why we have the appearances of bread at all; Aquinas
answers that the horror and mockery are avoided that would follow at our
eating human flesh and blood (*ST* 3.75.5). The setting of this answer can be
seen from the less inhibited language of Alger of Liège (d. 1132) in his *De
Sacramentis Corporis et Sanguinis Dominici*: we cannot receive Christ dead (he
is immortal), or as he was on earth (we could not swallow down, *deglutire*, a
thirty-year-old man), or as he is glorified (we could not bear it) (II, 3; *PL*
180, 817–18). Ritual is construed as camouflage, and what else is being
camouflaged but cannibalism?

EUCHARISTIC SACRIFICE IN EARLIER WRITERS

I have now surveyed something of the background to my main topic, and
turn to eucharistic sacrifice itself. We have seen that there was an interest in
the topic of transformation for the eucharist, a topic whose elaboration was
alien to ritual. For the theme of eucharistic sacrifice there is no such
elaboration, and we shall have to look in a variety of places, which will be
no bad thing. My intention in this section is to consider some writers earlier
than Aquinas, but I start from a text of his we met near the end of last
section – that 'mystery' in the eucharist means 'hidden'. It is the merit of
Henri de Lubac to have shown how, over the centuries that ushered in the
middle ages proper, a shift in interest took place; that the force of symbolism
in the eucharist gave way to dialectical argument (principally in Gaul) over
the presence of Christ; that the change showed itself in the preferred
vocabulary; and that a phrase like 'Mystical Body', which for Aquinas
already has its later meaning of 'The Church', signified in earlier times the
eucharist itself (Lubac 1949). Lubac's work can and should be complemented by the equally great achievement of Josef Jungmann's account of the

development of the Roman Rite, for words and worship go together. Jungmann shows how, in the course of the eighth century, the Christian Church in Gaul adopted the Roman Liturgy, but the Roman Liturgy in its most solemn and 'pontifical' form; the successive elaborations of liturgy led to its becoming ever more an activity distinctive of the clergy, with the laity in the role of spectators; the change (emphasized by the separation of vernacular speeches from Latin) showed itself not only in ceremonies, but in the very structure of the church and sanctuary; the participation in liturgy by communion grew rarer; and the mass, despite the survival of older concerns in its ancient prayers, came to by seen less as the *gratiarum actio*, the thanksgiving – the 'eucharist', in fact – than as a grace and favour, a *bona gratia* from God, a descent to us of his merciful power. (See Jungmann 1952, vol. I, I, section 9; and especially pp. 109–14).

I hope that the texts I discuss will supplement the contentions of these two authors, and I go first to Augustine (d. 430) and to Gregory the Great (d. 604). When Augustine is asked whether we can say that a newly baptized infant *believes*, he answers that we can, just as we can say on any Sunday 'The Lord rose *today*', or just as we say that Christ is *immolated* in the eucharist, whereas he suffered only once; there is a resemblance, and were there not there could be no sacrament (Letter to Boniface; *PL* 33, 363). For Gregory the Great, Christ dies no more, but is immolated again in the eucharist – his body is divided for the salvation of believers, and his blood is poured out, no longer by the hands of the wicked, but into the mouths of the faithful. The eucharistic sacrifice imitates the passion of Christ; earth and heaven are joined; let us then sacrifice ('mactemus') ourselves (*Dialogues*, IV, 58 and 59; *PL* 77, 425, 428). In neither of the texts is there any elaboration of the concept of eucharistic sacrifice, nor is there any attempt to focus its efficacy upon some transformational moment in the mass.

These two didactic texts I complement with two early miracle-stories. (I shall be giving others later, being persuaded that their offensive absurdity does not prevent them from exhibiting priorities in belief.) Among one collection, the *Vitae Patrum*, sixth-century in origin, we find that a worshipper who doubted the eucharistic presence saw, when the loaves had been placed on the altar, a small boy lying there. When the priest was about to break the bread, an angel came down with a sword, cut the boy and received his blood into a (the?) chalice. Later, when the priest broke the bread into pieces, the angel cut the boy's limbs up into little bits. The doubter approached to communicate (brave man!) and was given a piece of bloody flesh. He ceased to doubt, and at once the flesh appeared as bread (v. 18; *PL* 73, 979). Nauseating, to be sure – although admittedly funny – but we shall find a distinction in emphasis in later stories. This tale does not make the consecratory prayer the moment for the miracle – the child is there right from the offertory, first gets wounded and gets cut right up only when the consecrated bread is being broken for communion; moreover, the tale does actually end with communion being received. In a later section, we shall see that eucharistic miracles end by losing all contact with receiving, and are focussed on the consecration.

In the second story (once more from Gregory the Great's *Dialogues*) a priest is asked, by Gregory himself, to offer mass for thirty consecutive days for some departed spirit (IV, 55; *PL* 77, 421). The story is in a sense of a piece with notorious later practices and tales, which we have yet to meet. But, once more, the emphasis is not the same. The community where the thirty masses are offered (and it *is* a community) does not keep a tally of numbers, and it is only after an apparition of the newly released spirit that the calculation is made. To bring out the shift in emphasis, it will be useful to set beside the 'informality' of this tale the far more business-like report of Walafrid Strabo (fl. 850; was Abbot near Constance; presumably squinted), who foreshadows how things were to develop in the middle ages. There is no witness to daily celebration in the early Church (Browe 1938b, 3), but Walafrid records what he considers to be lawful differences of opinion over frequency. For some (St Boniface, for example) once a day is right, as Christ died once for our sins; for others, the more often Christ's passion is commemorated, the more God's mercy is moved, and hence a recent and respected pope (this means, puzzlingly, Leo III (795–816)) celebrated the eucharist seven or nine times a day (*De Ecclesiasticarum Rerum Exordiis et Incrementis*, 21; *PL* 114, 943). The mass is seen, as Gregory saw it, as a *bona gratia*, but the picture has indeed changed, and the change affects preoccupations and ceremonies alike.

It also affected speculation, as can be seen from looking at the reasons offered by medieval writers for the daily celebration of the eucharist. One general argument consists in the analogy with food, which needs to be taken daily if we are to continue in life (see how the view of the eucharist as a 'descent of grace' has come to overshadow all else). Thus Paschasius Radbertus (780–860) says that our weakness remains after baptism, that we fall daily, and so Christ is mystically immolated each day for us (*Liber de Corpore et Sanguine Christi*, 9; *PL* 120, 1293–4). Durandus of Troarn (d. 1088) makes the spread of the Church throughout the world and the daily occurrence of sin a reason for daily celebration (*De Corpore et Sanguine Christi*, 2: *PL* 149, 1381. Innocent III (born Lothar of Segni, c. 1160–1216; elected to the papacy in 1198) makes the cross save us from the power of sin, and the eucharist save us from the will to sin (*De Sacro Altaris Mysterio*, IV, 44; *PL* 217, 885; Innocent's phrases are 'potestas peccati' and 'voluntas peccandi'; and I give them because – as on other occasions – I feel that the jingle carried the weight of argument). Stephen of Autun (fl. 1136) had gone further: the cross saved us from original sin, while the eucharist saves us from sins that we ourselves commit. Christ offered himself upon the cross, the priest offers Christ at the altar (*Tractatus de Sacramento Altaris*, 9; PL 172, 1280).

Reasonings like these led to a further question: does not the frequency of the eucharistic celebration compromise the uniqueness of Calvary? All are agreed that there is no new immolation, for Christ dies no more; but differences in emphasis deserve attention. For Alger of Liège, Christ is offered *in figura*, in a *type* or figure (*De Sacramentis Corporis et Sanguinis Dominici*, I, 16; PL 180, 786–7). For Durandus of Mende (1230–96), an analogy is drawn with other ways of *remembering* the passion, such as a picture or a sermon (*Prochiron Vulgo Rationale Divinorum Officiorum*, XLII, 32; Durandus 1775, p. 162). For Guitmund of Aversa (d. *c.* 1080), 'immolation' can be used of the eucharist as 'breaking' can – both have there a *likeness* to what the name means (*De Corporis et Sanguinis Christi Veritate in Eucharistia*, I; PL 149, 1434). Here, we are back to the *disguise* of the last section pp. 133–4 – there is only a *likeness* of breaking, because there is no bread left to be broken, only its appearances. Indeed, Peter the Venerable (d. 1156) goes further, and says it might be fairly asked why the eucharistic presence should involve eating at all (*Adversus Petrobrusianos Haereticos*, PL 189, 815). A fair deduction, we might say, from what we read above (p. 134) in Alger of Liège; but a foretaste too of what was later to come.

The detachment of such speculations from the actual practice of worship can be illustrated by two answers offered to a question about a difference of *order* in eucharistic ritual. In the gospel, Christ blesses the bread, breaks it and gives to his disciples, commanding them to eat, for it is his body. In the mass, there is a long gap between consecration and communion, and the 'words' come before the giving. One solution is from Baldwin of Ford (d. 1190): the gospel's words 'he blessed' refer to a silently effected transformation of the bread, of which 'this is my body' was only Christ's subsequent announcement (*Liber de Sacramento Altaris*; PL 204, 654–6). For Durandus of Mende this could be the answer, but he suggests another: Christ said the words silently while *breaking*, and then aloud while *distributing* (*Prochiron*, IV, 51, p. 151). One has to have gone a long way in misunderstanding even to put such a question, let alone answer it.

One has to have gone even further to embark on an enterprise very popular in the middle ages, that of *allegorizing* the eucharistic ceremonies – the taking of gestures by priest and ministers to represent events in the redemptive story. Bowing at one point represents Our Lord's death; bowing at another represents his burial. And so on: in a game with no rules, why stop? The practice goes back to Symphosius Amalarius (d. 850) in his *De Ecclesiasticis Officiis* (PL 105, 985–6). It is interesting to notice that his contemporary, Florus of Lyons, who attacked the method as a mixture of nursery-rhymes and old wives' tales, admitted its popularity (*Adversus Amalarium*; PL 119, 80–2). And popular it remained; some besides the writer will remember being taught it at school. It was of course a natural accompaniment of the eucharist seen as a disguise: just as the visible appearances conceal Christ's presence, so the ceremonies can be decoded as his saving actions – and both disguises assume that all but the ministers are simply spectators.

The tests we have seen so far develop no speculation over eucharistic sacrifice, although their presentation of it grows more elaborate with the passage of time. They do exhibit a tension between a conception of the eucharist as a means of grace, whose frequency answers our need, and an insistence on the uniqueness of the cross. The former expresses itself in analogies with repeated nourishment, the latter in talk of likeness, memorial or type. We must now see what Aquinas made of such things.

EUCHARISTIC SACRIFICE IN AQUINAS

That Aquinas does not dwell on eucharistic sacrifice as he dwells on the eucharistic presence can be seen at once from the order of Questions in the *Summa* (*ST* 3. 73–83). Four are spent on the presence, two on the words and effects of the sacrament and four on its institution and use – and it is only in the last Question of all that, amid talk of ritual, he asks whether the eucharist is an *immolation*. Let us bear in mind that ritual is the context, as we see what his views are, there and elsewhere.

They are – as was his mature thought on the atonement – distinguished by an essential *moderation*: the qualifying phrases I mentioned earlier are used repeatedly, and must be given their fair place in any estimate we reach of what follows. He not only accepts the analogy with our need for food to elucidate the frequency of celebration (*ST* 3.73.1), but shows a sound grasp of the sacrament's very foundation in eating and drinking: it is still one, despite being in two kinds, because it has the unity of what constitutes nourishment (*ST* 3.73.2); bread is a fitting means of representation because of the sacrament's 'common use' (*ST* 3.74.1 ad 3); and the two kinds themselves are fitting, as we need both food and drink (*ST* 3.74.1). To this acceptance of the human placing of the eucharist, he joins an awareness of its proximate and ultimate purposes. It signifies the unity of the Church, which is why 'communion' is one of its names; and it has a reference to the future, being our *Viaticum* or journey-food, as it prefigures the vision to which we are called (*ST* 3.73.4). But these qualities do not eliminate the role of those who would share in it, since its effects are limited by their dispositions (here he refers to the widow's mite). Indeed, since reception signifies unity with Christ, sinful reception 'commits a falsehood' in the sacrament (*ST* 3.80.4; a delightful anticipation of Wollaston's reduction in the eighteenth century of all vicious actions to lying!).

This moderation, this unwillingness to push to the point of paradox, is found in the considerations used by Aquinas in specifying the sacrificial nature of the eucharist. It represents the sacrificial passion of Christ, and so itself is of such a nature ('habet rationem sacrificii', *ST* 3.79.7); it commemorates it, and so one of its names is 'sacrifice' (*ST* 3.73.4). But this representativeness is possessed also by the Old Testament Passover, not in a commemorative but in a prefigurative fashion; there had to be something for mankind at all times with such a relation to Christ's passion (*ST* 3.73.5). So the eucharist is called an immolation of Christ, because it is a certain (*quaedam*) representative picture of his passion; since – he cites Augustine – we can say 'That is Cicero' of a picture of the orator, so we can call the eucharist an immolation (*ST* 3.83.1). Christ offered himself once for all, the eucharist is an image (*exemplum*) of that sacrifice (*ST* 3.83.1 ad 1); there is no plurality of sacrifice in the New Law, for the eucharist commemorates the sacrifice once offered (*ST* 3.22.3 ad 2). Christ is not crucified in the eucharist, but the rite can be said to represent the passion, and so the altar be said to represent the Cross, on which Christ was immolated in the primary sense (*in propria specie* – I will return to the justice of this version – *ST* 3.83.1 ad 2).

Since representation, commemoration and allied notions are so important for Aquinas, we must now ask where they are placed by him in the eucharist. Some readers will already know of one placing – the separate consecrations of bread and wine represent the separation of Christ's body and blood on Calvary. Aquinas does allot a representative role here, but with his moderation places that role in a wider context. The double consecration is 'not for no purpose'; and the reasons for this modest claim include the human reference to nourishment we have already met (*ST* 3.76.2 ad 1). While the doubleness represents, or 'more expressly' represents, his passion, the whole sacrament is a memorial of it (*ST* 3.78.3 ad 2, ad 7 and those objections). The representative function of the eucharist, by which we are able to call it an immolation of Christ, is not to be confined to one point of the rite, for the whole rite represents. What is specific to the eucharist, what sets it apart from the sacrifices of the Old Law, is that in it we share in the fruits of Christ's passion and death (*ST* 3.83.1). This is the second reason given by Aquinas at *ST* 3.83.1 for calling the eucharist an immolation of Christ, where the first was the analogy with calling portraits by what they portray; and it is this second line of thought we must now pursue.

We saw that Aquinas makes the eucharist signify the unity of the Church and prefigure the beatific vision (*ST* 3.73.4). In the same Question he claims that the eucharist is in this sense necessary for salvation – it signifies the Body of Christ, which is his Church and the means of being saved (art. 3); and the representative force now in the eucharist is always needed, since so is faith in Christ's passion, represented by it (art. 5). Let us then see how

Aquinas places the institution of the eucharist. That time, he writes, was fitting for the institution. Christ was leaving his disciples, and he wanted faith in his passion to be preserved by a representation. But what is new was not unheralded; rites of the Old Testament, and especially the Passover Lamb, had done this. Moreover, the eucharist partakes of the nature of a farewell, and 'the last things to be said, especially by friends who are about to leave us, are those that are best remembered. At such a time, our love for our friends is greatest, and what we love most is what sinks most deeply into our hearts' (*ST* 3.75.5). It is to the concrete circumstances of the institution that Aquinas directs our attention: the ritual inheritance from the Old Testament, the imminence of the passion, which is to be the universal means of salvation, the impressiveness of the last farewell, the representation of the passion by the new rite for ages to come (*ST* 3.73.5, 6). It is in this essentially ritual setting that, I submit, we must see the representative function of the eucharist and the role of the two-fold consecration. And it is in this ritual setting that we must understand the claim of Aquinas that what is specific to the eucharist is our sharing by it in the fruits of Christ's redemptive work.

Aquinas, in introducing the sacraments, takes the eucharist to be their consummation (*ST* 3.63.6). The other sacraments fit us for the worship of God; but that worship rests upon the priesthood of Christ (*ST* 3.63.3), who is present in the eucharist; and so the eucharist is the principal act of that worship itself (*ST* 3.63.6). Our sharing in the fruits of his passion is not anything over and above what Christ won upon the cross, for the eucharist commemorates that unique sacrifice; it does not multiply it (*ST* 3.22.3 ad 2). The whole picture here is of *ritual* participation and representation. The eucharist crowns the other sacraments because it is the supreme ritual act of *worship*.

And that is the trouble. Aquinas has shown in these texts a conspicuous sensitivity to the human, shared and ritual setting of the eucharist. For good measure, I add another text, *ST* 3.78.1, where he considers the 'problem' seen at p. 137 above, the order of blessing and breaking at the Last Supper: he makes the observation that verbs in a narrative do not indicate a rigid order. Having grasped the point here, he deals brilliantly in the same Question with the *truth* of the eucharistic words (*ST* 3.78.5; and readers who know about 'performative force' of utterances will welcome here the phrase 'virtus factiva'). But when all that has been admitted, it must also be admitted that the time was not as propitious to ritual understanding as it was to speculations (not essentially linked with ritual at all) over the eucharistic presence. I shall now give some examples of defects in the thought of Aquinas, but I would stress that the texts we have just seen (scattered, the reader will have noticed) not only show an awareness of the central place ritual has; in their brevity and lack of synthesis, they are an odd and real tribute to his insight into where lay the heart of the matter.

And so to some limitations and defects. I noted earlier the ominous phrase 'use of consecrated matter' to describe communicating (*ST* 3.78.1 ad 2; see above p. 134). Just so, Aquinas denies that water need be mixed with the wine – it stands for the sharing of the faithful in the eucharist, which is not necessary (*ST* 3.74.7). Again, he disagrees with his contemporary St Bonaventure over 'paradoxes' such as attempts to consecrate all the bread in a market-place, or the eating of a host by a mouse. For Bonaventure, no eucharistic presence emerges or remains there, for no link is left with sacramental use. But Aquinas – more mechanically, it must be said – invokes a hypothetical multitude for the first case (*ST* 3.74.4) and (ugh) the extraction of the host from the beast's stomach for the second (4 *S* 9.2.3; 371/61). More seriously, he distinguishes between the sacramental effects of the eucharist (confined to those who receive) and the sacrificial (not so confined; *ST* 3.79.7). It is not that the distinction has no force, for the 'ecclesial' effect of the eucharist is obviously wider than the group physically present at a celebration. But the distinction can easily lead to making the faithful's communion only a sequel, to giving the ritual a structure where communions are rarities, and to obscuring the essentially sacramental nature of immolation here by isolating the consecration from all else. We have yet to see how far this process went, and can turn to what I think is a lighter count on the indictment: the use by Aquinas in *ST* 3.83.4–5 of the allegorical reading of ceremonies (see above, p. 137).

Jungmann's blaming of Aquinas here (1952, vol. 1, p. 150; 1.11) is, I think, slightly misdirected. It is not the allegorizing itself (standard and unremarkable) that is the trouble, it is the breath-takingly ingenious *rationalization* of all gestures that Aquinas provides. Such a specious inevitability is conferred thereby upon details of the rite that its intrinsic structure and sense are lost, and the loss can lead to lamentable missings of the point. Readers will already have noticed that the representative and commemorative functions of the eucharist have been directed so far to the passion not to the resurrection. Since Aquinas would have recited, each time he said mass, the prayer 'Unde et memores' immediately after the consecration, in which the unified pattern of passion, death, resurrection and ascension is explicitly recalled, we might expect his account of the rite to mention it. He does not – the resurrection gets mentioned only in the three signs of the cross made after the 'Pax Domini', which are allegorized as the Third Day.

All of which illustrates that lesson that what we grasp is more than what we speculate about; and that ritual practice both embodies and limits our awareness of what we do and of what we believe. The lesson we shall see reinforced in what follows.

THE LATER MIDDLE AGES

'What will you make of the Articles?' After the moderation of what Aquinas writes about eucharistic sacrifice, it may seem odd that one of the Thirty-Nine Articles should have spoken so harshly of 'the sacrifices of Masses' (see p. 129). Yet so it was, and the English Reformers were only taking up in their own way the attack Luther had launched. I gather from Iserloh (1950) that on this topic his language was peculiarly vehement. For him, the very idea of eucharistic sacrifice is against the truth of the gospel: that we accept by faith the free gift of grace offered through Christ (Iserloh 1950, 55). In a text cited there, Luther uses the word 'Winkelmesse' ('Mass-in-the-corner') to describe what he is attacking, and the word shows the picture he must have had in mind: the multiplication of private masses, with no congregation present except the server. Just so, the title of one of his treatises mentioned there by Iserloh is 'De Abroganda Missa Privata', and his name for a massing-priest, 'Messknecht', could be translated as 'mass-lackey': he would rather, he writes, be burnt to ashes than let a Messknecht be higher than his Saviour Jesus Christ (Iserloh 1950, 56). The vehemence of Luther's language has led to disagreement over just what was being attacked. Newman, we saw, interpreted Article xxxi as being directed only against abuses, not against the substance of inherited belief (see p. 000, above), and the same thesis has been propounded by Kidd (1898) and Mascall (1965). But Clark's now classic work (1967) denies the thesis. For him, the Reformers, German and English alike, were concerned with more than abuse, and those who say otherwise have to stretch the evidence; there were no theological innovations in the later middle ages for the Reformers to attack, and eucharistic theories that seemed to involve any 'new slaying' of Christ are later in date than the attacks by Luther and others. My purpose here stands somewhat apart from this debate. I want to exhibit the general pattern and 'feel' of later medieval eucharistic practice and belief, using a multiplicity of sources to ensure as fair a picture as I can. Then, as I said, I hope to show that the dissent points to a tension in belief that is quite independent of Reformation polemic; and from that tension I shall draw some conclusions.

Eucharistic sacrifice was treated in the later middle ages even more sparsely than in earlier generations (Lepin 1926, 213–17; Iserloh 1952, 12; Iserloh 1956, 275). The writings of William Ockham (d. 1347) (investigated in Iserloh 1956) may serve as a fair example. He has nothing to say about eucharistic sacrifice, and nothing about the tradition from which has been inherited eucharistic belief: it is an abstract consideration of transubstantiation that takes up all his attention (Iserloh 1956, 273). Just as worthy of note is Ockham's opinion that sacramental signs might be purely spiritual (Iserloh 1956, 277): symbolism and ritual of any sort sit very uneasily with a view like that. Clark (1967) gives an account of what was written on the topic by Gabriel Biel (d. 1495; he was studied by Luther): the texts Clark cites (1967, 84–99) show nothing beyond what we might expect – the mass represents and commemorates the cross and hence is called an immolation. Even Wycliffe, while rejecting other eucharistic beliefs, seems to have remained silent over eucharistic sacrifice (Fox 1962).

This lack of theological development has a partial – only partial – analogue in the liturgical and devotional practice of the later middle ages. Jungmann (1952, vol. 1, 168–9; 1, 12) gives some details and more are available in Browe (1933). We read in this monograph of Browe that tendencies and limitations of the immediately preceding centuries persisted: the central portion or Canon as a silent prayer by the priest, the ever-growing reverence for the consecrated elements, the lack of awareness of the faithful's active role in offering (despite the daily recitation of prayers that expressed it) and the general rarity of communion. The elevation of the host, Browe tells us, which was unknown at the end of the twelfth century, had become almost universal by the middle of the thirteenth (p. 28) – interestingly enough, Durham was one of the last to adopt it, in 1255 (p. 35). The host was set thereby into ever greater relief, so that in some places a black veil was extended behind the altar, in order that the elevation might be more impressive (p. 56). The sight of the host was held to have much power, and the dead were sometimes shown it (p. 57). Indeed, even Aquinas felt obliged to state his rejection of the view that to *look at* the host while in grave sin was itself sinful (*ST* 3.80.4 obj. 4 and ad 4; for details see Jungmann 1952, vol. 11, 258–64; 1v, 2.13). A natural result of this concentration was the growth of a whole apparatus of casuistry concerning the perils (*pericula*) that might befall the priest at the altar with the host. Jungmann (1952, vol. 1, 169; 1. 12) gives references, while Iserloh (1956, 275) reports a search of forty-six (yes) late-medieval commentaries on the Sentences. What is clear from the search is that the writers' attention was devoted to nothing as fundamental as the nature of eucharistic sacrifice, but rather to questions about mass said by a bad priest; about the apportioning of the fruits of the mass; about the place of celebration and so on. Nor was it only theologians. Few things can better place the *Missale Romanum* in its historical setting than its section 'On Defects in Celebrating' (as was seen by its revisers in the days of Paul VI: their clean-up removed much of the fun).

It is this lack of sustained thought that makes the analogy between later-medieval theology and later-medieval liturgy be only partial. I submitted in the preceding section that the real insights in what Aquinas wrote of eucharistic sacrifice were restricted by the limitations of the eucharistic rite as known to him. Later-medieval theology did nothing to develop what Aquinas had written, and it is fair to describe it with Clark as 'a rather apathetic conservatism' (1967; his general thesis is usefully summarized at pp. 78–80). But liturgical practice can, for good or evil, go its own way, and in the absence of any speculative development that is what it did. In Aristotle's terminology, *empeiria* prevailed over all else, offering devices to meet practical needs but having nothing to say about principles. Devotional texts assembled by Simmons (1879) show precisely this. The reader is presumed neither to communicate (p. 54) nor to understand passages from Scripture (p. 16) – indeed, the Dean of Norwich under Bloody Mary considered that understanding the priest's words would distract the faithful (p. 365). Many benefits of the mass are attributed to scripture – for St Paul, it makes childbirth easier (p. 368), while for St Matthew our steps to and from it are numbered (p. 371). Moreover, it preserves from blindness and sudden death (can this be why it was customary to communicate before fighting a duel (Browe 1938b)?), while food taken after it is digested better than food taken before (pp. 367–8). That the devotions also stressed the need for reverence and for a good life (pp. 122–7) does not touch the superstitious emptiness of all this, its meagre grasp of ritual, its childish ignorance of scripture.

That the emptiness was filled up by miracle-stories should not surprise us. I shall preface what specimens I offer with a comment upon Aquinas' views here; it will sharpen the contrast between his grasp of what mattered and the later failures to grasp anything. We have already met one early miracle-story (above, pp. 135–6), but there the apparition was temporary and ended in communion. The middle ages were bolder, and Aquinas was faced with tales of permanently blood-stained hosts and similar apparitions. The explanation he offers (to his credit, he seems embarrassed) is that in neither case is Christ's flesh or blood visibly perceived: God either 'creates an appearance' in the accidents or modifies the eyes of the spectators (*ST* 3.76.8; the second explanation was a godsend later for Catholic Cartesians, who thus dispensed themselves from belief in subsisting accidents). But his good sense was not widely shared, and Orvieto Cathedral still harbours the linen blood-stained by the 'miracle of Bolsena', a tale by which even the *Catholic Encyclopaedia* was embarrassed (older edition – stress, and by an arch-conservative author, upon the lateness and uncertainty of the historical testimonies; newer edition – profound silence). In the 1970s (perhaps still) visitors to the shrine were given a leaflet in which the miracle was said to culminate in the host's becoming 'living flesh, dripping blood'. That Paul VI should have visited the place and not been embarrassed (see Paul VI, 1964 and 1971) can be fairly set beside his eucharistic encyclical *Mysterium Fidei*. Clark contends, rightly, that not all tales were of this kind, many being rather of Christ appearing as a 'wonder-child' (1967, 413). He also contends that those which did involve blood were taken as signs of the real presence, not of some new slaying (pp. 424–6). Unfortunately, he is thus prepared to explain both St Dominic's vision of blood flowing into the chalice from the crucified Christ, and late-medieval art-forms like 'the mystic wine-press' (there is a famous example at Paris, in the ambulatory of the church of Saint-Etienne-du-Mont), where Christ's blood is being tapped into barrels. I am more than prepared to take his word for it.

Much information about such miracle-stories is in yet another work by Browe (perversely indefatigable man! Apart from his eucharistical mono-graphs, listed in the References Section below, he produced one that translates not too baldly as 'Contributions to the History of Castration'). We learn from him that the Blessed Agnes Blannbekin of Vienna (d. 1315) could detect a beautiful smell at the altar where mass had been said, and sometimes could even detect from the smell which priest had said it – her convent had Franciscan chaplains (Browe 1938a, 46). Her fellow-Dominicaness, Adelheid Langmann, was told during mass by a vision of Christ (not, one hopes, by one of Clark's *Wunderkinder*) 'dein mund smekt noch rosen und dein leip noch viol' (p. 109). A heretic refused to burn, by diabolic protection; a host was brought along 'and he went up like straw' (p. 91). A Jew who had concealed a host in his strong-box found later all his ducats turned into hosts (p. 93). One does not need to be a Marxist to find that these stories make the eucharist into a *commodity*. A twelfth-century text already prescribed the host's form as that of a coin (Jungmann 1952, vol. II, 46; IV, 1.3); in these tales, it has now lost any detectable link with ritual or eating altogether.

And talk of commodities brings me to a final characteristic, noted by Luther in the texts quoted at the beginning of this section. The waning of the middle ages saw growth in the number of clergy whose one source of livelihood was the mass-offering (Jungmann pleasingly calls them a 'geistliches Proletariat': 1952, vol. I, 172; 1.12). An industry arose (there can be no other word) of celebrating masses for the dead, votive masses for this or that intention, series of consecutive masses, masses celebrated with this or that solemnity as means of securing this or that favour (Jungmann (1952, vol. I, 168–74; 1.12) gives a wealth of examples, if that be the right collective noun). The elevation stood out here once again – some priests took extra money for prolonging it (Jungmann 1952, vol. I, 160; 1.11). Legacies produced ever-lengthening lists of foundation-masses (I have myself sung one for John of Gaunt's mother), and so the need for ever more *Messknechte*. The concrete reality of the eucharistic rite was exhibited in a plurality of such celebrants. Clark (1976, 190) provides us with a good example. His contention that the first reformers wished to abolish not just abuses, but 'the consecrated altars of Christian sacrifice', he illustrates by what happened in a country parish church: payment was made there for 'breckynge down forten awters in the cherche'. He makes no comment – but if Burnham, Bucks., could muster fourteen, how many must there have been in cathedrals? A decree of the Council of Trent against eucharistic abuses gives, in its honest indignation, an idea of where things had got to (it was used by Newman in Tract xc; most easily accessible in Marietti's edition of the *Summa* at *ST* 3.73.1, pp. 480–1).

Luther's attack was directed against this concrete reality, and went beyond it to a wider revaluation of inherited belief: both the concreteness and the revaluation need to be kept in mind if we seek to understand him. Iserloh (1950) makes it clear that some early polemic against Luther, such as that of Johannes Eck (d. 1543), did not seize the point at issue, because of Luther's challenge to the whole historical tradition that had led to how things were (pp. 57, 94, 196). The order at least of Trent's decrees showed that it did see more clearly what was at stake – it began with the place of scripture and tradition, went on to original sin and justification, and only then to the sacraments. My own considerations now move to a tension revealed by one dissenter from Luther.

THE RECURRING TENSION

Historians seem agreed that one of the first Catholic apologists did see the point at issue with Luther, and did offer an account of Catholic belief that was adequate – this was Kaspar Schatzgeyer (d. 1527), concerning whom Iserloh (1950 and 1952) gives details and references, including Schatzgeyer's admission that good things had come from Luther's dissent, such as reading the Bible, preaching that was sensible and the discarding of many useless things (Iserloh 1950, 11). In his reply to Luther's attack on eucharistic sacrifice, Schatzgeyer insists that the mass is more than a memory; if it were only that, then thinking of Calvary would be a mass. It is not a picture of what is past, but the past things themselves, renewed in belief before God the Father, just as if they were happening in the present upon the cross. But there is no repetition of the cross; the presence is *in mysterio, in sacramento*. There is a twofold offering of sacrifice: one is a real one (*wesentliche*), in Latin 'realis', the other is a spiritual one (*geistliche*), in Latin 'mysterialis'. As we sin each day, so do we need each day a representation (*Vergegenwärtigung*) of the passion and sacrifice of Christ for sin. An event that took place once can be so made present (*Gegenwärtsetzung*) because Christ is yesterday and today, yea and for ever, there is no past and future in him (Iserloh 1952, 42–3).

What interests me is that Schatzgeyer's terminology exhibits a tension that has run all through the sources we have examined. On the one hand, there is an insistence upon the presence and the renewal of what is past. Already in earlier texts we found the analogy drawn between the repetition of the eucharist and our daily need for food, and the conception – both ritually and speculatively expressed – of the mass as the *bona gratia*, the descent of grace to us. In medieval sources we found a stress upon transformation at the expense of symbolism and ritual, and we also found analogues of the stress. One was intellectual, the theory of transubstanti-ation. Others were popular, such as the tales of eucharistic miracles, oddities in its use, the multiplication of private masses and the multiplic-ation of specific and equally private purposes for its celebration. But, along with all this, we have also found an enduring denial that Calvary is repeated, and just as enduring an employment of *qualifiers* in what is said of the sacrificial nature of the mass: imitation, representation, memory and image are only some. The tension goes very far back, as a text cited at the beginning of this essay can show – the denunciation by Arnold of the mass for having corrupted the primitive Christian notion of sacrifice. Interest has been aroused by Daly (1978), because here a Roman Catholic's description of early belief concerning eucharistic sacrifice moves towards Arnold's account of it as an offering of ourselves. I would point out myself that some of Daly's conclusions were anticipated – in a far less developed way – as long ago as 1873, when an attack was made by Harrison on Pusey's Tractarian views of eucharistic sacrifice (Harrison 1873). Matters never are as clear-cut as they look here, and the first damage done by religious polemic is that it tempts us to forget this.

What Aquinas writes of eucharistic sacrifice can, because of its very qualifications and moderateness, be read in a minimalising way: to make eucharistic representation do no more than what a bust of Cicero does for the orator would set the mass beside sermons or pictures. I have suggested that Aquinas can accommodate qualifiers to a 'substantial' view of eucharistic sacrifice because he remains aware of the ritual context of it all. We have seen how he stresses its institution in the loving urgency of Christ's farewell and as a fulfilment of the sacrifices of the Old Law; how he sees it as our means of sharing in the fruits of his passion, and as the worship for which all other sacraments prepare us. Where ritual is thus made the setting for understanding, qualifiers can do their job of directing our attention to the rite, and to the whole range of activity, speculative and practical alike, that is concerned with the eucharist. But to the extent that ritual is not given this place, there is not the same density and variety of content to be noticed; and qualifiers take on either simply the negative function of denying that the mass is a sacrifice, or the 'displacing' function of saying that it is, but in some concealed and non-obvious way.

Concealment is perennially attractive – human curiosity likes a peep behind the scenes – and concealment has been involved in so much of what we have seen of the eucharist. There is the change in pattern of the rite itself, to a greater remoteness from the congregation; there is the increased emphasis upon it as a *bona gratia* descending to us, rather than the ascent of our thanksgiving through and in Christ; there is the elaboration of theories of eucharistic presence in terms derived from what we should now call natural science; there is the growth of stories and customs that damagingly remove the material of the eucharist from the setting of its original institution. All this we have seen; but having seen it, let us admit unreservedly that talk here of concealment does bear witness – even if distorted witness – to the truth that there is more to the eucharistic rite than the expression of human fellowship, and more to it than a reminder of Calvary. There is, we might say, more to it than there is to a bust of Cicero. But having made this admission, we must add that the way in which concealment bears witness here is dangerous. Concealment rests upon the presupposition that what is being concealed is of a piece with what conceals it, in the way that a disguise could mask a friend. In ritual, on the other hand, we have signs, and signs do not compete with what they signify. Nor is that the only important difference. Ritual is more than what can be talked about; ritual is inherited and lived. Concealment will always be more attractive, as far as crispness in argument goes, because talk in terms of disguise will always invite us to ask whether the concealed object is there or not. So it proved at the end of the middle ages, when the reformers' attack and the general pattern of eucharistic debate and polemic – is Christ really present there? Is he offered in sacrifice there? – invited discussion in terms of concealment, and bore little or no reference to categories or ritual. Moreover, as in all polemic, qualifications were felt to be weaknesses, so that when the study of ritual history began to remedy the great gaps in our understanding of earlier centuries, its pursuit also was polemical. Nor did ecclesiastical organization help. The Church of Rome, while condemning ritual abuses at the Council of Trent, froze the pattern of the liturgy, so that the haphazard and heterogeneous causes of its development were identified with loyalty and orthodoxy. Ritual itself was given an aggressive cast: Trent saw eucharistic processions as leading either to the conversion of heretics or to their wasting away, weakened and broken (Session XIII, Cap. 5; Denzinger and Schönmetzer 1963, n. 1644).

I would supplement these observations by noticing a family of theories of eucharistic sacrifice, now abandoned but once popular, that were devised by some (by no means all) Roman Catholic theologians after the Tridentine reforms. They faced the Protestant denial of any eucharistic sacrifice in what they deemed their own sense; they did not have an elaborate heritage of speculation about it to invoke against their adversaries; neither side had examined the sense and growth of its liturgical practice. It was natural enough that their much more elaborated belief in transubstantiation should find an analogy in what they came to say of eucharistic sacrifice. Just as the accidents of bread conceal the substantial presence of Christ, so in some way or other, just as imperceptible to the senses but none the less real, Christ was affected or changed in the mass – and in a way sufficiently embarrassing to qualify as 'immolation'. As to what the way was, opinions differed. He is reduced to an inferior (*declivior*) state; to the status of food; to a state where he cannot of himself move; to a state resembling the months between conception and birth; the separate consecrations are a sword that mystically separates his body and blood; and so on. (Readers can follow it all up in the second part of Lepin 1926, where I learn that William Allen (d. 1594), founder of what is now Ushaw College, played a part in its prehistory.) The grotesqueness came from reducing ritual qualifications to something else: immolation in the eucharist could not be a new crucifixion, so it had to be another kind of 'endurance'. They imagined the eucharist as a disguised presence of Christ, and the very mechanism of his disguise qualified as his immolation.

But although these theories offer a vivid *reductio ad absurdum* of confusing ritual with disguise, I have another reason for mentioning them. I introduce the reason by keeping a promise made on p. 139 above, where I gave Aquinas' view (*ST* 3.83.1 ad 2) that on the cross Christ was immolated *in propria specie*, rendering the phrase as 'in the primary sense'. I did so because of the direction of his argument there. He is dealing with the objection that, since Christ is not crucified in the mass, he is not immolated either; his answer was that the rite *represents* the passion, and so the altar *represents* the cross, where Christ was immolated *in propria specie*. The phrase – literally 'in his own form' – is meant to contrast with the eucharistic *representation* of his passion, a representation that involves no further crucifixion. I rendered it as I did to keep off any suggestion that, while Calvary has a *perceptible* immolation, the Mass has a *disguised* one ('in aliena specie', we might put it) – which would push us into the bizarre theories I have just mentioned. But now notice something else. The bizarre theories can and do claim that there is a concealed immolation, if only we could see it; what Aquinas writes does nothing but send us back to the eucharist as a ritual representation of the passion. There is, for him, no *competition*, if I may so put it, between what we perceive and what there really is – as there would be if the former were only deceptive appearance. We are sent back to the ritual reality, a reality which represents the saving actions of Christ. The answer offered by Aquinas is in its austerity less specious than the other theories: it does not pretend to point to some definite if disguised process; it directs us to the ritual itself. And there, I submit, is its strength and richness. Indeed, I would go further and, as I have argued elsewhere, and argue at greater length in the book mentioned earlier (p. 132). I would extend his style of answer about eucharistic sacrifice to the eucharistic presence, and reject transubstantiation as confusing ritual with disguise and conceal-ment. I would reject too the recent substitution by some Dutch and French authors of 'transignification' for transubstantiation, somewhat as I would reject behaviourism as an adequate replacement for a Cartesian view of the soul. I take ritual neither as physics nor as ethics, but as ritual. I give no argument here for this position, but I make a general point that will concern us in the next and final section. The deepest attraction of using categories of concealment in eucharistic theology is that they seem to offer an independent criterion in disagreements – something lies concealed or it does not. The style of answer I find in Aquinas when he considers eucharistic sacrifice is not only austere in sending us back to the rite itself; by sending us back to what we do, it does not pretend to stand outside ritual, as if the answers were independent of ritual. At the beginning of this section, I said that I had found a persistent tension in the texts we have examined, and I went to Schatzgeyer's vocabulary in his reply to Luther for an example of it. I now end the section by submitting that the style of the answers offered by Aquinas shows him living with the tension, rather than attempting a specious resolution of it. This thought I develop in the final section.

LIVING WITH IT

When studying texts to do with the atonement, I did not doubt that recent theologians must have baulked at a good deal of what I found there. I have since inspected some modern works, and was pleased to find resemblances to my own distaste for what I called 'the scenario of tit-for-tat', and even – in the work of Aulén (1970), which seems highly regarded – some sympathy for the older 'devil's rights' theory. Sykes admits that some documents do move towards 'a morally monstrous saga in which God engineers human salvation by means of the ritual slaughter of his own Son' (1980, 74). For Aulén, the atonement is a divine warfare against evil, and the triumph of Christ (1970, 159); for Young, God 'took upon himself the consequences of evil and sin' (1975, 125). For Barrington-Ward, the divinity 'exposed itself to the dereliction of our uncertain quests and conflicts' (1980, 132). These and similar statements I welcome. I should have welcomed further statements, not as to how these positions can be reconciled with so much in Christian tradition, but as to why so much Christian tradition accepted so placidly the views it did. I myself have rejected (see earlier, p. 132) views like those of Aquinas about our moral involvement with Adam through seminal descent from him, and rejected them on moral grounds. But I then pointed out that views we now hold on the origin of man remove the basis for that theological superstructure. To state what I think should be put in its place will lead me to say more of what I think can be salvaged.

It is not original sin that we should believe in; it is original aspiration. We are descended from other animals, who exhibit 'nature' in bounded and repetitive ways. In human beings, 'nature' is in some ways just as constricted, for we have all the physical needs of our ancestors. But in other ways, the constriction is broken. We have hopes and desires ever new; our devices and inventions extend them; our patterns of behaviour are ever adaptable; 'nature' for us is an exercise, not a fixed formula for a limited range of action. And yet in still other ways all this makes the constriction only the greater, and more tragic. Since our nature is not given and fixed, we lack the built-in safety-devices of other animals that could limit the damage we do; our devices and inventions confront us with burdens of choice and with temptations to evil that are just different in kind and in power from the fenced-in aggressions and desires of other animals. And as those other animals are faced with decay and death, so are we: but we have seen and hoped and made and failed so much more before we come to die, that our death is an affront in a way that theirs cannot be. Even in the intellectualist tradition of Greek moral speculation, we find texts of Aristotle that put this and other affronts into a few words: 'To be immortal in so far as it is given to us' (*Nicomachean Ethics*, x, 7); 'the nature of men being in many ways in bondage' (*Metaphysics*, A, 2). For the Judaeo-Christian tradition, the intellect is inadequate, for there is more to be known than we should like to think, including how much our very sight is darkened: the heart of man is deceitful above all things and desperately wicked; who can know it?

I offer a text of Aquinas that can link what I have just written with the notion of sacrifice. When considering the virtue of religion, he devotes one Question to sacrifices (*ST* 2/2.85). He regards them as natural, claiming that they are found in all times and places, and states that the defects man feels in himself are the grounds on which he concludes that he should be subject to something above him, by which he can be helped and guided. It is this (whatever it be) that is everywhere called God, and just as signs of honour are used to earthly superiors, so are they to God, in ways that custom dictates (*ST* 2/2.85.1 and ad 1). God is our origin and the goal of our being made happy, and sacrifices do but express the offering of ourselves to him (*ST* 2/2.85.2). Any good act has something sacrificial about it, in that it shows our desire to share his fellowship (*ST* 2/2.85.3 ad 1); but actions specifically sacrificial are those specifically directed to revering him (*ST* 2/2.85.3). Of these, the chief is the offering of what is good in ourselves ('bonum animae'), such as devotion and prayer; next come martyrdom, mortification and so on; last comes the offering of material things – either directly to him, or giving them to others in his honour (*ST* 2/2.85.3 ad 2).

Many themes that we have already met converge in this one Question, and are complemented by the way Aquinas here places the whole topic. Our origin and our unended quest for happiness lie at the root of sacrifice. Our whole endeavour to do good is its setting, where particular rites and ceremonies draw their virtue from the inner giving of ourselves to God. All this strengthens what Aquinas says about the institution of the eucharist (see earlier, p. 140). The urgency of Christ's farewell displays both our darkness which is to engulf him and the pledge through him of what still lies ahead, beyond that darkness. That a meal is chosen to preserve belief both exhibits the dependence and limitation to which we are subject (how often we have encountered texts that stress our daily need for food!), and consummates the hope of deliverance embodied in the older Passover rite that he and the disciples inherited. Fragility and strength, the past and the future, come together in the sign chosen, just as human cruelty and divine love, time and eternity, come together in what is signified. If the whole endeavour to do good, and so to move towards the end of all our desiring, is the setting of sacrifice, the endeavour and movement receive in the person and deeds of Christ a substantiality that we of ourselves cannot give them. What Aquinas writes of the redemption in the *Summa Theologiae* exhibits this: his treatment takes as central the divine work done through Christ, and his role as head of the Church that is his body, the unity of which is signified by the eucharist.

I have suggested that the gap and paradox in the human condition provide an intelligible starting-point for talk about redemption in a way that talk of a primal fault does not; and I have suggested that the starting-point is one that can go with some things that Aquinas himself has written. I now want to suggest that it is this 'gap', or whatever else we wish to call it, that can explain, even if not justify, things I have been attacking in the course of this essay. I took exception to what I called the scenario of tit-for-tat; I accused medieval theories of the eucharistic presence of offering, in a context of an outmoded natural philosophy, an account that verges on camouflaged cannibalism; I claimed that some medieval accounts of eucharistic sacrifice, while comparatively unelaborated, confused signs and disguises, harboured ambiguities as to the uniqueness of Calvary, and – most of all – failed to integrate speculation with any adequate expression in liturgical practice. I found in these and other errors a crudity that does not in my opinion stand up to a dispassionate examination. But I now make what may strike some as the damaging admission that religion seems to need a dash of crudity if it is to flourish. It is concerned with more than we can do and say and resolve of ourselves; it is concerned with our very being and its enlargement. Body, blood, food, drink, death: these have not been accidentally encountered in the course of our journey; our journey has led us rather into places where they were bound to be met. I do not make these admissions in order to withdraw my complaints; I still stand by them. Indeed, I would go further. Talk here of holding a balance can be little more than an avowal of optimism; it is nearer the mark to wonder how many conflicting attitudes we can support simultaneously. When the Judaeo-Christian tradition laments the darkening of our moral sight, it ought to add that testimonies to the darkening are provided by that tradition. (For the dark side to eucharistic miracles, see the *Jewish Encyclopaedia*, s.v. 'Host, Desacration of'.) Among the merits of what Aquinas writes about atonement in the *Summa* is the way he puts his 'Abelardian' considerations (example and so on) within the setting of seeing Christ as the Head of the Church, and of seeing his humanity as the instrument of divine power and love. To say that we have something far deeper here than example is not to deny that the two ultimately coincide: Christ is indeed the ground of our beseeching. But here and now we do not see them as one, and both need stating and safeguarding. And crudeness can, in some cases, help to do this: in the atonement it can witness to the reality of sin and evil in the world, and to the 'costingness', if I may use von Hügel's word, of our release from it; and in the eucharist, both as sacrament and as sacrifice, crudeness can prevent any reduction of what is done there to what is done by us.

Of the dangers that lie in the crudity, I hope I have given proof enough; here, I point out that, by means of selective amnesia and inspired inattention, it is possible for believers to profit by credal and devotional forms that, taken at their face-value, are indefensible. The theologian's task – well, one of his tasks – will be to attempt to understand and to confront the heterogeneous mass of formularies and practice in which his religious tradition has expressed itself. Understanding here will involve an acknowledgement of the complexity of the past, and confrontation will call for the acknowledgement that we cannot treat that past as something of no present concern to us. Of the many policies which he can pursue in trying to accomplish his task, I end by mentioning two. One is to preserve a variety and multiplicity in his approaches to what is believed. The second is a matter of knowing when to stop: a theologian must resist the tendency of what he has said to protract itself – the trouble is not that religious analogies limp, it is that limping does not stop them moving. The eucharistic texts of Aquinas we have examined can provide us with examples. A weakness in what he writes of the eucharistic presence is that all his talk of substance and change and appearances simply goes on too long. Conversely, a lack of system gives his scattered remarks on eucharistic sacrifice an illumination and a strength; just as his *Summa Theologiae* has more to teach us about Christ's redemptive work than has his *Commentary on the Sentences*, precisely because it is less touched by the pressure to explain everything. In theology – and not only in theology – it is a great gift to know when to stop. All too tardily, I now do so; and so do.

REFERENCES

I gladly acknowledge here the guidance I have received, in investigating primary texts, from works like Rashdall (1920), Rivière (1909) and Lepin (1926). To this acknowledgement I add two remarks: I do not share the esteem in which writers like Rivière and Lepin hold their authors; and I would stress that patristic and medieval sources alike need reading *in bulk*, if the stuff is to be made any sense of.

Patristic references are accompanied by the volume and column numbers in Migne's Latin and Greek patrologies, indicted by '*PG*' or '*PL*'. The works themselves are divided variously; I use the convention of letting Roman numerals number Books, and Arabic numerals number chapters. Readers who use the indices and tables in Migne (usefully tabulated by an anonymous Carthusian in 1952) should note that column numbers there sometimes refer to the numerals set in bold type in the text.

References to the *Summa Theologiae* are by '*ST*', followed by numbers for Part, Question, Article, with 'ad 1' for 'Answer to the First Objection', and so on. References to the *Commentary on the Sentences* of Aquinas are indicated by '*S*', preceded by the number of the Book, and followed by numbers indicating the successive subdivisions of the Book. The system there is clumsy and complicated; to mend the difficulty, page and paragraph numbers are given for the portion edited by Moos.

Anonymous Carthusian (1952). *Elucidatio in 235 Tabulas Patrologiae Latinae, Auctore Cartusiensi.* Rotterdam: De Forel

Aquinas, Thomas (1947). *Scriptum super Sententiis Magistri Petri Lombardi...* vols. III and IV ed. M. F. Moos [the first two volumes are not edited by Moos; they lack paragraph-numbers]. Paris: P. Lethielleux

(1948). *Summa Theologiae ... notis selectis ornata, Pars IIIa et Supplementum.* Turin and Rome: Marietti

Aulén, G. (1970). *Christus Victor: An Historical Study of the three main Types of the Idea of the Atonement,* trans. A. G. Herbert. London: SPCK

Barrington-Ward, S. and Bourdillon, M. F. C. A Place for Sacrifice in Modern Christianity? In Bourdillon and Fortes (1980), pp. 127–33

Bourdillon, M. and Fortes, M. (eds.) (1980). *Sacrifice.* London: Academic Press

Browe, P. (1933). *Die Verehrung der Eucharistie im Mittelalter.* Munich: Max Hueber

(1938a). *Die eucharistischen Wunder des Mittelalters.* Breslau: Müller und Seiffert

(1938b). *Die häufige Kommunion im Mittelalter.* Münster: Regenbergsche Verlagsbuchhandlung

Catholic Encyclopedia, The (1907–12). 15 vols. New York: Robert Appleton Company (*See also* New Catholic Encyclopedia.)

Clark, F. (1967). *Eucharistic Sacrifice and the Reformation* (2nd edn, with a forward by Cardinal John Heenan). Oxford: Basil Blackwell

Daly, R. J. (1978). *The Origins of the Christian Doctrine of Sacrifice.* Philadelphia: Fortress Press

Denzinger, H. and A. Schönmetzer (eds.) (1963). *Enchiridion Symbolorum...* Barcelona: Herder

Durandus of Mende (1775). *Prochiron, Vulgo Rationale Divinorum Officiorum.* Madrid: Roman

FitzPatrick, P. J. (1972). Some Thoughts on the Eucharistic Presence. *New Blackfriars* 53: 627 (August) and 628 (September) [This and the following item appeared under the pseudonym 'G. Egner'.]

(1973). More Thoughts on the Eucharistic Presence. *New Blackfriars* 54: 635 (April)

(1987a). Present and Past in a Debate on Transubstantiation. In *The Philosophical Assessment of Theology: Essays in Honour of Frederick J. Copleston*, ed. G. J. Hughes, pp. 129–53. Tunbridge Wells/Georgetown. Washington: Search Press/Georgetown University Press.

(1987b). Some Seventeenth-Century Disagreements and Transubstantiation. In *Language, Meaning and God: Essays in Honour of Herbert McCabe, O.P.*, ed. B. Davies, pp. 120–44. London: Geoffrey Chapman

(1987c). Some Thoughts on the Eucharistic Presence [and] More Thoughts on the Eucharistic Presence. In *God Matters*, ed. H. McCabe, pp. 130–45, 155–64. London: Geoffrey Chapman [A revised version of FitzPatrick 1972 and 1973, with an Appendix.]

Fox, M. (1962). John Wyclif and the Mass. *Heythrop Journal* 3, 232–40

Harrison, J. (1873). *The Fathers Versus Dr Pusey* . . . London: Longmans, Green & Co.

Iserloh, E. (1950). *Eucharistie in der Darstellung des Johannes Eck* . . ., Reformationsgeschichtliche Studien. Studien und Texte, 73–4. Münster: Aschendorffsche Verlagsbuchhandlung

(1952). *Der Kampf um die Messe in den ersten Jahren der Auseinandersetzung mit Luther*. Katholisches Leben und Kampfe, 10. Münster: Aschendorffsche Verlagsbuchhandlung

(1956). *Gnade und Eucharistie in der Theologie Wilhelm von Ockham. Ihre Bedeutung für die Ursachen der Reformation*, Veröffentlichungen des Instituts für Europäische Geschichte Mainz. Wiesbaden: Franz Steiner

Jewish Encyclopedia, The (1901–). New York: Funk & Wagnall

Jorissen, H. (1965). *Die Entfaltung der Transsubstantiationslehre bis zum Beginn der Hochscholastik*. Münsterische Beiträge zur Theologie, 28, 1. Münster: Aschendorffsche Verlagsbuchhandlung

Jungmann, J. A. (1952). *Missarum Sollemnia. Eine genetische Erklärung der Römischen Messe*, 2 vols. Vienna: Herder [I supplement page references by giving the successive subdivisions (Part, Chapter, etc.) used by Jungmann. These serve for the English translation as well.]

Kidd, B. J. (1898). *The Later Medieval Doctrine of the Eucharistic Sacrifice*, The Church Historical Society, 46. London: SPCK

Lepin, M. (1926). *L'Idée du sacrifice de la messe d'après les théologiens jusqu'à nos jours*. Paris: Beauchesne

Lubac, H. de (1949). *Corpus Mysticum. L'Eucharistie et l'église au Moyen Age* (2nd edn), Théologie: Etudes publiées sous la direction de la Faculté de Théologie S. J. de Lyon-Fourvière, 3. Paris: Aubier

Mascall, E. L. (1965). *Corpus Christi, Essays on the Church and the Eucharist* (2nd edn). London: Longmans

New Catholic Encyclopedia, The (1967–79). 17 vols. New York etc.: McGraw Hill

[Newman, J. H.] (1842). *Tract Ninety: Of Remarks on Certain Passages in the Thirty-Nine Articles* (4th edn). London: Rivington [The work, like most of the Tracts, appeared anonymously. Newman used brackets here to indicate matter added after the first edition. Nothing of substance was added to the consideration of Article xxxi.]

Paul VI, Pope (1964). Siamo lietissimi (address delivered 11 August 1964 at Orvieto Cathedral). *Acta Apostolicae Sedis* 751–7

(1971). Eucharistic Preparation requires Faith, Grace, and Reconciliation (address delivered to a General Audience, 9 June 1971). Reproduced from *Osservatore Romano* in *Adoremus*, 53: 4, 139–42

Rashdall, H. (1920). *The Idea of Atonement in Christian Theology*. London: Macmillan

Rivière, J. (1909). *The Doctrine of the Atonement: A Historical Essay*, trans. L. Cappadelta. London: International Catholic Library

Simmons, T. F. (1879). *The Lay Folks Mass Book* (etc.). London: Early English Text Society (no. 71)

Stanley, A. P. (1846). *The Life and Correspondence of Thomas Arnold, D.D.* London: Ward Lock

Sykes, S. W. (1980). Sacrifice in the New Testament and Christian Theology. In Bourdillon and Fortes (1980), pp. 61–83

Young, F. M. (1975). *Sacrifice and the Death of Christ*. London: SPCK

9

THE SACRIFICE OF THE MASS AT THE COUNCIL OF TRENT

J. F. McHUGH

It is almost universally believed, by Catholics and Protestants alike, that the Council of Trent defined that the mass is a sacrifice. That statement stood, in fact, in the penultimate draft of the first canon on the mass, but at almost the last moment, in deference to the pleas of a minority, the Council substituted for it a more subtle formula which affirmed only 'that in the Mass there is offered to God a true and proper sacrifice'. Even today, few appreciate fully the significance of this change in wording, for it is only with the publication of the proceedings of the Council in the last hundred years[1] that it has become possible to assess the decrees of Trent with exactitude, and these revised and more accurate assessments have not yet become part of the normal stock-in-trade of every theologian. Yet it is clearly of the utmost importance to grasp very precisely what the Council of Trent wished to lay down as the first and basic proposition upon which all Roman Catholic theology concerning the mass must rest. For failure to appreciate its exact meaning will almost inevitably lead a person to discuss the problem of 'the sacrifice of the Mass' in strictly pre-Tridentine terms, and in that case he will almost certainly find himself a prisoner of late-medieval categories and reformation controversies. The purpose of this essay is to elucidate the meaning of the Tridentine decree, and the story is most easily told historically.

Everyone knows that the great schism between the Churches of the Reformation and those Churches which remained in communion with Rome was triggered off by a dispute about indulgences, which quickly brought into the open profound differences about justification. But the most burning question of all, around which all the others in practice revolved, was the status of the mass. The question at issue here was something that anyone, however illiterate, could understand, even though he might be totally bewildered over justification in the abstract. Was the celebration of the mass a good work availing for the remission of sins for the living and the dead? And was it a good work to provide a stipend for a priest who would in return celebrate mass in order to secure such remission or forgiveness? Here was a practical problem affecting every Christian, for it is self-evident that it raised the question, 'Can the rich, by providing stipends and founding chantries, buy forgiveness and remission of punishment due to their sins, for themselves and their deceased relatives?' One need hardly add that, unlike the other doctrines in dispute, this one had massive economic implications, for many monasteries and university colleges were richly endowed precisely in order to secure the celebration of masses for the souls of the departed.

Martin Luther had no doubt about the importance of the question, or about the right answer. When Pope Paul III summoned the long-demanded General Council to meet at Mantua in 1537, Luther, assisted by Melanchthon and six other theologians, drew up a list of the doctrines which divided Protestants and Catholics upon which no compromise was possible, the Schmalkaldic Articles (Jedin 1957, 320). The second article of Part II reads:

The Mass in the papacy must be regarded as the greatest and most horrible abomination because it runs into direct and violent conflict with this fundamental article [i.e. no. I, on justification]. Yet above and beyond all others, it has been the supreme and most precious of the papal idolatries, for it is held that this sacrifice or work of the Mass (even when offered by an evil scoundrel) delivers men from their sins, both here in this life and yonder in purgatory, although in reality this can and must be done by the Lamb of God alone... There is to be no concession or compromise in this article either, for the first article does not permit it. (Tappert 1959, 293)

The projected Council did not in fact assemble until 1545, and then it was not at Mantua, but at Trent. After nearly two months' wrangling over procedure, with the Emperor's party urging that practical legislation to reform abuses should take precedence over doctrinal issues and the Pope taking the opposite view, a compromise was reached: dogma and reform should be discussed simultaneously, though in different sittings. As a result, the Council moved immediately into basic doctrinal questions, and enacted its decrees in a strictly logical order, beginning with the manner of the transmission of revealed truth in scripture and tradition (Session IV: 8 April 1546), and moving swiftly to the teaching of revelation on original sin (Session V: 17 June 1546) before embarking on the drafting of its longest, its most crucial and its most masterly decree, on justification (Session VI: 13 January 1547). With its broad doctrinal bases thus firmly stated, the Council was ready to proceed with the application of these principles in the fields where doctrinal differences with the Protestants were in practice most apparent, and where abuses were most rife, namely, the sacraments; and in Session VII (3 March 1547) it promulgated its decree on the sacraments in general, and on baptism and confirmation. The next step was to be the decree on the holy eucharist, and it is at this point that our topic comes into the story.

A month earlier, on 3 February 1547, ten propositions or 'articles' had been put to the theologians who acted as advisers to the Council for examination and comment. The first nine were all taken from the works of the reformers, and concerned the Real Presence, reservation of the sacrament, and the giving of the cup to the laity. The tenth article (the only one for which no source was cited) read: 'It is not lawful for anyone to give holy communion to himself' (CT v 871, 5–6). This rather odd tenth article attracted little comment, only passing condemnation, until almost at the end of the discussions, on 18 February, a French Franciscan, Jean du Conseil, put his finger on the point at issue there: 'The tenth article is maliciously thought up against the sacrifice of the mass ... This article is devised against the mass', being directed, as he clearly perceived, against the practice of 'private masses' where the priest alone received holy communion (CT v 958, 30–1; 959, 10–12). This was, as far as I can see, the point at which the sacrifice of the mass was first mentioned in the proceedings of the Council of Trent.

Three days after Session VII, on Sunday, 6 March 1547, the ten articles were presented to the Fathers with comments, together with eleven further propositions put forward by the theologians themselves as calling for condemnation. The third of these read 'That the Eucharist is not a true sacrifice' (CT v 1007–8), and so the issue was placed on the agenda. The following morning, however, the presiding papal legate, Cardinal Cervini (later Pope Marcellus II), proposed that the mass (note the change of term from 'the eucharist') should be reserved for separate treatment after all the sacraments had been discussed; and this proposal was accepted almost unanimously (CT 1 137 and 623).

This decision to enact a conciliar decree on the holy eucharist as a sacrament, while excluding from it any mention of the mass as a sacrifice, seems to us today an extraordinary judgement for Catholics to make. Indeed, it is to us unthinkable; but to the Fathers of Trent it was not so illogical. For what the Lutherans and other Protestants had rejected was not the celebration of the Lord's Supper, but the assertion that such a celebration, conducted in the form of the Roman mass, constituted a *propitiatory sacrifice* which had value in itself for the expiation of sin, even if no one except the celebrant received holy communion. For the Fathers of Trent, as for Luther, this was quite a separate issue from that of the Real Presence and its implications, however the Presence of Christ in the sacrament be understood; for both parties, the dispute about 'the sacrifice of the mass' was more closely and more logically linked with the status of holy orders as 'priesthood' than with the doctrine of the Real Presence in the sacrament. Hence at Trent it seemed more natural and more orderly to approach the problem by treating first of holy orders as priesthood, in the sequence of the seven sacraments; and perhaps Cervini had in mind to combine this doctrine with that of the Real Presence in the eucharist in order to formulate a decree drawing on the nature of two sacraments, which would thus provide a fairly comprehensive and balanced statement about the mass.

But it was not to be. On that Sunday evening, 6 March 1547, the Bishop of Capaccio died of typhus, and in view of the alarming number of recent deaths from this disease, much of Wednesday and all Thursday was spent assessing the danger of a large-scale epidemic, for 'once the fact of an infectious disease at Trent had been established, there was reason to fear that the Republic of Venice, whose strict health inspectors were regarded as exemplary, would close the frontiers and that the neighbouring States would do likewise' (Jedin 1961, 421). Hence an emergency Session (VIII) was hurriedly convened on Friday, 11 March, at which it was decided to transfer the Council to Bologna.

By 25 March a reassembled but much depleted Council was ready to start work, and from April to July it discussed the eucharist and the remaining sacraments. A purely formal Session (IX) was held on the day originally scheduled for the Eighth (21 April), simply to adjourn until the Thursday of Whit Week, 2 June; but when that day came, even though the canons on the eucharist had been fully discussed from 9 to 31 May, the Session (X) merely adjourned once more until 15 September because so many prelates who had not come to Bologna were daily expected, notably the French. In these circumstances, the first papal legate, Cardinal del Monte (later Pope Julius III), judged that it would be improper to proceed until those bishops had arrived (CT VI–1 181, 2–8), and all agreed.

The French never came, and the bishops who had stayed behind in Trent persisted in their refusal to go to Bologna, encouraged by the Emperor, who was pressing for the Council to be recalled to Trent. Of the three papal legates, Cardinal Pole had departed a year earlier (28 June 1546) because of poor health (CT I 557), and had his resignation accepted on 16 October (CT X 701, n. 1). Cervini, worn out by the internal squabbling, continual lack of funds and the politically inspired procrastination of the Pope (Paul III), had repeatedly begged to be replaced, and with the other legate, del Monte, had formally tendered his resignation on 30 October 1546 (CT X 709, 8–10; 711, 14–24), only to have his request not so much refused as ignored (see Pole's account of a papal audience, at which he pleaded their case, and Cervini's exhaustion, on 20 November, CT X 913, 9–15). Yet these two men loyally presided over the transfer to Bologna in the following spring, and there succeeded in maintaining the momentum of the Council's work; but two days after the non-event of Session x, on 4 June, both of them, totally dispirited, tendered their resignations once more (CT XI 211–12), again in vain. And to crown all, during that June and July of 1547, nearly half the bishops who had come to Bologna drifted away, unable to endure the appalling heat (Jedin 1970, 93–4). It was in these unpropitious conditions, with the Churches of Northern Europe virtually unrepresented, that the theologians were asked to begin their discussions on the sacrifice of the mass.

Among the closest of Cervini's friends was Girolamo Seripando, Master General of the Augustinians (Luther's Order) and one of the wisest men at the Council. He had had to leave Bologna on 28 April to attend a General Chapter of his Order, but before leaving, he had put together a list of statements from Lutheran sources concerning the mass (CT VI–1 323–5); and this list appears to have formed the basis of seven articles presented for comment to the theologians on 29 July 1547 (CT VI–1 323, n. 2). These seven articles thus became the starting point of the Council's deliberations, and since the text is not easily accessible, I give it here in an English translation:

1   The eucharist in the mass is not a sacrifice, nor an offering for sins, but only a commemoration of the sacrifice enacted on the cross, and to offer it is not a good work or meritorious.

2   The mass as a sacrifice is of no advantage to the living or the dead; nor can it be applied to others [who are not present].

3   The mass cannot be traced back to the gospel [*non esse ex evangelio*], nor was it instituted by Christ; on the contrary, it was devised by men for the sake of profit and gain.

4   Private masses are therefore unlawful and should be forbidden by law; and only one mass should be allowed on any one day in any one church.

5   It is not lawful for priests to celebrate unless there are people present to receive holy communion.

6   The canon of the mass should be abolished by law, and eschewed as the worst possible abomination.

7   Water should not be mixed with wine in the chalice, because we do not read in the gospel that this was done.

(The Latin text is given in CT VI–1 322–3 in a critical edition, with copious footnotes indicating the sources from which these articles may be illustrated. The principal sources are Luther's *Babylonian Captivity* and his *Abrogation of Private Mass*, along with Melanchthon's *Apologia* for the Confession of Augsburg.)

The last two articles need little comment. The sixth is there because the Lutherans objected strongly to phrases in the Roman Canon which spoke of the 'sacrifice' at the altar (e.g. 'sanctum sacrificium'; 'immaculatam hostiam'). The seventh is doctrinally trivial, and was included only because Luther had denounced the custom on the ground that some late-medieval theologians and preachers interpreted the drop of water put into the wine as symbolic of man's uniting his own sacrifice with that of Christ.[2]

The core of the argument, and its logic, is all contained in articles 1 to 5. From these, it is luminously clear that the target is not the Lord's Supper considered as a sacrament, but the private mass, celebrated by a priest without a congregation to receive holy communion, in order to secure some benefit, which might include atonement for sin, for persons either not present or not communicating, including the dead. All that the five articles have done is to break down this thesis into its logical components.

The first article is the foundation on which the next four rest, and it may be considered from two angles, which we may for convenience label 'liturgical' and 'doctrinal', though the argument in both is essentially the same – only the starting point is different.

First, 'liturgically'. If the very act of celebrating the holy eucharist on one's own can be considered as, and is in reality, the offering of a sacrifice which avails for the forgiveness of sins, then it is by the same token a good work and an act pleasing to God, and does not need the presence of communicants to justify it. If, on the other hand, the eucharist is merely a memorial service recalling the sacrifice of the cross and uniting the communicants with Christ and among themselves, then it is senseless to hold such a service unless there are bystanders to participate in it by holy communion.

Alternatively, we may look at the same issue from a doctrinal standpoint. For Luther, the holy eucharist was esentially the Lord's testament, that is, Christ's legacy and parting bequest to us; it is therefore God's gift to man, not something which man can 'give' to God, and therefore it is in no sense a 'good work' of man. Luther repeatedly stresses that the New Testament knows of only one sacrifice, once for all, the sacrifice of the cross, by which all the sacrifices of the Old Law have been annulled and abrogated, and all future sacrifices excluded. For him, to call the mass a sacrifice is to derogate from the one perfect sacrifice of Calvary.[3]

Stated in these terms, the problem facing the theologians at Bologna was to produce evidence from scripture alone (to satisfy or to rebut the Lutherans) and evidence also from tradition (to satisfy themselves) showing that the mass, even when celebrated privately and with no communicants, is a good work and a sacrifice which avails for the expiation of sins.

Yet the theologians at Bologna seem never to have grasped the nature of this challenge, for as one reads the record of their speeches (CT vi–1 321–91), still more if one reads the full texts which are now available (CT vi–2 433–627) and the written submission of the Jesuits Claudius Jajus and Salmeron (CT vi–3 383–534), modestly entitled 'Compendiosa responsio', one sees them constantly proving to their own satisfaction that 'Church tradition has always understood the relevant texts of scripture in this way'. Luther, who had died on 18 February 1546, would undoubtedly have concurred, adding that it only proved his point that Church tradition was from the earliest ages riddled with error, and that scripture alone was the one trustworthy source of divine revelation.

Why was it that at Bologna this manner of argument – so fundamental to the Reformation debate – was apparently never even questioned? First, it must be remembered that almost all the bishops from north of the Alps and east of the Rhine, with their attendant theologians, were still at Trent; all the theologians at Bologna were either Italian, Spanish, Portuguese or French (CT vi–1 390–1). Secondly, on 24 April 1547, the Emperor Charles V had inflicted a crushing defeat at Mühlberg on the alliance of Protestant princes known as the League of Schmalkalden; and it may be that this news led the people at Bologna to believe that a political solution was possible in Germany, after which the whole theological storm would either blow itself out or be settled in a wider context. All the time, they looked upon the Lutherans as a sect of errant Catholics whose day would quickly pass, like that of other heretical sects in the middle ages, never dreaming that they were dealing with a Western schism potentially more disruptive than the break with Constantinople.

But even if they did not, and could not, foresee the extent or the duration of the gulf that was opening in the Western Church, the theologians at Bologna fully appreciated how potentially dangerous for Catholicism were Luther's *ideas*. They therefore set to with a will to find biblical texts in support of the doctrine that the mass is a sacrifice for sin, truly searching the scriptures, and it is interesting to note that their main biblical arguments were in fact taken from the Old Testament, with the New Testament evidence in a somewhat subordinate place.

First, they repeatedly invoked the text of Mal. 1:11 according to the Vulgate, which may be translated: 'In every place there is sacrifice, and there is offered to my name a clean oblation.' This prophecy, they argued, cannot refer to Old Testament sacrifices, which were restricted to Jerusalem; nor to the sacrifice of the cross, for the same reason, and also because that was not a clean, but a bloody sacrifice. The fulfilment of this prophetical text can therefore be found only in the mass, as tradition has always maintained (CT vi–1 326, 338, 344, 346, 350, 362, 370, 377).

Secondly, the two texts concerning Melchizedek were of prime importance. According to Gen. 14, Melchizedek offered bread and wine; according to Ps. 110:4, Christ was to be a priest for ever according to the order of Melchizedek. Therefore Christ fulfilled his role as a priest in the order of Melchizedek when he offered bread and wine at the Last Supper; and since he is, in that order, a priest for ever, he must continue to offer sacrifice through bread and wine for ever, which he does, through the ministry of others, in the mass (CT vi–1 333, 338, 344, 346, 361, 367, 377, 387).

Thirdly, the words 'Do this in memory of me' mean 'Offer this sacrifice' because 'this' (which the apostles are commanded to 'do') denotes the *action* of Christ at the Supper. Now what he did was to offer or to sacrifice his body and blood to make atonement for the sins of others, as can be seen from the words 'this body which is delivered up for you' and 'the blood which is shed for you'; and immediately afterwards he commanded his apostles to do the same. Therefore, since it cannot be denied that the supper was a true sacrifice by Christ, so is the mass (*CT* VI–I 334, 346, 355, 361, 370, 376–7, 382, 387–8, 389–90).

Fourthly, the mass fulfils all the conditions of a sacrifice laid down in the Old Testament. There is a priest duly appointed (by virtue of Christ's command, 'Do this'), and an acceptable offering (namely, the body and blood of Christ) which is presented to God on behalf of men to atone for sins and to praise him. And to the Lutheran objection that in the mass there is no true immolation of Christ, because he is not put to death, the reply was that the slaughtering of an animal was not of the essence of sacrifice even in the Old Testament (for example, the bird in Lev. 14: 52–3 and the scapegoat in 16: 6–10, 20–22), only the offering of it to God (*CT* VI–I 327, 332, 344–5, 345–6, 355, 362, 367, 376–7, 383, 387).

Other, supporting, arguments were: (a) that to offer sacrifice is part of man's nature, so that if the mass were not a sacrifice, Christians would be worse off than Jews or pagans, in having no sacrifice to offer on earth (*CT* VI–I 334); (b) that since Christ our Passover is the antitype of the Passover Lamb (I Cor. 5: 7–8), the eucharist must be, like the Jewish Passover, a sacrificial meal (*CT* VI–I 376; 387); (c) that Paul would never have drawn the parallel between the table of the Lord and the tables of demons (I Cor. 10: 21) if he had not believed that sharing the table of the Lord was sharing in a sacrificial meal (*CT* VI–I 376). And throughout the whole discussion, speaker after speaker reiterated that the offering at the altar is, like the Supper, essentially the same as the offering on the cross.

One of the most learned speeches was delivered on 18 August by Alfonso Salmeron, a Spanish Jesuit delegated by the Pope, in which one finds almost all the points mentioned above illustrated in short compass with a wealth of patristic and scholastic references (*CT* VI–I 375–8). But two others also deserve mention, because they endeavoured to argue their way forward by drawing out the implications of the Catholic doctrine of justification (though, surprisingly, neither ever cited the recent decree from Session VI of Trent). Giovanni Antonio Delfino, Provincial of the Conventual Franciscans at Bologna, was the fourth to speak, and put forward very clearly a set of distinctions which are indispensable for any Catholic who wishes to answer the Lutheran arguments:

There is a difference between the eucharist as a sacrament and as a sacrifice, for as a sacrament it is of no avail except to those who receive it, whereas as a sacrifice it is of advantage to others also, for whom it is offered, and for whom the priest intends to offer it and to whom he intends it to be applied.

(Here Delfino's argument about the mass is really calling attention to the fact that the eucharist celebrated by Christ at the Supper was certainly of advantage to others who were not present, but for whom Christ intended to offer it, and to whom he intended its fruits to be applied.) Delfino continued:

In the Canon, the priest mentions both these advantages, when he says 'that as many of us as receive of the sacrament' of the altar, and in another place 'Remember, Lord, thy servants, men and women, for whom we offer this sacrifice of praise.' Furthermore, the Church does not allow sinners to approach or to receive the eucharist as a sacrament; but insofar as it is a sacrifice, it does not exclude them, since it may be to their advantage, in that it may lead them into righteousness, just as it is profitable to the righteous for an increase of grace. [CT VI–I 332, 29–36. Delfino spoke in fact three times, on 3, 9, and 20 August and his own summary of his three interventions, worked into one paper, is to be found in CT VI–2 605–15.]

Girolamo Muzzarelli, too, a Dominican of Bologna, in the very last speech on the subject (22 August), after stressing that the offering of Christ's body and blood in the mass is indeed a sacrifice, added:

But this sacrifice does not avail for the blotting out of sins by way of merit, only by way of successful petition, so that forgiveness is requested and granted, but not as if it were earned or deserved [Hoc autem sacrificium prodest ad peccata delenda, non meritorie, sed impetratorie, ita ut venia impetretur, non autem per modum meriti]. [CT VI–I 390, 6–7, giving the Latin verb impetrare, in the English version, its exact sense as 'to obtain a request']

All these distinctions are essential to the understanding of the doctrine of Trent, but it is interesting that Muzzarelli in fact assumed that the mass was a sacrifice offered by (sinful) man. In seeking to come to terms with one Lutheran objection (that the offering of mass does not obtain the grace of forgiveness as a matter of merit), he has momentarily forgotten that in Catholic doctrine the mass is truly a sacrifice offered by Christ.

The theologians concluded their discussions, begun on 2 August, on 22 August 1547, while the Pope, the Emperor and the bishops who had remained in Trent were still quarrelling furiously about the legitimacy of the move to Bologna, the manner of procedure and the whole future of the Council. History (or Providence) took the latter out of their hands. On 9 September the representatives of Henri II arrived, and with them nine French bishops, bringing the news that many others were already on their way; this would notably strengthen the anti-imperial party at Bologna. But on 11 September news arrived that the Duke of Piacenza, Pierluigi Farnese, the natural son of Paul III, had been assassinated the day before, and two days later, on the 13th, the Council heard that a detachment from the Emperor's forces in Milan had occupied Piacenza and expelled the Farnesi (CT VI–I 451, 456). On the 14th, Cardinal del Monte pointed out that since many bishops were still awaited, it would be imprudent to proceed without them, and the Session adjourned in June until 15 September was on the

14th, by unanimous vote, adjourned *sine die*, 'ad beneplacitum Concilii' (*CT* VI–I 464). Discussion continued, however, for the rest of the year, on abuses in the administration of the sacraments, while Pope and Emperor wrangled ever more fiercely about the legitimacy of the transference to Bologna, until on I February I548 Paul III suspended its proceedings (*CT* VI–I 727–38).

Paul III died on 10 November I549, and on 7 February I550, del Monte was elected Pope, taking the name Julius III. On 14 November I550 he summoned the Council to reconvene, not at Bologna but at Trent, on I May I551. The Session that day (XI) was purely formal, and merely fixed a date for a second meeting, I September. This Session in turn (XII) decided to hold Session XIII on 11 October I551, at which the long-delayed decree on the eucharist as a sacrament was promulgated. It looked as if the decree on the mass would quickly follow.

On 3 December I551, a series of articles concerning the mass and holy orders was put to the theologians. They are evidently based on the articles discussed four and a half years earlier at Bologna, but are more precise. It was by now evident that there was little hope of the Protestants coming to Trent: differences had sharpened, and Luther was no longer the only opponent. Calvin, Melanchthon, Bucer, Zwingli, Bullinger and Urbanus Rhegius are all cited by name, and with the decree on the holy eucharist as sacrament now definitely enacted, the entire discussion was concentrated on the sacrificial nature of the mass.

The Latin text of these articles is printed in *CT* VII–I 375–7 (cf. also VII–2 345–70. An English version of those concerning the mass (omitting the references to the works of the reformers) might read as follows:

I The mass is not a sacrifice nor an offering for sins, but only a commemoration of the sacrifice which took place on the cross; and though the Fathers call it, by a figure of speech, a sacrifice, it is not really and truly such, but only a testament and a promise of the forgiveness of sins.

2 The mass cannot be traced back to the gospel [*non esse ex evangelio*], nor was it instituted by Christ, but invented by men; nor is it a good work, or a meritorious one – indeed, in it the most manifest and multiple idolatry is committed.

3 It is blasphemy against the most holy sacrifice of Christ which took place on the cross, if anyone should believe that the Son of God is offered anew, in the mass, by priests, to God the Father; and to say that Christ is mystically immolated and offered means nothing other than that he is given to us to eat. And by those words 'Do this in memory of me', Christ did not ordain that the apostles should offer his body and blood in the sacrifice of the mass.

4   The canon of the mass abounds in errors and deceitful phrases, ought to be abolished by law, and eschewed as the worst abomination.

5   The mass as a sacrifice is of no advantage either to the living or to the dead; and it is impious to apply it for sins, for works of satisfaction or for other needs.

6   Just as no one can receive communion or absolution on behalf of someone else, so the priest in the mass cannot offer it for someone else.

7   Private masses, that is, those in which the priest alone receives communion and no one else, did not exist before Gregory the Great; are unlawful; and should be abolished. Moreover, they conflict with the institution of Christ, and represent rather excommunication than the communion instituted by Christ.

8   Wine is not the matter of this sacrifice; nor should water be mixed with wine in the chalice; and it is against the institution of Christ.

9   The rite of the Roman Church, by which the words of consecration are uttered secretly and in a low voice, is to be condemned; and the mass should be celebrated only in the common tongue, which all can understand; and it is preposterous to devote certain masses to certain saints.

10 In the celebration of masses, all the ceremonies, vestments and external signs are godless irritants, rather than works of piety. And just as Christ's mass was utterly simple, so the mass will be all the more Christian insofar as it is closer to, and resembles more clearly, that first of all masses.

The theologians examined these articles from 7 to 29 December 1551 (*CT* VII–1 378–437 for the minutes of their meetings; the full text of their submissions, where available, is in *CT* VII–2 370–689). The two Spanish Jesuits sent by the Pope, Diego Laynez and Alfonso Salmeron, opened the discussions, and after them eleven theologians sent by the Emperor, plus seven others from Germany or Austria, held the floor for two weeks, with strong representation (five) from Louvain. Much of the argument was repetitive of what had been said at Bologna, but one new element is worth noting. Melchior Cano, a Spanish Dominican sent by Charles V, strove to settle the basic issue by analysing the concept of sacrifice, arguing that though the death of an animal victim is by no means an essential constituent of sacrifice, the thing offered must in some way be changed or affected, and that this change must be brought about by a duly appointed priest in the course of a sacred ceremony (*CT* VII–1 388; cf. VII–2 536–8). The importance of his speech is that he raised the crucial question: what is a sacrifice? This question was taken up by Johann Gropper, a secular priest sent by the Elector of Cologne, and a man deeply anxious to build bridges to the Lutherans. Gropper, taking his definition from Augustine's *City of God*, x, 5 'a sacrifice is a visible sacrament – that is, a sacred sign – of an invisible sacrifice'), dwelt upon the necessary correspondence and inter-relationship of the invisible or internal offering, and its visible or externally observable expression. 'The sacrifice of the mass represents Christ's invisible sacrifice at the Supper, and his visible sacrifice on the cross, and that which he perpetually makes by interceding for us with his Father in heaven' (*CT* VII–1 406, 23–5). The essence of the sacrifice of the mass lies therefore in those three elements which were instituted by Christ: (a) the consecration, by which Christ once crucified now glorified becomes really present on the altar; (b) the offering of the body and blood of Christ by those who minister only in his name and at his behest; (c) the communion, by which the faithful share in this sacrifice, at his command. And since the consecration and the offering are effected by Christ himself (men are only his agents or ministers), the mass is in reality a sacrifice offered by Christ himself, and therefore cannot in any way detract from the sacrifice of the cross (*CT* VII–1 406–8; cf. also VII–2 442–7).

Another thirty theologians were still waiting to speak when discussion was abruptly terminated on 29 December 1551, on the ground that everything had been sufficiently examined (*CT* VII–1 437 and n. 9). At the same time, the draft of a decree (complete except for its canons) was prepared by a small group of theologians within the space of one week, starting on 26 December (for the date and authorship see the letter of Francisco de Toledo to Charles V in *CT* XI 741, and Jedin 1970, 524, n. 26). On 3 January 1552 the Fathers received both the draft of the decree on the mass and the report of the theologians on the ten articles given above pp. 166–7. Not surprisingly, the report rejected all the articles, but it was an exaggeration to say (as did the senior legate, Cardinal Crescenzio) that all ten were rejected 'unanimously, as heretical' (*CT* VII–1 438, 6); rejected they certainly were, but the official report is careful to note dissentient views and cautious qualifications (*CT* VII–1 440–1). Since the Fathers in their subsequent debate for all practical purposes endorsed the judgement of the theologians, there is no need to pursue this matter further. Suffice it to say that *if* the mass *is* a sacrifice expiatory of sin, offered by Christ himself, then the Protestant objections to it listed in articles 4 to 10 have no force (and any Protestant theologian would agree). The only issue at stake is *whether* the mass can truly (not by a figure of speech) be termed a sacrifice offered by Christ himself through the ministry of men.

The draft decree proposed on 3 January 1552 is obviously of immense historical interest, since it represents the first attempt at Trent to set out, in a positive form, Catholic teaching about the mass as a sacrifice; indeed, it was the first attempt by any council to do that. Yet it appears that only one copy of this document has survived. It is the copy which belonged to the Bishop of Vienna, who annotated it to indicate what alterations he thought needful or desirable and then sent it to the secretary of the Council; and by this happy accident it was preserved, in the Vatican Archives, and eventually published in 1960. Even so, it is not printed out straightforwardly in the proceedings of the Council: the reader must reconstruct it for himself by taking the revised version distributed on 20 January and printed in *CT* vii–1 475–83, and following in the footnotes the variants listed as *C 18*. *C 18* gives the original version of the text.

Since this document is about half the length of the present article, lack of space precludes its reproduction here. But that in turn is a blessing for the reader, for the text is not only long but long-winded: the kindest judgement one can make is that it does express clearly and fully virtually all the arguments which had been used at Trent up to that date. But one most important observation must be made. This first draft, in its second chapter, speaks explicitly of 'these two sacrifices' (of the eucharist and of the cross): its exact words are 'Ita autem de duobus his sacrificiis sermo habetur ...' True, this same chapter repeats time and time again that the sacrifice of the mass derives all its efficacy from the sacrifice of the cross; but in so doing, it clearly and repeatedly implies that there are here two distinct sacrifices (*CT* vii–1 477–8, footnote *n*). Such language was not calculated to mollify Protestants, and when the Fathers came to debate the draft, from 7 to 13 January, there was enough opposition to the notion of 'two sacrifices' for the whole of the second chapter to be abandoned, and replaced by a more acceptable version (given in *CT* vii–1 477–9).

But what had gone wrong, that a whole chapter which was so swiftly rejected by the Fathers ever got into a draft in the first place? The seven men mentioned by Francisco de Toledo as authors of the draft were all sound theologians; five of them in their speeches had stressed that the mass is not a different sacrifice from that of the cross (*CT* vii–1 386–7; 389; 404; 407; 436) and the other two had not spoken on this point. Hence Jedin (1970, 524, n. 26) may well be right in suspecting that their original draft was altered by the legate Crescenzio and his associates, probably by Laynez, for the offending chapter approximates most closely to his speech, towards the end of which we read: 'Nor does the sacrifice of the eucharist conflict with that of the cross; for it draws its strength from that sacrifice, and is its reward; it therefore adds to the passion of Christ rather than detracts from it [*arrogat igitur, non derogat passioni Christi*]' (*CT* vii–1 382, 34–36; cf. also vii–2 530–2. Salmeron, too, had argued that if the eucharist is not a sacrifice, then the sacrament of holy orders does not make men 'priests' (*CT* vii–2 532–4). Laynez and Salmeron had been thirty-four and thirty-one years old when they arrived at Trent in 1546, and they had not been slow to make their presence felt; indeed they had successfully opposed the fifty-four-year-old Seripando. By 1551 they were taking precedence (as the Pope's nominees) over all other theologians, speaking first and being allowed to speak far longer. Some found this less than congenial. 'Summus Pontifex habet hic duos jesuitas, doctissimos sane, sed adhuc iuvenes', wrote a Louvain canonist on 31 December 1551 (*CT* XI 753, 6). The only legate, Crescenzio, a friend of Ignatius Loyola and a stern upholder of the privileges and interests of the Papal Curia, no doubt regarded the two young Jesuits as his most dependable allies. The Fathers were less happy about his authoritarian ways. 'Il traite les évêques comme des esclaves', wrote one observer (*CT* XI 700, 11); the most learned theologians had come from the most remote parts of Spain and from Louvain, wrote another, 'à une assemblée, qui ne veut pas les emploier' (*CT* XI 699, 28–9). The seeds of the party divisions of the counter-reformation Church were already taking root, with the Jesuits standing firm for papal absolutism and an uncompromising rejection of everything that savoured of Protestantism, and the bishops searching for a more practical solution to a bewilderingly complex pastoral problem. The action of the bishops in striking out immediately the offending second chapter on the mass, and deleting all references to the 'two sacrifices' of Christ, shows that they were not prepared to be mere tools of the legate and that they were truly sensitive to the intricacy of the theological problems facing them.

In the short debate from 7 to 13 January 1552, two contributions are significant. Tommaso Campeggio, Bishop of Feltre and brother of the Cardinal, Lorenzo, who had dealt with Henry VIII's divorce, asked for a change in the wording of the text: 'he would prefer it to read *that in the Mass there is a sacrifice*, not *that the Mass is a sacrifice*' (*CT* VII–1 446, 16–17; cf. VII–2 611, 43–45, where the full text of his intervention is given on 610–12). Cornelio Musso, Bishop of Bitonto, was more adventurous still in his analysis:

He showed that the Mass was a sacrifice and propitiatory for sins, and that all the articles should be condemned as heretical. But when dealing with the formulation of doctrine [i.e. the draft decree], he opposed [*improbavit*] the suggestion that Christ offered himself at the Supper, because in that case his death would have been pointless [*alias gratis mortuus esset*], since the offering would have been sufficient to reconcile us with God. Nor does St Paul, when speaking about the sacrifice of Christ, ever speak of the Supper, but always of the cross. At the Supper, Christ instituted both sacrament and sacrifice, saying, *Do this*; but he offered only one sacrifice [*semel tantum sacrificavit*], namely, on the cross. (*CT* VII–1 449, 27–9, 34–5)

This latter speech is especially significant, for Sebastiano Pighi, the deputy president (but not a papal legate), sided with the Bishop of Bitonto against all the others who had spoken, stating that he too held that Christ did not offer himself at the Supper, and affirming that in the mass we commemorate the offering on the cross, not an offering at the Supper (*CT* VII–1 459).

After the debate, a commission formulated a set of canons on the mass and holy orders, which were distributed on Monday 18 January, and a revised version of the decree on the mass by Wednesday the 20th, plus a revised text on holy orders by Thursday morning. (The proposed canons are given in *CT* VII–1 460–1, the long decree on the mass on p. 475–83, that on the sacrament of Orders on pp. 483–9). The draft of the first canon on the mass read:

Si quis dixerit, in missa non esse sacrificium nec oblationem pro peccatis, sed tantum commemorationem sacrificii in cruce peracti, aut vocari translato nomine sacrificium, at vere et proprie non esse: anathema sit. (*CT* VII–1 460, 10–12)

If anyone should say that in the mass there is no sacrifice nor any offering for sins, but only a commemoration of the sacrifice which took place on the cross; or that it is by metaphor called a sacrifice, but is not truly and properly such: let him be anathema.

Campeggio, who was a member of the drafting committee (*CT* VII–1 459, 27), had won his point, and it was intended to enact the revised version of the decree and canons on the following Monday, 25 January 1552.

But, that very week, the Emperor made one last bid for reconciliation, if not between the Pope and the Protestants, at least between the Council and the Lutherans. On Monday the 18th, he wrote from Innsbruck to his ambassadors at Trent instructing them to press for a hearing of the Lutheran emissaries who had arrived in the city on the 10th, and urging them to ensure that the Council took no decisions on doctrinal matters until a deputation of Lutheran theologians, already *en route*, had arrived; and by the same post he wrote to Francisco de Toledo (*CT* XI 780–3). The two letters reached Trent on Tuesday (*CT* XI 784, 22). On the Wednesday, Don Francisco saw the papal legate and with some difficulty extracted from him a promise that the Council would not proceed to any doctrinal definitions until the Lutheran theologians came, since that was the wish of the Emperor (*CT* XI 787, 1–5).

Charles V's intervention came just in time, for the next formal Session, to enact and to promulgate a definitive decree on the mass, had for three months been fixed for the following Monday, 25 January, but with the proviso that the German Protestants should be guaranteed safe conduct to present their case before then. Indeed, the Council, in Session XIII (11 October 1551), had deferred pronouncing on giving the cup to the laity and on children's communion because it wished to hear the Lutherans first (*CT* VII–1 207). A public promise had been made at Session XIII; representatives of two Lutheran princes were already in Trent; and a decision was both urgent and imperative. (We may add that but for Charles' intervention the Roman Catholic Church would have had, as its Tridentine decree on the mass, the incredibly wordy, very unsatisfactory and hastily prepared draft printed in *CT* VII–1 475–83.)

On Saturday, 23 January the Council agreed to hear the two Lutheran delegations. So on Sunday the 24th, the embassy from the Duke of Württemberg presented its case in the morning, the first Protestants to appear there; and in the afternoon, a more important and more outspoken delegation put its argument, on behalf of their Prince, Maurice of Saxony. Both delegations not only requested the Council to halt all proceedings until their own theologians had arrived, but asked for a 'free, ecumenical, Christian and general council' of all Christian bodies, in which the Pope would not be the ultimate judge, and in which the decrees already enacted at Trent should be deemed not yet ratified, since the other party had not been heard. The Council heard them, and promised to consider their views (*CT* VII–I 465–75).

Hence Session XV (25 January 1552) merely adjourned until 19 March, to give the Lutherans time to arrive and to discuss the proposed texts. This was unanimously agreed, and the Lutheran theologians were daily expected; but by 19 March, Maurice of Saxony had broken with Charles V to ally himself with Henri II, and the subsequent war led the Council on 26 April 1552 (Session XVI) to suspend its activities for two years.

Wars dragged on, half of Europe committed itself to different forms of Protestantism, and it was not until ten years later, on 18 January 1562, that the Catholic bishops reassembled at Trent. On 19 July thirteen articles on the sacrifice of the mass were presented to the theologians for comment, but unlike the articles of 1551 (see above, pp. 166–7) they were not taken from the works of the Reformers, were phrased as questions and were not so precise. For example, the first reads: 'Is the mass merely a commemoration of the sacrifice at the Supper, but not a true sacrifice?' They are printed in *CT* VIII 719, and Jedin (1975, 338, n. 11) confesses that he can throw no light on their drafting or authorship; and they are so general that to translate them would not help our argument forward. Not surprisingly, some of the Fathers at Trent thought it a waste of time to go over the same ground again; why not take up the matter where it had been left in January 1552 (*CT* VIII 722, 1–4)?

Seripando, absent through ill-health in 1551–2, was now a cardinal, one of five papal legates and the deputy president. He pointed out that in 1552 only some seventy Fathers had been present, whereas now there were 180, of whom only three or four had been at Trent ten years earlier. It was only reasonable, therefore, to let the Fathers hear the theologians again – though the latter might with advantage be briefer (*CT* VIII 722, 4–8; also III–I 373, 1–5). And so they began to discuss the thirteen articles, with Salmeron once again leading the exposition, starting with Mal. 1 : 11 and working his way through the Melchizedek texts and Hebrews to the Pauline text on Christ our Passover and the words 'Do this in memory of me.' Before an audience of well over 2,000, 'he thus expounded this first article in a learned and godly fashion' for between two and three hours (*CT* VIII 722–4).

Truth to tell, there is little of interest in these 'wearisome and repetitive' speeches (21 July to 4 August, *CT* VIII 722–51; cf. Jedin 1975, 338, n. 12), for the questions which formed the agenda were too broad to permit anyone to develop an idea in depth. One question notable by its absence was whether the Last Supper was a sacrifice. Perhaps those who had compiled the list of questions took this for granted; if so, they were very soon to receive a rude shock.

On 6 August, a text with canons attached was distributed to the Fathers; it followed closely the order and often the wording of the draft of 1552, and the main improvement was that it ran to less than half the length (*CT* VIII 751–5). Chapter I repeatedly implied and affirmed that the Last Supper was in fact a true sacrifice, and deduced that therefore so was the mass ('hoc verum sacrificium divinissimum declarant', *CT* VIII 752, 1–2). But whereas the draft of 1552 had stated explicitly that Christ offered *himself* to his Father at the Supper ('se suo Patri sub sensibilibus panis et vini speciebus in ultima cena obtulit', *CT* VII–1 475, 23–4), the new draft contented itself with saying that he there offered a sacrifice, without specifying any further detail. This led to a heated debate (11–27 August), in which four broad lines of opinion emerged.

First, there were those who maintained that Christ offered himself to the Father at the Supper in expiation of the sins of the human race, and who therefore concluded that the Supper was an expiatory sacrifice. They argued that this visible communion-sacrifice does not derogate from the power of the redemptive sacrifice of the cross, but enables men to share in it, just as the Old Testament sacrifices enabled men to share by anticipation in the forgiveness of sins won only on Calvary. (And before the Fathers began their discussions, Salmeron circulated a long paper begging them to assert explicitly that Christ offered himself at the Supper as an expiatory sacrifice, *CT* III–1 375, 42–44.)

A second group was willing to admit that Christ offered and instituted a sacrifice at the Supper, but only a 'sacrifice of praise and thanksgiving', a perfect sacrifice indeed, but only a 'sacrificium eucharisticum', i.e. of adoration and thanksgiving, not a sacrifice in expiation of sin. Thus the sacrifice on the cross was still necessary.

A third group (which gathered strength, and even adherents from the first two) sought to restrict the decree to the essentials of Catholic faith, suggesting that the text should read simply 'that Christ offered himself', leaving the option open between the first two.

Under the fourth heading, we should group together all who held rather personal views which do not fall under the other three. One (from the Bishop of Chioggia) is important, namely, that the sacrifice at the Supper was the *beginning* of the sacrifice on the cross. (The speeches are reported in *CT* VIII 755–90, Chioggia's on p. 762, and summarized by a contemporary diarist in III–1 375–7.)

The one point on which everyone agreed was that the draft was far too long, and so a drastically shortened version was prepared, and distributed on 5 September 1562 (*CT* VIII 909–12). By stating in Chapter 1 that at the Supper Christ 'offered to God the Father his body and blood under the outward appearances of bread and wine', it left the way open for any of the four views just listed. This becomes even more evident if we contrast the wording of the first canon in each draft. On 6 August it had read:

Si quis dixerit, missam non esse sacrificium, sed commemorationem tantum sacrificii in cruce peracti, aut vocari translato nomine sacrificium, vere tamen et proprie non esse: anathema sit. (*CT* VIII 754, 25–7)

If anyone should say that the mass is not a sacrifice, but only a commemoration of the sacrifice which took place on the cross; or that it is by metaphor called a sacrifice, but is not truly and properly such: let him be anathema.

That text quite openly represents a reversal of the draft put forward on 20 January 1552 to the previous text of 3 January 1552 (see above, pp. 168–71), which was in practice a return to the view advocated by Salmeron. The new draft of 5 September 1562 reinstated the view held by Campeggio, though in a different form (because the canons had been restructured):

Si quis dixerit, in missa non offerri Deo verum et proprium sacrificium, aut quod offerre [*sic*] non sit aliud quam nobis Christum ad manducandum dari, vel tantum prodesse sumenti: anathema sit. (*CT* VIII 911, 30–2)

If anyone should say that in the mass there is not offered to God a true and proper sacrifice; or that the offering is nothing other than Christ being given to us to eat; or that it profits only the recipient (of Holy Communion): let him be anathema.

That the mass *is a* sacrifice, or that a sacrifice *is offered* in the mass: here we have two different statements. The first would logically imply that the mass is a sacrifice *additional to* that of the cross; the second does not, but allows one to hold that *what* is offered to God in the mass is the sacrifice of the cross.

Only one other point need be mentioned about this document. Though Chapter 1 leaves open the question whether Christ *at the Supper* offered only a sacrifice of praise and thanksgiving (that is, not a sacrifice expiatory of sin), canon 2 anathematizes those who would say the same about the mass: 'If anyone should say that the mass is only a sacrifice of praise and thanksgiving, but not propitiatory...' (*CT* VIII 911, 33–5). So the debate moved into its final phase.

Seripando, as a papal legate and deputy chairman, was unable to intervene in this debate, but he did write, for the peace of his conscience and for posterity, an admirable short paper 'concerning the Offering of Christ at the Supper', preserved in the Vatican Library and first published in 1967 (*CT* XIII–1 732–5). He complained that during the debate the most learned men at the Council had been ridiculed or ignored (*CT* XIII–1 735, 36–44) –

an evident reference to the lack of tolerance displayed by the party which wanted to define that the Last Supper was a sacrifice; and set forth his own opinion on the question. One short text may be cited to illustrate the lucidity and power of his thinking:

I have, too, been not a little influenced by St Thomas [Aquinas]. He dealt most carefully with the [Old Testament] types of the eucharist, yet did not put forward even one type as prefiguring the sacrifice which they talk of at the Supper. On the contrary, he compared the offering of Melchizedek with that which in the eucharist is merely the sacrament, namely, with the outward appearances of bread and wine, not with any offering; and when he was discussing the three kinds of sacrifice which were offered under the Old Law – the sin-offering, the peace-offering and the whole-burnt-offering – he related every one of them to the passion of Christ, making no mention of any other sacrifice at the Supper. (CT XIII–I 735, 19–26)

This paper, written between 7 and 15 September, while the Fathers were debating the new, shortened draft, was not circulated among them; but Seripando did show it to the principal legate, Cardinal Gonzaga, and there can be little doubt that it influenced the events to be narrated in the next paragraph.

The revising committee had introduced into Chapter 1 the statement that at the Supper Christ 'offered to God the Father his body and blood under the outward appearances of bread and wine' (see above, p. 174). Cardinal Madruzzo, the Bishop of Trent, proposed that there should here be inserted the words 'pro nobis verum sacrificium', 'a true sacrifice for us' (CT VIII 912, 17–18). This insertion, had it been accepted, would have affirmed not only that the Supper was a true sacrifice, but also that it was an expiatory sacrifice ('pro nobis', 'for us'). Madruzzo's proposal received considerable support, but was also opposed, and thus did not find a place in the final decree, the wording of which required the approval of the papal legates.

Thus on 16 September the new draft proposed on the 5th was approved with only minor alterations; and this, the final decree, promulgated on 17 September 1562 at Session XXII, while it firmly declares that Christ at the Supper instituted a visible sacrifice which is offered in the mass, carefully refrains from declaring that the Last Supper was, or that the mass is, in itself or by itself, a sacrifice. The Latin text from CT VIII 959–62 is easily accessible in Denzinger–Schönmetzer, 1738–59, and there is an English translation of the complete decree in Schroeder 1941 (pp. 145–50).

But for the convenience of the general reader, a translation of Chapters 1 and 2, and of canons 1–4, may be included here, with a few prefatory remarks. First, the words *oblatio* and *immolatio* are here used interchangeably and equivalently to signify in a general way 'a sacrificial offering', without specifying the nature of that offering; and they are certainly not used as in later theology (see below, p. 179) with two distinct meanings. Secondly, Chapter 1 affirms unambiguously that Christ redeemed mankind by his once-for-all sacrifice on the cross. Thirdly, the main thrust of Chapter 1 is an affirmation that Christ at the Supper instituted a visible sacrifice which was to be for ever continued in the mass *in order that* through this rite the once-for-all redeeming sacrifice of the cross might be rendered present ('repraesentaretur') to all future ages, so that men by participation in this communion-sacrifice which takes place in the mass might receive a share in the grace of forgiveness which comes from the sacrifice of the cross. The argument is expressed not in scholastic terms, but in Latin prose of unforgettable lucidity which weaves together all the biblical symbols used in the conciliar debates.

THE COUNCIL OF TRENT: SESSION XXII

CHAPTER 1

Under the former covenant (as the Apostle Paul tells us), because of the inherent imperfection of the Levitical priesthood, there was no possibility of reaching perfection. It was therefore necessary (since God the Father of mercies so ordained it) that there should arise another priest 'according to the order of Melchizedek', our Lord Jesus Christ, who would have the power to perfect, and to lead to perfection, as many as were to be made holy. He was to offer himself to God the Father once only [*semel*], at the moment of death, on the altar of the cross, there to secure for them eternal redemption. But since his priesthood was not to be terminated by death, he, our Lord and God, willed to leave to his beloved spouse the Church a visible sacrifice (as human nature requires). Its purpose was to symbolize and render present [*repraesentaretur*] that blood-stained sacrifice which was to take place once for all on the cross; to keep alive the memory of it until the very end of the world; and to apply its saving power for the forgiveness of those sins which we commit daily. At the Last Supper, therefore, 'on the night he was betrayed', making clear that he was appointed 'a priest according to the order of Melchizedek, for ever', he offered to God the Father, under the outward appearances of bread and wine, his own body and blood; and under the same symbols, he gave them to the apostles to eat. It was at that point too that he made them priests of the new covenant, and ordered them, and their successors in the priesthood, to make the same offering [*ut offerent*], through these words: 'Do this in memory of me', as the Catholic Church has always understood and taught. The multitude of the sons of Israel was accustomed to sacrifice the old Passover in memory of its exodus from Egypt; and he, after celebrating the old, instituted a new Passover, in which he himself was to be offered in sacrifice [*immolandum*] by the Church, through priests, under visible signs. This sacrifice was to be offered in memory of his own passing-over out of this world to the Father, when, by the shedding of his own blood, he redeemed us, 'delivered us from the dominion of darkness and carried us over into his kingdom' [Col. 1:13].

Furthermore, this is indeed a clean offering which cannot be defiled by any unworthiness or wickedness on the part of those who offer it. It is that which the Lord through Malachi foretold would be offered in every place, as a clean offering, to his name, which would be great among the Gentiles. The Apostle Paul, too, writing to the Corinthians, has a not obscure reference to it, when he says that those who have been rendered unclean by sharing in the table of devils cannot be admitted to share in the table of the Lord (understanding by the word 'table', in each case, an altar). Finally, this is that offering which was prefigured, in the era of natural religion and of the Law, by various types of sacrifice; for everything good that was signified in those sacrifices is contained in this one, which is as it were their consummation and perfection.

CHAPTER 2

In this divine sacrifice, which takes place in the mass, the very same Christ is present [*continetur*] and is, with no shedding of blood, sacrificially offered [*immolatur*], who 'once sacrificed himself amid blood' on the altar of the cross [cf. Heb. 9:27]. Therefore the holy Synod teaches that this sacrifice is truly propitiatory, and that through this same sacrifice it comes to pass that, provided we draw near to God with a sincere heart and true faith, with fear and reverence, in contrition and repentance, 'we obtain mercy, and find the grace which helps us in our time of need' [Heb. 4:16]. For by this sacrificial offering the Lord is indeed appeased, concedes the grace and gift of repentance, forgives great faults and even heinous sins. For it is one and the same victim, now offering himself through the ministry of priests, who offered himself long ago on the cross; only the manner of offering is different. And the fruits of that sacrificial offering (the one amid blood) are abundantly obtained through this other sacrificial offering, in which there is no shedding of blood: so far are we from saying that this one derogates from that. Hence it is duly offered not only for the sins of the faithful during their lifetime, for the punishments they have deserved and the deeds of satisfaction which they rightly owe, and for other needs, but also for those who have died in Christ, according to the tradition of the Apostles.

Canons 1–4

1   If anyone should say that in the Mass there is not offered to God a true and proper sacrifice; or that the offering is nothing other than Christ's being given to us to eat: let him be anathema.
2   If anyone should say that by the words 'Do this in memory of me' Christ did not appoint the apostles priests; or that he did not ordain that they and other priests should offer his body and blood: let him be anathema.
3   If anyone should say that the mass is only a sacrifice of praise and thanksgiving, or merely a service commemorative of the sacrifice which took place on the cross, but not a propitiatory sacrifice; or that it avails only to one who receives communion; or that it should not be offered for the living and the dead, for their sins, for the punishments they have deserved and the deeds of satisfaction which they rightly owe, and for other needs: let him be anathema.
4   If anyone should say that by the sacrifice of the mass blasphemy is committed against the most holy sacrifice of Christ which took place on the cross, or that it derogates from the sacrifice of the cross: let him be anathema.

It requires but a few minutes' reflection to perceive that *if* the doctrine set out here, with all its careful qualifications and distinctions, is true, a number of conclusions logically follow. The major ones are set out in the remaining chapters and canons of Trent: (1) when a mass is offered in honour of a saint, it is not offered *to* that saint, but to God alone, who bestows on the saints their crowns, in thanksgiving to him for their life and example (Chapter 3 and canon 5); (2) the doctrine of sacrifice implied in the canon of the mass is not erroneous (Chapter 4 and canon 6); (3) the external ceremonies which accompany the mass (such as the use of vestments and incense) are legitimate means of showing forth to men 'the majesty of so great a sacrifice' (Chapter 5 and canon 7); (4) even a mass in which the celebrant alone receives holy communion is none the less a public act of the Church, offered in the name of the Church for all who belong to the body of Christ (Chapter 6 and canon 8); (5) the custom of mixing a little water with the wine before the consecration is to be continued, because Christ is believed to have done so; because it reminds us that from his side there flowed water as well as blood; and because it signifies our union with his sacrifice (Chapter 7, cf. canon 9); (6) though it was not judged expedient to celebrate the mass in the vernacular, priests should frequently explain to their congregations the doctrine of the mass, and the meaning of the rites and ceremonies (Chapter 8). Finally, the Council firmly rejected two other complaints: (a) that the Roman custom of reciting part of the canon quietly was to be condemned, and (b) that the mass should be celebrated *only* in the vernacular (canon 9). The Latin text of these chapters and canons may be found in Denzinger–Schönmetzer 1963, 1744–50 and 1755–9.

The interpretation of this decree in Roman Catholic theology from Trent to the present day is a subject so vast that even the most sketchy outline would call for an essay of its own; those who wish to pursue the quest may be referred to the magisterial work of M. Lepin (1926), or to the equally comprehensive article by A. Michel (1928). For as a result of the Reformers' onslaught, Catholic theologians devoted the best of their abilities to this central point of difference, and began to explore in detail the problem of *how* the mass may be termed a sacrifice. Since their predecessors had hardly discussed it, and since the Tridentine decree was so carefully phrased as not to exclude any of the very divergent opinions held by the Fathers at the Council, these later theologians had a free field to develop their speculations and theories. All that Trent required was that Catholics should hold fast to the doctrine that in the mass a sacrifice is offered which is not merely a service of praise and thanksgiving, but also a sacrifice expiatory of sins, and a source of abundant grace, to the profit not only of the living, but also of the dead; that in this sacrifice, what is offered is Christ crucified; and that the priest who brings this offering before the Father is none other than Christ himself, acting now here on earth through the agency of his ministers (who thus fulfil on his behalf a priestly role).

Among all the post-Tridentine theologians who have written on this subject, one author is outstanding: Maurice de la Taille, S.J. His monumental work *Mysterium Fidei* (1921) finally disposed of much dead wood from previous centuries: theories of sacrifice applied to the mass of which some were curious, some bizarre and many simply unsatisfactory or incomplete. In their place he presented a clear and coherent theology along the lines advocated by Seripando and his friends, notably by the Bishop of Chioggia (see above, pp. 173–5).

De la Taille's thesis is essentially a very simple one. Every sacrifice must consist of the formal, liturgical offering of something to God (*oblatio*), and of an act by which what is offered is positively given over to God (*immolatio*); and it must be accepted by God (*acceptatio*). At the Last Supper, Christ offered himself and his life to God in a solemn liturgical act, as is evident from the words spoken ('the body which is given' ... 'the blood which is shed'). On the cross, his obedient acceptance of death turned the crime of his executioners into (on his part) an act of self-immolation, by which he gave himself totally to God. By the resurrection, God signified to the disciples his acceptance of that sacrifice. Thus the Supper was not a sacrifice complete in itself or by itself, but in it a sacrifice was offered, a sacrifice which was to be consummated only on Calvary.

In the mass, he continues, there is an analogous offering. Christ at the Supper offered his life for others, to die as a victim of his own obedience. Christ in the mass offers himself to the Father along with all the members of his body which is the Church (who in the mass join themselves with his self-offering) as the victim already given over into the Father's hands on Calvary, and eternally pleasing to him. The relationship between the Supper, the cross and the mass may therefore be expressed in this way (omitting the details about the Church, and the rather obvious fact that the mass is offered through the ministry of ordained priests):

THE LAST SUPPER	THE CROSS	THE MASS
The offering	The immolation	The offering
of Christ as victim	of Christ as victim	of Christ as victim
by Christ as priest	by Christ as priest	by Christ as priest
to be immolated	already offered	already immolated

The virtue of de la Taille's theology is that it undubitably safeguards the uniqueness of Christ's sacrifice, once for all, on the cross, and brings it into the very centre of the mass. And though not all Roman Catholic theologians would accept so precise a definition of sacrifice (*oblatio – immolatio – acceptatio*), or this theory of the relationship between the Supper, the cross and the mass, all are agreed that Christ's self-immolation at his death is sacramentally signified by the consecration of the bread and wine, and by the words there spoken: 'This is my body which is given up for you . . . This is the cup of my blood, which will be shed for you.'

The essence of Christ's sacrifice lies not in the fact that he was put to death, but in the fact that he willingly accepted death. There is no place in Christian theology, if it is to be consistent with the New Testament, for the view that an angry God had to be appeased by human suffering, or that he demanded that mankind should undergo a cruel punishment as just retribution for the unlawful pride and pleasure found in sin. The essence of Christ's redemptive sacrifice lies rather in his total obedience to the will of the Father, as Heb. 10: 5–10 makes clear; and it is equally clear in Phil. 2: 8, where the whole weight of the sentence falls on the assertion that Christ *became obedient*, and proved the completeness of his obedience by enduring unto death, even death on a cross. Thomas Aquinas makes much of this theme in the *Summa Theologiae* III, qq. 46–9, especially in q. 47, art. 2 ('Did Christ die out of obedience?') and q. 48, art. 3 ('Did Christ's passion achieve its effect by being a sacrifice?'). In the latter article, in his reply to the third objection, he writes: 'On the part of those who put Christ to death, the passion was a crime; on the part of Christ, who suffered out of love, it was a sacrifice. And that is why Christ himself is said to have offered this sacrifice, and not those who slew him.'

Stated in these terms, the doctrine of Christ's redeeming sacrifice has lost none of its relevance today. And it is this doctrine which lies at the heart of Roman Catholic faith and practice concerning the mass. Catholics believe that in the mass there is a sacramental re-enactment and rendering present (*repraesentatio*) of Christ's sacrifice, in which Christ crucified, now risen, becomes really and truly present on the altar. Such a belief confronts those who hold it with an awesome challenge as well as a comfortable word. For the mass is then in no sense a ritual good work on the part of men, dispensing them from moral effort and automatically (*ex opere operato*) cleansing them from sin without need of response on their part. On the contrary, it is a divine summons to unite oneself, by prayerful participation and especially by Holy Communion, with the total self-dedication of Jesus Christ the Redeemer in his obedience unto death, even to death on a cross.

NOTES

1 When Leo XIII opened the Vatican Archives to scholars, the German Catholic historical society known as the Görresgesellschaft decided in 1894 to undertake the publication of the proceedings of the Council of Trent. The first volume appeared in 1901, the most recent in 1980 (*Concilium Tridentinum: Diariorum, Actorum, Epistularum, Tractatum nova collectio*. Edidit Societas Goerresiana (Freiburg-im-Breisgau: Herder)). It is to this series that all the references bracketed as *CT* allude; references are to volume, page and (where relevant) lines. Four of the thirteen volumes (namely III, VI, VII and XIII) are being published in several

parts, and these are distinguished as III–1, VII–2, etc. Thus a reference to *CT* VIII 755, 2–3 gives volume, page and lines; but *CT* VII–1 325; 354; 368 gives volume, part and three page references without specifying any particular lines. The translations from this work are my own.

2 M. Luther, *Formula missae et Communionis* (1523), in *D. Martin Luthers Werke. Kritische Gesamtausgabe*, vol. XII (Weimar, 1891), pp. 211–12.

3 M. Luther, *De Abroganda Missa Privata* (1521), in the same edition, vol. VIII (1889), pp. 431–45.

REFERENCES

de la Taille, M. (1921). *Mysterium Fidei* (3rd edn, enlarged and revised, 1931). Paris: Beauchesne

Denzinger-Schönmetzer (1963). *Enchiridion Symbolorum*, first edited by H. Denzinger in 1854; 32nd edn, completely revised, extended and annotated by A. Schönmetzer. Barcelona, Freiburg, Rome, New York: Herder

Jedin, H. (1957). *A History of the Council of Trent*, trans. Ernest Graf, vol. I. London and Edinburgh: Nelson

(1961). *A History of the Council of Trent*, trans. Ernest Graf, vol. II. London and Edinburgh: Nelson

(1970). *Geschichte des Konzils von Trient*, vol. III. Freiburg, Basel, Vienna: Herder

(1975). *Geschichte des Konzils von Trient*, vol. IV (in two parts: all references are to Part 1). Freiburg, Basel, Vienna: Herder

Lepin, M. (1926). *L'Idée du sacrifice de la Messe d'après les théologiens*. Paris: Beauchesne

Michel, A. (1928). La Messe chez les théologiens postérieurs au Concile de Trente. In the *Dictionnaire de Théologie Catholique*, x: 1, cols. 1143–315. Paris: Letouzey et Ané

Schroeder, H. J. (1941). *Canons and Decrees of the Council of Trent*. Rockford, Illinois: Tan Books Inc. [Reprinted 1978.]

Tappert, T. G. (1959). *The Book of Concord: the Confessions of the Evangelical Lutheran Church*. Philadelphia: The Mühlenberg Press

IO

SACRIFICE IN PURITAN TYPOLOGY

S. HARDMAN MOORE

'The sacrifice Christ doth *placare Deo*, appease an incensed God; our sacrifices do but *placere Deum*, please an appeased God' (Mather 1705, 188). The Reformation saw a serious revaluation of the place of sacrifice in Christian theology, which if it in one sense firmly diverted attention from the present to the past, from human acts to divine, in another allowed new value to be given to 'sacrifice' in the Christian life. The significance attached to Christians' 'spiritual sacrifice' in one branch of developing Protestantism is to be investigated here, as it appears in devotional literature and commentaries produced by seventeenth-century puritans – English Protestants of the third or fourth generation. Sacrifice was not often a primary theme in their exposition of the Christian life, and yet, despite an untidiness of evidence, it is clear that certain allusions to sacrifice were conventional, part of a common rhetoric, a common imagery.

Returning to what they understood to be New Testament tradition, early Protestant reformers had taken up an Israelite distinction between propitiatory sacrifice for sin and a 'peace-offering' made in gratitude for present or hoped-for blessings. Christ's death was identified with the former and Christians' self-offering or petition in Christ with the latter. These fundamentally different kinds of sacrifice, it was argued, had been confused by the Church's teaching on the place of works done in grace 'making satisfaction' for sin, and above all by the belief that in a priest's offering of the mass Christ's sacrifice was again presented to God. To end such confusion, the sufficiency of Christ's past self-offering on the cross was exalted to exclude the necessity of present propitiatory sacrifice and any suggestion of a mingling of human activity with divine in atonement. The present dimension of sacrifice in the Church was transformed. 'Spiritual priesthood' was said to include all Christians: its limitation to the clergy had often been justified by the priest's role at the mass, but now it was claimed that all in Christ shared his priesthood, consecrated by his sacrifice, and could offer 'spiritual sacrifice' in him. Seventeenth-century puritans assumed these premisses.

'Puritanism' is a loaded and ambiguous term. Recent scholarship has shown how artificial it is to make a rigid distinction between 'Anglican' and 'Puritan' in the Elizabethan and Jacobean Church: it cannot be maintained on grounds of conduct or doctrine – there are too many exceptions to prove a rule. Not until the rise of Arminianism in the 1620s roused Calvinist orthodoxy to opposition did a divide appear, and yet still within the 'puritan' movement a wide diversity of views on doctrine and practice continued to co-exist (Tyacke 1973). Those whose writings will be mentioned (all ministers of predestinarian Calvinist persuasion who have been described in some context as 'puritan') amply demonstrate this ambiguity by their differing attitudes to, for example, forms of Church government and liturgy. However, two shared and on the whole non-controversial interests have brought them together here: a concern for 'practical divinity', and a belief in the instructive value of the Old Testament cultic rites for the Christian. It has been suggested recently that if puritanism is to be defined at all, it must be in terms of an 'internal spiritual dynamic, a dynamic that forced the believer to externalise his own sense of election through a campaign of works directed against Antichrist, the flesh, the devil, sin and the world' (Lake 1982, 282). 'Practical divinity' offered encouragement and guidance towards this end. For the significance attached to cultic rites, we must look to aspects of Calvin's thought. He placed great weight on the unity of the Old and New Testaments: the same covenant was present in each, accommodated to the capacity of a 'Church under age' in Israel. Christ appeared in the Old Testament in 'types', shadows of what was to come which had no meaning apart from him (Calvin, *Institutes* ([1559] 1960) 2.7–11; Frei 1974, 21–37). Sacrifice, considered apart from its role in pointing to Christ, was futile (*Institutes*, 2.7.1, 16; 2.17.4; 3.4.30; 4.14.21). Calvin understood the priesthood of believers to derive from Christians' incorporation into Christ's 'threefold office' as prophet, priest and king, which represented a fulfilment of Israel's sacred vocations (*Institutes*, 2.15). The elect lived in a union with Christ effected by the Holy Spirit, sharing his death and resurrection in 'mortification' and 'vivification', both in justification and the process of sanctification (*Institutes*, 3). To the moral law of the Old Testament Calvin gave a positive role, not as something to be kept in order to gain salvation, but as a rule to direct and spur on the Christian life (*Institutes* 2.7.12–13). While his own exposition of sacrifice focussed on the way it anticipated Christ rather than on the significance of the sacrificial rites for the Christian (see for example his sermon on Micah 6: 6–8 (1970)), his emphasis on typology and on the value of the Law for Christians opened the way for much closer study of the minutiae of the rites as 'shadows' important to Christians in Christ. As Calvinism matured, Protestant fascination with typology increased. Publication of tracts with a typological interest blossomed in England from the end of the sixteenth century (as is evident in the bibliography of Bercovitch 1972). While scholars disagree about the extent to which Israelite experience was seen in the seventeenth century as a divine paradigm for or type of the English people (compare Lewalski 1979, 129–35; Polizzotto 1975; and J. F. Wilson 1969, 143–6), sacrificial rites were certainly viewed by many at the time as 'neither dark and dumb, but mystical and significant, and fit to stir up the dull mind of man to the remembrance of his duty toward God' (Mather 1705, 197).[1]

In my preparation of this study, detailed explanations of Old Testament typology in biblical commentaries or works devoted to a survey of the types of Israel proved to be a central point of reference. Practical writings on the Christian life – 'guides to godliness', tracts on prayer, on preparation for communion, on meditation – yielded many allusions to 'spiritual sacrifice' showing the general use and application of the idea. Sermons provided some startling examples of sacrificial rhetoric. Among writers in the typological field are Henry Ainsworth (1571–1622/3), a separatist whose rabbinical scholarship was respected and cited by many later commentators; William Guild (1585–1657), in later life Principal of King's College, Aberdeen, and a rather reluctant presbyterian; Thomas Taylor (1576–1633), a London minister with a reputation for practical divinity whose career was tinged with nonconformity; and Samuel Mather (1626–91), a Dublin congregationalist raised in New England whose sermon series of the 1660s on typology was influential on both sides of the Atlantic. William Gouge (1578–1653) deserves special mention. His commentary on Hebrews was the fruit of almost a thousand sermons preached over thirty years at a weekly lecture in his London parish (Gouge 1655, Preface); and this, with his detailed exposition of Psalm 116, *The Saints Sacrifice* (1632), demonstrates a keen interest in Christian interpretation of the cult. He was active in puritan plans of the 1620s to secure an adequate preaching ministry and later became a staunch presbyterian member of the Westminster Assembly. With Taylor, Gouge is to be found among the 'Affectionate Practical English writers' Richard Baxter recommended in his *Christian Directory* (1673) for 'A Poor Mans Library': Baxter (1615–91), a leading moderate in post-Restoration Nonconformity, supplied in the *Directory* the first comprehensive handbook of Protestant casuistry. His catalogue of useful authors includes many others whose devotional works, popular in their day and not infrequently reprinted in Victorian times, will be cited below: Lewis Bayly (d. 1631), Bishop of Bangor; Jeremiah Burroughes (1599–1646), suspended for nonconformity by Wren and later one of the few congregationalists in the Westminster Assembly; Jeremiah Dyke (d. 1620), Vicar of Epping, Essex; Thomas Hooker (1586–1647), of New England; William Perkins (1558–1602), a Cambridge theologian of great influence in puritan circles, although never a nonconformist; Richard Rogers (1550?–1618), lecturer at Wethersfield, Essex; Henry Scudder (d. 1659?), Rector of Collingbourne Ducis, Wiltshire; and William Whately (1583–1639), Scudder's brother-in-law and Vicar of Banbury. Baxter also commended the sermons of an Elizabethan preacher, Henry Smith (1550?–1591), known as 'silver-tongued' Smith, on which we draw. Two other notable puritan preachers will often be mentioned: Thomas Adams (fl. 1612–23) of London and Samuel Ward of Ipswich (1577–1640).[2]

What were considered to be the Christian's 'spiritual sacrifices', sacred offerings of the new covenant?

To see worship and particularly prayer as spiritual sacrifice has been a constant note of Christian tradition. William Gouge offered a well-worn argument when he claimed that as sacrifice was divinely instituted as the form of due worship in Israel so 'the general equity of performing due worship to God doth still and ever shall remain in force': worship under the new covenant consisted of 'prayer, singing of psalms, reading, preaching, hearing the Word and celebrating the Sacraments', which 'are as sacrifices of bullocks and calves, goats and kids, sheep and lambs, turtles, pigeons and sparrows; and all manner of meat and drink offerings' (Gouge 1632, 243; see also Gouge 1655 on Heb. 7:27; *Annotations* 1645 on Exod. 30:1; Marshall 1641, 36; Perkins 1613, 18; R. Rogers 1620, 170; *Westminster* 1647, XIX iii, XXVII v; Wilkinson 1644, 3, 4). Sabbath worship, because a Sabbath offering is mentioned only once in the Pentateuch (Num. 29:9–10), was rarely discussed with reference to the sacrificial cult. Daily prayer on the part of a Christian, shadowed by burnt-offerings and incense presented each day in the temple (Ex. 29:38–42, 30:7–8, Num. 28:1–8), received far more attention. Such prayer, contended Richard Rogers, 'was one of the principal things God meant to teach us by the morning and evening sacrifice' (1603, 321; see also Adams 1629, 988; *Annotations* 1645 on Exod. 29:39; Bayly 1613, 300–1; Carter 1642, 35; Gouge 1632, 174, 234; W. Perkins, 'Directions how to live well' in Greenham *et al.* 1609; Guild 1620, 122–3; Hinde 1641, 73–4; Preston 1629, 16; Taylor 1635, 149). Paul Baynes (d. 1617), who preached in William Perkins' place at Cambridge after Perkins' death, until silenced for nonconformity, interpreted Paul's injunction 'pray always' (1 Thess. 5:17) in light of cultic practice, deriving the custom of morning and evening prayer from scriptural typology, not tradition: 'That we are said to do continually which we ... do at fit times daily, as Numb. 28, that was a continual sacrifice which was daily offered, morning and evening' (1620, 293). The principle of daily sacrifice applied not only to individuals in private but to households, each regarded as a 'little Church'. Thomas Wilson (1563–1622), Rector of St George the Martyr, Canterbury, and associate of William Gouge, told the puritan patron Sir Robert Harley, 'I need not commend unto you, one approved in Christ yourself, that your house should be a Church for doctrine and discipline, that there should be morning and evening sacrifice day by day continually . . .' (T. Wilson MS 1636; see also Baynes 1637, 185; Clarke 1662, 7,450; Hinde 1641, 113; Marshall 1641, 49–50; Worden 1664, 310). The householder, responsible for members of the little church, was seen as its minister. Gouge, using the notion of the threefold office of Christ, described the householder as in the home a lord to govern, a prophet to teach, and 'a priest to offer up the sacrifice of prayer' (1619, 437; see also R. Rogers 1603, 397; and for comment on puritan household religion Davies 1948, 281, Appx D; Wakefield 1957, 55–65).

Daily worship in Israel was supplemented by 'extraordinary' recourse to God on particular occasions or in times of crisis or rejoicing, and this too was taken as a model for Christian practice. In Israel, for example, the monthly feasts, the Feast of Trumpets and the Day of Atonement, required 'extraordinary' sacrifices (Num. 28–9), and sacrifice might mark a public or private fast or formal thanksgiving, offered for national or personal causes (Judg. 20:26; 2 Sam. 24:25; 2 Chron. 15:11; Lev. 3, 7:11–18; Ps. 116:17; Mather 1705, 191, 194–5). Days of fasting and thanksgiving with 'extraordinary' sacrifices of prayer, to petition God for mercies needed or aversion of judgement, or to offer special thanks, were common in the personal and public religion of 'the godly' in seventeenth-century England and New England (Love 1895; J.F. Wilson 1969). In a preface to a parliamentary fast sermon, Edmund Calamy (1600–66), Rector of St Mary Aldermanbury, London, declared with some pleasure of the Long Parliament's programme of monthly communions, fasts and thanksgivings, and the extension of fast-day preaching into the country:

We have not only our monthly sacrament feast . . . but also our New Moon Fasts, in which the Word is preached, trading ceaseth, and sacrifices of prayer, praises and alms are tendered up to God in the name of Jesus Christ. We have our Feast of Trumpets, in which our godly ministers throughout the whole kingdom lift up their voices as a trumpet, and all the whole day, are either the mouth of the people to God, or God's mouth to the people, showing unto England their sins . . . and calling them unto humiliation, and reformation. (Calamy 1642, 140)

Henry Scudder identified the Day of Atonement, 'the solemn day of the fast' (Num. 29:7–12) as the shadow of all religious fasts, occasions when Christians should offer God extraordinary sacrifices, seeking him more often and with special prayer (1635, 37–8). Thomas Taylor concluded from the high priest's duties on the Day of Atonement that every Christian as a priest must 'every year set apart a day of expiation, to make an atonement for himself, for his house, for all the people . . . a day of humiliation in serious fasting and prayer' (1635, 149–50). It is interesting to note that Taylor and others referred freely to Old Testament rites of expiation as types of Christian sacrifice, particularly as types of petitionary prayer, with no intention of jeopardizing the crucial significance of the rites as types of Christ's work in redemption (Greenhill 1643, 27; Marshall 1641, 24). To offer 'sacrifices of thanksgiving', antitype of peace-offerings (Burroughes 1641, 1; Marshall 1641, 24) and fundamental to New Testament 'spiritual sacrifice' (Heb. 13: 15), was considered obligatory for the Christian (Owen 1684, on Heb. 13: 15). The custom of keeping a record of providences to oneself or to the nation, well attested in the period, suggests practicalities associated with such sacrifice besides formal thanksgiving days or private prayer. Samuel Ward's Thanksgiving Day sermon 'A Peace Offering' (not an uncommon title for such sermons) encouraged his hearers to offer sacrifices of thanksgiving. When printed it included as a practical appendix 'A thankefull Mans Calender': an autobiography in outline suggesting to Christians aspects of their lives which should provide cause for thanksgiving (1627, 'A Peace Offering', 48–53). In the record of God's providences towards him kept by the Cheshire layman, John Bruen (1560–1625), something of Ward's principle was at work: after each mercy or judgement noted, Bruen habitually added a phrase such as 'Laus Deo' (Hinde 1641, 145–8). *The Journal or Diary of a Thankful Christian* (1656) by an Essex clergyman, John Beadle (d. 1667), was devoted to persuading the reader of the value of keeping an account of providences. In its preface the book was described as wood, as fuel, for a sacrifice of thanksgiving. Much later in the period Richard Baxter gave 'Directions for Thankfulness' which, regarding thanksgiving as a sacrifice, suggested:

Think much of those personal mercies which God hath showed thee from thy youth up until now ... though the common mercies of God's servants be the greatest ... yet personal favours peculiar to ourselves are apt much to affect us ... Christians should mark God's dealings with them and write down the great and notable mercies of their lives. (1678, 141)

Baxter himself practised this art in poetry and prose (1681, 10–50; 1696 *passim*). Although autobiography has often been interpreted as a means by which individuals charted their spiritual progress, looking for evidence of election, it could clearly also act as a spur to the religious duty of offering sacrifices of thanksgiving (Keeble 1982, 139–43). Other practices could also act as a spur. A parliamentary thanksgiving sermon, 'A Peace Offering', argued that the 'soul thankfulness' which was an essential part of a 'whole peace-offering' involved a 'laying up and registering ... mercies of God in our memories' aided by means of which keeping a record was but one:

This thankful memory feeds the heart with continual matter of praise ... thankful hearts have found so much good in remembering of God's mercies that they have been careful to keep registers, set up monuments to help their memory, indited

Psalms to bring to remembrance, gave names to places where mercies received, new names to times when they were received, write the names of their deliverance upon their children, that the sight of them might quicken their memories and thoughts. (Marshall 1641, 32–3; see also Calamy 1642, 14)

The close connection between vows and sacrifice in Israel (Lev. 7:16, 22:21 and 27:2, 9–13; Num. 15:3; Ps. 56:12, 66:13–15 and 116:17–18) led to an association of vows with extraordinary spiritual sacrifice. Joseph Caryl (1602–73), preacher to Parliament and member of the Westminster Assembly, described the relationship of vows, petition and offering praise: 'praise is the payment of vows... praise days are vow performing days ... vows are the dedication of our mercies to God before we receive them, and praise is the dedication of our mercies to God after we have received them' (Caryl 1644, 12; see also Carter 1642, 4–5; Case 1646, 17; Gouge 1632, 247–50; Mather 1705, 228). Whether of petition or thanksgiving, however, and whether or not associated with 'extraordinary' practices 'extraordinary' sacrifices were to be offered without disrupting the pattern of daily prayer. William Gouge noted that Nehemiah added to morning and evening prayer extraordinary prayer helped by fasting, and that extraordinary temple sacrifices were made in addition to the daily offering. Old Testament piety and ceremonial law alike showed that 'ordinary and extraordinary prayer, joined together, will add life to each other' (Gouge 1642, 150; Neh. 1:4–6; Num. 28–9).

'Spiritual sacrifice' was by no means restricted in puritan thought to acts of public or private worship. The injunction 'to do good, and to communicate, forget not: for with such sacrifices God is well pleased' (Heb. 13:16; see also Phil. 4:18 and Eccles. 35:3)[3] led to almsgiving and 'works of mercy and love' being included in enumerations of 'gospel sacrifices' (Adams 1629, 91,988; Cornwell 1646, 10; Gouge 1655, on Heb. 13:15; R. Greenham, 'Short Rules', rule 5, in Greenham *et al.* 1609; Gouge 1632, 246; Marshall 1641, 36–7; Owen 1644, 22; Perkins 1613, 20; Whately 1640, 246; the text appeared in the Book of Common Prayer as part of the exhortation to give to the poor). However, the definition could be much wider. John Owen (1616–83), a leading Congregationalist, believed 'every act and duty of faith' to have the nature of a sacrifice pleasing to God (1684, 252; see also Perkins 1613, 18; T. Wilson 1611, 419).

Behind Owen's inclusive description lay the commonly held view that Christians' offering of particular acts to God was part of the living sacrifice of themselves to God urged by Paul (Rom. 12:1). 'Living sacrifice' meant union with Christ, in his priesthood and self-offering. Thomas Hooker voiced an orthodox opinion when he claimed that the Christian, like Christ and in Christ should be both priest and sacrifice, 'to offer ourselves ... as a living sacrifice and acceptable' (1640, 25). His injunction was part of a discussion of Christ's threefold office which emphasized that incorporation should involve imitation of Christ in sincere and constant assent to the will of God in all conduct (pp. 26–9). In this instance, Hooker's exegesis dwelt on the theme of obedience. John Owen, in similar vein, equated 'gospel obedience' with 'living sacrifice', describing it as interdependent with a sacrifice of thanksgiving: 'thankfulness is the peculiar animating principle of all gospel obedience', and 'gospel obedience' consists of 'thanksgiving for Christ and grace by him' (1684, on Heb. 13:15; see, likewise, Marshall 1641, 33–4). However, Owen reflected a different but equally common nuance of interpretation when he referred to living sacrifice as 'Autothusias or self-slaughter, crucifying the old man, killing sin and offering up our souls and bodies ... to God', linking Rom. 12:1 with the wider Pauline theme of Christians' incorporation into the death of Christ, or Christian 'mortification' (Owen 1644, 24; see Owen 1684, on Heb. 13:15; *Annotations* 1645, on Rom. 12:1). In light of Rom. 6:6, 'our old man is crucified with him, that the body of sin may be destroyed, that henceforth we should not serve sin' (see also Rom. 6:11, 2 Cor. 5:15, Gal. 2:20, Coloss. 3:5), Christ's death was seen as effective in killing sin. John Cotton (1584–1652), a minister in Boston, Massachusetts, whose works were popular in England, argued that 'the body of sin in us is crucified by the death of our Lord Jesus Christ ... we draw virtue from Christ crucifying and mortifying our lusts'. He drew extensive parallels between Christian mortification and Christ's crucifixion: as crucifixion was a lingering death, for example, so it would be 'a lingering work to get a proud heart humbled' (1641, 257, 264; see Adams 1629, 826–7; Pemble 1628, 16).

Typology gave a vivid means of illustrating 'living sacrifice', whether conceived as obedience or mortification. Samuel Ward was graphic and direct in preaching that

the whole duty of all men is to give themselves wholly to Christ, to sacrifice not a leg or an arm or any other piece but soul spirit and body and all that is within us: the fat, the inwards, the head and hoof, and all as a holocaust to him, dedicating, devoting ourselves to his service all the days and hours of our lives, that all our days may be Lord's Days. (1627, 'Christ is All in All', 35)

Thomas Taylor drew on the typology of daily sacrifice to put forward as a precept: 'Every Christian, as a priest unto God, must daily labour in his own mortification; every day must kill some beast or other, some lust or other' (1635, 149; see also Adams 1629, 988; Ward 1627 'A Peace Offering', 15). Imaginative meditation on the crucifixion, particularly at communion, was praised in puritan writing. 'Living sacrifice', interpreted in accord with Old Testament types, could be used to characterize Christians' renewal of their covenant with Christ in the rite. Jeremiah Dyke's manual for communicants argued that at the Lord's Supper it was a duty 'to represent unto ourselves the bitterness of Christ's passion' (1636, 519). He suggested, as an appropriate private 'Communion resolution', 'I will use my sins as I see they have used Christ. They pierced him, I will pierce them ... I will kill, crucify, put them to death' (1636, 540; see also Burroughes 1653, 264–8; Pemble 1628, 8). As the Israelites had renewed the covenant by sacrifice, so must Christians, by 'the covenants of offering themselves a living and acceptable sacrifice, of mortification of their sottish lusts, of an holy and obedient life' (Dyke 1636, 542; Arrowsmith 1643, 17; Burges 1641a, 27; Calamy 1643, 13. This theme is reminiscent of the Prayer of Oblation after Communion introduced in *The Book of Common Prayer*, 1552. On sacramental devotion and the Lord's Supper as a 'seal' of the covenant in puritan thought see Holifield 1974, 109–38; Wakefield 1957, 42–53). Outside the context of communion, entering into covenant could be described as a sacrificial act: 'give up yourselves in covenant with God, that is the peace-offering or thank-offering he expects this day, even yourselves given up to him a living sacrifice' (Carter 1642, 36; see also pp. 4–5, Burroughes 1641, 26, and Taylor 1635, 37–8).

The 'sacrifice of a broken and contrite heart' (drawn from an Old Testament spiritualization of sacrifice which emphasized the importance of sincere devotion accompanying the outward act, Ps. 51:16–17) stood alongside 'living sacrifice' (Marshall 1641, 35). Like living sacrifice it could represent mortification: brokenness, repentance and contrition in meditation on the brokenness of Christ in his sacrifice (Burroughes 1653, 67–8, 246–9; Cornwell 1646, 9–10). (John Bunyan and the parliamentary preacher Francis Roberts devoted whole tracts to discussing such 'brokenness': Bunyan 1689; Roberts, 1647.) It could represent the slaying of 'beastly lusts' (Adams 1629, 90; Owen 1684, 253). The necessary crushing of incense before it was offered was understood as a type of the broken and contrite heart. Thomas Wilson argued that the sacrifice of prayer should be 'perfumed with a concomitancy of several graces as so many spices and some of it to be broken very small having ever the broken heart, the very sacrifice of God most pleasing to him' (T. Wilson MS 1636; see also Guild 1608, 11; Keach 1682, 426; Mather 1705, 403). Like living sacrifice this sacrifice informed all particular acts of sacrifice, but (in accord with biblical tradition) bore most closely on purity of intention in offering duties to God. John Preston (1587–1628), for a time chaplain to Prince Charles, alleged that the sacrifice of a broken, contrite heart 'is that which sets a high price upon every sacrifice we offer' (1629, 124; see also Crooke 1614, 319; Herle 1631, 297; Taylor 1630, 247; Whately 1640, 246; Wilkinson 1644, 9). Henry Smith told his congregation that the essence of living sacrifice was an offering of the heart, 'because he that gives the heart gives all: for out of the abundance of the heart the mouth speaketh, the eye looketh ... the foot walketh to good or evil' (1589, 6v–7; Matt. 12:34–5; Ezek. 36:26). It is not unusual to find on the title pages of the period illustrations of the sacrifice of the heart: a heart-shaped vessel on an altar issuing incense, or a heart, sometimes broken, burning on wood. Samuel Ward, apparently the designer of his own title pages, gave 'A Peace Offering' (1627) such a frontispiece; among works on the Christian life already cited, those by Bayly (1613) and Baxter (1673, 1678) also offer examples. These illustrations reflect the much wider Catholic and Protestant emblematic tradition of the *Schola Cordis* (Harvey 1647, 76–9; Freeman 1948, 134–9, 178–9; Lewalski 1979, 193–6; the radical John Pym did not object to this element of John Cosin's title page for *A Collection of Private Devotions* ([1627] 1967) although he took exception to others). Because of its association with repentance the sacrifice of a broken heart was considered particularly appropriate for a day of humiliation, which should be a 'heart-breaking day' (Wilkinson 1644, 31; Roberts 1647, Preface).

Samuel Mather's reverence for the minutiae of cultic ritual as 'mystical and significant, and fit to stir up the dull mind of man to the remembrance of his duty toward God' (1705, 197) has already been mentioned. The ceremonial law was 'one of the richest cabinets of divinity, full of inestimable jewels' (1705, 61). Mather is typical of those who tried, by exploring the intricacies of ritual, to make the nature and proper manner of offering spiritual sacrifice yet more plain. It will be impossible to do more than hint at the complex and diverse typological identifications put forward, but some themes call for particular comment.

With an intensity that must impress, layer upon layer of typological exegesis pointed out that Christians and Christian sacrifice were acceptable to God only in and through Christ. Discussion of every aspect of the cultic rites elaborated this idea. The ceremonial law commanded, for example, that the sacrificial lamb be unblemished. This was said to represent the perfection of Christ and Christians' purity in him (Ainsworth 1616–19, on Lev. 1: 3, Exod. 12: 5; Mather 1705, 196; Taylor 1635, 217–18; Weemse 1632, 57). It is perhaps worth noting that a hostile witness described early London Anabaptists as calling each other 'unspotted lambs of the Lord', although, as Professor Collinson has pointed out, this was almost certainly not a title they themselves used (Collinson 1967, 86). As sacrificial rites could be performed only by a priest, so Christian sacrifice must be made in Christ (Baillie 1643, 24–5; Wilkinson 1644, 12). The fate of those who offered without a priest was held up as a warning (Owen 1644, 13–14; Preston 1629, 10–11, 140–1; see 2 Chron. 26: 16–20, Lev. 17: 1–7). Writers whose primary concern was the explanation of types analysed ritual surrounding the choice and consecration of priests in great detail: priestly garments shadowed higher spiritual 'clothing', for example, and sacrifice at a priest's consecration, and the smearing of his ear, toe and thumb with blood, denoted the expiatory sacrifice and cleansing blood of Christ which consecrate Christians to spiritual priesthood (Ainsworth

1616–19, on Exod. 28:40, *Annotations* 1645, on Exod. 29:20; Guild 1620, 68–9, 72–3; Keach 1682, 421; Mather 1705, 499–527; Taylor 1635, 107–15). The salt seasoning all offerings shadowed, according to William Perkins, a believer's becoming 'savoury and acceptable to God by virtue of the sacrifice of Christ upon the cross ... as flesh that cannot be seasoned with salt putrifies, so men that cannot be seasoned and changed by the sacrifice of Christ do rot and perish in their sins' (1612, 221; see also Burroughes 1653, 67; Guild 1620, 131; T. Wilson 1611, 410). 'Temple furniture' held deep mysteries. The brazen grate within the altar (Exod. 27:4), for example, which allowed ashes of animal sacrifice to fall through but a 'sweet savour' to ascend, prefigured Christ's purging of all imperfection from Christian sacrifice (Burroughes 1653, 110–11; Guild 1620, 113; Worden 1664, 178–80). The altar which sanctified the offering and the blood sprinkled on it also shadowed Christ (Matt. 23:19; Heb. 9:14; Adams 1629, 89, 97; *Annotations* 1645, on Lev. 4:6, Bunyan 1688, 23; Cawdrey 1600, 858; Gouge 1655, on Heb. 2:17, Guild 1608, 4–6, 1620, 108–13, 117–18; Keach 1682, 427; Mather 1705, 201; Perkins 1612, 220, 221; Taylor 1635, 144; Whately 1640, 98, 246; T. Wilson MS 1636; Worden 1664, 138–43). The importance attributed to the heart led some writers to identify Christians' hearts (as well as Christ) with the altar on which sacrifice should be offered (Adams 1629, 89, 988; Ainsworth 1616–19, on Exod. 24:5, followed by Keach 1682, 427; Bayly 1613, 301, 320; Cawdrey 1600, 609; Gouge 1632, 234; Guild 1608, 126–7). Samuel Mather thought this usurped the place of Christ: 'it is not thy heart that sanctifies thee' (1705, 368). As the priest alone could mingle incense with the sacrifice and use the golden censer, so Christ alone 'must offer the sacrifice, wherein the Lord smells savour of rest' (Preston 1629, 143; see also Adams 1629, 828; Clarke 1662, 38; Gouge 1655, on Heb. 9:12; Guild 1620, 103, 109).

Sacrificial instruments – knife, fleshhooks, cords for tying animals to the altar – suggested to some writers God-given 'means' to help Christians offer spiritual sacrifice. The Authorised Version's translation of Ps. 118:27, 'bind the sacrifice with cords, even unto the horns of the altar', led Edmund Calamy to argue, in recommending the making of spiritual vows at communion, that 'as the beast was tied to the horns of the altar ... so these blessed vows and resolutions are heavenly cords to tie the soul faster to God' (1680, 199), elaborating both the typology of renewing the covenant at communion by 'living sacrifice' and the association of vows with spiritual sacrifice. It was a useful image with respect to vows: their value in 'binding' to good duties or from particular sins was part of the common stock of puritan casuistry (Gouge 1632, 129–30, 191; Whately 1640, 2nd pag., 51). Similar interpretations of the cords were offered by other writers outside the context of communion and with no direct reference to vows. To

Thomas Adams, binding the sacrifice to the altar denoted constant devotion to Christ (1629, 89, 93–5). Thomas Worden thought that if believers 'would not have their sacrifices and duties miscarry', they should tie them closely to Christ with cords of faith, understanding, love, sincerity and zeal (1664, 181–7). The text was used as a plea for mortification by William Guild: 'Tie carnal affections to the altar's horns by captivating them to Christ' (1620, 112; see also Perkins 1613, 112). Samuel Mather, however, usually intent on drawing significance from small detail, saw binding with cords as simply 'an action of natural necessity unto such a work as the slaying of a beast' (1705, 104–5).

Sacrificial knives were seen as types of the Word of God, the sword of the Spirit (Eph. 6:17), crucial in mortification. William Perkins described preaching as

a sacrificing knife whereby the old Adam must be killed in us ... and we made an holy and acceptable sweet smelling oblation ... everyone that heareth God's word ... must endeavour that by profitable hearing thereof his sins and whole nature may be subdued and killed, as the beast was slain and sacrificed upon the altar by the hand of the Levite ... (1612, 221)

He thought of it as part of the 'priest's' office a Christian minister should fulfil (1613, 112), in terms reminiscent of Paul's priestly description of his work (Rom. 15:16). Thomas Taylor alluded to Paul's words when he placed first among a minister's duties that of preparing 'not dead beasts but living Christians' as 'sacrifices to the Lord': 'as the poor beast must be killed, and cut in pieces, and then offered, so we must by the sharp knife of the Law (urging repentance and mortification) cut asunder the heart-strings of sin and let out the life-blood of man's lusts and corruptions' (1635, 147; see also Owen 1644, 24). 'Labour in mortifying sin' should be followed by efforts to 'bring men to the lavour of sanctification, separate them from their foulness, and bring them to full holiness', just as slaughter was followed by washing and purging the carcass (Taylor 1635, 147). Taylor made much of the significance of priests' duties for Christian ministers: it seems to have been a particular concern. For Mather, as the knife cut open the beast, so the Spirit searched out hypocrisy in a Christian offering (1705, 202). Henry Ainsworth's earlier typological commentary had referred in more general terms to the shovels, fleshhooks and censers used in the burnt-offering as shadows of 'the ministry of the Word in the Church of Christ, which serveth to purge the filth and corruption of the flesh and to kindle the fire of the Spirit for the pure service of God, Rom. 12:1–2 and 15:16, Zech. 14:20, 21' (1616–19, on Exod. 27:3; see also Guild 1620, 112; Worden 1664, 215). John Bunyan, however, preferred to see the instruments as shadowing the sins which had inflicted death on Christ, and encouraged communion meditations on the type as an aid to repentance (1688, 103, 105).

Precepts and prohibitions hedging the sacrificial rites provided rich sacred analogies to help Christians distinguish true sacrifice from false, and to evaluate their own intent. As Moses was instructed to make the Tabernacle exactly according to God's pattern (Heb. 8:5, Exod. 25:40) so spiritual sacrifice, to be acceptable, must be offered as God required (Wilkinson 1644, 31; Mather 1705, 193). William Gouge believed 'we were as good to be ignorant of the duty itself, as of the manner of performing it ... to know what ought to be done, and not to know how it ought to be done, will be a great aggravation of sin' (1655, on Heb. 8:5, Section 17, 'Of the Right Manner of Doing Duty').

Accordingly, a number of writers stressed that spiritual sacrifice should be voluntary: even if the offering of sacrifices had been laid down in the Law, 'yet none of them were to be offered against the will' (*Annotations* 1645, on Lev. 1:3; see also Wilkinson 1644, 9; Worden 1664, 185). The voluntary nature of sacrifice was a type of Christ, who 'died willingly and offered up himself a sacrifice and a whole burnt offering unto God for us' (Mather 1705, 197, 213; see also Guild 1620, 116–17). Type and antitype were an example to the Christian: 'so should we in all our services be a willing people' (Mather 1705, 197; see also Gouge 1632, 245; and Gouge 1655, on Heb. 10:5, 6 and 11:24). Edmund Calamy applied this to the nation in a parliamentary sermon, arguing 'If England's mercies come from free grace, let England serve God freely. God loves a free-will offering' (1642, 2). Henry Wilkinson echoed these sentiments in a later parliamentary sermon:

that which we offer to God, we must offer freely, without constraint, of a ready mind and willingly; we must offer our hearts in the sacrifice we give, and service we perform to God ... whatever we offer to God ... if it be with the heart, we may say in a theological sense that it is a free-will offering; when we offer our hearts, wills and affections, we offer freely ... (1644, 8; see also p. 13 and Ashe 1647, 18)

Spiritual sacrifice must not be tainted by hypocrisy. Ritually unclean offerings shadowed hypocritical service. A sacrifice of prayer made in empty words without 'further proceeding in obedience' was, according to Richard Rogers, 'all lame and maimed, and as odious to God as the mortlings and untimely first born of the beasts' (1603, 282–3, alluding to Mal. 1:14; see also Baynes 1637, 157; Calamy 1643, 2–3; Cotton 1641, 419–20; Marshall 1641, 30, 34). Thomas Adams pictured a blemished living sacrifice: 'The drunkard is without a head, the swearer hath a garget in his throat, the covetous hath a lame hand, he cannot give to the poor ...' (1628, 91). Sacrifices offered in act alone without inner devotion were condemned as dead and stinking carcasses (Adams 1629, 92; Baxter 1678, 105; R. Rogers 1616, 176); as the 'sacrifices of fools' (Eccles. 5:1–2; Calamy 1680, 89; Hooker 1640, 232; Ward 1627, 'A Peace Offering, 7) or of the wicked (Prov. 15:8; Caryl 1644, 10–11); as the offering of the skin of a sacrifice without the substance (Adams 1629, 90); or as a niggardly sacrifice like that of Cain (Gouge 1655, on Heb. 8: 5, Section 17; Perkins 1613, 15–16; Whately 1640, 24, 31–2). To offer acts without conviction was a subtle form of hypocrisy, but could not escape God's notice. Thomas Adams told his congregation: 'All outward works a hypocrite may do, only he fails in the heart . . . man judgeth the heart by the works; God judgeth the works by the heart' (1629, 947; see Scudder 1635, 318–19). Hypocrisy might tarnish Christians who offered spiritual sacrifice without due preparation of their hearts (R. Rogers 1603, 163). William Gouge urged his readers to avoid this: 'Think on duty beforehand, and endeavour to prepare thyself thereto. Sudden, hasty, rash, unprepared enterprising on sacred duty is one occasion of failing in the manner of doing it' (1655, on Heb. 8: 5, Section 17). It was because of the importance of the heart in Christian sacrifice that 'preparing', 'preserving' or 'keeping' it was so vital. John Cotton's *Way of Life*, for example, particularly his exposition of Prov. 4: 23, 'Keep thy heart with all diligence', documented the necessity for constant vigilance: the heart could easily become drowsy or dead, and was always deceitful (1641, 203–4, 216–26, 419–29. Thomas Adams warned, 'God values not the offerer by the gift, but the gift by the offerer. Let not thy heart be as dead as the beast thou immolatest' (1629, 92; see also Calamy 1680, 80; Cooper 1615, 164–82: Hall 1607, 25; Preston 1629, 124; Owen 1684, on Heb. 13: 15 Taylor 1631, 8–9). This stress on 'preparation for duty' reflects a general emphasis in puritan literature (Baynes 1637, 123; Burroughes 1653, 42, 55, 71; Calamy 1680, *passim*; Dyke 1636, 47, 51).

Misplaced religious enthusiasm, human meddling in God's rites and 'lukewarm' religion all found condemnation in interpretations of sacrificial fire. The fate of Nadab and Abihu, who offered sacrifice with fire God had not commanded and were consumed by a holy fire of judgement (Lev. 10: 1–3), was a cautionary tale. Jeremiah Burroughes concluded from it that 'in God's worship there must be nothing rendered up to God but what he hath commanded . . . it must be what we have a covenant for out of the Word of God' (1653, 8–9; see also Ainsworth 1616–19 on Lev. 10: 2; Downame 1608, 250–1; Geneva 1560, on Lev. 10: 3; Greenhill 1643, 44; Keach 1682, 426; Smith 1644, 30–2; T. Wilson 1611, 156). John Preston thought the incident showed that ordinances must be used with due reverence, instancing God's punishment of contemporary Sabbath-breakers (1634, 271; see also, in general, Bayly 1613, 551–3); Francis Cornwell, Rector of Marden, Kent, and a Baptist, found in it an argument against 'set prayer', since 'God is so jealous of his glory that he cannot endure his worship should be corrupted with the least mixture of man' (1646, 50; see Mather 1705 on false incense, p. 403). According to Samuel Ward, 'false fire' igniting sacrifice might be the counterfeit devotion of hypocrisy, the blind fervour of a separatist or 'devout Papist', a fire of malicious anger or the 'wild fire' of enthusiasts, who 'instead of burning bright and shining clear ... sparkle and spit at others, or, like ill-couched fireworks, let fly on all sides' (1627, 'A Coale from the Altar', 10–24; see also Adams 1629, 91–2; Bayly 1613, 316–17; Burges 1641/2, 60; P. Smith 1644, 30–2).

Yet the necessity of fire to make sacrifice burn with 'a sweet savour unto the Lord' (Gen. 8: 21; Lev. 1: 9, 13, 2: 9, 3: 5 etc.) called for comment on the true heavenly zeal with which Christians ought to burn. To William Guild, the cooking of the meat-offering demonstrated that 'our worship of God should not be raw or zeal-less'. He referred Christians to the condemnation of the 'lukewarm' church of Laodicea, and Christ's command to its members 'be zealous' (1620, 130, on Rev. 3: 15–16; see also Guild 1608, 3, 10). Ward's sermon 'A Coale from the Altar', its title rich in allusion to sacrificial fire and in content outspoken against 'Nadabs and Abihus', took Christ's command as its text, likening 'our common Christians' to the Laodiceans (1627, 'A Coale from the Altar', Preface). Cornelius Burges (1589?–1665) identified zeal's opposite as 'that lukewarm temper in distempered Laodicea'; claiming of the true 'holy fire of zeal', 'no acceptable sacrifice can be offered without it, no oblation itself so pleasing to God ... yet no one grace so much in disgrace' (1625, 10, 1–2; see also Wilkinson 1644, 11, and for comment on contemporary identification of the Laodiceans with English Christians see Christianson 1978, Firth 1979 and Olsen 1973). Henry Smith defined zeal as love of God: 'Therefore every sacrifice was offered with fire, to show with what they should burn, which come to offer prayer or praise, or thanks unto God.' He berated his congregation to be 'more than statute Protestants ... which go to church and hear a homily, and receive once a year, but will not offend any person, nor leave any custom, nor bear any charge, nor suffer any trouble for the glory of God' (1595, c3; see also H. Smith 1589, 15; Ashe 1647, 18; Greene 1644, 31; Guild 1608, 3, 10; Keach 1682, 426). True fire, true zeal, was of heavenly origin, as the perpetual fire on the altar had been: 'a holy fire of love kindled by the Spirit whereby our sacrifices are burned' (Sibbes 1639, 57; see also Adams 1629, 988; Guild 1620, 109; Harvey 1647, 79; Herle 1631, 297; Mather 1705, 404; Taylor 1630, 3; Ward 1627, 'A Coale from the Altar' 6; T. Wilson MS 1636), a purifying fire (Adams 1629, 122; Ainsworth 1616–19, on Exod. 27: 5; Perkins 1613, 200).

Finally, the typology of sacrifice could play a part in the quest for assurance of election. The fire kindling the sacrifices, making a 'sweet savour' ascend, could be identified with the heavenly fire which ignited sacrifices, showing God's approval (Lev. 9: 24; 1 Kings 18: 20–40; Judges 13: 15–23; 2 Chron. 7: 1; Ainsworth 1616–19, on Gen. 4: 4 and Lev. 9: 24; Cotton 1641, 342–3). According to Jeremiah Dyke, 'when a man in prayer ... feels his heart set on fire with fervency of holy affections, this is the fire of the Spirit ... that comes down from heaven: a sensible testimony of God's acceptance, thus God turns our sacrifices into ashes...' (1636, 133; see also Burges 1625, 23–4, and Ward 1627, 'A Coale from the Altar', 9–10). If people found themselves cold in wanting to praise God, William Gouge believed, 'the fire that descends from heaven hath not fallen upon the altar of their heart' (1632, 234). Evidence from fire was evidence from 'fervency of holy affections', but the principle of gaining assurance from the offering of spiritual sacrifice was also applied to Christians' capacity to offer sacrifice, shown in obedience. Henry Smith suggested a test by which Christians could discern whether they had offered their hearts to God as the essence of a 'living sacrifice':

By this thou shalt know whether thou hast given it to him or no: if thy heart be gone, all will follow. As the sun riseth first, and then the beasts arise from their dens, the fowls from their nests, and men from their beds: so when the heart settles forward to God, all the members will march after it. The tongue will praise him, the foot will follow him, the ear will attend him, the eye will watch him, the hand will serve him. Nothing will stay after the heart, but everyone goes like handmaids after their Mistress... (1589, 9v–10; see also Adams 1629, 946)

William Whately, discussing Isaac's worship as a 'prototype', challenged his readers: 'Would you confirm to your own consciences that you be true Isaacs? Ask yourselves then, do you offer these burnt offerings? If not, you be not as Isaac, children of the promise; if yea, you may assure your souls that you be' (1640, 246, and see also 97 and 2nd pag. 54; Cooper 1615, 131; for similar references to obedience attesting election, outside the context of sacrifice, see Cooper 1622, 136; Dyke 1636, 604; Hooker 1640, 29; Pemble 1628, 16; Kendall 1979).

A popular enhancement of 'spiritual sacrifice' is evident in this strand of Protestant tradition; and the number of characteristic themes of puritan piety which derive justification or added conviction from the typology of sacrifice is striking. These themes, to be sure, have vigour outside the context of sacrificial terminology: most often discussed without reference to sacrifice, they were frequently attached to other types – as mortification was to circumcision, for example. However, it is hard to find another Old Testament type which so adequately gathers such themes together. Perhaps this is inevitably so, because of the place of sacrifice in Israelite religion as a religious duty. It provided the most coherent model for Christian duty. Even though the prophetic critique of sacrifice found willing hearers (like the prophets, these writers knew 'formal religion' and feared God's judgement for it), the figural value of the Levitical rites was defended. Richard Rogers' interpretation of Samuel's words to Saul, 'to obey is better than sacrifice' (1 Sam. 15:22), in terms of 'sacrifice pleaseth God not without obedience' typifies a general reluctance to surrender the 'mystical significance' of cultic rites as shadows of life under the new covenant (R. Rogers 1620, 170–93).

The adequacy of sacrifice as a paradigm for Christian duty underlines the voluntarism of puritan thought on the Christian life. Faith is evidenced in an attitude of the will rather than in conviction of the intellect. The perceived voluntarism of Israelite worship – devotion shown in 'freewill offerings', with the will perhaps bound by a vow – becomes a fruitful type, 'baptised in Christ', for voluntarism in the new Israel. The details of Christian duty expounded in this way speak eloquently about the nature of 'voluntary religion' in the age, the call to be 'more than statute Protestants'. And it is not improper to ask (although admittedly impossible to determine) whether notions of religious duty found a helpful analogy in Israelite sacrifice, or whether brooding on the types of Israel reinforced voluntarist tendencies in puritanism.

The material collected for this study has proved to be of an exhortatory nature, devoted to one end: persuading its audience to Christian duty, to offer sacrifice in a right manner. It 'wields the sacrificial knife', acting on the will; its genre is that of an 'instrument' God has provided to aid sacrifice. Against this background, it may be useful to mention some negative evidence. Although sacrificial rhetoric seems to be a rhetoric of exhortation, the Fast Sermons of the Long Parliament, with their interpretation of the significance of the affairs of Israel for England, do not much use it. A lack of interest in texts from Leviticus has been noted (J. F. Wilson 1969, 148n.). Sacrificial allusions are quite frequent, but they centre on the individual rather than describing 'spiritual sacrifice' as part of a programme of national reform. This can perhaps be understood in light of the trait of voluntarism in puritan sacrificial typology. Although a national sacrifice may be on occasion extolled and encouraged (Burroughes 1641, 26), or Parliament entreated to offer a 'representative sacrifice' (as in Marshall 1641, 47–8), the sincerity of these sacrifices – and therefore their value in God's sight – is determined at an individual level. Christians must engage in a constant dialogue between inner devotion and outward act – do actions proceed from a proper brokenness of heart, and is this brokenness evidenced in appropriate action? Discussion of national or representative 'spiritual sacrifice' devolves to consideration of each parliamentarian's sacrifice: sincere 'Selfe-surrender unto God' will issue in proper reforming acts (Ashe 1647; Roberts 1647; Wilkinson 1644). It is also noticeable and somewhat surprising that sacrificial typology plays little part in collections of autobiographical testimonies (such as J. Rogers 1653, 354–450), and that there appears to be no convention in funeral sermons or biography of speaking of the exemplary individual as a 'living sacrifice' (see, for example, Threnoikos 1640; Clarke 1662). Interest in sacrificial typology seems to be characteristic of literature and preaching which is concerned to make clear the 'use' of a text, doctrine or biblical image. Nor, perhaps more unexpectedly, is there a concentration on sacrifice as a type of Christian duty and a means of entering into a covenant with God in writers such as Ames, Cotton, Sibbes and Hooker, who, it is often claimed, make a 'theology of covenant' the governing principle of their thought – this despite the intense focus in their work on individual religious experience and intention.

One area in which Protestant use of sacrificial typology later developed was hymnody. It is evident in the freely composed hymns which became acceptable to nonconformists early in the eighteenth century, replacing or supplementing the customary singing of metrical psalms. An early collection of communion hymns published by the Baptist Joseph Stennett (1663–1713) (see Stennett 1697) employs the theme, and it is not uncommon in the hymns of Isaac Watts and Charles Wesley.

The irony of a lively sacrificial typology, indeed of wider puritan interest in 'the figures and types of Israel', is that those most disinclined 'to dig Moses out of his grave' (Mather 1705, 277) – rejecting remnants of 'Israelite' ceremony such as the surplice – were themselves accused of a 'judaizing puritanism' (Burges 1641a, 75). It demonstrates the curiosity and particularity of their interest in the Old Testament. With this in mind, a provocative comment by William Haller is telling:

the Puritan saga did not cherish the memory of Christ ... on the cross, that is of the lamb of God sacrificed in vicarious atonement for the sins of man ... the mystic passion was the crucifixion of the new man by the old, and the true propitiation the sacrifice of the old to the new. (Haller 1939, 151)

NOTES

I am indebted to Professor P. Collinson and Dr G. F. Nuttall for their comments on an earlier version of this paper.

1 Spelling, punctuation and capitalization have been modernised throughout, except in the citation of book titles.
2 Biographical sketches of those mentioned in this paper appear in the *Dictionary of National Biography* or *Dictionary of American Biography* (with the exception of Francis Cornwell, for whom see *Transactions of the Baptist Historical Society*, vol. VII (1920–1), p. 194).
3 Biblical quotations are from the Authorised Version.

REFERENCES

Primary sources (Published in London unless otherwise stated. '*F.S.*' in a reference means that the work has been reprinted in the facsimile series *The English Revolution*, general editor R. Jeffs, 1: *Fast Sermons to Parliament* (Cornmarket Press, 1970–1); the following number refers to the volume in the series.)

Adams, T. (1629). *The Workes of Thomas Adams*
Ainsworth, H. (1616–19). *Annotations upon the Five Bookes of Moses*

Annotations (1645). *Annotations upon all the Bookes of the Old and New Testament, published by order of the Westminster Assembly*
Arrowsmith, J. (1643). *The Covenant-Avenging Sword Brandished.* [F.S. 5]
Ashe, S. (1647). *Selfe-Surrender unto God* [F.S. 30]
Baillie, R. (1643). *Satan the Leader in Chief to All who Resist the Reparation of Sion* [F.S. 10]
Baxter, R. (1673). *The Christian Directory (1st edn) (1678). The Christian Directory* (2nd edn)
  (1681). *Poetical Fragments*
  (1696). *Reliquiae Baxterianae*, ed. M. Sylvester
Bayly, L. (1613). *The Practice of Piety*
Baynes, P. (1620). *The Spirituall Armour*
  (1637). *Briefe Directions unto a Godly Life* (2nd edn)
Beadle, J. (1656). *The Journal or Diary of a Thankful Christian*
Bunyan, J. (1688). *Solomon's Temple Spiritualised*
  (1689). *The Acceptable Sacrifice: Or, the Excellency of a Broken Heart*
Burges, C. (1625). *The Fire of the Sanctuarie newly uncovered, or A Compleat Tract of Zeal*
  (1641a). *The First Sermon* [F.S. 1]
  (1641b). *Another Sermon* [F.S. 1]
Burroughes, J. (1641). *Sions Joy* [F.S. 1]
  (1653). *Gospel Worship* (2nd edn)
Calamy, E. (1642). *God's Free Mercy to England* [F.S. 2]
  (1643). *The Noble-mans Patterne of True and Reall Thankfulnesse* [F.S. 6]
  (1680). *The Art of Divine Meditation*
Calvin, J. ([1559] 1960). *The Institutes of the Christian Religion* (first published 1559), ed. J. T. McNeill. Philadelphia: The Westminster Press, 1960
  (1970). Calvin's Saturday Morning Sermon on Micah 6: 6–8, trans. A. D. Lewis. *Scottish Journal of Theology* 23 (1970), 166–82
Carter, W. (1642). *Israel's Peace with God* [F.S. 3]
Caryl, J. (1644). *The Saints Thankfull Acclamation* [F.S. 10]
Case, T. (1646). *A Model of True Spirituall Thankfullnesse* [F.S. 21]
Cawdrey, R. (1600). *A Treasurie or Storehouse of Similes*
Clarke, S. (1662). *A Collection of the Lives of Ten Eminent Divines*
Cooper, T. (1615). *The Christians Daily Sacrifice* (3rd edn)
  (1622). *The Wonderfull Mysterie of Spirituall Growth*
Cornwell, F. (1646). *A Description of the Spirituall Temple*
Cosin, J. ([1627] 1967). *A Collection of Private Devotions* (reprinted, ed. P. G. Stanwood, Oxford: Oxford University Press, 1967)
Cotton, J. (1641). *The Way of Life*
Crooke, S. (1614). *The Guide unto True Blessednesse*
Downame, J. (1608). *Lectures upon the Foure First Chapters of the Prophecie of Hosea*
Dyke, J. (1636). *A Worthy Communicant*
Geneva (1560). *The Geneva Bible.* (Facsimile of the 1560 edn, Madison: University of Wisconsin Press, 1969)
Gouge, W. (1619). *The Whole Armour of God*
  (1632). *The Saints Sacrifice*
  (1642). *The Saints Support* [F.S. 3]

(1655). *A Learned and very useful Commentary on the Whole Epistle to the Hebrews*

Greene, J. (1644). *Nehemiah's Teares and Prayers* [F.S. 11]

Greenham, R.,'M.M.', Perkins, W., Rogers, R. and Web, G. (1609). *A Garden of Spiritual Flowers* (9th edn)

Greenhill, W. (1643). *The Axe at the Root* [F.S. 6]

Guild, W. (1608). *The New Sacrifice of Christian Incense*
   (1620). *Moses Unvailed*

Hall, J. (1607). *Holy Observations, Lib. I*

Harvey, C. (1647). *Schola Cordis*

Herle, C. (1631). *Contemplations and Devotions on the Severall Passages of our Blessed Saviours Death and Passion*

Hinde, W. (1641). *A Faithful Remonstrance of the Holy Life and Happy Death of John Bruen*

Hooker, T. (1640). *The Christians two Chiefe Lessons: Self-Deniall and Selfe-Tryall*

Keach, B. (1682). *Tropologia: A Key to Open Scripture Metaphors*

Marshall, S. (1641). *A Peace Offering to God* [F.S. 1]

Mather, S. (1705). *The Figures or Types of the Old Testament*, 2nd edn. (Reprinted New York: Johnson Reprint Corporation, 1969)

Owen, J. (1644). *The Duty of Pastors and People Distinguished*
   (1684). *Exercitations on the Epistle to the Hebrews*. vol. IV

Pemble, W. (1628). *An Introduction to the Worthy Receiving of the Sacrament of the Lord's Supper*

Perkins, W. (1612). *The Workes of ... William Perkins*, vol. I
   (1613). *The Workes of ... William Perkins*, vol. III

Preston, J. (1629). *The Saints Daily Exercise*
   (1634). *Remaines*

Roberts, F. (1647). *A Broken Spirit, Gods Sacrifices* [F.S. 25]

Rogers, J. (1653). *Ohel or Beth-shemesh. A Tabernacle for the Sun.* (Dublin)

Rogers, R. (1603). *Seven Treatises* (1st edn)
   (1616). *Seven Treatises* (4th edn)
   (1620). *Samuel's Encounter with Saul*

Scudder, H. (1635). *The Christians Daily Walke in holy Securitie and Peace* (6th edn)

Sibbes, R. (1639). *Bowels Opened, Or a Discovery of the Neere and Deere Love, Union and Communion betwixt Christ and the Church*

Smith, H. (1589). *The Christians Sacrifice*
   (1595). *Jacobs Ladder, Or the High Way to Heaven*

Smith, P. (1644). *A Sermon* [F.S. 11]

Stennett, J. (1697). *Hymns in Commemoration of the Sufferings of our Blessed Saviour Jesus Christ. Compos'd for the Celebration of his Holy Supper*

Taylor, T. (1630). *The Progresse of Saints to full Holinesse*
   (1631). *Circumspect Walking*
   (1635). *Christ Revealed: Or the Old Testament Explained* (reissued 1653 under the title *Moses and Aaron*)

Threnoikos (1640). *Threnoikos. The Household of Mourning* (Collection of sermons by 'D. Featly, M. Day, R. Sibbes, T. Taylor.')

Ward, S. (1627). *A Collection of such Sermons and Treatises as have beene written and published by Mr. Samuel Ward*

Weemse, J. (1632). *An Explanation of the Ceremoniall Lawes of Moses*

Westminster (1647). *The Westminster Confession*. Reprinted in *The Creeds of Evangelical Protestant Churches*, eds. P. Schaff and H. B. Smith (London: Hodder and Stoughton, 1877), pp. 600–74
Whately, W. (1640). *Prototypes, or, The Primarie Presidents out of the Booke of Genesis*
Wilkinson, H. (1644). *The Gainefull Cost* [*F.S.* 14]
Wilson, T. (1611). *A Christian Dictionarie*
    (MS 1636). British Museum Loan MSS 29/172, fol. 105 (Wilson to Sir Robert Harley, 19 May 1636). Cited by kind permission of Lady Anne Bentinck
Worden, T. (1664). *The Types Unvailed, or the Gospel Pick't out of the Legal Ceremonies*

Secondary sources

Bercovitch, S. (ed.) (1972). *Typology and Early American Literature*. Amherst, Mass.: University of Massachusetts Press
Christianson, P. (1978). *Reformers and Babylon: English Apocalyptic Visions from the Reformation to the Eve of the Civil War*. Toronto, Buffalo, London: University of Toronto Press
Collinson, P. (1967). *The Elizabethan Puritan Movement*. London: Jonathan Cape
Davies, H. (1948). *The Worship of the English Puritans*. Westminster: The Dacre Press
Firth, K. R. (1979). *The Apocalyptic Tradition in Reformation Britain, 1530–1645*. Oxford: Oxford University Press
Freeman, R. (1948). *English Emblem Books*. London: Chatto and Windus
Frei, H. W. (1974). *The Eclipse of the Biblical Narrative*. New Haven and London: Yale University Press
Haller, W. (1938). *The Rise of Puritanism*. New York: Columbia University Press
Holifield, E. B. (1974). *The Covenant Sealed: The Development of Puritan Sacramental Theology in Old and New England, 1520–1720*. New Haven and London: Yale University Press
Keeble, N. (1982). *Richard Baxter: Puritan Man of Letters*. Oxford: Oxford University Press
Kendall, R. T. (1979). *Calvin and English Calvinism to 1649*. Oxford: Oxford University Press
Lake, P. (1982). *Moderate Puritanism and the Elizabethan Church*. Cambridge: Cambridge University Press
Lewalski, B. K. (1979). *Protestant Poetics and the Seventeenth-Century Religious Lyric*. Princeton, N.J.: Princeton University Press
Love, W. D. (1895). *The Fast and Thanksgiving Days of New England*. Boston and New York: Houghton, Mifflin and Company
Olsen, N. (1973). *John Foxe and the Elizabethan Church*. Berkeley, Los Angeles and London: University of California Press
Polizzotto, C. M. (1975). *Types and Typology: A Study in Puritan Hermeneutics*. Unpublished Ph.D. Thesis, University of London
Tyacke, N. (1973). Puritanism, Arminianism and Counter-Revolution, in *The Origins of the English Civil War*, ed. C. Russell, pp. 119–43. London: Macmillan
Wakefield, G. S. (1957). *Puritan Devotion*. London: The Epworth Press
Wilson, J. F. (1969). *Pulpit in Parliament: Puritanism during the English Civil Wars, 1640–1648*. Princeton, N.J.: Princeton University Press

III

THE CONSCIOUS AND THE UNCONSCIOUS SACRIFICE: KIERKEGAARD ON ART, SUFFERING AND RELIGION

GEORGE PATTISON

'When Christians are exposed to public insult, when they suffer and die for his sake, Christ takes on visible form in his Church.' These words of Dietrich Bonhoeffer (1959, 273) reflect an approach to Christian life and witness which had all but disappeared from mainstream Protestantism by the late eighteenth century but which was then rediscovered in the wake of the Romantic movement. One of the main contributors to this rediscovery was Søren Kierkegaard (1813–55) whose late diaries and (simultaneous) polemics against the established Church return again and again to the question of what it means to be a witness to Christ. Kierkegaard's answer to this question was that a true witness did not testify by preaching from a well-endowed and socially respected pulpit but by suffering for and because of the gospel. A true witness is a blood-witness, a martyr in what Kierkegaard, rightly or wrongly, took to be the universal and undisputed sense of the early Church. Such witnesses are 'the sacrificed ones' (Kierkegaard 1967–78, vol. IV, 562).[1]

No doubt there is much that is morbid in Kierkegaard's preoccupation, one might even say obsession, with the themes of martyrdom, sacrifice and freely chosen suffering; nor can it be disputed that there is something stifling in the intensity and repetitiveness with which he treats these matters; nor, finally, can it be denied that Kierkegaard himself would make a fascinating 'case' in the annals of the psychopathology of religious melancholy. However, having said all this, it also needs to be said that he was a great philosopher and a major Christian writer and that what he actually says about suffering is frighteningly lucid and is consistent with much popular Christian writing and devotion. We are therefore well-advised to take these writings seriously on account both of their place in Kierkegaard's authorship as a whole and of their influence on subsequent Christian thought.

Kierkegaard's own approach to most questions is what he himself called 'indirect', and it is therefore appropriate to develop our own exegesis of his thought indirectly and to start not with his understanding of the Christian life, but with his vision of another sort of life, a life as remote as possible from the Christian life, a life he calls 'the poetic' or 'the aesthetic' life. An entry in one of his early diaries says of this poetic life that:

this is the glory of the world; this is the highest and the best on earth: the poet – this illustrious name to which one attaches the most elevated conceptions, the most lofty expectations – and yet this is his fate: to know a thirst which is never satisfied. The poetic life in the personality is the unconscious sacrifice, the *molimina* of the divine, because it is first in the religious that the sacrifice becomes conscious and the misrelationship is removed. (J & P 1 450/III A 62)

This is a striking text, not least on account of the rather odd description of the poetic life as 'sacrificial', albeit the sacrifice concerned is also described as 'unconcious'. What then does it mean to call the poetic life 'the unconscious sacrifice'? An answer to this question will prepare the way for a full understanding of what Kierkegaard means by calling the religious life a life of 'conscious' sacrifice and, it may be added, by proceeding in this way we follow the course of Kierkegaard's own authorship: from the aesthetic to the religious.

Kierkegaard's understanding of the poetic life was moulded by the two great streams of contemporary idealist thought: Romanticism and Hegelianism. When he speaks of the poetic life as 'the highest and the best on earth' he shows the influence of the Romantic concept of poetic genius, but when he goes on to argue that this same poetic life is limited by a certain lack of consciousness he shows that, here at least, he has learnt from the Hegelians. Let us now look first at the poetic life as that was understood by the Romantics.

The Early Romantic movement (German: *die Frühromantik*), which can be dated to the last decade of the eighteenth century, comprised such literary figures as Friedrich and A. W. Schlegel, Tieck, Novalis and Hölderlin, as well as philosophers such as Schelling and his Norwegian disciple Henrik Steffens and, not least, the theologian Friedrich Schleiermacher. The influence of this circle of writers and thinkers pervaded Danish as well as German cultural life, although by the time Kierkegaard went to university in the 1830s these 'Early Romantics' were the old men and a second wave of Romantic figures – Byron, Shelley and Heine, for example – had appeared, who represented a nihilistic development of Romantic themes. Nonetheless the Early Romantics continued to be a major force in the intellectual climate of the age: Schleiermacher visited Copenhagen while Kierkegaard was a student and, in Berlin, he heard both Schelling and Steffens lecture.

The philosophy of Early Romanticism laid great stress on aesthetic experience. With regard to the Kantian division of life into the two realms of transcendent freedom (selfhood, ethics) and of finite appearance (nature, experience) the Romantics asserted that aesthetic experience was the sole means of reconciling these otherwise irreconcilable dimensions, for, in their understanding of it, aesthetic experience involved the intuition of Absolute Spirit (freedom) in, with and under a sensuous, finite appearance (or form). The imaginative creation and reception of art is thus the true climax of human life in which man echoes the creative activity of the divine Being. The poet communicates 'radiant, holy images of the eternal' (Steffens 1905, 22). In such aesthetic experience man experiences himself as an harmonious being; the divisions and contradictions which characterize the rest of his existence are overcome, or at least set to one side. All men may participate in such aesthetic experience from time to time, but for the poet such a condition is the nature of his whole existence. A poetic genius of this kind is described, with typical Romantic pomposity, by Coleridge, who was an eager disciple of the German Early Romantics:

The poet, described in ideal perfection, brings the whole soul of man into activity, with the subordination of its faculties to each other according to their relative worth and dignity. He diffuses a tone and spirit of unity, that blends, and (as it were) *fuses*, each into each, by that synthetic and magical power, to which I would exclusively appropriate the name of Imagination. (Coleridge 1906, 166)

This is the poetic life which Kierkegaard describes as 'the highest and the best on earth'.

The Romantics soon found critics. Not least among these was Hegel, who broke with his former friend and colleague, Schelling, on the issue of whether Absolute Spirit could be known or merely intuited, comprehended or merely apprehended. Hegel argued that the Romantic glorification of intuition and feeling amounted to little more than 'rapturous haziness' (Hegel 1977, 6), and that the true road to knowledge of the Absolute was only open to those who were prepared to think doubtingly, critically and historically, and who were willing to set forth their thoughts in a logical systematic way. The aesthetic intuition or apprehension of the Absolute is described by Hegel as merely 'immediate', and such immediate awareness is, he claims, surpassed by the religious and philosophical forms of consciousness. Art, in other words, is relegated to third place, and Hegel wrote that 'the peculiar nature of art no longer fills our highest need... Thought and reflection have spread their wings above fine art' (Hegel 1975, 10).

Kierkegaard took over from the Hegelians the point that art, or the poetic life, yields only an imaginary, as opposed to a *real*, unification of the polarities of existence. The harmonious feeling which art bestows can only be a temporary or momentary experience. In such blessed moments the being of the whole world, the being of God, and my own being are poetry in which all the multiplicity, the wretched disparities of life indigestible for human thought, are reconciled in a misty, dreamy existence. But then, regrettably, I wake up again, and the very same tragic relativity in everything begins worse than ever... (*J & P* I, 448/II A 125)

But Kierkegaard did not, as is well known, go all the way with Hegel. For whereas Hegel believed that the contradictions of the world could be made an object for detached, philosophical study, Kierkegaard *experienced* the contradictions, the 'wretched disparities of life', as an agonal dimension of existence which could only be lived through – not 'known'. For this reason his criticism of aesthetic experience was not so much that it was an inadequate form of consciousness (by comparison with rational knowledge), but because it masked the real contradictions of the personal life which had to be suffered rather than sublimated. Thus he saw the poetic life as an attempt to distract man's attention from his real condition of suffering and pain. The best-known, and most forceful, presentation of this view occurs at the beginning of his first major work, *Either/Or*:

What is a poet? An unhappy man who in his heart harbors a deep anguish, but those lips are so fashioned that the moans and cries which pass over them are transformed into ravishing music. His fate is like that of the unfortunate victims whom the tyrant Phalaris imprisoned in a brazen bull, and slowly tortured over a steady fire; their cries could not reach the tyrant's ears so as to strike terror into his heart; when they reached his ears they sounded like sweet music. (Kierkegaard 1959, I, 19)

This understanding of the poetic life turns the tables on the Romantics and anticipates Nietzsche's concept of art as a necessary illusion. The comparison with the Romantics can usefully be focussed on Coleridge's 'Dejection: An Ode' (Coleridge 1912, 362ff.). In this poem Coleridge describes a condition which he experiences as

> A grief without a pang, void, dark and drear,
> A stifled, drowsy, unimpassioned grief,
> Which finds no natural outlet, no relief,
> In word or sigh, or tear...

In such a mood even the beauty of the natural world can only be seen, not felt, and the poet laments the failing of his 'genial spirits' as he remembers the times when visions of beauty met him in all his ways, visions which were the offspring of his own 'shaping Spirit of imagination'. The operation of this 'shaping Spirit' is described as a 'strong music in the soul'; it is a 'light', a 'glory', a 'fair luminous mist', a 'beautiful and beauty-making power', whose whole essence is 'joy'. The point of the poem is that 'dejection' is the result of the drying-up of this spring of joyous imagination. Kierkegaard, however, would argue the opposite case: that the poetic work of the imagination is in fact a sublimation of the nagging consciousness of an underlying despair. Art is, in fact, a product of dejection or, to use a typical Kierkegaardian word, melancholy. Such dejection may follow the youthful ecstasies of the imagination in the order of time, but it precedes them in the order of causes. There are crises and contradictions which the poet, as poet, never faces, let alone overcomes; indeed his poetry is precisely a way of dissipating the reality and the force of his repressed suffering. In a poem such as 'Dejection' the poet actually gains a sort of insight into his true condition, and, albeit still obliquely, testifies to the inadequacy of his own poetic life.

Nietzsche passes a similar judgement on Romantic art. Like Kierkegaard he is profoundly aware of the suffering inherent in existence, and he admits to being impressed with the wisdom of Silenus that man is an 'ephemeral wretch, begotten by accident and toil . . . What would be best . . . is . . . not to have been born, not to *be*, to be *nothing*. But the second best is to die soon' (Nietzsche 1956, 29). Yet, Nietzsche argues, art provides us with a way by means of which this unbearable life can be made bearable. Art is a 'rapt vision and delightful illusion' by which the 'ever-suffering and con-tradictory' life of man redeems itself (Nietzsche 1956, 32):

If we could imagine an incarnation of dissonance – and what is man if not that? – that dissonance, in order to endure life, would need a marvellous illusion to cover it with a veil of beauty. This is the proper artistic intention of Apollo, in whose name are gathered together all those countless illusions of fair semblance which at any moment make life worth living and whet our appetite for the next moment. (Nietzsche 1956, 145)

Art is thus a kind of safety-valve for the psychic turmoil of human existence. Both Nietzsche and Kierkegaard see the artist as a kind of liar – but there is a significant difference: for Nietzsche it is axiomatic that 'God is dead', that religion, like art, is an illusory form of consciousness. Indeed, he would claim that religion and art are inextricably involved with one another; both occupy the same plane of existence. Kierkegaard, however, separates them utterly. Religion, he asserts, is not an evasion of the agonal dimension of life, but faces it and embraces it. The religious life works on the assumption that 'Keeping a wound open can also be very beneficial: a healthy and open wound; sometimes it is worst when it skins over' (*J & P* IV, 369/VI A 16).

We are now in a position to see what Kierkegaard means by calling the poet an 'unconscious sacrifice'. Poetry – like all art – masks the deep pain of life with beautiful images and harmonies so that, for a while at least, we forget what life is really like, and escape into a dream-world. This, Kierkegaard would argue, is a universal need and experience. But the actual production of art, the poetic life itself, the life of the 'genius', presupposes an intensification of the normal human condition, and consequently an intensification of the suffering which belongs to this condition. The intensity of this suffering acts as the motor force of the genius's productivity. The greater the pain, the more beautiful the music. The poetic genius, however, does not seek out suffering, since he is unaware of his true situation, and his poetry is precisely an attempt to avoid the consciousness of pain. He believes, as he must, in the reality of his dream. Indeed he is unable to separate his real life in the world from the dream-world of art. Kierkegaard wrote down in his diary a line from the Romantic writer von Eichendorff which expresses this poetic confusion of reality and imagination with great precision: '"Träume ich denn, oder träumt diese phantastische Nacht von mir?"' ('Do I then dream, or does this fantastic night dream of me?') (II A 405). The poet is what Hegel calls an 'unhappy consciousness'; his genius is the fruit of a more than usual suffering, and yet as he does not realize this he cannot really, decisively, escape from this suffering.

The poetic dream hovers on the edge of reality; it is born out of the needs of life, but it does not give a true reflection of life, only an illusory promise:

The poetic ideal is always a false ideal, for the true ideal is always the real. So when the spirit is not allowed to soar up into the eternal world of spirit it remains midway and rejoices in the pictures reflected in the clouds and weeps that they are so transitory. A poet-existence is therefore, as such, an unhappy existence, it is higher than finiteness and yet not infiniteness. The poet sees the ideals, but he must flee away from the world in order to rejoice in them, he cannot bear about in the midst of life's confusion these divine images within him... (Kierkegaard 1959, II, 214)

Such a poet, weeping over the transitory nature of his images, is the figure portrayed by Coleridge in 'Dejection'. But in this passage Kierkegaard makes it clear that although the poetic life is 'as such' a failure, 'an unhappy existence', it is an attempt to transcend the merely finite, animal life of man devoid of ideals; it is an attempt to achieve some kind of transcendence and is, if only on this account, worthy of honour. Nietzsche, as we have seen, is happy to leave it at that: what he calls his 'honesty' compels him to see the aesthetic redemption of life as purely illusory – and yet the only possible redemption there is. Sartre and other existentialist writers similarly deny the possibility of man's breaking through to a position where existence is accepted and affirmed in the light of a totally free act of self-choice. Our uttermost possibility on such a view is simply to accept the meaninglessness of it all, and to make do with such broken and inadequate dreams as art can offer. Kierkegaard, however, believes that in addition to the false ideality of art there is a true ideal, an ideal which can endure 'life's confusion'. This true ideal is the religious life. The poet is an *unconscious* sacrifice, vainly and blindly labouring to become – in his self and in his work – an image of the true eternal freedom: the religious person actually lives this freedom, the freedom of the new being in Christ which no image or set of images can ever adequately convey. Kierkegaard's faith in the reality of what he calls an 'eternal blessedness', a fully personal immortal life with God in which the dissonances of this life are replaced by the unending strains of adoration and praise, is nowhere more clearly stated than in the words which he chose to be inscribed upon his tombstone, words taken from one of the great pietistic hymn-writers of the Danish Church:

> In yet a little while
> I shall have won;
> Then the whole fight
> Will all at once be done.
> Then I may rest
> In bowers of roses
> And perpetually
> And perpetually
> speak with my Jesus.
> (Kierkegaard 1978, 27)

But – in contrast to the poetic vision – he does not wish this vision of a heavenly existence to mask the reality of existence here and now. The religious life presupposes a clear and unblinking recognition of the universal and inescapable agony of life. The 'honesty' of the religious view means that joy is seen not merely as something which comes 'after' life, but is to be affirmed *in* this life *despite* everything which seems to work against it. The religious life strikes a 'note of joy in the strife of suffering'.[2]

Before proceeding to look more closely at this religious life a final point needs to be made concerning the poetic life of aesthetic experience. What Kierkegaard says about the poet and about art in general is both narrower and broader than we might at first be tempted to think. It is narrower because the view of art which he espouses is not really capable of dealing with the manifold of artistic enterprises which constitute the whole field of 'art'. Indeed, the notion that the ultimate purpose of art is to provide a beautiful image of an harmonious existence is a notion which was already being questioned in his own time. The twentieth century seems to have abandoned it altogether. Many of the major movements in twentieth-century art (in all fields of art) have explicitly set themselves the task of undermining or subverting the sort of 'beautiful' aesthetic experience which Kierkegaard regarded as the main aim of all art. Of course Kierkegaard would simply retort (as many people do!) that such works are not 'real' art; but it must constitute a major criticism of any view of art that it is unable to make a place for what is actually produced as art. Kierkegaard's understanding of the poet is as much a programme for art as an interpretation of it. But his treatment of this issue is also broader than it at first appears, since the aesthetic experience which he is concerned with is not confined to what we would recognize as art. It is rather a basic dimension of consciousness which can manifest itself in many ways. One of the most important, in Kierkegaard's work, is the way in which religion can be used 'aesthetically', used, that is, to conceal the dissonances and discords which true religion is concerned to expose. In this sense he is able to speak of the priest as a kind of poet whose message anaesthetizes his 'audience' instead of challenging it (Kierkegaard 1968, 201–2). The 'aesthetic' then is not just a matter of poetry and art: it is rather a basic attitude to life. The consequences of such an aesthetic life are what Kierkegaard deals with in his major 'novels': 'Either/Or'; 'Repetition'; 'Stages on Life's Way'. It is one of the ironies of literary history that in these analyses of the failure of aesthetic existence Kierkegaard anticipates, perhaps even sets in motion, those forms of modern literature which he would have had difficulty in recognizing as 'art'. For what he shows in these works is figures who are far from 'beautiful'; they are, on the contrary, described in terms of *angst*, despair, boredom and suffering. This, in Kierkegaard's view, is the reality which lies behind the glittering surface of the poetic life. It is to the religious way of coping with this reality that we now turn.

This religious life, as we have already seen, is prepared to face up to the suffering and anguish of existence. The religious man does not flee suffering but freely and honestly affirms it as a true part of his total selfhood. At this point, however, we come to a tension in Kierkegaard's thought. For this conscious affirmation of suffering can take two very different forms. On the one hand it can be simply an attitude of resignation; on the other it can involve the quest for voluntary suffering and, ultimately, for martyrdom. The question is whether the Christian is called to take upon himself the suffering which is an inescapable part of the human condition, or whether he is to go further, to seek out additional sufferings, sufferings which, in the natural course of things, he could avoid. Either way we can speak of the free affirmation and acceptance of suffering, but there is a real difference, a difference which may indeed be that between a healthy and a pathological attitude to suffering. Admittedly the line is not always easy to draw; but although Kierkegaard often seems to hold the two positions in tension he increasingly seems to have opted for the cult of martyrdom. The difference between the two approaches is clearly reflected in the following quotation from his journal: 'To suffer patiently is not specifically Christian at all – but freely to choose the suffering which one could also avoid, freely to choose it in the interest of the good cause – this is Christian' (*J & P* IV, 376/VIII¹ A 259).

Why does Kierkegaard choose this latter course, the way of the martyr? The easy answer is, of course, because he was a psychologically disturbed man. But that is to ignore the theological dimension of the question; for, theologically, we must ask whether his 'solution' was a genuine interpretation of the New Testament teaching (as he claimed it was), or whether he was unduly influenced by a non-biblical metaphysical bias, a Manichaean rejection of finite, material existence as such – a bias which has often made itself felt in Christian theology, but which is not, in essence, truly biblical. In other words, is the world a 'vale of tears' on account of some fundamental ontological flaw which vitiates created being as such (with the result that we are well advised to escape from 'life' as soon as possible), or is the suffering of existence a superficial excrescence on the face of a basically good and beautiful creation?

This question is, in fact, no easier to answer in the limited context of Kierkegaard's authorship than it is in the face of life itself. Kierkegaard, however, tried, as so many apologists have tried, to unite a vision of God as pure love with an almost Schopenhauerian horror of the seething ferment of biological existence. But his affirmation of God's love was an increasingly desperate cry 'in spite of' all appearances, and he more and more tended to the view that it was best to die, literally die, to this world, to be with the Lord in the next. The terrible abyss of his torment is made clear by the following excerpts from what was to be, dramatically, the final entry in his journal:

The destiny of this life is that it be brought to the extremity of life-weariness. The person who when brought to that point can maintain or the person whom God helps so he is able to maintain that it is God who has brought him to that point – such a person, from the Christian point of view, passes the examination of life and is nurtured for eternity ... what, specifically, does God want? He wants souls able to praise, adore, worship, and thank him – the business of angels. Therefore God is surrounded by angels ... what pleases Him even more than the praise of angels is a human being who in the last lap of this life, when God seemingly changes into sheer cruelty and with the most cruelly devised cruelty does everything to deprive him of all zest for life, nevertheless continues to believe that God is love, that God does it out of love. Such a person becomes an angel. (*J & P* VI, 575–6/XI^2 A 439)

From this perspective Kierkegaard is able to reduce Christianity to the two theses that 'because you are a sufferer, therefore God loves you', and that 'because you love God, therefore you must suffer' (*J & P* IV, 412/X^4 A 593). It seems hard to avoid the conclusion that he was indeed motivated by an almost Manichaean disgust – or perhaps we should say an almost Sartrean 'nausea' – at the natural life of the material world, and that it was this disgust which led him to champion the way of the martyr, the way of freely chosen self-sacrifice. Yet if we follow him through the course of his authorship we see that he himself seemed to fight against following his thought through to this conclusion. His short essay 'Has a Man the Right to Let Himself be Put to Death for the Truth?' gives a negative answer to the question posed by its own title (Kierkegaard 1940). He did not wish to condone, still less encourage, all manner of romantic self-immolating gestures. Suffering, in his view, is the matter of a lifetime of endurance, and to embrace suffering is not to take a short cut out of the stressful condition of existence but is a matter of patient endurance. This emphasis on endurance indicates that for Kierkegaard the whole issue of our experience of suffering has to be set against the background of a providential ordering of life, which in turn means that he can never just write off the created order as such. The vale of tears is also the vale of soul-making.

The theme of patient endurance is one which he takes up again and again in his *Upbuilding Discourses*. Indeed, the titles of two of these, 'In Patience to Acquire One's Soul' and 'In Patience to Preserve One's Soul', show the importance he attached to this idea (Kierkegaard 1943–6). In the former of these he argues that patience is not a means by which one acquires a soul (or self), such that the means is external or incidental to the end attained, but it is precisely *in patience*, in becoming patient, that one comes to one's self. Why is this so? Because patience means the voluntary immersion of the self in the stream of its own essential temporality. Human existence is inescapably temporal. This subjection to time is tied up with the ultimate nothingness of life, with what we have referred to as the agonal dimension of existence. This, after all, is a point which recurs throughout the mainstream of Western religious thought ('The days of man are but as grass...'). Here again we can contrast the religious acceptance of temporality with the aesthetic attempt to freeze or neutralize time. The religious person accepts his life as a process of becoming, however painful this acceptance may be, whereas the poetic life tries to compress life into moments of intense and penetrating insight or intuition, moments which are somehow 'timeless'. The religious acceptance of time, however, alone paves the way for man to acquire what Kierkegaard calls an inward or interior history; and it is only in the context of such an interior history that we can penetrate what is meant by seeing life as the way of the cross. For

a cross-bearer who every day takes up his cross cannot be represented either in poetry or in art, because the point is that he does it every day. If I would imagine a hero who stakes his life, it can very well be concentrated in the moment, but not the business of dying daily, for here the principal point is that it occurs every day. Courage can very well be concentrated in the moment, but not patience, precisely for the reason that patience strives with time. (Kierkegaard 1959, II, 138)

Such patience is an integral part of what Kierkegaard means by the Christian life being a life of suffering. Despite the differences in terminology what he is talking about in such passages is essentially similar to Tillich's concept of 'absolute faith which makes the courage of despair possible'; it is the courage to be 'even in the despair about meaning' (Tillich 1962, 167ff.). Like Tillich, Kierkegaard argues that the experience of despair can be transformed by a conscious and resolute willing of despair itself. That is just another way of saying that we are to accept, to affirm, to live through the essential nothingness of our temporal being. For, he claims, we continually tend to absolutize what is intrinsically temporal and therefore passing. In this way we are constantly threatened by despair since what we regard as absolute, what we regard as making life worth living, is something which may well at any moment vanish or fade. To recognize this situation, however, is to see the relativity of all temporal existence and thus, paradoxically, to be liberated from its claims.

Kierkegaard's advocacy of despair – or, as he also calls it, resignation – can be defended as a bleak but nonetheless realistic approach to the search for authentic selfhood (Mullen 1981). Nor need it lead to a complete break with worldly existence as such. And yet there is a point here where the pursuit of suffering which we find in the later writings is clearly anticipated. For by arguing that our clinging to what is transient is the real ground of despair, Kierkegaard opens the door to an ethic of renunciation which can easily lead on to a deliberate policy of self-inflicted suffering. There is a delicate balance between such an idealization of suffering and the realistic appraisal and acceptance of life's stresses and dissonances which belongs to the attitude of patient resignation. Edward Young, whom Kierkegaard read approvingly, wrote in his poem on the theme of 'Resignation':

> For the course of Providence;
> This course it has pursued,
> 'Pain is the parent, woe the womb,
> Of sound, important good'.

> Our hearts are fasten'd to this world
> By strong and endless ties,
> And every sorrow cuts a string,
> And urges us to rise. (Young 1806, IV, 130)

Such counsel may help us to accept inevitable suffering, but it is also a short step from here to the deliberate pursuit of pain and suffering; the more the pain and the woe, the sounder the good we receive from it!

But is there not the possibility of a third way? Is this step from resignation to the pursuit of suffering really necessary? Is it not rather itself a form of impatience, of wanting to leap over the anxious tedium of time? It may be, as Kierkegaard argues, that human existence is utterly immersed in time, a process of becoming which is incapable of constructing itself into a new totality, and, as such, having no end (in the sense of *telos*: goal, or aim) in itself; but does it follow that its goal or meaning is to be sought elsewhere, outside it? Why should we have to cut loose from temporal existence to find the meaning to that existence? Indeed, Kierkegaard's critique of the aesthetic flights from reality, and his notion of accepting our despair and our nothingness in an attitude of patient resignation, suggest another way. Patient resignation is not, as he himself says, a means of getting to a realm of meanings behind or beyond the veil of appearance: it is rather itself the appropriate expression of meaning experienced in the encounter with a transcendent, completely creative divine Being, who stretches out the whole sphere of relativity as the milieu in which finite, temporal beings, such as ourselves, have their proper existence. We prove our transcendent freedom, our god-likeness, by acknowledging and accepting the wisdom of this order – not by striving to get out of it nor by seeking to anticipate its end. As Alan Watts has said, 'You do not play a sonata *in order* to reach the final chord and if the meanings of things were simply in ends, composers would write nothing but finales' (Watts 1978, 105).

Although there are elements of Kierkegaard's thought which point to just such an acceptance of the relative in all its relativity as the actual form of the created order (and thus the milieu in which we meet with the divine) it is hard to escape the conclusion that his final judgement owes a great deal to a dualistic metaphysical bias (as well, it must be admitted, as to the morbid aspects of his personal outlook). And yet there is a final point worth considering. It is simply this: that people do not take kindly to the demythologizing of what they regard as absolute ends or values. The person who lives without illusions, and who takes away others' illusions that things are more than they really are, will not tread the path of easy popularity. It is Kierkegaard's view that men prefer the services of an idealizing (and falsifying) poet, since

man in his natural condition is sick, he is in a delusion, a self-deceit, and therefore desires most of all to be deceived, so that he can get permission not merely to continue in the delusion, but to make himself at home in the self-deceit. And a deceiver, suitable for this task, is, precisely: the poet. Therefore man loves him above all. (Kierkegaard 1968, 201)

Not only the artists but also, in Kierkegaard's judgement, the priests of the established Church and, we may add, ideologues of all kinds who announce peace when there is no peace, are 'poets' in this sense. It also follows that whoever sees the illusions of such poets for what they are will draw down upon himself the wrath of the crowd. This will not necessarily lead to martyrdom in the sense of the actual suffering of death; it may, as Kierkegaard found in his dealings with the popular press, lead to being made an object of ridicule, but it may also lead further. A name such as that of Oscar Romero reminds us that it is perilous to speak the truth, to expose cruelty and corruption for what they are. It is not exactly what Kierkegaard meant by his distinction between the conscious and the unconscious sacrifice, but it is worth considering that consciousness of the false idealizations by which men conform themselves to the pattern of this passing age may well lead to a conscious decision such as that faced by the early martyrs: a decision to risk life and goods for the sake of truth. Such a consideration is not morbid or pathological. It is simply facing facts. It is for this reason that the Christian witness may (even to-day!) find himself or herself becoming 'a sacrificed one'.

NOTES

1 Kierkegaard's *Journals and Papers* have been translated into English and edited in six volumes by H. V. and E. H. Hong, and published by Indiana University Press from 1967 to 1978 (we gratefully acknowledge permission from Indiana University Press for permission to quote from this edition). Hereafter all references to this work will be given in the text in the following form: *J & P* 1, 450 (meaning vol. 1, p. 450). They will be followed by the corresponding reference number to the standard Danish edition of the *Papirer* in the following form: x 4A 381 (meaning vol. x, section 4A, number 381).
2 'Joyful Notes in the Strife of Suffering' is the title of a set of Kierkegaard's *Christian Discourses*; see Kierkegaard 1971.

REFERENCES

Bonhoeffer, D. (1959). *The Cost of Discipleship*. London: SCM Press
Coleridge, S. T. (1906). *Biographia Literaria* (Everyman edn). London: Dent
    (1912). *Poetical Works*. Oxford: Oxford University Press
Hegel, G. W. F. (1975). *Aesthetics*. Oxford: Oxford University Press
    (1977). *Phenomenology of Spirit*. Oxford: Oxford University Press
Kierkegaard, S. (1940). *The Present Age*. Oxford: Oxford University Press
    (1943–6). *Edifying [or Upbuilding] Discourses*, 4 vols. Minneapolis: Augsburg
    (1959). *Either/Or*, 2 vols. Princeton: Princeton University Press
    (1967–78). *Journals and Papers*, 6 vols. Bloomington: Indiana University Press
    (1968). *Attack upon 'Christendom'*. Princeton: Princeton University Press
    (1971). *Christian Discourses*. Princeton: Princeton University Press
    (1978). *Letters and Documents*. Princeton: Princeton University Press
Mullen, J. D. (1981). *Kierkegaard's Philosophy: Self-Deception and Cowardice in The Present Age*. New York: New American Library
Nietzsche, F. (1956). *The Birth of Tragedy*. New York: Doubleday (Anchor)
Steffens, H. (1905). *Inledning til Philosophiske Forelaesninger i København*, new edn. Copenhagen: Gyldendal
Tillich, P. (1962). *The Courage to Be*. London: Collins (Fontana)
Watts, A. (1978). *The Wisdom of Insecurity*. London: Rider
Young, E. (1806). *Poetical Works*, 4 vols. London: Whittingham and Roland

12

PEARSE'S SACRIFICE: CHRIST AND CUCHULAIN CRUCIFIED AND RISEN IN THE EASTER RISING, 1916

S. W. GILLEY

The idea of sacrifice occurs in Christian cultures in realms remote from high theology, and the invocation of the soldier's sacrifice in war became highly topical in 1982, when even sensitive Anglican bishops defended the British onslaught in the Falklands with the text 'Greater love hath no man than this, that a man lay down his life for his friends.' The pacifist might reply that the scripture does not say that a man should kill for his friends; yet it needed only this little war to remind us of the power of sacrifice even in modern language, in the ambiguous willingness to give up one's own life while taking the lives of others. It was this understanding of sacrifice in war, while invoking the model of the passion of Christ, which inspired and justified the first ultimately successful 'anti-colonial' revolution of the twentieth century, the Irish Rising of Easter 1916; and the speeches and poetry of the leaders of the Rising, of Joseph Mary Plunkett and Thomas MacDonagh, and more especially of Padraic Pearse, drew upon the sacrificial Christ of a prayerful Irish Catholicism.

The Easter reference in the Rising has always attracted attention. As James Stephens declared at the time, on Easter Sunday in Dublin they cried 'Christ has risen' in the churches; they cried 'Ireland has risen' on Easter Monday (A. Martin 1966, 38). 'Elsewhere Easter is celebrated as the Feast of the Resurrection', remarks Terence de Vere White; 'In Dublin it is celebrated as the Feast of the Insurrection' (O'Brien 1973, 308). The resurrection of Ireland at Easter derives its power from a long tradition: the identification of Ireland and the Irish people with Jesus, as the suffering Christ of the nations martyred by the British, runs deep through nineteenth-century Irish Catholic culture. Yet in the wider European setting, the metaphor of suffering like Christ was so far from revolutionary violence as to incur the Marxist indictment of religion for offering an otherworldly justification for present suffering, and certainly the political conservatism of the court of Rome, in its century of warfare with revolutionary Italian nationalism, discouraged even Irish Catholics from developing the case for a just war into an argument for armed rebellion. There *were* Catholic revolutions in the nineteenth century, in Poland and Belgium, as well as a strong movement of Catholic civil disobedience in Prussia and the German Empire; and in Ireland there was a minority of revolutionary priests, from the 'croppy' clerics of Wexford in 1798 to the irrepressible neo-Fenian Father Patrick Lavelle. But the Church in general opposed the Irish rebellions of 1798, 1848 and 1867, supporting instead the non-violent nationalism of O'Connell and later Home Rule (Lyons 1971; Norman 1965). Archbishop Paul Cullen, later a cardinal, as ruler of the Irish Church for more than a quarter of a century from 1850, earned the undying hatred of the revolutionary Fenians by refusing them the sacraments (Norman 1965), yet deep-seated anticlericalism failed to develop (McCartney 1967; Newsinger 1979), and the bridges with constitutionalist, not violent, nationalism were mended by Cullen's episcopal successors. Despite the survival of an underground insurrectionary tradition in the tiny Irish Republican Brotherhood, founded and funded from America, the victory of the constitutionalist school seemed complete by 1900, through an alliance between the priesthood and the parliamentary politicians (Larkin 1975, 1978, 1979; Miller 1973; Tierney 1976). To the outward eye, the non-violent character of Irish Catholicism seemed secure until the very eve of the Rising, which satisfied none of the Church's conditions for a just rebellion (Horgan 1948, 285; Shaw 1972, 118): so that Pearse and his fellow rebels were in revolt not only against the British, but against the explicit teaching and the dominant element in Irish Catholicism itself.

Yet the Rising was overwhelmingly the work of Catholics; only one of the 1916 leaders, Tom Clarke, an old Fenian and sometime convict in England, remained true to the Fenian past by dying without the last rites, and the principal Protestant connected with the Rising, Roger Casement, was received into the Church before his execution. Some other nationalists like Maud Gonne had already taken a nationalist path to Rome (Levenson 1977, 94). Catholicism had baptized revolution: and that by means of an understanding of Christ which carried revolution into the heart of Catholicism.

The revolutionary ideal was no more exclusively Catholic or even Christian in origin than Irish nationalism itself. Irish constitutionalism was partly a product of English Utilitarian influence, and revolution came to Ireland from republican France, firing the imagination of the rebels of Protestant background if not Protestant conviction, like Robert Emmet and Wolfe Tone. The Irish nationalist pantheon was always an ecumenical one, and Catholic nationalists were never narrow sectarians, but readily accepted Protestant leaders like Isaac Butt and Charles Stewart Parnell. Yet from the 1820s the great majority of Presbyterians and Church of Ireland

Protestants became militantly Unionist and often No-Popery Evangelical, and so Irish nationalism became Catholic in its mass membership, as the expression of the wrongs of an impoverished and persecuted people. This trend was enhanced in the second half of the nineteenth century as the ardours of Italianate devotion (Larkin 1972) warmed nationalist feeling (O'Farrell 1971), and as the language revivalists set to work to rescue the dying tongue and culture of the Gael. Here again, in the revival of Gaelic culture, the leaders were often Protestants opposed by the great mass of their co-religionists: most of the professional Gaelic scholars were Catholics, some were priests, but Douglas Hyde, the famous President of the Gaelic League, and Standish O'Grady, whose histories of heroic pagan Ireland so stirred the emotions of the young Padraic Pearse, were both sons of Church of Ireland rectors. The greatest writers of the literary revival, Yeats and Synge, were also Protestants by birth, while another, non-Catholic, element came into the revolutionary tradition through James Connolly (O. D. Edwards 1971), a curious Catholic Marxist who might be said, like many of the early socialists, to have believed in a devout Christianity all his own (Ransom 1980, 29, 94).

Yet the fires of 1916 burnt out the foreign matter in Catholic nationalism. The idealism of literary nationalism was accepted, but not its ventures towards the wild romantic realism of J. M. Synge's depiction of the peasantry. As Pearse's lieutenant in the Dublin Post Office, Connolly, crippled by British bullets, made his confession and was anointed by a Capuchin friar to die a Christian hero, and his socialism never came to mean anything to the great mass of Irishmen. O'Grady's semi-pagan heroism and a Jacobin republicanism purged of anti-Catholicism and anticlericalism became part of the spiritual endowment of the most Catholic state in Europe, a state which was the creation of a Catholic revolution.

Pearse's life and thought lie at the heart of that transition, the translation of ideals not specific to Catholicism into language seemingly Catholic. Like many another an Irish rebel (Horgan 1948, 9), he was of mixed English–Irish parentage, his father being an Englishman, a successful ecclesiastical sculptor of radical London and Birmingham Unitarian background, converted with his English wife to Catholicism in Dublin (R. D. Edwards 1977). His second wife, Padraic's mother, was an Irish Catholic, and from his Irish great aunt the boy got his taste for Irish folk culture. His Gaelic was an acquired tongue which he never spoke with the fluency of a native, and his schooling, by the Christian Brothers, though much more nationalist than most Irish education, was wholly geared to a gradgrind English examination system which he later described as a 'Murder Machine'.

Pearse qualified as a barrister, but his one notable appearance in court, if an oratorical triumph, was a legal failure. His early work was as a teacher and as Secretary of the Gaelic League's Publications Committee, and in both his educational and linguistic endeavours he showed an efficiency and wisdom out of sorts with his literary reputation as a dreamy idealist. As editor of a famous Gaelic journal from 1903, he was responsible for encouraging many practical good works. After 1908, he founded two schools, St Enda's for boys and St Ita's for girls, in which a wide-ranging curriculum emancipated students from the examination treadmill and from coercion and corporal punishment, while under an honours system drawing its inspiration from the 'fosterage' practised in the courts of Irish kings, the students enjoyed considerable freedom from authority in a 'Child Republic' with its own elected officers (Ryan 1919, 80). Pearse is a clear exception to the rule that no man is a hero to his pupils, who seem almost without exception to have loved their school. Like the Gaelic League itself, St Enda's did not seek to be monolingually Irish, but was based on a bilingualism taken from Catholic Belgium. It is true that the pupils sometimes 'ran wild' (Thornley 1971, 343) and that the schools were in chronic financial difficulties, and because Pearse's programmes for expansion and building outran his meagre income, St Ita's had to close. Yet here again, as F. S. L. Lyons declares in his Introduction to Séamas Ó Buachalla's recent collection of Pearse's letters, Pearse was a man 'meticulous and systematic' (Ó Buachalla 1980, xvii) in his business arrangements, and, except perhaps in his own eyes, was by no means a worldly failure, when he took the path to hopeless revolution.

But the first paradox of Pearse's nationalism was that spiritual success was the reward of worldly failure. 'The Gael is not like other men', he wrote in a famous early address:

the spade, and the loom, and the sword are not for him. But a destiny more glorious than that of Rome, more glorious than that of Britain awaits him: to become the saviour of idealism in modern intellectual and social life, the regenerator and rejuvenator of the literature of the world, the instructor of the nations, the preacher of the gospel of nature-worship, hero-worship, God-worship ... (Pearse 1924, 221)

The passage might have been written by a Deist nationalist enthusiast like Mazzini on behalf of Young Italy; it is notable, moreover, for the uncompromising, superhuman standards which it sets for Irish nationhood. Pearse's idealist refusal of the decadent realism of contemporary European literature is just as absolute, for the Gaelic race is the only one possessing 'a literature natural and uncontaminated ... as different from the unnatural literature of to-day as the pure radiance of the sun is different from the hideous glare of the electric light ...' (Pearse 1924, 225). Though he was later to change his mind on the value of the realism of Synge, the young Pearse was a passionate believer in the purity and perfection of Irishness, and that made him no moderate Home Ruler, but an exponent of separatism from the very first. Yet the lesson here – 'the spade, and the loom, and the sword are not for him' – is one of conquest by the spirit not the sword, by the weapons appropriate to the schoolteacher and Gaelic Leaguer. Indeed the lecture concludes with Newman's vision of an international Catholic University in Dublin, and Pearse's early political intransigence remained firmly rooted in the realm of absolute ideas.

Pearse was, however, offering as severely censored a reading of the Gaelic inheritance as of foreign literature, a Puritan Victorian understanding of heroic Ireland common to the Gaelic movement as a whole. The considerable traditional elements of bawdy and eroticism (Connolly 1982, 192–4) were strained out in the translation in the interests of an Ireland pure and holy; not so the violence, which it was impossible to purge, and which is so grandiloquently idealized as Christian chivalry in the rhetorical volumes of O'Grady (1878 and 1880). The hall of King Concobar Mac Nessa of the Red Branch of Ulster is hung with 'the naked forms of great men clear against the dark dome, having the cords of their slaughter around their necks and their white limbs splashed with blood' (O'Grady n.d., 3–4); and Concobar's court is the setting for the coming of the young Cuchulain whom Pearse was to make 'an important if invisible member of the staff' of St Enda's (Pearse 1917b, 90). 'A.E.', the mystic George William Russell, describes Cuchulain in his tribute to O'Grady, as '*that incarnation of Gaelic chivalry, (of) the fire and gentleness, the beauty and heroic ardour*' displayed in a hundred gory battles against overwhelming odds (O'Grady n.d., xiii). Cuchulain's ending is like Christ's, 'strapped to a post and shedding his life's blood in the defence of his people' (O. D. Edwards and F. Pyle 1968, 45). Pearse declared that 'the story of Cuchulainn [sic] symbolises the redemption of man by a sinless God' (Pearse 1924, 156), and wanted an Ireland 'teeming with Cuchulains ... a Cuchulain baptised' (Thompson 1967, 76–7), and the mingling of Christian and pagan elements appears in his ideal for St Enda's:

the knightly tradition of the macradh of Eamhain Macha, dead at the Ford 'in the beauty of their boyhood,' the high tradition of Cuchulainn, 'better is short life with honour than long life with dishonour,' 'I care not though I were to live but one day and one night, if only my fame and my deeds live after me;' the noble tradition of the Fianna, 'we, the Fianna, never told a lie, falsehood was never imputed to us,' 'strength in our hands, truth on our lips, and cleanness in our hearts;' the Christ-like tradition of Colm Cille [sic], 'if I die, it shall be from the excess of the love I bear the Gael.' (Pearse 1917b, 7)

This famous 'non-Christian' saying of Colum Cille, St Columba, inscribed on the walls of St Enda's, with Cuchulain's 'better short life with honour', comes from a late and suspect source (Shaw 1972, 134); but even in a different idiom, the same mingling of warlike sentiment and patriotism with Christianity could be also found in schools in England, in the years before the First World War (Marrin 1974, 127–8). There is, however, an easy transition in Pearse's work from the blood of Cuchulain to the blood of Christ, and from there to the blood of the Irish political martyrs, and so to a more explicit enunciation of the underlying doctrine that the shedding of blood makes men holy.

The full statement of this position belongs to the last years of Pearse's short life: as late as 1912, he welcomed the Home Rule Bill as a first step to separation, while warning 'that if we are again betrayed there shall be red war throughout Ireland' (R. D. Edwards 1977, 159). There was a significant turning of a minority of nationalists in this year to the physical-force school (F. X. Martin and F. J. Byrne 1973, 108), out of disillusionment with the power of the moderates to win Home Rule; and it was also in 1912 that Pearse published his canonization of non-Catholic rebels in a ferocious litany intended in no sense of blasphemy, but in deadly reverence:

> In the name of God,
> By Christ His only Son,
> By Mary His gentle Mother,
> By Patrick the Apostle of the Irish,
> By the loyalty of Colm Cille,
> By the glory of our race,
> By the blood of our ancestors,
> By the murder of Red Hugh,
> By the sad death of Hugh O'Neill,
> By the tragic death of Owen Roe,
> By the dying wish of Sarsfield,
> By the anguished sigh of Fitzgerald,
> By the bloody wounds of Tone,
> By the noble blood of Emmet,
> By the Famine corpses,
> By the tears of Irish exiles,
> We swear the oaths our ancestors swore,
> That we will free our race from bondage,
> Or that we will fall fighting hand to hand. Amen.
> (R. D. Edwards 1977, 161–2)

So Pearse saw no incongruity in proclaiming at the grave of Wolfe Tone, who had loathed Catholicism (Shaw 1972, 128–9):

We have come to the holiest place in Ireland; holier to us even than the place where Patrick sleeps in Down. Patrick brought us life, but this man died for us... He was the greatest of Irish Nationalists; I believe he was the greatest of Irish men... it must be that the holiest sod of a nation's soil is the sod where the greatest of her dead lies buried. (Pearse 1922, 53–4)

So too, Pearse on Davis, a Protestant: 'The highest form of genius is the genius for sanctity, the genius for noble life and thought. That genius was

Davis's' (Pearse 1922, 328). Last, there is the ringing peroration to Pearse's elegy over the grave of the Fenian O'Donovan Rossa:

This is a place of peace, sacred to the dead, where men should speak wth all charity ... but I hold it a Christian thing, as O'Donovan Rossa held it, to hate evil, to hate untruth, to hate oppression, and, hating them, to strive to overthrow them. Our foes are strong and wise and wary; but ... they cannot undo the miracles of God who ripens in the hearts of young men the seeds sown by the young men of a former generation. And the seeds sown by the young men of '65 and '67 are coming to their miraculous ripening to-day ... Life springs from death; and from the graves of patriot men and women spring living nations. The Defenders of this Realm have worked well in secret and in the open. They think that they have pacified Ireland ... They think that they have foreseen everything, think that they have provided against everything; but the fools, the fools, the fools! – they have left us our Fenian dead, and while Ireland holds these graves, Ireland unfree shall never be at peace. (Pearse 1922, 136–7)

The theme of resurrection is a law of nature, as well as God's: 'It is murder and death that make possible the terrible beautiful thing we call physical life. Life springs from death, life lives on death', and death can give birth to life (Pearse 1917b, 61).

Pearse found the roots of his identification of Ireland's cause with God's in some of the seventeenth-century poetry (but see Shaw 1972, 141–2) mourning over Cromwell's Ireland, which Pearse had translated from the Irish, as in 'Prophecy':

> 'Victory shall be to the host of the Gael
> Over Calvin's clan – the trickster, the thief, the liar;
> Their nobles shall triumph over heretics,
> And shout at the routing of Clan Luther ...
>
> 'I pray God, if He deign to hear me,
> I pray Jesus Who seeth all this,
> And the Holy Ghost again with one will,
> Mother Mary and Patrick White-Tooth,
>
> 'Kindly Colum and Holy Brigid,
> That they may weld the Gael together,
> And that thus they may compass this deed:
> The banishment of the Gall and the freeing of Ireland.'
> (Pearse 1924, 69, 71)

The Irishman's proper emotion is hatred of the Gall. 'Just as in early Irish manuscripts,' writes Pearse, 'Irish love of nature or of nature's God so frequently bursts out in fugitive quatrains of great beauty, so in the seventeenth- and eighteenth-century manuscripts we find Irish hate of the English (a scarcely less holy passion) expressing itself suddenly and splendidly ...' (Pearse 1924, 34–5). If love of Ireland was holy, then so was hating England.

Yet Pearse's ferocity was directed against abstractions, not individuals. No man of violence himself, but a radical deeply opposed to capital punishment, he would 'weep over a dead kitten, and once stopped gardening for a whole day because he had killed a worm by accident' (Ryan 1919, 126). HIs plays and stories about women and children have a tenderness verging on the lachrymose: of the dying Old Matthias, who loved children, and was rewarded with a vision of Iosagan, 'Jesus-kin', the Christ child, to fetch him a priest, though Matthias had frequented neither clergy nor mass: of the Virgin and Child's visit to a barren woman, who later conceives; of the Christ-devotion of Mary Magdalen:

> O woman, of the snowy side,
> Many a lover hath lain with thee,
> Yet left thee sad at the morning tide;
> But thy lover Christ shall comfort thee...
>
> O woman that no lover's kiss
> (Tho' many a kiss was given thee)
> Could slake thy love, is it not for this
> The hero Christ shall die for thee? (Pearse 1917a, 80)

'God loves the women better than the men', remarks Pearse with the voice of the narrator. 'It's to them He sends the greatest sorrows, and it's on them He bestows the greatest joy' (Pearse 1917a, 135). Pearse's psychology is a passionate intensity of extremes, and his ferocity is near neighbour to tenderness; great hate is born of great love, hate of the Gall, love of the Gael.

A hostile critic roundly declares that these direct emotions arise from Pearse's immaturity of vision, which places children before adults, and favours the rustic culture of the peasantry over urban sophistication, primitivism over civilization, and an ideal moral and literary simplicity over realist complexity (Thompson 1967, 58–82). All the favoured qualities, however, are also those of Irish Catholic devotion, whether in the joyous tenderness of Iosagan and his mother, or in the reiterated theme of the *mater dolorosa*, the sorrowing mother, who becomes the mother of Christ, and is also Mother Ireland. The Keening Woman cries for twenty years for her dead son killed by the British: the story ends with prayer for the soul of the son, and the saying of the Rosary. Mother Ireland bears Cuchulain to her glory, and traitors to her shame. In the three Mother poems written just before his execution, Pearse addressed his own mother on the 'dolorosa' theme:

> My gift to you hath been the gift of sorrow,
> My one return for your rich gifts to me ... (Ó Buachalla 1980, 382)

'The Mother' offers Pearse and his gentle brother Willie, the ecclesiastical sculptor who died with him, to God:

> I do not grudge them: Lord, I do not grudge
> My two strong sons that I have seen go out
> To break their strength and die, they and a few,
> In bloody protest for a glorious thing,
> They shall be spoken of among their people,
> The generations shall remember them,
> And call them blessed... (Pearse 1917a, 333)

These last lines recall the Magnificat. Willie Pearse's statue of the 'Mater Dolorosa' still stands in a Dublin chapel, and 'A Mother Speaks' is an address to the sorrowing Virgin, and was taken by the Capuchin Father Aloysius to Mrs Pearse on the day of Padraic's death:

> Dear Mary, that didst see thy first-born Son
> Go forth to die amid the scorn of men
> For whom He died,
> Receive my first-born into thy arms,
> Who also hath gone out to die for men,
> And keep him by thee till I come to him.
> Dear Mary, I have shared thy sorrow,
> And soon shall share thy joy. (Ó Buachalla 1980, 383)

Pearse's identification of his mother with Mary is also an identification of himself with the Christ of the passion, a preoccupation which originally arose out of his brilliant Passion Play in Irish, performed by his family, friends and pupils on the stage of the famous Abbey Theatre in 1911, with the blessing of Yeats, and with women keeners to provide an Irish setting: 'the Irish medium', recalled Pearse's pupil Desmond Ryan, 'had not veiled but intensified the meaning and pathos of the story. Some of us, too, thought, though to many it may seem an irreverence, that our national and individual struggle was in ways a faint reflection of the Great One just enacted. Is it not so? The Man is crucified as the Nation...' (Pearse 1917b, 108). This theme is made explicit in Pearse's morality 'The King', again enacted by his schoolboys, in which a sinless child-king from a monastic school takes the place of his sinful monarch to die in battle for the freedom of the people. 'Do you think', asks his teacher Abbot, 'I would grudge the dearest of these little boys, to death calling with that terrible, beautiful voice?' (Pearse 1917a, 55). There is, then, an identity between the nation, Christ, the victim who dies for it and Pearse. 'The people who wept in Gethsemane, who trod the sorrowful way, who died naked on a cross, who went down into hell, will rise again glorious and immortal, will sit on the right hand of God, and will come in the end to give judgment, a judge just and terrible' (Pearse 1922, 345). These themes all come together in the hero of his play *The Singer*, the revolutionary schoolteacher MacDara, who loses his faith, but refinds it in the passion of the people: 'The people, Maoilsheachlainn, the dumb, suffering people: reviled and outcast, yet pure and splendid and faithful. In them I saw, or seemed to see again, the Face of God. Ah, it is tear-stained face, blood-stained, defiled with ordure, but it is the Holy Face!' (Pearse 1917a, 34–5). And as the people are as Veronica's Veil to Christ, so MacDara is again the Son of Mary 'on the Dolorous Way', and is Christ in his triumphant conclusion: 'One man can free a people as one Man redeemed the world. I will take no pike, I will go into the battle with bare hands. I will stand up before the Gall as Christ hung naked before men on the tree!' (Pearse 1917a, 24, 44). Or as Pearse said in his last address to his pupils at St Enda's: 'It had taken the blood of the Son of God to redeem the world. It would take the blood of the sons of Ireland to redeem Ireland' (Pearse 1917b, 98).

The means, then, to this salvation is by the shedding of blood. Pearse wrote of the carnage of the first years of the war that 'Heroism has come back to the earth... The old heart of the earth needed to be warmed with the red wine of the battlefields...' (Pearse 1922, 216). Or, as he declared in anticipation of his own coming revolution, 'We may make mistakes in the beginning and shoot the wrong people; but bloodshed is a cleansing and a sanctifying thing, and the nation which regards it as the final horror has lost its manhood' (Pearse 1922, 98–9). This doctrine is not, again, specifically Catholic in origin, though it occurs in the popular novels of the Catholic Canon Sheehan (Lyons 1979, 91). Rather, it derives from Cuchulain and from the favourite nationalist image of Ireland as the rose which needed to be watered with blood, as immortalized by Pearse's exchange with Connolly in Yeats' famous poem:

> There's nothing but our own red blood
> Can make a right Rose Tree. (Yeats 1950, 206)

The rose, however, has its relation to the passion, as in Joseph Mary Plunkett's 'I see His blood upon the rose' (Plunkett 1916, 50); and even Connolly, no conventional Catholic, had been impelled to give the idea a religious cast: 'of us, as of mankind before Calvary', he wrote, 'it may truly be said "without the shedding of blood there is no redemption"' (Lyons 1979, 90).

In less dramatic form, the same idea existed in Protestant Britain in the generalized notion that the First World War would purge sin and selfishness through the redemptive shedding of blood (Wilkinson 1978, 188; Thornley 1971, 342). Some Irish Catholics also gave the war a religious justification, like the Irish MP Tom Kettle, who died on the battlefield, one of the half a million soldiers of Irish ancestry to fight in the British and Dominion armies:

> Know that we fools, now with the foolish dead,
> Died not for flag, nor King, nor Emperor,
> But for a dream, born in a herdsman's shed,
> And for the secret Scripture of the poor.
> (Martin 1976b, 63; O. D. Edwards and Pyle 1968, 100)

But here again, there are links with Pearse: Kettle dies for the dream of the poor, not for the king, while as in the theme of the sacrifice of the fool, the connection between the planned Rising and the Passion is completed by the boast of their holy foolishness. The Rising was a theatrical gesture, an act of imagination, rather than a serious military affair (Martin 1968, 110–12). It was the work of a tiny conspiracy within the wider separatist movement: Sinn Féin had no part in it, though Sinn Féiners were to reap the reward, Casement's German mission had failed, and the leaders of the Irish Republican Brotherhood had also failed in their attempt to trick the mass of Professor Eoin MacNeill's Volunteers to join them. They took on the British Empire knowing that they must be beaten: yet for that Pearse was already prepared. 'I speak that am only a fool', he had written:

> I have squandered the splendid years that
>   the Lord God gave to my youth
> In attempting impossible things, deeming
>   them alone worth the toil.

The impossibility of the Rising is part of its attraction, for the consummate Christian hero is the fool:

> Was it folly or grace? Not men shall
>   judge me, but God . . .

Sacrifice of self is the chief message of the gospel:

> For this I have heard in my heart, that a
>   man shall scatter, not hoard,
> Shall do the deed of to-day, nor take thought
>   of to-morrow's teen,
> Shall not bargain or huxter with God; or
>   was it a jest of Christ's
> And is this my sin before men, to have
>   taken Him at His word?
> The lawyers have sat in council, the men
>   with the keen, long faces,
> And said, 'This man is a fool,' and others
>   have said, 'He blasphemeth;'
> And the wise have pitied the fool that hath
>   striven to give a life
> In the world of time and space among the
>   bulks of actual things,
> To a dream that was dreamed in the heart,
>   and that only the heart could hold.
>   (Pearse 1917a, 334–5)

The lawyers in council, declaring 'He blasphemeth', are the Sanhedrin, and respectable Society; they are also the enemy, with Political Economy, of

Christianity, as well as the British legal system which Pearse the barrister had forsaken (Pearse 1917b, 81; McCay 1966, 45). They all stand for the judgement of the world on Christ, which forgets that he triumphed through failure. Pearse's final act – recalling MacDara's nakedness – is one of total sacrificial 'Renunciation':

> Naked I saw thee,
> O beauty of beauty,
> And I blinded my eyes
> For fear I should fail . . .
>
> I turned my back
> On the vision I had shaped,
> And to this road before me
> I turned my face.
>
> I have turned my face
> To this road before me
> To the deed that I see
> And the death I shall die.
>   (Pearse 1917a, 324–5)

Pearse foresaw and chose this destiny, even to the final dereliction of rejection by his people. The image arose from his dream about one of his pupils of St Enda's about to die for a cause, confronted by a silent indifferent crowd. Pearse applies it to himself in the person of MacDara: 'I seemed to see myself brought to die before a great crowd that stood cold and silent; and there were some that cursed me in their hearts for having brought death into their houses' (Pearse 1917a, 25). Again, Pearse was to experience this himself, in reading the Proclamation of the Irish Republic to indifferent bystanders on the steps of the Post Office, and in enduring the more actively hostile jeers of Dubliners outraged by the destruction of their city. Yet the initial hostility of both Church and Nation to Pearse was to pass, as British bullets immortalized him as hero: '"Kings with plumes may adorn their hearse," ran a popular tribute . . . "but angels meet the soul of Patrick Pearse"' (Ryan 1919, 1–2). And so the religious imagination made true the sub-title of Ruth Dudley Edwards' brilliant life of Pearse, 'The Triumph of Failure', turning fine rhetoric and indifferent poetry into a nation's creed.

It was Yeats, of course, who saw that these mildly comic fools, poets and schoolmasters, had been transformed by the power of their sacrifice into something deadly serious:

> Being certain that they and I
> But lived where motley is worn:
> All changed, changed utterly:
> A terrible beauty is born.
>   (Yeats 1950, 203)

The final immortal oxymoron is almost a quotation from Pearse: the Abbot's 'terrible, beautiful voice' of death. Yeats concludes on the theme of love and death:

> And what if excess of love
> Bewildered them till they died?
> I write it out in a verse –
> MacDonagh and MacBride
> And Connolly and Pearse
> Now and in time to be,
> Wherever green is worn,
> Are changed, changed utterly:
> A terrible beauty is born.
>   (Yeats 1950, 204–5)

Pearse was not the finest poet of the Rising: that was Thomas MacDonagh. The dying tubercular Joseph Mary Plunkett, with his bejewelled fingers and bejewelled verses and eve-of-execution marriage, is also a more complex and interesting writer than Pearse, as he places Ireland's resurrection and Christ's against a background of cosmic imagery drawn from the mystic St John of the Cross (Ryan 1963). Yet Pearse was arguably 'the most influential thinker, the most inspirational personality of the Rising' (A. Martin 1966, 39). One of his many brilliant and grateful pupils wrote of him and his companions, with no sense of irony, that 'we are now living the dream they died for' – that is, modern Ireland (Reddin 1943, 241).

There was of course more to the Catholicism of the Rising than Pearse. The confessionals crammed on Easter Saturday with men and boys, 'the striking fact that the rank and file of the Volunteers, almost to a man, prepared for the rising by going to confession and holy communion' (Martin 1967b, 20); the steady pace of the Rosary through the British bombardment; the O'Rahilly kneeling for a final blessing; even, in lighter vein, the impression of a modern writer 'that a few hundred British soldiers, dressed as priests, could have walked into the Post Office unhampered and put a sudden end to the entire rebellion' and the anxiety of combatants confronted with Friday chicken, until their chaplain, Father Flanagan, had taken his fork to the bird (Coffey 1971, 126, 202). For these men, the religious legitimation of the Rising, even in the face of clergymen whom they had often defied, was of desperate importance, and Pearse provided that legitimation through the very symbols of the Faith. The consequences for Ireland were of course disastrous. Foolish talk costs lives, and as some Irish historians now recognize, the rebellion discredited the constitutionalist tradition and permanently alienated the Protestants of Northern Ireland from Irish nationhood. The passionate purity of the young firebombers of Belfast is Pearse's legacy, and an increasing number of Irish Catholics, like

the splendid Jesuit Professor Francis Shaw, in his posthumously published
challenge to the canon of Irish history (Shaw 1972), have dared to say that
Pearse's ideals were hardly Christian.

It has been for some of the novelists and poets to reject Pearse most
unambiguously: Sean O'Casey's prostitute sourly remarking of the nationalists, 'they're all in a holy mood to-night' (A. Martin 1966, 40); Joyce
creating a deliberately bourgeois anti-hero and sure that 'heroism is, and
always was, a damned lie' (Watson 1979, 221); Yeats withdrawing into the
tower of his old-age poetry from the Catholic nation he had helped to make:

> Did that play of mine send out
> Certain men the English shot?
> (Yeats 1950, 393)

or in another concluding oxymoron which occurs in Pearse:

> A revolutionary soldier kneeling to be blessed;
> An Abbot or Archbishop with an unpraised hand
> Blessing the Tricolour. 'This is not', I say,
> The dead Ireland of my youth, but an Ireland
> The poets have imagined, terrible and gay.'
> (Yeats 1950, 368)

Yet it was an Ireland dreamed of by the young poet Yeats, who had lived in
fascinated horror to disown his dream. 'Too long a sacrifice can make a
stone of the heart', and for Yeats that stone was the heart of Catholic
Ireland:

> Out of Ireland have we come.
> Great hatred, little room,
> Maimed us at the start.
> I carry from my mother's womb
> A fanatic heart.
> (Yeats 1950, 288)

In that sense, of turning the heart to the stone of a fanatic hate, it must be
said of Pearse's sacrifice that it was magnificent, but hardly Christianity.
Perhaps there is a lesson here for the liberation theologies of our time, which
can be so free with the blood of the oppressor. Yet I had written this
conclusion when I heard an army chaplain in Falklands Cathedral telling
his men that war had changed them utterly, with a deeper knowledge of
God and of themselves. How far is it from that to the doctrine that blood
purifies? The crucified Christ has many contradictory faces in the history of
the Church, and the true Christ is difficult to find. It is too hard a saying that
even this Irish Christ-modelled sacrifice of a Christian man and nation
should be accounted wholly wrong.

There is also the uncomfortable consideration that Pearse's sacrifice, like
Christ's, succeeded by its failure:

O wise men, riddle me this: what if the dream come true?
What if the dream come true? and if millions unborn shall dwell
In the house that I shaped in my heart...? (Pearse 1917a, 336)

Yet Pearse's victory cannot in the nature of things be final. History has many odd turnings, and the successful sacrifice demands another if the very spirit of sacrifice is to continue to succeed. As William Morris said in *The Dream of John Ball*, 'Men fight and lose the battle, and the thing that they fought for comes about in spite of their defeat, and when it comes turns out to be not what they meant, and other men have to fight for what they meant under another name.'

REFERENCES

Coffey, Thomas M. (1971). *Agony at Easter. The 1916 Irish Uprising.* London: Penguin

Connolly, S. J. (1982). *Priests and People in Pre-Famine Ireland 1780–1845.* New York: Gill and Macmillan

Dangerfield, George (1977). *The Damnable Question: A Study in Anglo-Irish Relations.* London: Constable

Edwards, Owen Dudley (1971). *The Mind of an Activist – James Connolly.* Dublin: Gill and Macmillan

Edwards, Owen Dudley and Pyle, Fergus (1968). *1916: The Easter Rising.* London: MacGibbon & Kee

Edwards, Ruth Dudley (1977). *Patrick Pearse: The Triumph of Failure.* London: Victor Gollancz

Egan, Desmond (1966). Attitudes to Catholicism in the Modern Irish Novel. Unpublished M.A. thesis, University College, Dublin

Horgan, John J. (1948). *Parnell to Pearse: Some Recollections and Reflections.* Dublin: Browne and Nolan

Larkin, Emmet (1972). The Devotional Revolution in Ireland, 1850–75. *The American Historical Review* 77, 625–52

    (1975). *The Roman Catholic Church and the Creation of the Modern Irish State, 1878–1886.* Philadelphia: American Philosophical Society

    (1978). *The Roman Catholic Church and the Plan of Campaign in Ireland, 1886–1888.* Cork: Irish University Press

    (1979). *The Roman Catholic Church in Ireland and the Fall of Parnell, 1888–1891.* Liverpool: Liverpool University Press

Levenson, Samuel (1977). *Maud Gonne.* London: Cassell

Lyons, F. S. L. (1971). *Ireland since the Famine.* London: Weidenfeld and Nicolson

    (1979). *Culture and Anarchy in Ireland 1890–1939.* Oxford: Clarendon Press

McCartney, Donal (1967). The Church and the Fenians. *University Review* 4, 203–15

McCay, Hedley (1966). *Padraic Pearse: A New Biography.* Cork: The Mercier Press

Marrin, Albert (1974). *The Last Crusade: The Church of England in the First World War.* Durham, N.C.: Duke University Press

Martin, Augustine (1966). To Make a Right Rose Tree. *Studies. An Irish Quarterly Review* 5, 38–50

Martin, F. X., OSA (ed.) (1967a). *Leaders of Men of the Easter Rising: Dublin 1916*. London: Methuen

(1967b). 1916 – Myth, Fact and Mystery. *Studia Hibernica* 7, 7–126

(1968). The 1916 Rising – A *Coup d'État* or a 'Bloody Protest'? *Studia Hibernica* 8, 106–37

Martin, F. X. and Byrne, F. J. (eds.) (1973). *The Scholar Revolutionary: Eoin MacNeill, 1867–1945, and the Making of the New Ireland*. Shannon: Irish University Press

Miller, David W. (1973). *Church, State and Nation in Ireland, 1898–1921*. Dublin: Gill and Macmillan

Newsinger, John (1979). Revolution and Catholicism in Ireland, 1848–1923. *European Studies Review* 9, 457–80

Norman, E. R. (1965). *The Catholic Church and Ireland in the Age of Rebellion, 1859–1873*. London: Longmans

O'Brien, Conor Cruise (1973). *States of Ireland*. London: Hutchinson

Ó Buachalla, Séamas (ed.) (1980). *The Letters of P. H. Pearse*. Gerrards Cross: Colin Smythe

O'Farrell, Patrick (1971). *Ireland's English Question: Anglo-Irish Relations, 1534–1970*. London: Batsford

O'Grady, Standish (n.d.). *The Coming of Cuculain*. Dublin: The Talbot Press

(1878 and 1880). *History of Ireland: The Heroic Period*, 2 vols. London: Sampson Low [Reprinted 1979, New York: Lemma]

Pearse, P. H. (1916). *The Separatist Idea*. Dublin: Whelan & Son

(1917a). *Collected Works of Padraic H. Pearse: Plays, Stories, Poems*. Dublin and London: Maunsel

(1917b). *The Story of a Success, Being a Record of St. Enda's College September 1908 to Easter 1916*, ed. Desmond Ryan. Dublin and London: Maunsel

(1922). *Collected Works of Padraic H. Pearse: Political Writings and Speeches*. Dublin and London: Maunsel & Roberts

(1924). *Collected Works of Padraic H. Pearse: Songs of the Irish Rebels and Specimens from an Irish Anthology, Some Aspects of Irish Literature, Three Lectures on Gaelic Topics*. Dublin, Cork, Belfast: The Phoenix Publishing Co.

Plunkett, Joseph Mary (1916). *The Poems of Joseph Mary Plunkett*. Dublin: The Talbot Press

Ransom, Bernard (1980). *Connolly's Marxism*. London: Pluto Press

Reddin, Kenneth (1943). A Man called Pearse. *Studies. An Irish Quarterly Review* 32, 241–52

Ryan, Desmond (1919). *The Man called Pearse*. Dublin and London: Maunsel

(1934). *Remembering Sion*. London: Arthur Barker

(ed.) (1963). *The 1916 Poets*. Dublin: Allen Figgis

Shaw, Rev. Professor Francis, SJ (1972). The Canon of Irish History – A Challenge. *Studies. An Irish Quarterly Review* 61, 113–53

Thompson, William Irwin (1967). *The Imagination of an Insurrection: Dublin, Easter, 1916, A Study of an Ideological Movement*. New York: Oxford University Press

Thornley, David (1971). Patrick Pearse and the Pearse Family. *Studies. An Irish Quarterly Review* 60, 332–46

Tierney, Mark (1976). *Croke of Cashel: the Life of Archbishop Thomas William Croke, 1823–1902*. Dublin: Gill and Macmillan

Watson, G. J. (1979). *Irish Identity and the Literary Revival: Synge, Yeats, Joyce and O'Casey*. London: Croom Helm

Wilkinson, Alan (1978). *The Church of England and the First World War*. London: SPCK

Yeats, W. B. (1950). *The Collected Poems of Yeats*. London: Macmillan

13

THE CONCEPT OF SACRIFICE IN ANGLICAN SOCIAL ETHICS

ALAN M. SUGGATE

In the tradition of Anglican social ethics which harks back to F. D. Maurice, Charles Kingsley and J. M. Ludlow the concept of sacrifice has had a considerable vogue. In his teaching about the Divine Order Maurice himself opposed every kind of individualism in the name of the true law of creation, which was the law of sacrifice and love. It was this outlook which lay behind the producers' cooperatives founded by the small brotherhood Maurice led (Christensen 1962, 23–6). Half a century later Bishop Westcott claimed that in the steady march of progress towards an ideal the labours of men became fruitful through sacrifice (Westcott 1901, 395). In Scott Holland's estimation no one who insisted on the centrality of the cross could help believing that human life is realized not through egoistic self-assertion but through altruistic self-sacrifice. The language of sacrifice was taken up by non-conformists too. When Philip Snowden wrote *The Christ that is to Be*, designed to convert Christians to socialism, he said that Christ's law of sacrifice, love and cooperation was the foundation of all the great ethical religions of the world, and he looked forward to a political Christianity and an earthly paradise won through sacrifice (Snowden 1905). The same high moral tone runs through the speeches and writings both of the half-secularized leaders of the emerging Labour Movement, like Keir Hardie, and of out-and-out secularists such as George Odger. They exemplify what Beatrice Webb called 'the transference of the emotion of self-sacrificing service from God to man' (Webb 1926, 112). Common to Christian thinkers in this tradition was the desire to slay the dragon of 'individualism'. Against this they sallied with two basic weapons: first, the insistence that the social, political and economic spheres of human life were not wholly autonomous, but subject to Christian moral criteria; and secondly, that a proper understanding of man involved the recognition not only of his individual dignity and responsibility, but also of his social nature. Throughout there was a tacit assumption that the concept of sacrifice could be applied directly to the social order.

235

In this goodly company of idealists moved the young William Temple. He was educated at Rugby in Arnold's ideal of strenuous service, and at Balliol, where his mentor was the British Hegelian Edward Caird. Right from his Glasgow days Caird had shown a passionate social concern. At Oxford he encouraged his pupils to go down to the East End of London to study the problem of poverty at first hand. Beveridge and Tawney were notable respondents. Temple too sampled the university settlements. At the Oxford Medical Mission at Bermondsey he risked his ample frame on a rickety tin bed and passed the night in the company of vicious bugs (Iremonger 1948, 42). In 1905 he joined the Workers' Educational Association, and within three years was President. His speeches, printed in *The Highway*, were full of the airy language of faith, hope and love; the vastness of the cause demanded the spirit of absolute self-denial. His contact with a rather unrepresentative section of the working class spurred on his enthusiasm for the Labour Movement. In 1908 his cry was 'socialism or heresy' (Temple 1908, 199). Ten years later he joined the Labour Party for a while, maintaining that its ideals were basically Christian (Chronicle of Convocation 1918, 349–53).

The depressing aftermath of the First World War drove Temple towards a modification of his idealism. In 1920 we find him saying, 'Our duty is the very difficult one of maintaining an ideal while adopting in the most realistic manner the steps which are in fact best calculated to lead to its attainment.' There is no absolute moral claim independently of all actual consequences. We must simply do the best thing for humanity in all the circumstances (Temple 1920). Because the term 'ideals' seemed to many to suggest absolute action-rules, Temple increasingly distinguished ideals from principles. The way of principles, he claimed in 1923, avoided on the one hand conceiving an ideal system and implementing it regardless of circumstances, and on the other hand a timorous acceptance of, or tinkering with, the *status quo*. This method is idealist in that it goes beyond the remedying of admitted evils and suggests positive relationships to be established; but it is realist in that it is always concerned with the application of principles to what is, rather than with dreams of what might be. Then for the first time Temple coordinates into a set of four the social principles which he (and many other churchmen) had come to use: respect for personality; fellowship; the duty of service; the power of sacrifice (Temple 1923a). This thinking was part of Temple's personal preparation for the 1924 Conference on Christian Politics, Economics and Citizenship (COPEC), which he chaired.

Nearly twenty years later Temple summarized this working method of principles in *Christianity and Social Order* (1942). There is no fundamental change from 1923. Yet sacrifice has disappeared as a social principle. It is too exacting, we are told, to force on societies; it is for individuals to practise it voluntarily. As there is no full explanation given, we have to try to infer the reasons from a study of the mass of Temple's writings in their historical context. The chief clue lies, I believe, in some remarks he made in the religious weekly *The Guardian* on 24 November, 1939:

I think that it is an open question whether an actual preference by one of the interests of the other over its own is ethically right; but, even if the question is open, it is purely academic; when we reach the stage of justice in the relations between capital and labour or between one nation and another, we shall have moved a very long way. We had better aim at this before we preach corporate self-sacrifice. I used to preach it once; I thereby gained much applause, which I very much enjoyed; but I have long been convinced that such talk is only 'uplift'; it does not affect anything which actually happens. It is a super-human thing when an individual is lifted above his self-centredness; but the egotism of any corporation except a genuine fellowship of the Spirit is something far more intense than that of an individual, because it enlists in its service alike the idealism and the selfishness of its members. To establish justice here is an achievement far beyond our present attainment, perhaps beyond our resources. (Temple 1940a, 26–7)

I shall explore what was Temple's earlier 'preaching' about self-sacrifice, to see whether he correctly characterizes it; what was its social, theological and philosophical context; what chiefly brought about his change of mind.

There are a number of passages in Temple's earlier work, mainly in the period between 1920 and 1926, where Temple uses the terms 'sacrifice' and 'self-sacrifice' in connection with the social order. Some examples will suffice:

(a) In 1920 he notes a better climate in industrial relations: the capitalist press now proclaims the true principle of the natural fellowship of Capital and Labour. Temple appeals to Labour to accept voluntarily a principle which Capital is in no position to practise: the brotherhood of man and the duty of forgiveness. He calls on all to refrain from allocating blame:

'Judge not' is a Christian maxim of supreme importance in industrial politics . . . We shall find peace only when those who have both the right and the power to punish choose instead to promote the common interest. For the moral foundation of peace in a perfectly ordered world is justice. But our world is disordered. And when evil has come in, it can only be expelled through suffering voluntarily accepted by the innocent; in our world the moral foundation of peace is self-sacrifice. (Temple 1920, 65–70)

Obviously the language here is very idealistic. Yet Temple does not really advocate the abandonment by Labour of all claims. He does not actually call for the preference by Labour of the interests of Capital. He is pleading that men should not fix their thoughts on 'abstract justice' based on a spurious notion of absolute moral claims; for this is the level of retribution, and it is liable to degenerate into vindictiveness. He calls on men to look to the future and to promote the highest general welfare. This requires the cultivation of 'moral opportunism', that combination of idealism and realism which we have already noted. So we see that Temple is using 'self-sacrifice' and 'forgiveness' in the rather peculiar sense of 'declining to even the scores'. 'Judge not' in industrial politics turns out to be quite compatible with realistic judgements of consequences.

(b) The article 'Christian Social Principles' (Temple 1923b) is similarly ambivalent over the applicability of the term 'self-sacrifice'. On the one hand Temple writes that sacrifice is at the very heart of the Christian religion. 'Real progress comes by self-sacrifice. In a society that had never become corrupted, fellowship might rest on justice; but when once corruption has set in, it can only be based on self-sacrifice ... The Cross is the means of salvation.' Temple believes that neither Labour nor Capital is yet ready to suffer rather than risk receiving unrighteous gain. On the other hand he recognizes that 'it may be right for Labour to resist by force a forcible aggression by Capital', and thinks that real progress comes from men's sacrificial constancy in the hardship of a strike. It is very difficult to reconcile these two gambits, and Temple's own uncertainty is reflected in the remark, 'We have scarcely dared to apply the principle of sacrifice to social or international questions even in thought.'

(c) In *Personal Religion and the Life of Fellowship* (Temple 1926, 68) there is a passage which seems to advocate corporate self-sacrifice quite straightforwardly. Temple contrasts the victory of pride won by force over beaten enemies with the victory of love won by sacrifice over enemies who are thereby converted into friends. The latter is the only sort of victory God cares to win, and progress can only come in his way. Here Temple certainly does advocate corporate self-sacrifice, for he makes the contrast in an exposition of the principle of sacrifice, which is offered along with the other three principles mentioned earlier as 'capable of, and demanding, application to the structure of society'.

However, this should be taken with what Temple says earlier in the same work (1926, 12–13). There he argues that a God who was only Creator and Judge might make men just, but this would not be enough to save the world. For the pursuit of justice becomes a vice in disputants, making them defend their self-interest with the passion of a moral crusade. Now 'the spirit of ultimate Reality' is a God who does not stand above the conflict, awarding all their due, but is within it, receiving without recrimination what is not his due. His credentials are his pierced hands and side. We must choose between the way of pride and the way of self-sacrifice. So Temple calls for nations to renounce their pride through sacrifice. However, he also speaks highly of justice as 'the virtue of the judge who stands outside the quarrel and decides between the disputants'. Thus Temple is clear about the ultimate solution to man's sin, but we are left with the awkward question, What do we do in the meantime? Do we abandon all claims and practise complete corporate self-sacrifice? Or do we pursue claims but accept arbitration? No clear reply is given.

Our answer to the question whether Temple correctly characterizes his earlier 'preaching' is hardly a simple 'Yes'. It is rare to find unambiguous advocacy of corporate self-sacrifice in the sense of a policy of heedless altruism instead of the pursuit of justice. Temple writes idealistically as if sacrifice were directly applicable to social issues, but he tends to adapt the meaning of Christian phrases and to show a realistic approach within the same article. Temple's ambivalent thinking in the 1920s fits well with a remark made by Reinhold Niebuhr in 1943: Christian social pronouncements in Britain seemed to be taken from the pages of the old American 'social gospel', yet radicals in practice showed great shrewdness of analysis (Niebuhr 1943a).

Temple's position in the period from 1920 to 1926 needs to be understood against his social and philosophical-theological background. The immediate context is the widespread use of the Christian language of sacrifice during and after the First World War. This has been set out by Alan Wilkinson in his excellent book, *The Church of England and the First World War* (1978). It is hardly surprising that an identification of the trenches with Calvary was made, as men struggled to make some sense of the maelstrom into which they had stepped. The mood was captured during the war by James Clark's picture 'The Great Sacrifice', showing a decorously dead soldier lying with one hand on the feet of the crucified Christ (Wilkinson 1978, 191). After the war came the practice of superimposing a cross on a sword on gravestones and war memorials. Even those who protested against the romantic jingoism of men like Winnington-Ingram, the Bishop of London, adopted the language of sacrifice. This was quite noticeable among liberal Catholics. Neville Figgis said in 1917: 'When the Cross of Christ is held before us, it is not as a strange, unique phenomenon. It is the inner meaning of all our struggles, the symbol of all sacrifice for distant ends' (Wilkinson 1978, 188). Paul Bull glorified the self-sacrifice of the soldiers as congruent with the Catholic faith which had at its centre the sacrifice of the mass (Wilkinson 1978, 55).

The call for sacrifice ran through the National Mission of Repentance and Hope, in which Temple was very active. As he toured the country, he contrasted the capacity for heroism which the war had evoked with the failure of the Church to evoke a similar sacrificial allegiance. The National Mission was not designed simply to rouse men and women to sacrifice during the war. Archbishop Lang recognized that at the end of the war the old order of society would have gone, and that repentance and hope were prerequisites if the nation was to purge the stains of civilization and seek 'a new order in a new world'. True to this outlook Henry Scott Holland declared that men, right in the heart of the hell of war, had found a strange heaven. 'They have been nearer to the mind and heart of Christ than they had ever attained to in the life of peace. They have known what it is to give away their hope of life out of love of others ... they have been initiated into the secret of sacrifice, into the inner meaning of life through death' (Wilkinson 1978, 258). The problem after the war, he said, would be how the spirit of heroic devotion could be retained. There must be an extension of cooperative industrial enterprise. The Church too must ask for sacrificial heroism from its members. The whole Church needed 'Sons of Thunder', those in monastic communities who could 'afford to take on their lips the language of the Sermon on the Mount without offence, so presenting Christianity in its most romantic and heroic shape'. The motifs of cooperation and self-sacrifice are also very prominent in the thought of Studdert Kennedy both as First World War chaplain and then as messenger of the Industrial Christian Fellowship (Hopkinson 1978, esp. chapter 6).

This ready use of the language of sacrifice was not simply the result of the availability of biblical and romantic images in a time of intense personal and national stress. The ground had also been prepared in the British Hegelian tradition, especially by T. H. Green, who was born in 1837. Green was educated in the tradition of Thomas Arnold at Rugby, and performed the remarkable feat of popularizing Hegel by developing a distinctive form of Hegelianism which was attuned to the Arnoldian ethos. Scott Holland once said of Green, 'He gave us back the language of self-sacrifice, and taught us how we belonged to one another in the one life of organic humanity. He filled us again with the breath of high idealism' (quoted in Richter 1964, 35). Green restored the ideas of self-denial and self-sacrifice through his criticism of utilitarianism. He believed that all forms of utilitarianism involved their adherents in a conflict between their logical premisses and their philanthropic motives. Practically it was vain to suppose that egoistic hedonism could be transmuted into altruistic hedonism. Green substituted a doctrine of self-sacrifice in the interests of altruism. He was passionately concerned with social reform, and highly sensitive to the needs of his contemporaries, who found their faith crumbling and looked to secular outlets for the impulses to altruism and sacrifice which their believing parents had inculcated into them. Although few accepted Green's position *in toto*, many of the hallmarks of his philosophy exercised a strong influence: the quest for synthesis, especially of reason and religion; the belief that reality could be rationally comprehended; the accent on divine immanence, whereby God realizes himself progressively in men and in society; the stress on the development of character to perfection through self-sacrifice and devotion to a cause; the belief that sin is essentially selfishness, eradicable by intense discipline.

Green died young in 1882. His influence was at its height in the period between his death and the outbreak of the First World War – the very period when Temple grew to manhood. Green provided much inspiration not only for the writers of *Lux Mundi*, who aimed to set the Christian faith, conceived incarnationally and sacramentally, in its right relation to contemporary intellectual and moral problems, but also to the founders of the Christian Social Union, who sought to draw out the implications of the Christian faith for the ordering of society. Basically, as Richter writes, these men believed that the great forces operating in modern culture were beneficent and ought to be regarded as the fulfilment of Christianity, especially democracy and the new kind of citizenship it made possible in a state moralized by the values immanent in Christian teaching (Richter 1964, 124). British Hegelianism was the matrix out of which Temple developed his own Christian philosophy. The First World War was regarded merely as an interlude, and in due course Temple produced his *Christus Veritas* in 1924 and his crowning philosophical work, *Nature, Man and God*, in 1932–4. Though in several respects he rebelled against Hegelianism, he continued to share its basic optimism and significantly dedicated the latter work to Edward Caird.

These were some of the influences disposing Temple to write as he did in the 1920s about sacrifice as a principle applicable to society. What brought about his change of mind? Doubtless there were many factors both in Britain and abroad: the whole course and outcome of the miners' strike in 1926; the financial crisis of 1931 and the Government's inability to solve the problems of economics and unemployment; the chaos in Germany and Spain; and the weakness of the League of Nations. Yet one man, I suggest, acted as a catalyst more than any other factor: Reinhold Niebuhr. Temple first met him in 1923. It was some time before Niebuhr emerged from his own liberal phase and launched his devastating attacks on American liberal Christians. His position crystallized in the 1930s and 1940s, from *Moral Man and Immoral Society* (1932) through *An Interpretation of Christian Ethics* (1936) to the Gifford Lectures, *The Nature and Destiny of Man* (1941–3). John C. Bennett has said that

Reinhold Niebuhr's social ethics are close to the centre of his thought. The centre is doubtless to be found in his theology; but more than with other theologians, his theology has developed in response to his reading of contemporary history and to his reflections upon his own social and political responsibility in that history. His thought as a whole is a unity. His theology is in immediate control over his social ethics... (Bennett 1961, 46)

At the heart of the social ethics is a dialectical understanding of the relation of love and justice, and this is firmly rooted in an understanding of the cross. The first point at which Temple was challenged was over Niebuhr's conception of *agape* as self-sacrifice, in contrast to mutual love, which Niebuhr tended to dub as *eros* and see as having the root of selfishness in it (Niebuhr 1943b, 86). It is true that Niebuhr does speak of love in terms of mutuality: 'the law of (man's) nature is love, a harmonious relation of life to life in obedience to the divine centre and source of his life' (Niebuhr 1941a, 17). But that is an ultimate state, and Niebuhr's preoccupation is with the confrontation of that law of love with this fallen world. Heedless, uncalculating love must entail self-sacrifice in this life:

> The perfect disinterestedness of the divine love can have a counterpart in history only in a life which ends tragically because it refuses to participate in the claims and counterclaims of historical existence. It portrays a love 'which seeketh not its own'. But a love which seeketh not its own is not able to maintain itself in historical society. (Niebuhr 1943b, 75)

The second point at which Temple was challenged was over the dialectical understanding of love and justice (Harland 1960, chapter 2). If Niebuhr is right about love as sacrificial *agape*, then it is clearly impossible to construct a social ethic out of the ideal of love in its pure form. Yet if Niebuhr denies the direct applicability of the law of love to the world of contending claims, he also denies its irrelevance. The law of love has a transcendent eschatological reference which is related *dialectically* to this life. First, love and justice are not identical, for love is heedless and sacrificial, whereas justice is discriminating and concerned with balancing interests and claims. Love *fulfils* justice: it goes beyond the general provision for need prompted by a sense of justice to meet the other man's particular needs. 'Love is the end term of any system of morals. It is the moral requirement in which all schemes of justice are fulfilled ... because the obligation of life to life is more fully met in love than is possible in any scheme of equity and justice' (Niebuhr 1941a, 313). Secondly, love *requires* the pursuit of justice. Justice is not alien to love; it is the way in which love must find expression in complex human relations. Thirdly, love *negates* justice, 'because love makes an end of the nicely calculated less and more of structures of justice. It does not carefully arbitrate between the needs of the self and of the other, since it meets the needs of the other without concern for the self.' Whatever our achievements in the realm of justice, they always stand under the judgement of love. The laws of justice, since they always take sinful self-interest for granted, 'are therefore always in danger of throwing the aura of sanctity' upon that sinful self-interest. 'They must consequently stand under the criticism of the law of love' (Niebuhr 1938, 72). 'There is no justice, even in a sinful world, which can be regarded as finally normative. The higher possibilities of love, which at once is the fulfilment and the negation of justice, always hover over every system of justice' (Niebuhr 1941a, 302). Love is not only 'the source of the norms of justice' but also the 'ultimate perspective by which their limitations are discovered' (Niebuhr 1941b, 150). Yet love also redeems what remains incomplete and distorted by sin. In this sense too love fulfils justice. Justice needs draughts of love if it is not to degenerate into something less than justice. Just as mutual love needs *agape* to prevent it descending into a calculation of interests, so justice without love is merely the balance of power.

A study of the Temple of 1934–44 reveals how extensively he drew on Niebuhr, especially in his discussion of the problem of pacifism. I have set out the evidence elsewhere (Suggate 1980). Temple had no difficulty in accepting that love transcends justice and love requires justice. His own understanding of the relationship of Church and Nation, set out in 1914, paves the way for this ready response to Niebuhr. 'Both State and Church are instruments of God for establishing His Kingdom; both have the same goal; but they have different functions in relation to that goal.' The nation is a natural growth. It emerges to meet the elementary needs of man, but having emerged it has a spiritual value far beyond this as an instrument of the growth of culture and family life. The nation's organ of action is the State. Being natural, it appeals to men on that side of their nature which is lower, but is not in itself bad. 'Justice is its highest aim and force its typical instrument, though force is progressively less employed as the moral sense of the community develops; mercy can find an entrance only on strict conditions.' The State's action is for the most part in the form of restraint; it 'is concerned to maintain the highest standard of life that can be generally realised by its citizens'. By contrast the Church is

a spiritual creation working through a natural medium. Its informing principle is the Holy Spirit of God in Christ, but its members are men and women who are partly animal in nature as well as children of God. The Church's primary quality is holiness; mercy will be the chief characteristic of its judgement. Its action is mostly in the form of appeal. It is concerned with upholding an ideal to which not even the best will fully attain. (Temple 1915, 51–5, 57)

This was basically a position which Temple still maintained in *Citizen and Churchman* in 1941.

However, on the central question of whether *agape* is essentially self-sacrifice and whether the relation between love and justice is dialectical, there is a divergence between Temple and Niebuhr, and this is rooted in a difference over the way in which Christianity is fundamentally related to social affairs. Unfortunately Temple does not discuss either issue, or exhibit a position as coordinated as Niebuhr's.

First, in his social ethics the dominant note in Temple's understanding of love is mutuality. This is evident in his preoccupation with the social principle of fellowship. The goal for Temple is a world completely in fellowship with God and completely at harmony with itself. Now when we look at the idea of sacrifice in Temple's theology we find that he belongs among those who look on sacrifice as subordinate to God's will for mutuality. Sacrifice becomes necessary where the fellowship or mutuality has broken down. But it would perhaps be even truer to say that Temple's understanding of sacrifice is so wide as virtually to merge with mutuality:

Sacrifice is not always painful; that depends on the response. The form of sacrifice is that one chooses for love's sake to do or to suffer what apart from love one would not have chosen to do or to suffer... Sacrifice expressing a love that is returned can be such a joy as is not otherwise known to men. (Temple 1924, 273)

Underlying this language are Temple's doctrines of God and of the eucharist. First, there is a complete mutuality of self-giving within the Godhead: 'God loves; God answers with love; and the love wherewith God loves and answers is God: Three Persons, One God' (Temple 1924, 284). Secondly he insists on the importance of the doctrine of the eucharistic sacrifice. Drawing on Bishop Hicks' *The Fullness of Sacrifice* (1930), he stresses that the essence of animal sacrifice was not the killing of the victim but the offering of the life, which in its acceptance by God is lifted from its earthly limitations into full association with God in Heaven:

But full self-giving is precisely that of which we are least capable... What I cannot do in and for myself, Christ has done for me and will do in me. He offers His life – the life of perfect love expressed in the uttermost self-sacrifice – that I may receive it as my own, and in its power I become able to give myself more completely to God. (Temple 1931, 149–51)

Thus if *agape* is construed primarily as mutuality, it must also be construed essentially as sacrifice. For any expression of mutuality *is* sacrifice. Indeed precisely what is new in the Christian doctrine of God is the idea that self-sacrifice is integral to the Godhead, revealed to man in the agony of the cross. Temple admits that even his beloved Plato could not rise to a vision of the excellence of sacrifice.

Secondly, the evidence suggests that Temple does not see love and justice in a fully dialectical relationship. True, there are instances of a radical negation of our attempts at justice: all our efforts, he says once, stand condemned as sinful; concern for justice may be no more than self-interest in decent habiliments (Iremonger 1948, 542–3). As early as 1914 he stresses the inability of men and nations to live by the law of Christ, and quotes the text which was later a favourite of Niebuhr: 'Wretched man that I am, who will deliver me from the body of this death?' (Temple 1914, 13). However the prevailing impression is of a smooth upward movement of infinite gradations, starting from total selfishness and working up to a point where perfect love and perfect justice coincide. Careful study confirms the judgement of Robert Craig in his *Social Concern in the Thought of William Temple* that Temple 'failed to insist sufficiently on the sin and contradiction of love inherent in political organisation', and did not rise to Niebuhr's insistence on the dialectical relationship of love to justice (Craig 1963, 99–103).

Temple's change of mind between the 1920s and the late 1930s was a remarkable feat, comparable to his recognition of the inadequacy of his Christian philosophy in an article in *Theology* in November 1939. Sacrifice was deleted as a social principle, and appears in *Christianity and Social Order* (1942) only as an invitation to individuals. Temple does, as we might expect, use the word 'sacrifice' during the Second World War, in the sense of 'endurance in the cause of justice', 'As by sacrifice and fortitude we shall win the war, so by sacrifice and magnanimity we must establish true peace' (Temple 1940b, 44). It is however used sparingly, and never in the idealistic way in which Temple had applied it to collectivities in the 1920s.

It is questionable whether Temple ever quite grasped the theological roots of Niebuhr's position, and here I believe we touch on a basic difference of orientation. Anglican social ethics had been rooted principally in such doctrines as the Trinity, Creation and Incarnation, and had in effect a realized eschatology. Temple stood in this line, as is most evident in his *Readings in St John's Gospel* (1939–40). Niebuhr's outlook is more evidently Pauline, and he succeeds better than Temple in grasping the character of history between the cross and the End in the light of the cross itself (Harland 1960, 111ff.). He takes up the motif of the cross as the Wisdom of God. The cross clarifies the mystery of a divine power which bears history, and thereby reveals the mystery of life and history. God has a resource of mercy beyond his law and justice, which is effective only because he takes the consequences of his wrath and judgement upon himself. That love requires justice is rooted in God's demand for justice; that love negates justice is rooted in God's judgement on our behaviour; that love redeems justice is rooted in the ultimate dimension of the justice of God where love takes on itself our violations of law of love. Further, Niebuhr pursues the idea of the power of the cross. Grace for Niebuhr is not only God's power in us (the dominant accent in Temple), but God's power over us in judgement, mercy and forgiveness. On the one hand, in the Interim, grace is effective in us – there are indeterminate renewals of life, significant realizations of the Kingdom of God. On the other hand the contradictions of life remain; man is still in rebellion against God (even Christian man); therefore there is still judgement, and man must rely on God's power of forgiveness and his resources of mercy. All good is tainted, every structure of justice is incomplete, all achievements need divine mercy. In this way the heedless self-sacrificing *agape* of the cross remains permanently related to social life.

REFERENCES

Bennett, J. C. (1961). Reinhold Niebuhr's Social Ethics. In *Reinhold Niebuhr, His Religious, Social and Political Thought*, ed. C. W. Kegley and R. W. Bretall, pp. 45–77. New York: Macmillan

Christensen, T. (1962). *Origin and History of Christian Socialism, 1848–1854.* Aarhus Universitetsforlaget

Craig, R. (1963). *Social Concern in the Thought of William Temple.* London: Gollancz

Harland, G. (1960). *The Thought of Reinhold Niebuhr.* New York: Oxford University Press

Hopkinson, W. H. (1978). The Religious Thought of G. A. Studdert Kennedy (1883–1929) in Relation to its Social and Intellectual Context. Unpublished M.A. thesis, Durham University

Iremonger, F. A. (1948). *William Temple, Archbishop of Canterbury.* London: Oxford University Press

Niebuhr, Reinhold (1938). The Christian Faith and the Common Life. In *Christian Faith and the Common Life,* vol. IV of the Oxford Conference, 1937, on Church, Community and State. London: Allen and Unwin

(1941a). *The Nature and Destiny of Man,* vol. I. London: Nisbet (New York: Scribners)

(1941b). *An Interpretation of Christian Ethics* (3rd edn). London: SCM Press

(1943a). Christianity and Politics in Britain. *Christianity and Society,* Summer 1943

(1943b). *The Nature and Destiny of Man,* vol. II. London: Nisbet

Richter, M. (1964). *The Politics of Conscience.* London: Weidenfeld and Nicolson

Snowden, P. (1905). *The Christ that is to Be.* London: Independent Labour Party pamphlet

Suggate, A. M. (1980). William Temple's Christian Social Ethics: a Study in Method. Unpublished Ph.D. thesis, Durham University

(1987). *William Temple and Christian Social Ethics Today.* Edinburgh: T. & T. Clark

Temple, W. (1908). The Church and the Labour Party. *The Economic Review* 18, April 1908, 190–202

(1914). *Christianity and War.* London: Oxford University Press

(1915). *Church and Nation.* London: Macmillan

(1920). The Moral Foundation of Peace. *The Contemporary Review* 118, July 1920, 65–70

(1923a). Principles or Ideals? *The Pilgrim* (January), 218–25

(1923b). Christian Social Principles. *The Pilgrim* (April), 337–46 [Also reprinted in *Essays in Christian Politics* (London: Longmans Green, 1927), pp. 9–18.]

(1924). *Christus Veritas.* London: Macmillan

(1926). *Personal Religion and the Life of Fellowship.* London: Longmans Green

(1931). *Thoughts on Some Problems of the Day.* London: Macmillan

(1940a). *Thoughts in War-Time.* London: Macmillan

(1940b). *The Hope of a New World.* London: SCM Press

(1942). *Christianity and Social Order.* Harmondsworth: Penguin

Webb, B. (1926). *My Apprenticeship.* London: Longmans Green

Westcott, B. F. (1901). *Lessons from Work.* London: Macmillan

Wilkinson, A. (1978). *The Church of England and the First World War.* London: SPCK

14

EUCHARISTIC SACRIFICE: THE PROBLEM OF HOW TO USE A LITURGICAL METAPHOR, WITH SPECIAL REFERENCE TO SIMONE WEIL

A. L. LOADES

My interest in Simone Weil is not primarily in her very many merits, but in what helped to bring her to her death. I would not deny that she was one of the great minds of this century, and that whatever she wrote, whether for publication or for her own needs, is marked by her own inimitable authority. We can rely on argument for her merits from writers as different as Professor D. Allen, with his critique of that egocentrism which infects our culture, and is at odds with Christianity's doctrines of co-inherence in their many forms; and Professor D. Z. Phillips, not least with regard to her hunger for the transcendent.

We may recall that terrible prayer she wrote towards the end of her life (Weil 1970b, 243–4, see also Weil 1978b, 196) though she did insist to herself that one could not voluntarily demand what the petitions were for, that such prayer was despite oneself, though with consent, entire and without reservation, a movement of the whole being. The prayer included petition to the Father to grant her in the name of Christ, 'That I may be unable to will any bodily movement, or even any attempt at movement, like a total paralytic. That I may be incapable of receiving any sensation, like someone who is completely blind, deaf, and deprived of all the senses. That I may be unable to make the slightest connection between two thoughts . . .' She asked for will, sensibility, intelligence, love to be stripped away, 'devoured by God, transformed into Christ's substance, and given for food to afflicted men whose body and soul lack every kind of nourishment. And let me be a paralytic – blind, deaf, witless, and utterly decrepit.'

At the very least, she is one of those of whom Margaret Masterman wrote in a remarkable article (1948), who skip certain levels of contemplative religious development and start with 'Passionist' manifestations. Someone operating at this level presents themselves as a total physical sacrifice to the destructive elements of the world, rather than 'hitting back'; and it is worth noticing that the next level is what Margaret Masterman identified as the 'Hostic' level, 'only sacramentally portrayed', at which the saint desires not only to be killed but eaten. And indeed we find Simone Weil noting: 'To live the death of a being is to eat him. The reverse is to be eaten by him. Man eats God and is eaten by God – and that in two senses, one in which he is lost, and another in which he is saved. Communion' (Weil 1976a, 329; see also Teilhard de Chardin 1965, 126; Weil 1974, 119). Or again, 'Catholic communion. God has not only made himself flesh once; every day he makes himself matter in order to give himself to man and be consumed by him. Conversely, through fatigue, affliction, death, man is made matter and consumed by God. How refuse this reciprocity?' (Weil 1976a, 99).

It is of course the case that we can find examples of those who write and pray in what may appear at first sight to be not wholly dissimilar terms, though I think that profound differences in meaning become evident. There was, for instance, that other most remarkable Frenchwoman, Thérèse of Lisieux, who made on 9 June 1895 (aged 22, and but a year away from the first haemorrhage that signalled her death in September 1897) her 'Act of oblation as victim of holocaust to God's merciful love' (Ulanov 1967, 228). Thérèse pleaded to God that he 'consume me unceasingly, while you let the floods of *infinite tenderness* pent up in you flow into my soul, so that I may become a *Martyr* to your *Love*, O my God...' As Ulanov points out in his study of her, she was here experiencing all the stages of the mystical life – purgation, illumination and union all at once (Ulanov 1967, 234). Thérèse, however, was different from Simone Weil in many obvious ways. She was brought up in a passionately and overtly affectionate home, secure in a Catholicism since her baptism and with spiritual gifts evident from the age of three or four. We may recall that at the age of ten, almost dying from kidney disease, she was learning that what the cross might mean for her was the absence of those closest to her when she most desperately needed them. At this point, her father and two of her sisters were away; she was the youngest in her class at school and felt the least befriended; her adoptive mother and favourite sister had entered Carmel. Yet precisely at this point she found an image of the Virgin glowing with beauty for her, 'A beauty beyond any I had ever experienced before', she said, 'her face radiated an indescribable kindness and love...' (Ulanov 1967, 85).

It was a kiss of love. I felt myself loved, and I said in my turn, 'I love you and I give myself to you forever.' There had been no demands, no struggles, no sacrifices; we had exchanged looks a long time ago, Jesus and poor little Thérèse, and we had understood each other. And now, on this day, it wasn't a look any more, but a perfect joining together; there was no longer two of us... (Ulanov 1967, 100)

Small wonder then if, when she took the veil on 8 September 1890, her faith took absolutely seriously her union with her divine bridegroom, and made it possible for her to accept from her monastic family the verbal and physical caresses which were balm to her soul in this world. 'She did not fight them off. Her spirituality required no such bleakness of response to human warmth' (Ulanov 1967, 173). Moreover, her trust in God's ever-available presence in his natural world was a constant and ready means to assuage grief and pain for her. For Céline, the last sister to enter Carmel, on her father's death she wrote:

> In you Jesus, I have all things;
> I have the wheat, the half-open flowers,
> Forget-me-nots, buttercups, exquisite roses;
> I have the bloom of the lily of the valley,
> I have its fragrance. (Ulanov 1967, 215)

Ulanov may well say that she was 'stunned, dazed, drunk with love' (p. 177), although she normally suffered long periods of aridity, and her prayer of surrender to God, her 'Act of oblation as victim of holocaust to God's merciful love' was to receive a response, on 14 June, in choir, as she was beginning to say the Stations of the Cross: 'It was as if an invisible hand had plunged all of me, completely, into fire. Oh! and what fire and what sweetness at the same time! I was burning up with love and I felt that not for a minute, not even for another second, could I stand such violent feelings' (Ulanov 1967, 236). It is absolutely clear that she never sought suffering for its own sake, and that her central weapon when it attacked her was cheerful acceptance, which she somehow managed, however intermittently, through the progress of her tuberculosis from lungs to intestines, complicated by gangrene, ulcers and hideous medical treatment. She was canonized in 1925 when Simone Weil was sixteen.

Small wonder it is that Thérèse became the saint for the soldier on the battlefields of the First World War and beyond. In any case, the conditions had arrived for the application of Christ's sacrificial death as a metaphor for military death. This meant that those actions which at first in early Christian understanding would make the eucharistic ritual ineffectual and false, that is, acts of violence which affect the state of the heart of the worshipper, would in time help to change ritual practice. Fear of unworthy participation in the eating and drinking of the bread and wine, together with a sense of awe at the presence of the eucharistic miracle which recapitulated in the present the effectiveness of the once-for-all sacrifice of Christ, made non-communicating attendance at the eucharist the norm, thus protecting its worshippers from having to confront the issues of what made the ritual ineffective and false. (I owe these points and some subsequent ones to a lecture by Professor S. W. Sykes given in connection with a performance of Britten's *War Requiem*.) It need come as no surprise to

find Simone Weil advancing a project for frontline nurses in the Second
World War, who would be prepared 'to offer their lives as a sacrifice' (Weil
1965, 147; see also pp. 150, 171) and begging Maurice Schumann for 'the
amount of hardship and danger which can save me from being wasted by
sterile chagrin' (Weil 1965, 156). She wanted to try to use her pain
creatively but in a way that would assuage it, and was unable to find any
way of doing so (Lake 1966), and was certainly not to be allowed to share
the soldier's conditions of death in the front line.

There is in any case a problem about treating Christ's death as a sacrifice,
but that is not my concern here. At least one may say that Christ's death
metaphorically described as sacrifice was that which in principle ended any
necessity for further sacrifice. The mass became a ritual which made present
the benefits of Christ's death, and elements within the ritual, such as acts of
contrition, thanksgiving and offering could also, by metaphorical extension
within the ritual context, be described as sacrifice. They could then be
regarded as sacrificial *outside* the ritual context, as could those acts of self-
denial, however faint or overt, which were both judged by the standard of
what Christ alone could do, whilst being merged with what he alone had
done. What could mark the limits to the re-deployment of the language of
sacrifice when once the process had begun? Stephen Sykes' lecture
indicated one point beyond which the limit has been over-stepped. For the
present purpose, however, my concern is with another such point.
Whatever is to be made of all the details of Hyam Maccoby's argument in
The Sacred Executioner, his reflections on the Akedah, the binding of Isaac by
a wholly good Abraham, at a supreme moment of crisis in obedience to the
command of God which leads to the abrogation of human sacrifice,
conclude that for the Jew, no excuse whatsoever was left for its reinstitution
in any lesser emergency (Maccoby 1982, 76). For the Jew, then, there was
'the conviction that the great sacrifice (the Akedah) had taken place long
ago, that the Covenant had resulted from it, and that the worshipper thus
lived in spiritual security within it'. It was for those without this security
that another sacrifice was required (Maccoby 1982, 105). Simone Weil is,
as it were, doubly outside the bounds of security, neither part of a practising
Jewish community, nor incorporated by baptism into the Christian one
inaugurated by Christ's sacrifice. Further, Maccoby is acutely alert to the
way in which it is extremely hard to disguise the literal sense of sacrifice by
using it metaphorically. He remarks on how such disguise may go against
the grain of the psyche which tries to slip into the real thing (as in the
military context) despising as inadequate the substitutes for the literal, such
as the sacrifice of prayer and praise, even the practices of the ascetics
(Maccoby 1982, 82).

It seems to be to this problem that Eugène Masure addressed himself in *Le
Sacrifice du chef*, translated into English by Dom Illtyd Trethowan and

published in Britain in 1944. Masure argued against what he called the 'unconscious Cartesianism' which counteracted Catholic sacramentalism and its respect for the flesh (1944. 71). He wrote of the way in which the spirituality of the Gallican Church yielded too easily to 'a destructive pessimism under the real or merely verbal influence of Jansenism', and of how he and some of his fellow liturgical theologians had fought to rectify and contest the theory of sacrifice as annihilation. This latter he described as a poison in a system of morality and spirituality which separated the Church from the 'deepseated rational desires of mankind' (Masure 1944, 31). The sacrifice of the mass was meant to express the surrender to good of a humanism face to face with God, of the intelligent creature refusing to make itself its final end (Masure 1944, 78). The mystery of the mass had then to do with appropriating the fruits of the merits of Christ, and *not* of renewing them. We might think that it is Simone Weil's political philosophy rather than her spirituality as expressed in certain ways which illustrated Masure's contention. With these preliminary remarks in mind, we may turn to some features of what she says about the eucharist and about God's dealings with his creatures.

Simone Weil believed that the mass was 'a sacrifice in which the passion is repeated day by day' (Weil 1974, 189; see also 1976b, 119) and had to do with the eternal crucifixion of God, '"The Lamb slain from the foundation of the world"' (Weil 1976a, 564; see also p. 222; Weil 1970b, 300–1). She provided an interpretation of the sacrament with which she could manage, selecting elements already existing in the tradition. One could read her as a certain kind of orthodox believer when she affirms that 'my heart has been transplanted, for ever, I hope, into the Blessed Sacrament exposed on the altar' (Weil 1974, 42), even that 'Eternal beatitude . . . is a state where to look is to eat' (Weil 1976a, 367; 1974, 121). It goes almost without saying that this would cohere all too well with her distaste for food. She wrote of the philosophical mystery of the eucharist (Weil 1976a, 322; 1974, 141) and used the analogy of a 'blind man's stick' to indicate means of apprehending the inapprehensible. 'Blind man's sticks making it possible to touch God . . . it is also a question of *contact*' – 'Blind man's sticks for touching eternity' (Weil 1976a, 252–3; see also p. 322). In the same set of notes she wrote 'Ceremonies? Sacred chants? Sacraments?' and 'the story of the centurion indicates sufficiently that we exaggerate the role of the sacraments' (see Weil 1970b, 298). She had made her own assessment. 'In my eyes, a Christian sacrament is a contact with God through a sensible symbol, employed by the Church and whose meaning derives from a teaching of Christ's' (see Weil 1970b, 289). No conventional exegesis was offered:

Whoever looked up at the brazen serpent lifted on a pole was preserved from the poison of snakes. I think it is a sacrament simply to look at the host and the chalice during the elevation with this thought in mind. For analogous reasons, I think the same about reciting the Lord's prayer in Christ's own words (I am convinced the Greek text goes back to Christ; it is too beautiful), provided one's desire is to be nothing but an instrument for the repetition of Christ's own prayer. (Weil 1965, 171-2)

The saying of that prayer was clearly central to her 'inner life'. It was, together with the text of the gospel and the sacraments, one of the three elements of Christianity which retained their redemptive power. 'It is only in this sense that hell had not prevailed' (Weil 1979b, 295; see also p. 305, 360-2). The daily recital of the Lord's Prayer in Greek was for her like 'hanging from a rope and passing, hand over hand, across the abyss of hell' (Weil 1970b, 270). It was necessary to her vocation that she believed that Christ himself had deprived her of 'sharing in his flesh in the way that he had instituted' (Weil 1974, 51) with the exception of one circumstance – if intellectual work was made definitively and totally impossible for her.

She wrote a miniature story, which may express the position at which she had arrived, much perhaps as Ann Cavidge's vision does in Iris Murdoch's novel *Nuns and Soldiers* (Murdoch 1982, 293–300). It was found loose among her papers, and could be juxtaposed with her terrible prayer, so that one can see that she was at least aware of resources other than the deadly imagery of sacrifice. She wrote it as though it were about someone else, not by using a Kierkegaardian-style synonym, but simply by using the masculine gender, and two-thirds of the analogy (quoted here to begin with) give no hint of the emotional 'twist' of the last part:

He entered my room and said: 'Poor creature, you who understand nothing, who know nothing. Come with me and I will teach you things which you do not suspect'. I followed him. He took me into a church. It was new and ugly. He led me up to the altar and said: 'Kneel down'. I said 'I have not been baptised'. He said 'Fall on your knees before this place, in love, as before the place where lies the truth'. I obeyed. He brought me out and made me climb up to a garret. Through the open window one could see the whole city spread out, some wooden scaffoldings, and the river on which boats were being unloaded. The garret was empty, except for a table and two chairs. He bade me be seated.

We were alone. He spoke. From time to time someone would enter, mingle in the conversation, then leave again.

Winter had gone; spring had not yet come. The branches of the trees lay bare, without buds, in the cold air full of sunshine.

The light of day would arise, shine forth in splendour, and fade away; then the moon and the stars would enter through the window. And then once more the dawn would come up. At times he would fall silent, take some bread from a cupboard, and we would share it. This bread really had the taste of bread. I have never found that taste again.

He would pour out some wine for me, and some for himself – wine which tasted of the sun and of the soil upon which this city was built.

At other times we would stretch ourselves out on the floor of the garret, and sweet sleep would enfold me. Then I would wake and drink in the light of the sun.
He had promised to teach me, but he did not teach me anything. We talked about all kinds of things, in a desultory way, as do old friends. (Weil 1976a, 638)

This may perhaps be regarded as her attempt in prose to re-express Herbert's poem 'Love' which she used as a prayer, albeit unintentionally to begin with (Weil 1965, 142). There are points to notice appropriate to both. Nuttall has sharpened the problem of reading Herbert's poem by commenting that Herbert is 'so clever as to come within an ace of resolving the old paradox of humility, which may be explained thus: is "I am humble" a self-refuting sentence?' (Nuttall 1981, 41). In the poem the paradox is set aside by God himself, though the poet's humility is still self-regarding (see Weil 1976a, 239; 1978a, 135). One of her most devoted friends wrote of her that 'Her humility is still partly inspired by a *negative* preoccupation with self: she carves her *ego* by hollowing it out as the proud carve theirs in relief. The ideal would be to make of it a perfectly smooth surface on which one could glide without stopping ...' (Thibon 1953, 138). Moreover, it has been pointed out that she assigned to prayer the kind of anxiety and anguish proper to the writer, or the poet whenever words seem to fail his experience (Jennings 1959, 355). She shared with Herbert the anxiety of religious solipsism. He did not solve the problem of the 'divine' voice and she attempted to solve it by paradox: 'The word of God is silence. God's secret word of love can be nothing else but silence. Christ is the silence of God ... When the silence of God comes to the soul and penetrates it and joins the silence which is secretly present in us, from then on we have our treasure and our heart in God' (Weil 1968, 197; see Bambrough 1978, 210). This silence is essential to love, for if the soul

does not renounce loving, it happens one day to hear, not a reply to the question which it cries, for there is none, but the very silence as something infinitely more full of significance than any response, like God himself speaking. It knows then that God's absence here below is the same as the secret presence upon earth of the god who is in heaven. (Weil 1976b, 199; see also 1976a, 240, 267, 626–7)

In her case, the experience of silence and absence had something to do with her lack of self-worth. She thought that as far as other people were concerned, there was a sense in which she did not exist for them. 'I am the colour of dead leaves, like certain insects which go unnoticed' (Weil 1974, 64; see also 1965, 141). Hence the 'reversal' of the last third of her 'garret' analogy:

One day he said to me: 'Now go'. I fell down before him, I clasped his knees, I implored him not to drive me away. But he threw me out on the stairs. I went down unconscious of anything, my heart as it were in shreds. I wandered along the streets. Then I realized that I had no idea where this house lay.

I have never tried to find it again. I understand that he had come for me by mistake. My place is not in that garret. It can be anywhere – in a prison cell, in one of those middle-class drawing-rooms full of knick-knacks and red plush, in the waiting-room of a station – anywhere, except in that garret.

Sometimes I cannot help trying, fearfully and remorsefully, to repeat to myself a part of what he said to me. How am I to know if I remember rightly? He is not there to tell me.

I know well that he does not love me. How could he love me? And yet deep down within me something, a particle of myself, cannot help thinking, with fear and trembling, that perhaps, in spite of all, he loves me. (Weil 1976a, 638–9)

She found her emotional pain echoed in the Greeks, haunted as they were by the thought that love is not loved (Weil 1976b, 65). Her intellect provided the anodyne for her pain, the 'nail' in her soul (Weil 1965, 137; see also 1968, 184–5). To the long-suffering and kind Thibon she wrote,

I . . . like to think that after the slight shock of separation you will not feel any sorrow about whatever may be in store for me, and that if you should sometimes happen to think of me you will do so as one thinks of a book one read in childhood. I do not want ever to occupy a different place from that in the hearts of those I love, because then I shall be sure of never causing them any unhappiness. (Weil 1963, xiv)

She concluded with words very like those she sent to another friend, by saying, 'I shall never forget the generosity which made you say and write to me some of those things which warm and cheer us even when, as in my case, it is impossible to believe them. They are a support all the same – perhaps too much so' (Weil 1963, xiv). It may be that this other friend was even more important to her. Joë Bousquet had been permanently paralysed as a result of serving in the First World War. Because of his own affliction, she perhaps could learn from him that 'loved ones' were needed, even when she went on affirming that *her* suffering was such that she could not imagine the possibility that anyone could feel friendship for *her*. So to Bousquet she wrote that if she believed in his friendship, 'it is only because I have confidence in you and you have assured me of it, so that my reason tells me to believe it. But this does not make it seem any the less impossible.' At least she managed to affirm her tender gratitude to those who managed to stay her friends:

Because friendship is an incomparable, immeasurable boon to me, and a source of life – not metaphorically but literally. Since it is not only my body but my soul itself that is poisoned all through by suffering, it is impossible for my thought to dwell there and it is obliged to travel elsewhere. It can only dwell for brief moments in God; it dwells often among things; but it would be against nature for human thought never to dwell in anything human. Thus it is literally true that friendship gives to my thought all the life it has, apart from what comes to it from God or from the beauty of the world. (Weil 1965, 141; see also 1970b, 12, 43–4, and 1976b, 195)

Bousquet above all represented to her the fragility of her loved ones (Weil 1963, xii–xiii; 1974, 48). Of the images which 'touch and pierce the soul' one such was

a human body and face which arouse not only desire but also and more strongly the fear of approaching because of the risk of spoiling them, whose decay we cannot imagine although vividly aware of their extreme fragility, and which, by almost wrenching our soul away, make it violently aware that it is nailed to a point in time and space. (Weil 1968, 18)

Unfortunately and typically of her, she interpreted her fears for those she loved as disobedience on her part: 'Because of death, human affections are all irremediably doomed and futureless. What we love barely exists. What is more, for the objects of our love, existence is not a good. We need to grasp this with the mind and accept it out of love for God' (Weil 1976a, 582; see also Weil 1970b, 323–4). She apparently never considered that there might be something inadequate in her understanding of her relationship to God even in her terms of 'consented obedience' (Weil 1970b, 127), 'the only pure motive' (Weil 1976a, 150; see also Weil 1970b, 41), and disobedience when the fate of her friends upset her so deeply (Oppenheimer 1966, 233; see also Weil 1965, 177; 1974, 55; 1978a, 275).

Nevertheless, one constructive point that she learned from her longing for and experience of affection was that it provided her with clues for the use of its language in theology:

The longing to love the beauty of the world in a human being is essentially the longing for the Incarnation. It is mistaken if it thinks it is anything else. The Incarnation alone can satisfy it. It is therefore wrong to reproach the mystics, as has been done sometimes, because they use love's language. It is theirs by right. Others only borrow it. (Weil 1974, 126; see also Weil 1970b, 176, 316)

She may well be referring here to her 'conversion experience' (for want of a better phrase) and its aftermath. By her own account she had felt compelled to kneel in a chapel closely associated with St Francis when visiting Assisi in 1937. The following Easter her father arranged for her and her mother to attend the Easter Week services at Solesmes, and in and through the pain of her constant splitting headaches she experienced what she believed to be the presence of Christ:

The joy of Easter is not the joy that comes after pain, like freedom after chains, repletion after hunger, or reunion after separation. It is the joy that soars above pain and perfects it. In Gregorian chant, for example, the songs themselves make this clear (*Salve, festa dies* . . .) Pain and joy are in perfect equilibrium. Pain is the contrary of joy; but joy is not the contrary of pain. (Weil 1970b, 69)

She wrote of this in a few years' time only to Father Perrin and to Joë Bousquet. To the former she said that she had never foreseen the possibility of 'a real contact, person to person, here below, between a human being and God' though she had vaguely heard of it, without believing in it. She insisted that in her experience neither sense nor imagination played their part – it was not a form of consolation: 'I only felt in the midst of my suffering the presence of a love, like that which one can read in the smile on a beloved face' (Weil 1974, 35). To Bousquet she wrote that in her pain she was making the effort to love, 'although believing that I had no right to give any name to the love', and completely unprepared in the sense that she had never read the mystics. Then she felt 'a presence more personal, more certain, and more real than that of a human being; it was inaccessible both to sense and to imagination, and it resembled the love that irradiates the tenderest smile of somebody one loves' (Weil 1965, 140). Also to Father Perrin she admitted that sometimes during her repetition of the 'Our Father' or at other moments, 'Christ is present with me in person, but his presence is infinitely more real, more moving, more clear than on that first occasion when he took possession of me' (Weil 1974, 38). No doubt is being cast on the sincerity of her account, by the suggestion that the remedy for some of her loneliness and pain was being provided in connection with her developing capacity for human relationships. Her biographer wrote: 'A pure love, a love that does not seek egotistical satisfactions, that seeks the good of others, that does not confuse what is truly other with what one desires for oneself, such a love can be believed when it declares that it has encountered a reality that goes beyond itself and is not a thing of this world' (Pétrement 1976, 341). There is no evidence to show that she knew of it, but the Benedictine tradition contains some prayers of perhaps its greatest abbot which express something of that 'smile' which was her own analogy for Christ's presence to her. St Anselm had written in the context of a prayer to St Paul:

> And you, my soul, dead in yourself,
> run under the wings of Jesus your mother
> and lament your griefs under his feathers.
> Ask that your wounds may be healed
> and that, comforted, you may live again.

> Christ, my mother,
> you gather your chickens under your wings,
> this dead chicken of yours puts himself under those wings.
> For by your gentleness the badly frightened are comforted,
> by your sweet smell the despairing are revived,
> your warmth gives life to the dead,
> your touch justifies sinners.
> Mother, know again your dead son,
> both by the sign of your cross and the voice of his confession.
> Warm your chicken, give life to your dead man,
> justify your sinner. (Ward 1973, 155–6)

Simone Weil's incapacity to believe in the possibility of love and affection for herself, despite all its manifestations (Phillips 1966, 325–8), left her with an assessment of herself as a positive nuisance to others, not only in their relationships between themselves but to God: 'I am not the girl who is waiting for her lover, but the tiresome third party who is sitting with two lovers and has got to get up and go away if they are to be really together' (Weil 1976a, 404). She wrote as a general statement what she seems to have regarded as being true for her personally, and which parallels her statement about eternal beatitude:

Friendship is a miracle by which a person consents to view from a certain distance, and without coming any nearer, the very being who is necessary to him as food. It requires the strength of soul that Eve did not have; and yet she had no need of the fruit. If she had been hungry at the moment when she looked at the fruit, and if in spite of that she had remained looking at it indefinitely without taking one step towards it, she would have performed a miracle analogous to that of perfect friendship. (Weil 1974, 157; see also 1970b, 18, 286)

So whenever she approached a possible relationship which might be life-giving to her she was clearly terrified that the relationship equally likely might involve her in something other than the mutual respect she rightly valued (Weil 1970b, 42, 53). She had learned that only in connection with the language of eucharistic sacrifice was it proper to talk of eating and drinking someone. The greatest mystery of all about the eucharist was that Christ 'wanted to nourish us with himself'. What gets trans-signified in the eucharist is not the bread and wine, but the body and blood of the Lord, which are trans-signified into food and drink (Anscombe 1981). Doris Lessing in *The Golden Notebook* uses this sort of language in a way which expresses Simone Weil's fear, where she writes a conversation between a man and a woman about real people radiating serenity:

Every bloody one of them's got a history of emotional crime, oh the sad bleeding corpses that litter the road to maturity of the wise serene man or woman of fifty-odd! . . . Mind you, from time to time one of the corpses will let out a small self-pitying bleat – remember me? . . . it doesn't make it less depressing, the way the victims are always so willing to contribute their flesh and blood.

And a little later:

The people who are oh so willing to be victims are those who've given up being cannibals themselves, they're not tough enough for the golden road to maturity and the ever so wise shrug. They know they've given up. What they are really saying is: *I've* given up, but I'll be happy to contribute my flesh and blood to you.

One possible response is that of the couple in the dialogue – 'Crunch crunch crunch' (Lessing 1981, 603–4). Simone Weil thought that she loved her friends because

We love like cannibals . . . Thanks to their companionship, their words, or their letters, we get comfort, energy, and stimulation from the people we love. They affect us in the same way as a good meal after a hard day's work. So we love them like food. It is indeed an anthropophagous love. And our hatred, our indifference, are anthropophagous too. You were hungry and you have eaten me. And indeed we ought to eat him. (Weil 1970b, 284–5)

She insisted that such affection was legitimate only towards 'Those in whom Christ lives', that is, an unpossessive love, for 'Pure food eludes all particular relationships. Apart from this kind of love, all human relation-ships are ghoulish. To love someone means to love drinking his blood.' Inevitably, then, 'One can only love purely if one has renounced life' (Weil 1970b, 284–5).

The language of eucharist as well as of sacrifice thus ministered to her 'imaginative act of self-destruction' (Oates 1980, 163) and this in turn helped to precipitate her interpretation of the doctrine of creation (Weil 1974, 133; 1976a, 183). For instance:

Sacrifice is a gift to God, and giving to God is destroying. It is right, therefore, to think that God abdicated in order to create and that by destroying we are making restitution to him. God's sacrifice is creation; man's sacrifice is destruction. But man has the right to destroy only what belongs to him; that is to say, not even his body, but solely and exclusively his will. (Weil 1970b, 212; see also pp. 96–7, 123, 354)

Both incarnation and passion are implied by creation (Vetö 1965, 277; Little 1970) so ruthlessly she wrote that 'The birth of Christ is already a sacrifice. Christmas ought to be as sad a day as Good Friday' (Weil 1970b, 213; see also pp. 70, 81, 83, 91).

She would have done better to have trusted to clues other than those provided by the imagery of sacrifice and eucharist. For instance, she was deeply appreciative of the beauty of the world (Weil 1976a, 291; 1968, 198), a beauty which she saw as the creative gift of God's Son (Weil 1976b, 101–4): 'The beauty of the world is Christ's tender smile for us coming through matter. He is really present in the universal beauty. The love of this beauty proceeds from God dwelling in our soul and goes out to God present in the universe. It also is like a sacrament' (Weil 1974, 120; see also 1970a, 77). Such joy could then have become 'joie de vivre', or 'vivre d'amour' as it did for Thérèse of Lisieux (Ulanov 1967, 223) and as Simone Weil herself indicated when she began to develop a sacramental view of work (Weil 1976a, 170; 1978a, 288). For example, 'What is required is that this world and the world beyond, in their double beauty, should be present and associated in the act of work, like the child about to be born in the making of the layette' (Weil 1978a, 91).

It was, however, to be a tragedy that experience and imagery which offered the possibility of survival and even of hope were in no way as powerful as the alternatives, which had bitten all too deeply into her intellect and emotion, corroding her vitality especially at the time when she was to become adrift briefly in North America and then in war-time Britain, in alien cultures in which her role was anything but clear, or even promising. In these circumstances, the slavery both physical and spiritual of her own time gave the gospel comparisons drawn from slavery significance again. She maintained that in Christ's mouth the word 'slave' was an artifice of love, indicating those 'who have wanted with all their hearts to give themselves to God as slaves', to be converted into something analogous to nothingness, albeit by their consent (Weil 1978a, 264; see also 1974, 102). This was the sort of fidelity raised to the point of madness which compelled Orestes to reveal himself to Electra (Weil 1976b, 17; see also 1976a, 389, 583) and yet, here again, the moral sensibility that she deployed so effectively in some contexts deserted her entirely when she explored some metaphors for such grace. Sexual violence rightly horrified her (Pétrement 1976, 192–4) yet she had found nothing morally monstrous in using metaphor from what horrified her to inter-react with analogies for sacrifice and eucharist. So in the case of grace she produced some equalling appalling analogies, of which the two worst are as follows: 'Death and rape – two metaphors for describing the action of the Holy Spirit on the soul. Murder and rape are crimes owing to the fact that they constitute illegitimate imitations of God's actions' (Weil 1976a, 390); and, 'Tearing a girl away from her mother's side, against her will – the greatest and most painful form of violence that it is possible for men to commit – is what serves us as an image of grace' (Weil 1976a, 401). The one comment which should of course be made in her favour is the point she herself made when she wrote her prayer about sacrifice, and followed it with metaphors somewhat comparable with those quoted above. For then she wrote, 'But all these spiritual phenomena are absolutely beyond my competence. I know nothing about it. They are reserved for those who possess, to begin with, the elementary moral virtues. I can only speak of them haphazard. And I cannot even sincerely tell myself that I am speaking haphazard' (Weil 1970b, 245).

Without her fascination with particular elements of the Christian tradition she might have survived to become an even greater political philosopher than indeed she was, with her exceptional independence and clarity of mind, generosity and courage harnessed to a complete maturity of which I think we have here only the beginnings. One may say of her that she was an exponent of 'minority religion at its bleakest' (West 1966, 146) and that she died of love (Rees 1966, 191). She quoted Augustine's *Confessions* with approval at one point: '"Amare amabam." If he had stuck to that, he had found the way' (Weil 1970b, 261). It could, after all, have been a mistake to interpret such love as of a kind to fit with her opinion that 'Christmas ought to be as sad a day as Good Friday.' She had indeed begun to realize that there were resources by which to live, but by then it was too late. Among her last notes, written as she lay dying, she suggested that there was an alliance between matter and real emotions. She wrote of the importance of meals on solemn occasions, festivals, family reunions, even that of two friends. Special foods were then important – turkey, marrons glacés, Christmas pudding, Easter eggs and many local and regional traditions (although these were in danger of disappearing). The joy and the spiritual significance of the festival lay in the special tit-bits associated with the festival (Weil 1970b, 368). It was that *alliance* between matter and emotion she was unable to live to explore, and which might have put the elements of Christianity that she did explore into their proper perspective, and thus discover their possible proper meaning. It is one thing to employ the metaphors of sacrifice in the context of love and then to be sustained by it in a situation of extremity, but quite another to make the possibility of being in that situation a focus of attention outside the context of love. Without that context, life may be eaten away by metaphor, with those who employ it literally tested to destruction by it.

NOTE

An early, much shorter version of this chapter appeared in the journal *Religion and Literature* (17: 2, Summer 1985); the author is grateful to its editors for permission to reprint some material from it here.

REFERENCES

Anscombe, G. E. M. (1981). On Transubstantiation. In *Collected Philosophical Papers*, vol. III, pp. 107–12. Oxford: Blackwell

Bambrough, R. (1978). Intuition and the Inexpressible. In *Mysticism and Philosophical Analysis*, ed. S. Katz, pp. 200–13. London: Sheldon

Jennings, E. (1959). A World of Contradiction: A Study of Simone Weil. *The Month* 22, 349–58

Lake, F. (1966). *Clinical Theology*. London: Darton, Longman & Todd

Lessing, D. (1981). *The Golden Notebook*. St Albans: Granada

Little, J. P. (1970). The Symbolism of the Cross in the Writings of Simone Weil. *Religious Studies* 6, 175–83

Maccoby, H. (1982). *The Sacred Executioner: Human Sacrifice and the Legacy of Guilt*. London: Thames and Hudson

Masure, E. (1944). *The Christian Sacrifice*, trans. I. Trethowan. London: Burns & Oates

Murdoch, I. (1982). *Nuns and Soldiers*. Harmondsworth: Penguin

Nuttall, A. D. (1981). Gospel Truth. In *Ways of Reading the Bible*, ed. M. Wadsworth. Brighton: Harvester

Oates, J. C. (1980). The Art of Suicide. In *Suicide: The Philosophical Issues*, ed. M. Pabst Battin and D. J. Mayo. New York: St Martin's Press

Oppenheimer, H. (1966). Moral Choice and Divine Authority. In *Christian Ethics and Contemporary Philosophy*, ed. I. T. Ramsey, pp. 219–33. London: SCM Press

Pétrement, S. (1976). *Simone Weil: A Life*, trans. R. Rosenthal. London: Mowbrays

Phillips, D. Z. (1966). The Christian Concept of Love. In *Christian Ethics and Contemporary Philosophy*, ed. I. T. Ramsey, pp. 314–28. London: SCM Press

Rees, R. (1966). *Simone Weil: A Sketch for a Portrait*. Carbondale: Southern Illinois University Press

Teilhard de Chardin, P. (1965). *Le Milieu divin*, trans. B. Wall. London: Fontana

Thibon, G. (1953). Part 2 of J. M. Perrin and G. Thibon, *Simone Weil As We Knew Her*, trans. E. Crawford. London: Routledge and Kegan Paul

Ulanov, B. (1967). *The Making of a Modern Saint: A Biographical Study of Thérèse of Lisieux*. London: Cape

Vetö, M. (1965). Simone Weil and Suffering. *Thought* 40: 157, 275–86

Ward, B. (ed. and trans.) (1973). *St Anselm: The Prayers and Meditations*. Harmondsworth: Penguin

Weil, Simone (1963). *Gravity and Grace*, trans. E. Crawford. London: Routledge and Kegan Paul

(1965). *Seventy Letters*, trans. R. Rees. London: Oxford University Press

(1968). *On Science, Necessity and the Love of God*, trans. R. Rees. London: Oxford University Press

(1970a). *Gateway to God*, ed. D. Raper. London: Fontana

(1970b). *First and Last Notebooks*, trans. R. Rees. London: Oxford University Press

(1974). *Waiting on God*, trans. E. Crawford. London: Fontana

(1976a). *The Notebooks*, trans. A. Wills (2 vols.). London: Routledge and Kegan Paul

(1976b). *Intimations of Christianity among the Greeks*, trans. E. C. Geissbuhler. London: Routledge and Kegan Paul

(1978a). *The Need for Roots*, trans. A. F. Wills. London: Routledge and Kegan Paul

(1978b). *Lectures on Philosophy*, trans. H. Price. London: Cambridge University Press

In Simone Weil's work, material printed as aphorisms has sometimes been cited as though printed in paragraph form.

West, P. (1966). *The Wine of Absurdity: Essays on Literature and Consolation*. London: Pennsylvania University Press

IV

15

THE SEMANTICS OF SACRIFICE

EDWARD HULMES

INTRODUCTION

The subject of sacrifice has occupied the attention of students in fields as distinct as theology, psychology, sociology and social anthropology. These discrete intellectual disciplines employ different investigative techniques, and proceed from different presuppositions about the nature of the enquiry itself. Independent investigations from a variety of disciplined approaches offer different perspectives on a given subject, but the knowledge which accrues is impressionistic in consequence. Workers in one field are often unaware of what has been done in others, and sometimes prefer to remain so.

In the case of a subject such as sacrifice, precision may be gained by concentrating on what is taken to be primitive, or early, religious ritual within a designated community, but only at the expense of limiting the importance of what sacrifice continues to signify in the living language of tradition and daily usage. The semantic shift in the meaning of the word 'sacrifice' can be detected in different religious traditions. Meaning shifts from the ritual slaughter of living beings as part of the religious cultus, to the inner disposition of the worshipper which renders unnecessary the taking of life. Thence, by way of attenuation, the meaning shifts in general usage to denote heroic attitudes and costly acts which have no transcendent reference of a specifically religious nature.

The primary meaning of the verb 'to sacrifice' is to make sacred to deity the offerings provided, particularly (but not exclusively) those animals ritually slaughtered for such a purpose. The widespread practice of sacrifice in religion furnishes evidence of the need for human beings to enter into a relationship with the powers that are believed to influence the course of daily life, but which are beyond the range of normal human comprehension. The propitiation of deities, the attempt to remain in contact (even in communion) with them, to solicit their help, to deflect their anger or to neutralize their potentially baleful influence, requires not merely the offering of the sacrifice, but the precise use of rituals prescribed in the cultus.

Sacrifices made to deity in earlier times (though by no means unknown in many parts of the world today) were of various kinds. Human sacrifices, animal sacrifices, libations, presentations of food and other gifts were accompanied by offerings of worship, prayer, thanksgiving, penitence and submission. In addition to this, the ritual offering of sacrifice (especially sacrifices of blood) had an important moral as well as religious purpose in controlling the effects of violence in society. In the absence of the cathartic and substitutionary functions of authorized religious sacrifice, it has recently been argued that violence might erupt with catastrophic effects for the community (Girard 1977, 2).

Ambiguity, rather than ambivalence, attaches to the various uses of the word 'sacrifice', either as noun or verb (Girard 1977, 1, 181–5). In different places and periods the word refers to human activities directed to different ends, and proceeding from different motives. In the prescribed rituals of institutionalized religion it calls to mind activities and beliefs with specific cultic significance. Within the sphere of religious observance the word assumes a figurative meaning, never wholly divorced from the literal, but spiritualized during the development of the tradition. The significance of this development is not so accessible to outside observers, and is seldom thought by those inside to require external explication. The word has, thus, another set of meanings for observers who have no personal experience of what it is to be united with a believing and worshipping community. Secular usage of the word 'sacrifice' is primarily metaphorical. Whether or not this is consciously so depends upon the residual influence of religious beliefs and practices no longer deemed to be either useful or necessary.

The origins of sacrifice are not known, though there has been a good deal of reasonable speculation. Intuitions of transcendence, intimations of immortality and an awareness of the numinous no doubt contribute to the development of sacrificial rites which make possible a more profound understanding of critical moments in human experience (Otto 1929). These include the rites of passage associated with birth, puberty, marriage and death. They also include rituals in which the deity is not only solicited, but constrained to answer with favour the needs of human creatures dependent upon an orderly succession of the seasons, the success of crops, the provision of water and continuing good health (Schimmel 1960).

The history of religious sacrifices is replete with the ritual slaughter of animals (and – in certain cases – of human beings). These offerings frequently involve the consumption by fire of the remains of the sacrifice as an earnest of its total dedication to the deity. From the fire which consumes the sacrificial remains rises a mixture of smell and smoke, bearing upwards the evidence of submissive intent from the individual or group on whose behalf the sacrifice is offered.[1] The cost to the involuntary victim of sacrifice is life itself. The cost to the one who sacrifices varies according to the degree of solemnity which attaches to the occasion of the sacrifice, and according to the means available for the proper conduct of the appropriate rite.

The protection of the cultic tradition and its transmission to the next generation always call for a nice balance between conservation and development. It is a balance seldom achieved, but the resulting tension prepares the way for renewal. The balance between the old and the new is difficult to achieve, even within a society which is shielded by historical and geographical factors from outside influences. Except in rare cases (and even these are not likely to remain isolated indefinitely), such protection is no longer afforded in the modern world. Society is developing to an apparently irreversible level of religious pluralism, requiring a reconsideration and requiring the surrender (or sacrifice) of many cherished traditional beliefs.

In a figurative sense 'sacrifice' increasingly comes to mean the voluntary and whole-hearted surrender to God of that which is his proper due. What is expressly required is a *living* sacrifice of the worshipping self, the surrender of the whole personality, in every aspect of its manifestation (Rom. 12:1–2). Yet there is still a sense of human inadequacy in presuming to approach God at all. The recognition of the baseness of human beings in comparison with the holiness of God, as revealed in monotheistic religions, exposes the unacceptability of *any* offering made to God unaccompanied by submission to the divine will.[2] With the habituation of centuries even the practice of a bloodless and spiritualized sacrifice may become perfunctory, and degenerate into ritual that has grown stale in the service of tradition. The resulting declension from the original purpose of sacrifice requires the cleansing of renewal.

DIFFERENCES OF APPROACH

Students of religion with an interest in comparative studies – sociological, psychological, anthropological or theological – have been tempted to generalize from the particular, to presume to have discovered the underlying unity of the sacrificial system, or to formulate theories which are supposed to account for the universality, or near universality, of sacrifice. Despite the many independent efforts to observe, describe and interpret sacrifice, the subject remains mysterious, and probably essentially so. Prudently for his purposes, yet damagingly for the wider interpretation of the significance of sacrifice, Max Weber categorically excluded from his study of religion what he assumed (presumably in private) to be its essence (*das Wesentliche*):

To define 'religion', to say what it *is*, is not possible at the start of a presentation such as this. Definition can be attempted, if at all, only at the conclusion of the study. The essence of religion is not even our concern, as we make it our task to study the conditions and effects of a particular type of social behaviour. (Weber 1963, 1)

Weber's consideration of sacrifice falls under the same reductionist ban. Both 'characteristic elements of "divine worship"' (i.e. prayer and sacrifice) 'have their origin in magic'. Sacrifice is 'a magical instrumentality' which, *inter alia*, coerces the gods. It is also a *communio*, 'a ceremony of eating together which serves to produce a fraternal community between the sacrificers and the god'. Weber notes that this already marks a shift in the significance of sacrifice, that is to say, a development from an earlier emphasis on the magical transference to the participants in the sacrifice of the qualities of the slaughtered animal (Weber 1963, 26).

A classic example of a social-anthropological approach to the subject of sacrifice is contained in a work by H. Hubert and M. Mauss first published in French in 1898 and in English in 1964 (Hubert and Mauss 1964). Noting that the sociological and social-anthropological contributions to the 'enormous' literature on sacrifice have been few, the writer of the Foreword to the English edition, Evans Pritchard, modestly confesses his inability to comment on what his two authors say about the details of Vedic and Hebrew sacrifices, but naively assumes that these details are intended to have a general application to all sacrificial acts. Even allowing that he may have in mind only blood sacrifices, it is not clear why he should conclude that the examples cited have a universal significance. Hubert and Mauss are more prudent. Their stated intention is to define the nature and social function of sacrifice within a self-contained cultural system (Hinduism) that has led 'to pantheism', and a self-contained cultural system (that of the biblical Hebrews) that has led 'to monotheism' (Hubert and Mauss 1964, 8). What emerges from their researches is that the unity of the sacrificial system derives from a common procedure, employed for different purposes in different ways. Sacrifice, in short, establishes a means of communication between the 'sacred' world and the 'profane' world, through the mediation of a victim which is ritually destroyed (Hubert and Mauss 1964, 97).

This is modest enough, but apparently sufficient for the narrowly defined interests of sociology (Hubert and Mauss 1964, 103). That sacrifice is a peculiar element in systems of consecration was never in doubt. The possibility that the significance of sacrifice exceeds the narrow aims assigned to it by 'elementary theologies' is apparent after a moment's reflection. The authors of this monograph are unaware of, or choose to exclude, the important refinement of the concept of sacrifice in what may be called – in response to their own phrase quoted above – advanced theologies.

In studies of this kind it is not only the level of theoretical abstraction that is disconcerting but what can only be described as the manipulation (however unintentional) of vast systems of belief and practice for the purposes of a specific enquiry. It is at this point that the social anthropologist might profitably turn to students with a more comprehensive grasp of theology in order to question the appropriateness of the statement (on which so much depends) that the one religion 'leads to' monotheism, and 'the other to pantheism'. *Theological* reflection about the purpose and continuing significance of the prescribed rituals is constantly required, lest sacrifice (for example) become, or be thought to be, an end in itself.

Reference to the origins and purposes of sacrifice has been a periodically recurring feature of the challenge presented to tradition by would-be instigators of reform. This renewal is a vital part of the *internal* development of the tradition, although it sometimes leads to a separation of the new from the old, and to independent and even mutually hostile beliefs and liturgical practices. Reformation need not prove to be disastrous for the ancient tradition, provided that it is continuous, and does not itself become institutionalized to the point where, in turn, it requires reform. The consequences of the tension between conservation and development, between reformation and counter-reformation, can be seen in several parts of the world today.

IDEAS IN THE OLD TESTAMENT AND IN THE NEW TESTAMENT

Where there could be little or no understanding of the mysterious nature of what was 'wholly other', sacrifices proceeded out of a sense of awe in the presence of the unknown and the unknowable, and also out of experience that the gods were not malevolent aliens but natural protectors. But the assertion 'Primus in orbe deos fecit timor' does not carry much conviction.[3] With the advent of revelation the response from the human side developed on the basis of increasing trust and, ultimately, of love. The Old Testament concept of revelation is rooted in the belief that the creator God, the Lord of history, graciously discloses his purpose to those whom he has chosen to receive it (Gen. 17:18–19; Exod. 4:15–16; Jer. 7:25–8; Dan. 9:10; Lk 1:68–79). In the New Testament the self-sacrificial love of God for his creatures is shown in the mystery of the incarnation, death and resurrection of Jesus, the lamb of sacrifice, who reveals to believers the manner in which a sinful creation is reconciled to its creator (2 Cor. 5:17–21; Eph. 2:13–22; Col. 1:15–23).

In the New Testament, altar and sacrifice are familiar enough as part of the accepted pattern of worship (Matt. 5:23–4; 23:18–39),[4] although Jesus himself regards them as obsolete (Matt. 12:6; John 2:19: 4:20–5). They are part of the old dispensation, a feature of the old covenant, to be replaced by the new covenant. No sacrifice is necessary in the new covenant, once the work of Jesus is finished. Under the terms of the old covenant the purpose of sacrifice was to effect a personal relationship between God and man. This purpose is

finally fulfilled in the personal act of Christ, in the voluntary and unique offering up of his life. Sacrifice is thus brought to an end in him. Cultic sacrifice is not merely transcended but ended by the unique self-offering of Christ because the person of Christ as High-priest is unique. The New Testament experience of salvation frees the author of Hebrews from the cultic conception of sacrifice which dominates his world of thought. (Behm 1979, 185–6)

The interpretation of the death of Jesus as sacrificial, both in the New Testament and subsequently throughout the development of Christian theology, requires a considerable shift in the meaning of the word 'sacrifice'. The crucifixion of Jesus was the culmination of a judicial process, in which the representatives of political power and legal authority were only adventitiously engaged in fulfilling the divine purpose (Sykes 1980, 62; and compare Isa. 44:24–8; 45:1–13).[5]

In the Old Testament the propitiation of a capricious deity is replaced by devotion to a God who now reveals himself in a series of compassionate acts, and by a desire to respond with offerings of self-dedication, obedience and repentance for sins committed against the divine will. What God requires is clearly stated:

> With what shall I come before the Lord,
> and bow myself before God on high?
> Shall I come before him with burnt offerings,
> with calves a year old?
> Will the Lord be pleased with thousands of rams,
> with ten thousands of rivers of oil?
> Shall I give my first-born for my transgression,
> the fruit of my body for the sin of my soul?

After this passage the prophet provides the answer to these questions within the space of a sentence, epitomizing the requirements of religion – legal, ethical and spiritual – and reminding the people of all that is involved in walking humbly with God:

> He has showed you, O man, what is good;
> and what does the Lord require of you
> but to do justice, and to love kindness (steadfast love),
> and to walk humbly with your God.
> (Mic. 6:6–8; cf. Isa. 1:12–17; Amos 5:23–4)

There were critical periods in the life of the Hebrew people, as recorded in the Old Testament, when God's relationship with his chosen people needed to be renewed. Ideally, the sacrificial order of the covenant relationship pointed to the dynamic presence of a gracious God who reveals his will to his people, and who requires their obedience if the unique relationship is to prosper. The sacrifices which the Israelites offered acknowledged the divine initiative in establishing the covenant. From the eighth century BC onwards the Old Testament prophets criticized sacrifice. They did so because its original purpose had been abandoned, neglected or forgotten. This is clear from a number of passages: Amos 5:21–4; Hos. 6:6 and 8:11–14; Isa. 1:11–17 (cf. 56:6–8); Jer. 6:16–21 and 7:21–6. The Lord delights in justice and righteousness, and not in the multiplicity of festivals and sacrifices (Amos 5:24). During their nomadic desert period the Israelites enjoyed a relationship with God which rendered sacrifice redundant (Amos 5:25).

The examples which have been cited in this section reflect the shift in the meaning attached to the word 'sacrifice' as recorded in the Old Testament and in the New Testament. This is not to say that the development was continuous and evolutionary. It is already clear from the story in Gen. 22 that it was the obedience of Abraham, and the binding (not the sacrifice) of Isaac, that God required. The figure of Abraham is of the greatest significance for Jews, Christians and Muslims. For Muslims, he (Ibrāhīm) was the first Muslim (ḥanīfan musliman): 'Abraham was not a Jew, nor yet a Christian; but he was an upright man who had surrendered (to Allāh), and he was not of the idolaters.'[6] It was Abraham's faith in the providence of God that was put to the test before the symbolic offering was provided. The Old Testament prophets consistently recalled their people from the practice of time-honoured ritual, performed without an awareness of its inner significance, to the faithfulness exemplified by Abraham, and to the personal sacrifice it signified.

DEVELOPMENTS IN OTHER RELIGIOUS TRADITIONS

(a) A Hindu approach

There is testimony from other religious traditions to the difficulties experienced during the course of spiritual renewal. The attenuation of the life of the spirit is not limited to a single religious tradition. Further to the east, at approximately the same time as the Old Testament prophets were inveighing against the neglect of the inner significance of sacrifice in their own tradition, the Indian experience was allowing for a comparable adjustment to meet the growing awareness of the need to reinvigorate religious practices that had lost much of their meaning. The Hindu tradition had developed over a period of centuries to the point where the ancient religious rites had become the means for perpetuating divisions in society between groups with different religious duties and social functions.

The Aryan people who crossed the Indus from the north-west, some time during the second millennium BC, brought with them their own religion.

They were unable to eradicate the indigenous beliefs of the peoples who already inhabited the sub-continent east and south of the Indus. The interaction between the religion of the conquering invaders and the religion of the conquered led to the rise of Hinduism. Sacrifices to the gods were a feature of religious practices, with offerings of food and drink as well as of animals. In this early phase of its development Hindu worship found poetic expression in a collection of hymns (of which the *Ṛg Veda* – 'Royal Knowledge') is perhaps the best known:

To thee, O Agni (Fire), illuminator of the darkness, day by day with prayer bringing worship we come;

To thee that rulest over the sacrifices, protector of Law, radiant one, increasing in thine own abode.

Be thou, as a father to a son, O Agni, easy of access to us. Abide with us for blessing. (Thomas 1923, 26)

Simple belief in the divinity of (for example) the fire, the sun, dawn and lightning began to make way for a belief in beings who influence the course of events. Worship and sacrifice were their due, not least in order that favours might be granted, the wicked punished, and evil deflected:

O Maruts (the Storm-Gods), that man in whose dwelling you drink (the Soma), ye mighty (sons) of heaven, he indeed has the best guardians.

You who are propitiated either by sacrifices or from the prayers of the sage, hear the call, O Maruts!

Aye, the strong man to whom you have granted a sage, he will live in a stable rich in cattle.

On the altar of that strong man Soma is poured out in daily sacrifices; praise and joy are sung.

To him let the strong Maruts listen, to him who surpasses all men, as the flowing rain-clouds pass over the sun.

For we, O Maruts, have sacrificed in many a harvest, through the mercies of the swift gods (the Storm-Gods).

May that mortal be blessed, O worshipful Maruts, whose offerings you carry off.

You take notice either of the sweat of him who praises you, ye men of true strength, or of the desire of the suppliant.

O ye of true strength, make this manifest by your greatness! Strike the fiend with your thunderbolt!

Hide the hideous darkness, destroy every tusky (tusked, toothed) spirit. Create the light which we long for! ('Hymn to the Maruts (Storm-Gods)', in Müller 1869, 137).

The hymns of the Veda are addressed to different deities. Agni is Fire.

Indra, perhaps the most prominent god in the Veda, is the god of Thunder. Varuna is the upholder of the universe. Whilst ignoring (but not denying) the existence of other gods worthy of praise and sacrifice, the devotee invested the god of his choice with supremacy, and with all the nobler qualities of the deities he otherwise ignored. In this henotheism was the seed of an attitude characteristic of contemporary Hinduism, namely, the belief that there is one Reality at the heart of things, which is approached and worshipped under different names.

This doctrine was re-interpreted, and then expressed in a radically different way, during the later Upaniṣadic period. The sacrificial rites were presided over by the priestly class, the Brahmins. The *Brāhmaṇas* were their manuals of ritual. W. E. Hocking has well noted the problem for religion when it becomes perfunctory and external: 'There can be no valid worship except that in which man is involuntarily bent by the presence of the Most Real, beyond his will' (Hocking 1912, 152). But the elaborate rituals, and the dominance of ceremonial by the Brahmins, were incapable of crushing a spirit of enquiry about the *inner* significance of sacrifice. Such speculations led ultimately to the teachings of the Upaniṣads. In the Upaniṣads the doctrine that all the different powers are manifestations of but one reality eliminates the reality of the distinction between the worshipper and the worshipped, between the Absolute (*Brahman*) and the individuated self (*Ātman*): Tat tvam aṣi – 'That art Thou!' When the doctrine reached this developed form it was clear that sacrifice in its ancient forms was redundant. A bridge between the old and the new needed to be constructed.

Owing to the gradual growth of rationalism in society, growing abhorrence to animal sacrifice in *Vedic* rites, and the increasing dissatisfaction with various outward and complex practices in ceremonials there came into being different Schools also in the *brāhmaṇic* class who doubted the value and validity of sacrifices. They considered them to be frail rafts for crossing the oceans of the world (*saṃsāra*), and allegorical explanations of sacrifices were sought to be offered. (Vidhushekhara 1952, 173)

The shift in understanding to what the author quoted above calls 'allegorical explanations of sacrifice' helps to preserve the significance of ancient sacrificial ritual without destroying the continuity of the tradition. The *aśva-medha* (horse sacrifice), the ancient and most elaborate animal sacrifice, assumes a cosmic significance:

Aum, the dawn, verily, is the head of the sacrificial horse, the sun the eye, the wind the breath, the open mouth the *Vaiśvānara* fire; the year is the body of the sacrificial horse, the sky is the back, the atmosphere is the belly, the earth the hoof, the quarters the sides, the intermediate quarters the ribs, the seasons the limbs, the months and half-months the joints, days and nights the feet, the stars the bones, the clouds the flesh; the food in the stomach is the sand, the rivers are the blood-vessels, the liver and the lungs are the mountains, the herbs and the trees are the hair. The rising (sun) the hind part, when he yawns then it lightens, when he shakes himself, it thunders, when he urinates it rains; voice, indeed, is his voice. (From the *Bṛhad-āraṇyaka-Upaniṣad*, in Radhakrishnan 1953, 149)

Radhakrishnan, whose translation this is, subsequently comments on this passage:

In this sacrifice a horse is let loose and a guard of three hundred follows his track. If anyone hinders the horse's progress, the guard will have to fight. When the horse completes a victorious circuit of the earth and returns to the capital, he is offered as a sacrifice and the king who performs the sacrifice assumes the title of sovereign, emperor ... The idea of sacrifice as a means to account for creation goes back to the *Puruṣa Sūkta* of the *Ṛg-Veda* (x. 90–129), where from each of the members of the primeval person, Puruṣa, some part of the world is made. (Radhakrishnan 1953, 149–50)

(b) A Buddhist perspective

When the identification of *Brahman* and *Ātman* was finding expression in the Upaniṣads, there came another development in India which was to have a profound effect on attitudes to the practice of sacrifice. Buddhism began to emerge in the sixth century BC in north-eastern India as a direct result of the religious awakening of Siddharta Gautama, the Buddha. The word 'Buddha', a title not a name, signifies one who has become enlightened by the reality of what *is*, or one who has awakened from the sleep of ordinary existence to see things as they really are. His was one of the most influential and lasting stirrings of renewal inside India. The Buddha responded to the inadequacy of institutionalized religion, and to the prevailing inescapable divisions of caste. Important as the awakening of the Buddha was (and still is), it is also significant that his message of enlightenment was increasingly acceptable to those who were questioning the need for sacrifice, and the excess sometimes associated with it:

In Magadha, a revered teacher, along with three hundred disciples, was performing a great sacrifice. He had been given plenty of land and wealth by Bimbisara. For the sacrificial purpose, seven hundred bullocks, seven hundred calves, seven hundred she-calves, seven hundred goats and seven hundred rams had been brought to the sacrificial ground. This gigantic preparation for blood-spilling in the name of religion is indicative of the dismal degeneration of the contemporary cults. (Varma 1973, 74)

The Buddha's teaching on the subject of sacrifices involving the death of animals is clear enough, and given in a number of short folk-tales. Typical of these are the stories called 'On Offering Food to the Dead', and 'On Offerings given under a Vow'. The first of these is prefaced by the following paragraph:

'If people would but understand.' This the Teacher told when at Jetavana, about food offered to the dead. For at that time people used to kill sheep and goats in large numbers in order to offer what is called 'The Feast of the Dead' in honour of their deceased relatives. When the monks saw men doing so, they asked the Teacher, saying, 'Lord! the people here bring destruction on many living creatures in order to provide the so-called "Feast of the Dead". Can there possibly, Sir, be any advantage in that?'

The Teacher said, 'Let not us, O mendicants! provide the Feast of the Dead: for what advantage is there in destroying life? Formerly sages seated in the sky preached a discourse showing the evils of it, and made all the dwellers in Jambu-dīpa give up this practice. But now since change of birth has set in, it has risen again.' (Rhys Davids 1977, 226–31)

The Buddha taught his followers to refrain from the taking of life. The cessation of ritual sacrifice follows from the Buddhist belief that the very notion of gods, to whom sacrifice or prayer are appropriate offerings, is part of the unreality from which human beings need to be awakened. At one level, therefore, sacrifice was not merely disadvantageous for a Buddhist, but unnecessary. At the same time the Buddha took the trouble to reinterpret for his disciples the significance of sacrifice, and to invest it with new meaning. Once again this shift in meaning was conveyed in the form of a story, in which the new is contrasted with the old, and the earlier disposition to make ritual sacrifices is adapted to serve the needs of a later and higher truth.

The story concerns a king whose sovereignty was unquestioned and who ruled his kingdom with serenity and wisdom (see Müller 1895, 93–104). Having secured peace inside as well as outside the borders of his kingdom, and having subdued his passions, he devoted his efforts to promoting the happiness of his subjects. He performed all the religious duties proper to his station, and sought to act in an exemplary way in order to encourage his subjects to do likewise. But the time came when drought afflicted several parts of his kingdom. He sought the advice of the Brahmins, headed by his family priest. Their advice was that a solemn sacrifice should be made, according to Vedic precedence, which would ensure the onset of abundant rain. Nothing less than the sacrifice of many hundreds of human beings would suffice:

[The king's] innate compassionateness forbade him to approve of their advice in his heart; yet out of civility, unwilling to offend them by harsh words of refusal, he slipped over this point, turning the conversation upon other topics. They, on the other hand, no sooner caught the opportunity of conversing with the king on matters of religion, than they once more admonished him to accomplish the sacrifice, for they did not understand his deeply hidden mind.

The king began to reflect on the advice he had received, and to question its value. 'What connection', he asked himself, 'may there be between righteousness and injuring animals?' Another question followed. '[And if] the victim killed in sacrifice really go to heaven, should we not expect the Brahmans to offer themselves to be immolated in sacrifice? A similar practice, however, is nowhere seen among them. Who, then, may take to heart the advice proffered by these counsellors?' Having decided to ignore the advice given to him, the king resolved to practise a little deception, pretending to be in favour of the sacrifice, but instead being determined to bring about by other means that which the sacrifice alone was believed capable of achieving. He agreed to make a sacrifice of a thousand human beings, at the appropriate time and place. He announced his intention to his people, but added that 'nobody behaving honestly is fit to be designated for immolation on my part.' Thus forewarned, the populace took good care to see that the emissaries sent out by the king to monitor their conduct found nothing untoward. [The people] 'avoided every occasion of hatred and enmity, and settling their quarrels and differences, cherished mutual love and mutual esteem'. With their minds thus concentrated on the prospect of death, the king's subjects began to practise virtue for reasons of prudence. But as their circumstances improved in every respect they continued on the path of virtue more for its own sake.

'By the power, then, of the king's performing his sacrifice [*sic*] in this manner in accordance with [the precepts of] the Law, the sufferings of the indigent were put to an end together with the plagues and calamities, and the country abounded in a prosperous and thriving population offering the pleasing aspect of felicity.' After a time one of the highest royal officials said to the king, 'You have obtained the happiness of your subjects both in this world and in the next, as the effect of your sacrifice being performed in righteousness, free from the blameable sin of animal-slaughter. The hard times are all over and the sufferings of poverty have ceased, since men have been established in the precepts of good conduct. Why use many words? Your subjects are happy.' The story shows that what is good is unattainable by 'a vile act, accompanied as it is by injury done to living beings' and ends with an interpretation of the kind of sacrifice which alone is necessary. In the course of time Buddhism itself needed to be reinvigorated by continuing and radical reform.

'Injuring animals never tends to bliss, but charity, self-restraint, continence and the like have this power; for this reason he who longs for bliss must devote himself to these virtues.' (Müller 1895, 104)

(c) A Muslim view

One of the shortest sūrahs of the Qur'ān is the one entitled *al-Kawthar* ('The Abundance').

In the Name of Allah, the Beneficent, the Merciful.
1. Lo! We have given thee Abundance;
2. So pray unto thy Lord, and sacrifice,
3. Lo! it is thy insulter (and not thou) who is without posterity. (Sūrah 108; in Pickthall 1930, 673)

The last part of the sūrah is a reminder of the fact that those who were not Muslims used to taunt the prophet Muḥammad because he had no male heir, and that he would, therefore, have no one to uphold the religion of Islam after him. The rest of the sūrah is important for a study of Islamic attitudes to sacrifice. Two things are immediately apparent. The first is that it is God (Allāh) who provides that which is necessary for their good to those obedient to his will. And the provision is an abundant one. The second is the injunction to pray and to sacrifice, as a response of gratitude to the Provider. But what kind of sacrifice is required?

It has already been noted above that Ibrāhīm (Abraham) 'the first Muslim' continues to have an exemplary role in Islam. The sacrifice of his son was not required by God, once Ibrāhīm had proved the extent of his faithfulness. The survival in Islam of the practice of animal sacrifices, offered in thankful remembrance of God's abundant provision – particularly during the month of the Pilgrimage (ḥajj) to Mecca at the time of the 'īd al-aḍḥā (the Feast of Sacrifices), signifies the readinesss of those who sacrifice the animals to lay down their own lives, if necessary, in the service of God. The sacrifice is not an appeasement of an offended deity, nor has it an atoning symbolism or effect. The outward acts of ritual sacrifice are present, but the sacrifice is one which epitomizes the surrender of self:

It is by the mention of Allah's name that an animal is sacrificed... [The hearts of Muslims] should tremble at the mention of that name, and they should bear in mind, if they have sacrificed an animal over which they hold control, how much more necessary it is that they should lay down their lives in the way of Allah, Who is not only their Master but also their Creator and their Sustainer, and thus exercises a far greater authority over them than they do over animals. (Ali 1917, 670, n. 1692)

The flesh of the animals sacrificed is not to be wasted, but it should serve as food for the poor and the needy. Thus, while inwardly laying down one's life in the cause of truth, it is to be borne in mind that outwardly a Muslim should devote himself to the service of humanity... It is not the outward act of sacrifice which is acceptable, but the deep meaning of *sacrifice* which underlies it... It is the righteous whom Islam requires to sacrifice. (Ali 1917, 670–1, nn. 1694 and 1695)

One who strives on behalf of God (in Arabic literally 'in the way of God') is a *mujāhid*, and this is the root meaning of the related Arabic word *jihād*. Surrender to the will of God is required of the faithful Muslim, who is called upon to make daily acts of witnessing to the sovereignty of God in every aspect of life. Sometimes the *mujāhid* is required to sacrifice his own life as the noblest act of witness. Here again there is an exemplary figure in Islam.

One of the most important dates in *Shī'ī* Islam is the 10th of Muḥarram, known as *'Āshūrā*. Each year the tragic death and martyrdom of the third Imam, Abū 'Abd'ullāh Ḥusayn ibn 'Alī, is recalled by the faithful. Ḥusayn, known to Shī'īs as 'Prince of the Martyrs' (*Sayyid al-Shuhadā'*) for what happened on the plain of Karbala on the 2nd of Muḥarram AH 61 (2 October AD 680), had been encouraged by his supporters to proceed to Kūfa in Iraq to claim succession to the caliphate in place of Yazīd, the son of Mu'āwiya. Such a succession, had it taken place, would have reinstated what many Muslims believed to be the legitimate line of 'Alī, fourth of the 'Rightly-Guided Caliphs', cousin of the Prophet Muḥammad, and father of Ḥusayn. The course of the continuing, and sometimes bloody, struggle for leadership following the death of Muḥammad in AH 10 (AD 632), does not need to be detailed here (see Momen 1985, 11–33). The struggle intensified the animosities between Muslims which began with Muḥammad's death. It led to the emergence of the *Shī'ah*, or 'party' of 'Alī, and the lasting division in the Islamic community between Shī'īs and Sunnīs:

It would be difficult to exaggerate the impact and importance of the martyrdom of Ḥusayn for Shi'is. Although it was the usurpation of 'Ali's rights that is looked upon by Shi'is as the event initiating their movement and giving it intellectual justification, it was Ḥusayn's martyrdom that gave it its impetus and implanted its ideas deep in the heart of the people. To this day it is the martyrdom of Ḥusayn that is the most fervently celebrated event in the Shi'i calendar. During the first ten days of Muḥarram, the whole Shi'i world is plunged into mourning. Above all, the martyrdom of Ḥusayn has given to Shi'i Islam a whole ethos of sanctification through martyrdom. (Momen 1985, 32–3)

What is important for present purposes is to recall the situation at Karbala faced by Ḥusayn, the small group of friends who went with him (women and children as well as men) and the continuing significance for Shī'īs of the sacrifice which ensued. Disregarding his own safety, and the safety of his party traditionally numbering seventy-two men bearing arms, eighteen from the house of 'Alī and fifty-four supporters, not counting the women and children, Ḥusayn went on to Kūfa, even though he had been warned in advance of the dangers that were waiting for him there. Several thousand of Yazīd's soldiers surrounded him and his supporters, cutting them off from water supplies until Ḥusayn would pledge his allegiance to Yazīd. This was not given, and in the slaughter which followed many were killed, including Ḥusayn and his infant son.[7]

These are the barest details of an event which has assumed the greatest importance in the lives of Shī'ī Muslims. It is an event which exemplifies the personal sacrifice to be made by anyone who would strive on behalf of Allāh. The sacrifice of Ḥusayn and his followers remains exemplary, and its interpretation a matter on which observers remain divided. To those inside the believing community the event has a significance which escapes the uncommitted observer. Given that Ḥusayn was ill-prepared for battle, Shiʿīs take the view that his purpose in going to Kūfa against great odds was to show that military defeat cannot finally deflect the purposes of God, and that military success can guarantee no lasting victory. Lasting success and permanent influence are the fruits of suffering and sacrifice.

It is rather disappointing to note that Western scholarship on Islam, given too much to historicism, has placed all its attention on the discrete external aspects of the event of Karbala and has never tried to analyse the inner history and agonizing conflict in Ḥusayn's mind ... [Ḥusayn] realized that mere force of arms would not have saved Islamic *action* and consciousness. To him it needed a shaking and jolting of hearts and feelings. This, he decided, could only be achieved through sacrifice and sufferings. This should not be difficult to understand, especially for those who fully appreciate the heroic deeds and sacrifices of, for example, Socrates and Joan of Arc, both of whom embraced death for their ideals, and above all of the great sacrifice of Jesus Christ for the redemption of mankind ... Ḥusayn succeeded in his purpose ... [The] change of thinking which prevailed after the sacrifice of Ḥusayn always served as a line of distinction between Islamic norms and the personal character of the rulers. (Jafri and Husain 1979, 200–4)[8]

THE ESSENCE OF SELF-SACRIFICE

The essence of sacrifice has shifted from the external act to the inward disposition of the heart. The essence of sacrifice is personal, expressed in terms of Paul's exhortation to Christian believers, 'to present your bodies as a living sacrifice, holy and acceptable to God, which is your spiritual worship' (Rom. 12:1). This is an interiorization of the notion of sacrifice that develops in each of the religions considered here. In its turn this idea finds a still deeper expression in acts which require of the one who makes the sacrifice the voluntary surrender of life itself, in the service of what is held to be the higher authority. This is something to which the king, in the Buddhist story considered above, could only draw attention, when he asked, 'should we not expect the Brahmans to offer themselves to be immolated in sacrifice?' In Christian belief the story is taken further, beyond the point at which the god is sacrificed and then brought back to life. The mystery of the Incarnation adds a new dimension to an otherwise familiar story. On this occasion it is God himself who takes the initiative, in the pursuit of love (Phil. 2:1–11). For the believer who uses the word 'sacrifice' in a religious context, the demands are inclusive and total, including the *sacrificium intellectus* as the preliminary step for receiving in return (as part of what Muslims would describe as the measure of God's Abundance), an intellect liberated to serve.

NOTES

1 This basic meaning of 'sacrifice' is used of burnt-offerings, with its Indo-Germanic root, 'to swirl, esp. of dust, mist or smoke' (Behm 1979, 180).
2 On the inadequacy of human beings faced with the presence of God see, for example, Exod. 3:4–6 and 33:30.
3 On the 'Wholly Other' see Otto (1929). On the rejection of the idea that fear was the primary motive for religion in 'primitive' societies, see Durkheim 1915, pp. 223–9.
4 In Matt. 12:7 Jesus reminds his hearers of the words of Hosea 6:6: 'And if you had known what this means, "I desire mercy and not sacrifice", you would not have condemned the guiltless.'
5 For an unusual re-creation of the events of the passion and crucifixion of Jesus, based on the experiences of the principal characters involved, and as understood by a twentieth-century Muslim scholar, see Hussein 1959.
6 Qur'ān 3.67, as translated by M. M. Pickthall (1930, 74). Exemplary faithfulness, obedience and surrender to God earned for Abraham the title of 'the friend of God' among Muslims. On the binding of Isaac/Ismā'īl, see Robert Hayward (1980) and James Swetnam (1981).
7 Among the women and children taken prisoner was Ḥusayn's son 'Alī, who became the fourth Imām.
8 There is an echo here of what Christians understand by the Agony of Christ in the Garden of Gethsemane (see Matt. 26:36–46).

REFERENCES

Ali, Muhammed, Maulvi (trans.) (1917). *The Holy Qur-án*. Lahore: Ahmadiyya Anjuman-i-Isháat-i-Islam
Behm, J. (1979). Sacrifice. In *Theological Dictionary of the New Testament*, vol. III, ed. G. Kittel, pp. 180–90. Grand Rapids: Eerdmans
Bourdillon, M. F. C. and M. Fortes (eds.) (1980). *Sacrifice*, London: Academic Press
Durkheim, E. (1915). *The Elementary Forms of the Religious Life*. London: Allen & Unwin
Girard, R. (1977). *Violence and the Sacred*. Baltimore: Johns Hopkins University Press
Hayward, Robert (1980). The Aqedah. In Bourdillon and Fortes (1980), pp. 84–7
Hocking, W. E. (1912). *The Meaning of God in Human Experience*. New Haven: Yale University Press
Hubert, H. and M. Mauss (1964). *Sacrifice: Its Nature and Function*. Chicago: Chicago University Press
Hussein, M. K. (1959). *City of Wrong: A Friday in Jerusalem*, trans. K. Cragg. Amsterdam: Djambatan
Jafri, S. and M. Husain (1979). *Origins and Early Development of Shī'ah Islam*. London: Longmans
Momen, M. (1985). *An Introduction to Shi'a Islam. The History and Doctrines of Twelver Shi'ism*. New Haven: Yale University Press
Müller, M. (trans.) (1869). *Rig-Veda-Sanhita. The Sacred Hymns of the Brahmans*, vol. I. London

(ed.) (1895). *Sacred Books of the Buddhists*, vol. 1. London: Henry Frowde

Otto, R. (1929). *The Idea of the Holy*. Oxford: Oxford University Press

Pickthall, M. M. (1930). *The Meaning of the Glorious Koran*. London: Allen & Unwin

Radhakrishnan, S. (ed.) (1952). *History of Philosophy Eastern and Western*, 2 vols. London: Allen & Unwin

(1953). *The Principal Upanishads*. New York: Harper & Row

Rhys Davids, T. W. (trans.) (1977). *Buddhist Birth Stories, or Jataka Tales*. New York: Arno Press

Schimmel, A. (1960). Opfer (Religionsgeschichtlich). In *Die Religion in Geschichte und Gegenwart*, 3rd edn, vol. IV, pp. 1637–41. Tübingen: Mohr

Swetnam, J. (1981). *Jesus and Isaac*. Rome: Biblical Institute Press

Sykes, S. W. (1980). Sacrifice in the New Testament and in Christian Theology. In Bourdillon and Fortes (1980), pp. 61–83

Thomas, E. J. (trans.) (1923). *Vedic Hymns from the Rigveda*. London: Murray

Varma, Vishwaneth Prasad (1973). *Early Buddhism and Its Origins*. New Delhi: Munshiram Manoharlal

Vidhushekhara, Bhattacharya (1952). Historical Introduction to the Indian Schools of Buddhism. In Radhakrishnan (1952), vol. 1

Weber, M. (1963). *The Sociology of Religion* (4th edn). Boston: Beacon Press

16

OUTLINE OF A THEOLOGY OF SACRIFICE

S. W. SYKES

The only adequate reason for recognizing in sacrifice the central notion, or one of the central notions, of a systematic Christian theology lies in the centrality of worship for the Christian tradition. A theology of sacrifice will be, therefore, a theology in which worship plays a central role. It will be forced to raise, in an acute form, the question of what theological activity actually is, and how it is related to the total activity of the Christian Church.

None of the matters which are referred to above can be treated as self-evident. Above all, there is no established locating of worship in relation to theology or ethics. The tag, *lex orandi, lex credendi*, is capable of numerous different interpretations (Wainwright 1980, 218ff.); attempts to para-phrase it are occasionally false because of an over-generous evaluation of the precision of liturgical tradition ('one ought to believe, as one prays'), or vacuous through a willingness to balance worship and intellectual formulation ('how one ought to pray, is how one ought to believe'). Accordingly this essay will have to proceed methodically through several stages.

THE CENTRALITY OF WORSHIP

In his analysis of the dimensions of religions, Ninian Smart (1971) lists six, which together constitute a single organism. The aspects, or dimensions, are rituals, myths, doctrines, ethical teachings and social institutions, all animated by the sixth dimension, religious experiences. By rituals Smart means religious services of various degrees of elaborateness, and also techniques of self-training (such as yoga). He asserts that rituals have both an inner and an outer aspect, and may degenerate into 'mere rituals'. He also argues that rituals cannot be understood apart from the environment of belief in which they occur, and are thus closely related to both myths and doctrines (see further Sykes 1984, 28f.).

Smart's analysis is, in effect, an elaboration of a threefold scheme offered by John Henry Newman in the preface to the third edition of *The Via Media* (1877). Here, the Christian Church is described as existing in a threefold form, corresponding to the threefold offices of Christ. As Christ was at once prophet, priest and king, so the Church 'after this pattern, and in human measure' has a threefold office, of teaching, of rule and of ministry. Christianity is at once a philosophy, a political power and a religious rite (Newman 1877, xi). The 'philosophical' dimension of Christianity is rendered by Smart as myths, doctrines and ethical teachings, the 'political' as social institution and the 'religious' as ritual. It may be added that the experiential dimension of Christianity is fully represented in all that Newman has to say about the illative sense.

While there is little doubt that Christianity lends itself to multidimensional analysis, there is an obvious problem in the mutual relation of these dimensions. Newman himself gives primacy to the theological dimension; 'theology is the fundamental and regulating principle of the whole Church system'. Why? Newman argues that because revelation is the 'initial and essential idea' of Christianity, and because theology is commensurate with revelation, it must be given primacy. Theology commensurate with revelation, indeed, is what alone constitutes the subject matter of the prophetical office (the philosophical dimension), and has brought the regal (i.e. political) and sacerdotal (i.e. ritual) into being. It has, therefore, 'in a certain sense' a power of jurisdiction over them, and may of course protect them from excess (Newman 1877, xlvii).

One can readily appreciate the rationality of this position. Rituals are not necessarily self-interpreting or self-explanatory. To explain them one needs a discursive discipline, capable of refining in words meanings which may otherwise be obscure or fallacious. Is there a correct or incorrect, helpful or misleading, ritual veneration of the eucharistic elements? Not *every* form of veneration is necessarily congruent with the Christian doctrine of the real presence. Only if ritual is 'policed', so to speak, by theology can it be protected from error. Newman has in mind, in particular, the errors of extravagance and superstition.

The fact, however, that theology may have a critical role to play in relation to the ritual or social embodiment of Christianity does not entitle one to speak of the primacy of theology. What is at fault here is Newman's assumption that revelation and theology are simply congruent with each other. Since Newman's day theologians have been forced to recognize the sheer variety of theological perspectives at the very fountain-head of Christian revelation. Take, for example, the central matter of resurrection belief. From a close study of the separate accounts of the resurrection it emerges that 'the resurrection' functions in a different way in each account, making problematic any simple notion of 'the revelatory datum' constituted by 'the resurrection' (Evans 1970, 128ff.). Under such circumstances discursive accounts of revelation inevitably lose any simple status of primacy. The theologies of the New Testament writers become documentary evidence for, on the one hand, an obscure or conjectured original experience, and, on the other, continuing experiences of 'resurrection faith' of various kinds.

How, then, are the relations between the various dimensions to be understood? Progress in the direction of an answer to this seems to lie in a hint given by Smart that the dimension of experience is not merely one dimension among others, but animates all the other five dimensions. Religious experience, of course, unlike the other dimensions, is not itself externally inspectible. We do not have 'experience' as a datum, in the sense in which we have texts giving ethical teaching, or the social structures of a given denomination. What we have, rather, is oral or written reports of religious experience, which are already shaped in some way by the myths or doctrines of a given form of religion. Nonetheless religious experience is an animating principle to the whole, and might be regarded as standing in some sense at the heart of the organism of a religion, provided that interplay involving the promoting and structuring of such experience by external factors (especially by socially transmitted rituals or techniques) was also allowed for.

A second hint of importance is given by Smart when he notes (1971, 17) that rituals, related to myths, precede theological reflection. It is widely agreed by anthropologists that most people act out their rituals first and philosophize about them afterwards (Leach 1968, 524; Beattie 1980, 33). In this sense theology is a derivative and dependent discipline, though it would be mistaken to conclude that it does not have a critical or corrective function. Nonetheless it depends upon the existence of a social organization, animated by corporate and individual experiences, which are at once promoted and interpreted in rituals and myths. The situation might be represented diagrammatically as in Figure 1, while Figure 2 shows a cross-section of the same diagram.

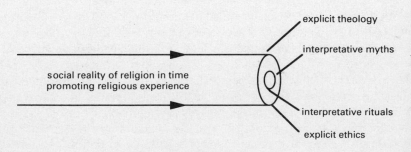

Figure 1

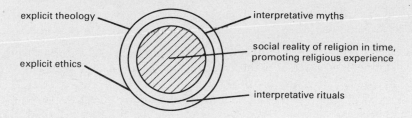

Figure 2

It is some such picture of interrelationships which makes sense of the origins of Christianity. Christianity originates in a 'transformation of Judaism' (Riches 1980). That is to say, it presupposes the existence and activities of the complex social organization known as Judaism. This social organization is not abolished by a revelatory legislative fiat; it is transformed from the inside by new conduct and example, supported by shifts of emphasis in fundamental mythology. It takes full advantage of the wide diversity and, to an extent, vacuity of religious ritual, to promote new freedoms. These freedoms both reflect and are supported by claimed new experiences. The total outcome of the transformation ia not entirely clear or certain; the new ways of being, acting and thinking do not emerge in a single coordinated package. The documentary evidence reveals what one would expect, namely a movement in process of taking shape at different paces and in a variety of ways.

In his study of this process of transformation, John Riches argues that Jesus substantially modified the conventional associations of the notion of kingship, and then totally rejected the prevailing teaching about purity. The significance of purity for the cult is too apparent to require comment. Holiness is the very heart, goal and purpose of sacrificial worship (see Jones, above, chapter 1). In rejecting, therefore, the concept of purity in its entirety, Jesus necessarily renders the continued performance of sacrificial ritual unnecessary. He does this, moreover, without any explicit attack on sacrifice itself. But the reason for the rejection of the purity teaching lies in his sense of God as loving and forgiving. Jesus' depiction of the quality of God's activity, both in his own teaching and still more in his behaviour, constitutes a new account of God's disposition and behaviour towards and ultimate treatment of humanity. In a word, Jesus tells and embodies a new story of God.

Riches states:

The fundamental springs of Jesus' understanding of God lie in his vision of a God who enters the world as a merciful, loving, forgiving reality, who is in the world healing and overcoming darkness and evil, who – simply – loves his enemies.' (Riches 1980, 166)

In other words, the story attaching to the entire religious vision is being transformed; Jesus achieves this transformation, not merely by teaching, but by embodying a new social reality.

It is this picture which enables us to argue for the centrality of worship. Worship is the interior acknowledgement of God. It is the reality of the divine–human relationship. This understanding of worship must be distinguished from that which sees in worship the outcome or effect of the acceptance of some religious proposition. In such a view worship necessarily becomes a secondary phenomenon, consequent upon a particular intellectual conviction. The view of worship which is, by contrast, adopted here regards worship as the divine–human relationship itself (Hardy and Ford, 1984). The terms of this relationship are reconstructed by Jesus in a transformation of Judaism. Viewed from the outside, what changes is the story (or myth) told of God. But that change is, in fact, a reflection of a changed interior reality.

Two pieces of evidence must be cited in support of this position. The first is Jesus' teaching about prayer. In the Lord's Prayer, which is regarded as the distinctive possession of the Christian disciple, the new vision of God offered by Jesus is expressed in three elements: in the intimate address to the Father, in the prayer for the coming of the kingdom and in the petition for forgiveness. God's will and nature are thus reinterpreted at the precise point where the interior reality of the divine–human relationship is expressed. The text of the common prayer of the transformed community contains the fundamentals of the new vision of God. The second piece of evidence, which is still more striking, is the fact of Jesus' fellowship meals with his followers and with various supposedly impure persons. This new social practice likewise embodies the changed vision of God in a way peculiarly offensive to the Pharisees, and difficult enough to assimilate in the new community (as the episode involving Peter illustrates). Our earliest account of the supper is to be found in 1 Cor. 2 in the context of an argument against those who were putting the poorer members of the community to shame. To 'discern the body' seems to mean to perceive the new unity of all humanity, already realized in Jesus Christ (Bartchy, 1979). Jesus Christ has restructured social relationships, not by new ethical teaching on its own, but by reconstructing the divine–human relationship itself. To worship in the body of Christ is the prior reality, from which the social implications must be allowed to follow, unless one wishes to incur judgement.

The centrality of worship in Christianity is, I have argued, based on the consideration that we have, in Jesus Christ, a new vision of the divine–human relationship. This new vision is, to be sure, *taught* by Jesus.

But the teaching is itself the verbal expression of a new interior reality, the new relationship of God and humanity. Moreover that relationship is seen, not as though laid on human beings as a taught obligation, but as embodied in who Jesus was, God's own initiative in drawing human beings to himself and to each other in a new fellowship. Thus worship is, for Christians, acknowledgement of that fellowship. It is externalized in the myths or stories told of God, a God whose story *is* our story. It is also externalized in the rituals, especially of baptism and the eucharist, which with the stories enact the terms of entry to and of continuance in the new fellowship. And it is analysed and explored, and accounts of it are criticized, in the discursive activity known as theology, which seeks to ensure that every aspect of Christian living does proper justice to the prior reality of the divine initiative by which the new social reality of the Church is brought into being. Worship then is central, because it is the acknowledgement of the divine initiative (Sykes 1984, 264–86).

WORSHIP AND SACRIFICE

The New Testament evidence, it will be universally admitted, does not immediately suggest that the idea of sacrifice is the prime category for the interpretation of the death of Christ. Apart from in the Epistle to the Hebrews, the word 'sacrifice' and its cognate terms is neither numerically prominent, nor apparently conceptually crucial. It is, as many have argued, but *one* of the ways of attempting to clarify the new reality signified in Christ's death and resurrection. Its helpfulness or unhelpfulness may legitimately vary from time to time, and context to context.

Now this position is certainly intelligible. But it will be argued here that the place accorded to worship turns the flank of the argument. If, as has been shown in the previous section, worship is the new reality of Christian fellowship with God in Jesus Christ, then an argument which shows that the symbol of sacrifice is inherent in that of worship has gone a long way to justifying the claim for the centrality of sacrifice in the interpretation of the event of Christ. The next stage of this chapter must necessarily, therefore, concern itself with the relationship between sacrifice and worship.

But first it must be established that the mere numerical incidence of words of a particular stem is no guide to the centrality or otherwise of the thought conveyed. No one who argued for the centrality of the notion of justification, for example, could hold such a view. Whether or not a concept is central depends rather on its capacity to illuminate Christian thought in depth. In this sense there is value in demonstrating that there are other symbolical structures by which the atonement is illuminated. That is not in dispute. The case for the centrality of sacrifice, or of any other theological symbol, must rest on the cogency or otherwise of a theological argument. In this case what the tradition of the Christian centuries has made of the evidence from the Old and New Testaments is as important as the numerical incidence of the term. Crucial here, of course, is the denomination of the eucharist as a sacrifice (Daly 1978a, 1978b; Hanson 1979; Williams 1982; Buchanan *et al.* 1984). Confronted daily by a form of worship spoken of as 'the Christian sacrifice' from the days of Justin Martyr (mid-second century), Christians have, rightly or wrongly, combined the thought of the centrality of the eucharist with the thought of the centrality of sacrifice in their thinking of the terms of the divine–human relationship. If the eucharist is central to the worship of the Church, if it is *the* sacrament of the fellowship between God and humanity, then there may exist something like a presumption in favour of the thought that sacrifice provides us with the most profound terms for speaking of how God and humanity are related.

That, however, is to advance too far, too fast. We must first enquire about the relationship between sacrifice and worship. One temptation must be resisted, which is to take advantage of the extraordinary complicated state of Jewish sacrificial thought and practice at the time of Jesus by imposing a definition of sacrifice upon the material, which definition neatly delivers the interlocking character of sacrifice and worship. Nothing, however, is achieved by such a tautological procedure. The argument has to be more lengthy and painstaking.

The basis of it is the observation that all worship requires a focus; prayer, precisely, is attention to the focus (Smart 1972, 26–7). In the Christian case the focus is, of course, God – God, that is, as 'storied forth in Jesus and the Holy Spirit. To attend to God, to worship him in truth, is to have that unique vision of him as the initiator of the new relationship of fellowship in Jesus Christ, through the Holy Spirit. He descends, he lives, he dies, he rises again, he ascends, he sends the Holy Spirit. All these must be 'in mind' as the worshipper focusses his or her attention. But it is a particular kind of attention which is required, and there must be a match between the 'storying forth' of God, and the quality of the believer's attention (Sykes 1983).

The quality of this attention is, in the last resort, signified by the gulf to be overcome in the distinction between secular and sacred. Human beings are not related to God as to other human beings. The qualification to stand before God is membership of God's holy people. Throughout the Psalms this membership is referred to in a number of terms, the righteous (*tsaddiq*), the saint (*chasid*), the oppressed (*uni*), and the humble (*anaw*). What is intended by these terms is the community standing within and maintaining the covenant, and living the qualities described. The covenant is the source of Israel's identity, bestowing both privileges and obligations. The qualification to stand before God is, therefore, bestowed by God in and with the covenant, and continuously realized by the worshipper. The point is made concretely in Psalm 81, of which the first five verses consist of an affirmation that cultic jubilation was prescribed by God as a remembrance of the delivery from Egypt, and the last six verses of a call to Israel to repent and return to the duties of the covenant.

The notion or concept of a covenant between God and Israel is, of course, a formalization of the terms of the relationship between God and a particular people. The covenant is made with 'the faithful' specifically by sacrifice (Ps. 50: 5); and not merely with external sacrifices, but with sacrifices expressive of the inward thankfulness of the heart, 'sacrifices of thanksgiving' (Ps. 50: 14). There are, in other words, two theatres in which the terms of the relationship between God and his people are continuously ratified, the external world of cult and the inner theatre of the heart. Furthermore it is intrinsic to the qualification of appearing before God that both of these be in agreement; hence the requirement of integrity or consistency in inner and outer holiness or purity.

At the time of Jesus it appears that the rationale for sacrificial rituals had ceased to play much part in religious profession, and that sacrifices were performed for no greater reason than that they had been commanded. The evidence is far from easy to interpret. But it may not be far from the truth to say that for the first-century Jew of Palestine the concept of worship and the occurrence of sacrifice were simply interlocked, as internal and external expressions of the one reality. It is for this reason that Jesus' break with the Pharisees' traditions about purity is of such importance. The point is that such a break entails a new understanding of the relation between God and humanity, of which the formalization is the notion of a new covenant. Thus for Paul to speak of the tradition of the cup as 'a new covenant in my blood' (1 Cor. 11: 25) attributes to the intention of Jesus the giving of his own life as the cost of the establishment of this new relationship. The new qualification for appearing before God is thus Jesus' giving of his own life. This introduces a decisive transformation of the tradition. The external theatre in which the qualification to appear before God is established is that of a particular event in human history; one man died once for all. The internal theatre of the heart is redirected by its attitude towards that event. Fellowship with God means participation in the body and blood of Christ, given for us.

But why should this event be given the term 'sacrifice'? Can it not equally be spoken of as 'ransom', or 'judgement', or even as 'saving obedience'? So interlinked in conventional Christian theology are these terms, that the significance of the question may elude us. But the point is simply enough made. Granted that the death of Christ is constitutive of the new relationship, that it is death 'for us', there are, it appears, a number of alternative ways in which this 'soteriological fact' can be expressed

(Jeremias 1963). It can be expressed cultically in terms of sacrifice, or juridically in terms of a judgement against sin, or by the commercial language of ransom from slavery, or by the moral category of freely willed obedience to the good.

The reply to this question is, as a matter of fact, no less simple. It is granted that there *are* other ways of giving the death of Christ metaphorical expression. But the metaphors drawn from the cult have priority, because it is these alone which make worship the central constitutive reality of the divine–human relationship. The juridical, the commercial and the moral-obedience metaphors are also enlightening, but they are enlightening precisely to the world of worship. They provide us, in other words, with further ways by which to elucidate the fundamental and central symbol of sacrifice.

Before turning to the significance for our argument of the category of story, it is well to pause and consider the formidable support for the central contention of this section from St Augustine of Hippo (see further Bonner, above, chapter 6). In the attention which Augustine pays to the question of sacrifice in Book x of *The City of God*, his main point is precisely this: that true sacrifice is a worship of God which unites us to him. In his celebrated statement,

The true sacrifice is offered in every act which is designed to unite us to God in a holy fellowship, every act, that is, which is directed to that final Good which makes possible our true felicity. (x, 6, 1; Augustine 1972, 379)

The mere quotation of this identifying description inadequately represents its force in the context of the argument. For Augustine has already in Book IX expounded his theory of false and true mediation, maintaining that in contrast to demonic mediation, Christ alone, being both God and human being, is able to bring humanity 'from mortal misery to blessed immortality' (IX, 15, 4):

He is the Mediator in that he is man, by this very manhood making it plain that for the attainment of that good, which is not only blessed but beatific also, we have not to look for other mediators, through whom, as we may think, we can achieve the approach to happiness. God himself, the blessed God who is the giver of blessedness, became partaker of our human nature and thus offered us a short cut [*compendium praebuit*] to participation in his own divine nature. (IX, 15, 52; Augustine 1972, 361)

It is this already defined final good, namely participation in the divine nature, which constitutes the purpose of true sacrifice. The realization, therefore, of this end is *only* achieved by the sacrifice of the mediator.

In the exposition of sacrifice found in Book x the strongest emphasis must be laid upon the words 'verum sacrificium'. It has been pointed out that Augustine has three points in mind: first, that true sacrifice is that which is owed to the one true God; second, that true sacrifice is the real interior sacrifice, most adequately summed up as love for God and for neighbour; and finally, that it refers supremely to the sacrifice of the cross (Frankovich 1976, 78–84). For Christians there is no access to the Father except by means of the sacrifice of the cross. It is, of course, true that Augustine is concerned to show, exegetically, the connection between Old Testament sacrifices and the new covenant. But for him the *concept* of sacrifice (hence 'verum sacrificium') is determined or defined by the mediatorial activity of Christ as human being, offering in his flesh the one sacrifice for sin (*On the Trinity* IV, 13, 17). The destruction of the body in death destroys the symbolic barrier between humanity and God:

To take then away the separating wall, which is sin that Mediator has come, and the priest has himself become the sacrifice ... He was made a sacrifice for sin, offering himself as a whole burnt-offering on the cross of his passion. (*Tractate on the Gospel of John*, 41, 5; Augustine 1874, 35)

It is for this reason that the sacrifice of Christ is the basis or fundament of the Church, which is his body. This conclusion is reached at the end of a long discussion in Book x of *The City of God*, the context of which has again to be carefully noted. The argument of the whole of Book x is concerned with the nature of the true worship of God. Even Platonists have become corrupt, Augustine argues, to the extent that they think that ceremonies and sacrifices ought to be rendered to demons. There is in fact but one object of worship and we owe this one God our service (or *latreia*), in various 'sacraments' or in ourselves. We are his temple, collectively and as individuals; he dwells both in the union of all and in each individually. When we lift up our hearts to him our heart is his altar. We propitiate him by our one high priest, his own Son. He is the source of our bliss and the goal of all our striving. Hence the command to love God with all our strength: all our powers are to be bent to the worship of God.

Augustine thus refuses to separate worship and the notion of a true sacrifice. But he very carefully denies that sacrificial offerings, despite their antiquity, are necessary to God. Here he joins hands with a long-standing Christian polemic against propitiatory sacrifices. Quoting Psalm 16, he maintains that God has no need of cattle and other material offerings. The fundamental intention of ancient sacrifice is not the propitiation of God, but cleaving to God and the good of the neighbour. 'Thus the visible sacrifice is the sacrament, the sacred sign, of the invisible sacrifice' (x, 5, 15; Augustine 1972, 377). Here Augustine's understanding of sacrifice links up with his general theory of signs expounded in *On Christian Doctrine*.

Thus what God desires is the *invisible* sacrifice, the offering of a broken heart, which cleaves to its maker. The Christian, however, is able to rely for such an act not on his or her own strength but on the self-oblation of Christ.

In a number of texts in other places, Augustine makes clear that there is only one true sacrifice, that of the cross:

Before the coming of Christ, the flesh and blood of this sacrifice were foreshadowed in the animals slain; in the passion of Christ the types were fulfilled by the true sacrifice; after the ascension of Christ, this sacrifice is commemorated in the sacrament. (*Reply to Faustus*, 20, 21; Augustine 1887, 262)

The reference to the sacrament of the eucharist makes clear the contemporaneity of the means whereby the Christian's interior sacrifices are offered to God. Visible sacrifices do not become redundant, since 'they are the symbols of the invisible offerings, just as spoken words are the symbols of things' (x, 19, 4; Augustine 1972, 399). By means of words we offer *ourselves*, through the true Mediator, both High Priest and Victim:

This is the reality, and he intended the daily sacrifice of the church to be the sacramental symbol of this; for the Church, being the body of which he is the head, learns to offer itself through him. (x, 20, 7; Augustine 1972, 401).

The Augustinian character of the argument of this section of this chapter, linking worship and sacrifice, is thus plain. We should also note that the emphasis which Augustine places upon the mediatorial character of the death of Christ closely coheres with the logic of sacrifice, as perceived by the contemporary anthropologist, Edmund Leach (Leach 1976, 81–93). According to this, in the sets of signs by which we order our world there exists a dangerous and ambiguous boundary area or marginal state in which there is established a channel of communication between temporal existence and the beyond. A sacrifice is not properly a bribe or exchange but a gift, enabling a transfer to take place. Alternatively the victim can be seen as playing the part of the initiate, moving into the new status across the boundary. Leach's emphasis on communication and gift is the crucial factor, which establishes the applicability of what he calls the 'logic' of sacrifice to Augustine's thought. 'Communication', in Augustine, is 'holy fellowship, the cleaving of the soul to God'; similarly 'gift' is, in Augustine, the grace of God in the provision of a mediatorial way. It should not surprise us that Augustine's thought corresponds so closely with the scheme laid out by Leach. Christian culture has been deeply influenced by the Augustinian development of a theology of sacrifice, and Leach's treatment of this theme should provoke the question: what would a Christian culture be which refused or marginalized not just the language of sacrifice, but the understanding of grace and of fellowship which underlay it?

SACRIFICE AND STORY

There are three ways in which the institution of sacrifice receives metaphorical extension in the traditions of the Old Testament. The first, to which reference has already been made above, is the sacrifice of thanksgiving. 'He honours me who brings sacrifice of thanksgiving', says the psalmist, not in opposition but in addition to the cultic celebration of a festival (Ps. 50:24, compare Ps. 27:6, 69:30, 107:22, 116:17). The second extension is the sacrifice of contrition: 'the sacrifice of God is a broken spirit: a broken and contrite heart, O God, you will not despise' (Ps. 51:17). Here the possibility of an actual replacement of sacrifice as a means of cleansing from wickedness seems to be envisaged. The third extension is comparable, namely the sacrifice of obedience: 'sacrifice and offering you do not desire: but my ears you have marked for obedience' (Ps. 40:8). This last example expresses that conformity to the covenant which is the behavioural hallmark of the righteous person. It may be that in relation to these three uses of the concept it is right to speak of the 'spiritualisation' of sacrifice (Hermisson 1965 and Daly 1978a, 8). At least what is involved is the extension of the term 'sacrifice' to cover dispositions and actions other than the ritual presentation of an offering.

Why is the term extendable? The basic reason lies in the nature of a symbol, and of symbolic actions. Symbolism is never precisely determinable. Its power lies in the breadth of its resonances, not in the clarity of its definition. A symbol establishes itself in a system of communication and may in time respond to changes taking place in other parts of the system. In the case of sacrifice, which is a symbolic means of communication with the divine, there are considerable possibilities for interpretative development. In these instances the ritual activity of sacrifice, having to do with ceremonies of thanksgiving or of contrition and implying the enacting of a covenant, promotes under certain specific circumstances the interpretative activity of including in the concept of sacrifice the disposition of thanksgiving or contrition, or the activity of obedience.

'Metaphorical extension' is thus the process whereby thanksgiving to God or an outpouring of contrition comes to be spoken of as a sacrifice. This need by no means entail the displacement of ritual sacrifices; but plainly in a situation in which for other reasons sacrifices had come to be less highly regarded, the metaphors could come to bear the weight of the original thought, the thought that God may be approached through *this* particular means. Sacrificial ritual as a specific instance of religious symbolism lends itself to this kind of development (Fernandez 1974).

The idea of development helps to explain the combination of similarities and differences between the Old and New Testaments precisely in relation to sacrifice. For what occurs in the New Testament is both an inheritance of earlier traditions together with a further development amounting in effect to a thoroughgoing transformation. The death of Christ itself is now seen as a sacrifice; and not merely *a* sacrifice, but *the* sacrifice, the new event establishing covenantal relationship between God and humanity itself (Barth 1961).

The startling thing about speaking of Jesus as a sacrificial victim is, of course, that it apparently de-personalizes the death which he died. As a slaughtered victim, it might seem as though his own involvement in the event is purely passive. But the world of the symbol has its own logic. It is precisely the category of sacrifice which throws into greater relief the exact course of Jesus' way to death. The author of 1 Peter has accurately caught the significance of the patience of Jesus under unjust punishment, and explicitly invokes Deutero-Isaiah's image of the 'lamb led to the slaughter' (Isa. 53:7) in order to interpret Jesus' guilelessness and innocence.

The statement that Jesus is *the* sacrificial victim, therefore, actually serves to emphasize the story by which he came to suffer that death. In particular, it is both stated and implied in the story that he perceived the likely outcome of his teaching and activities and accepted the 'cup' of his own future suffering. By means of this feature of the story the concept of offering implicit in sacrifice is rendered as *self*-offering. Jesus is not a victim only, he is the offerant. And yet such is the quality of the story that there is no suggestion that the death of Jesus could be seen as suicide. It is integral to the narrative that Jesus should be betrayed, not give himself up; and that those who put him to death do so unjustly, incurring guilt. Moreover the events of the garden of Gethsemane illustrate the wholly credible struggle involved in turning the *passio* of betrayal into an act of consent. The precise way in which Jesus' death may be spoken of as *the* sacrifice includes, therefore, the particular narrative of his way to death which is given us in the four gospels; and these narratives themselves constitute a further interpretation of the notion of sacrifice, transforming it for its new role in the Christian tradition.

But there is more to the transformation of sacrifice than the question of Jesus' own self-offering. For is not Jesus himself sent? What then of the motive of the One who sent him? The story constituted by the narration of the events of Jesus' life is set itself in a larger context provided by the claim of Jesus' sonship. May we not ask why this Son had to suffer and to die? Is there not another narrative interpreting the whole action of the sending of the Son as an act of steadfast love, having to do with the disaster of human rebellion against God? Analysis of the New Testament passages relating to sacrifice shows that there are two principal narrative sequences in which the principal agents are, respectively, God and Jesus (Sykes 1980). These are not independent of each other, but neither, on the other hand, are they assimilable into each other; nor, in fact, does any New Testament passage render the two narratives as one single epic (as Milton was to do). The one story has to do with God's appointment of Jesus as his 'means of dealing with sin'. The other story has to do with Jesus' own voluntary self-offering. Told as a single trinitarian drama, this becomes all too easily a monstrous saga in which the Father plans the immolation of his own Son in appeasement of his wrathful rejection of the human race. But it is highly significant that at no stage is this inference explicitly drawn in the New Testament, where the two narrative sequences tend to occur in somewhat different contexts. Nonetheless the potential of both narratives is present in the paradoxical ascription to Jesus of the roles of sacrificial victim and of High Priest, which is clearest in the Epistle to the Hebrews. If a *single* narrative were to lie behind this apparent paradox, then it would amount to a story of high-priestly suicide. The symbolic imagination is such, however, that it is capable of grasping both sides of the symbolism, and of both the narratives which underlie them, at the same time, without drawing the inference of suicide.

SACRIFICE AND CHARACTER

The final stage of the argument involves a brief indication of one further potential in the notion of sacrifice, arising directly out of the interpretation of Jesus' sacrificial death as a self-offering. This sacrifice is seen as the consistent expression in time and place of both words and intentions. There is demonstrated in his life-history, in other words, a consistent desire for the good both underlying and expressed in observable conduct.

The failure to achieve such consistency is identified as hypocrisy in Jesus' religious contemporaries, and its unrelenting exposure and harsh criticism demonstrates the seriousness with which Jesus views it. Hypocrisy is lying to God; it is futile, because God sees into human motives, but it may deceive or mislead others and, worse still, it may deceive oneself. Unconscious hypocrisy internally corrodes the will.

It is here that two features of the Old Testament development of sacrificial teaching are of such importance, the insistence on genuine contrition and on the genuine and obedient fulfilment of the terms of the covenant. The criticism of 'ritualism', that is, trust in the mere performance of the obligatory sacrificial cult, achieves the association of the category of worship with that of a genuine interior and exterior conformity to the divine will. If the sacrifice of Christ is consistent with his intentions, words and deeds, then the relationship between God and humanity established by that sacrifice entails an equally consistent interior and exterior conformity to the divine will. Human beings are to offer themselves as living sacrifices, both in body and soul (Rom. 12: 1–2).

It is crucial that the notion of sacrifice employed here should be closely related to the sacrifice of Christ, and to the terms of the divine–human relationship. Carelessly used, 'sacrificial' language about human behaviour could be a way of legitimating masochism, or ostentatious heroics, or grossly manipulative forms of blackmail (see Gilley and Loades, above, chapters 12 and 14). But for Christians the sacrifice of Christ is a theological symbol, set in a specific context provided by the doctrines of creation and last things. Its centrality by no means renders otiose the placing of it provided by its occurrence in the total organism of Christian doctrine. The failure of sacrifice to provide the hoped-for key to problems in, for example, social ethics lies in the failure of particular theologians properly to locate the doctrine in its relevant context (see Suggate, above, chapter 13).

That the human situation requires nothing less than the self-oblation of the Son of God provides an emphatic negation of romantic or optimistic theories of human self-offering. That his offering was offered voluntarily, in the human form, is likewise the death-blow to masochistic or pessimistic theories of human self-offering. The criterion of the divine self-offering, as expounded in the narrative and teaching of the Son of God, commits one who believes in it to a searching exploration of his or her own motives and deeds.

The New Testament contains two remarkable examples of the power of this criterion, applied in the one case to self-understanding and in the other to social activity. The first is in Romans, where St Paul has expounded the new divine principle of salvation apart from the law, the God-provided expiatory death of Christ, a gracious gift received by faith (Rom. 3:21–5). This death, St Paul believes, entails our death to law (Rom. 7:4); and his resurrection is our resurrection to new life. But St Paul perceives that the kind of victory which rising with Christ involves is no easy matter, since it involves a horrendous struggle between a principle of flesh, and the 'inmost self' (Rom. 7:22). It is, I would argue, the quality of the narratives of Christ's expiatory death which lead to this insight into the wretchedness of the divided human condition, a remarkable example of self-understanding and insight into the complexity of human motivation.

In the second place, we may point as evidence for the searching quality of the criterion of the sacrifice of Christ to the argument St Paul conducts with his Corinthian congregation about their social divisions. It is an argument whose presupposition is the importance of table-fellowship for Jews. The crucial conclusion is that 'any one who eats and drinks without discerning the body eats and drinks judgement upon himself' (1 Cor. 11:29). This body, the Corinthians evidently assumed, was that of the sacrificial lamb (1 Cor. 5:7). The celebration of the Christian festival was, further, with 'the unleavened bread of sincerity and truth'; malice and evil is, or ought to be, wholly foreign to the community. But it was not, and St Paul devastatingly observes that their meetings to eat the Lord's Supper disqualify themselves as the Lord's Supper because of the divisions which occur at them. The new covenantal relationship in the blood of Christ entails a proclamation in word *and deed* of the sacrificial death of Christ. Such a proclamation does not take place if the Church is socially divided. The nature of the body is not perceived; the Lord's Supper does not truly take place.

In this instance, the story of Jesus' own interpretation (so St Paul believes) of his death is determinative of the social practice of the congregation. Participation in the fellowship meal, which is participation in Christ's self-offered body and blood, requires a particular quality of human self-offering. Social relations are included in that self-offering. The natural divisions of class, or of status, are put to death as part of the old order, as a new reconciled humanity is proclaimed in and with the proclamation of the death of Christ.

Character is the arena in which inherited social conventions and selfish individual motivation struggle with the will for the good. To actualize the character of Christ in history is the supreme vocation of the Christian Church. But the concepts of sacrifice, of story and of character require each other. The sacrifice of Christ is told by means of the narratives of God's response to human rebellion, and of Jesus' self-oblation; the stories constitute event and character in interaction, and provide the criterion for the human realization of the divine purpose in history. And all three concepts – sacrifice, story and character – are located in worship. Sacrifice defines the terms of the divine–human relationship, which is worship; the recollection of the stories of God's dealings with humanity is the source of both the praise and contrition of worship; and character is formed in the matrix which worship constitutes, where the natural human centres of self and society are challenged by the displacement provided by the divine focus. A theology of sacrifice would be a theology of worship, of story and of character. It would neither overestimate nor underestimate the power of evil. It would neither overvalue nor undervalue the place of theology. It would not neglect the moral for the aesthetic, nor the aesthetic for the moral. It has, therefore, a reasonable claim to be regarded as a central concept of theology, with a power to order theological content in a credible vision of the whole of Christian living.

REFERENCES

Augustine (1874). *Lectures or Tractates on the Gospel according to St. John*, trans. J. Innes, vol. II. Edinburgh: T. & T. Clark
   (1887). *The Writings against the Manichaeans and against the Donatists*, Library of Nicene and Post-Nicene Fathers, 4. Oxford: Parker
   (1972). *The City of God*, trans. H. Bettenson. Harmondsworth: Penguin Books
Bartchy, S. S. (1979). Table Fellowship with Jesus and the 'Lord's Meal' at Corinth. In *Increase in Learning: Essays in Honor of James G. van Buren*, ed. R. J. Owens *et al.* Kansas: Manhatten College Press
Barth, M. (1961). *Was Christ's Death a Sacrifice?* Edinburgh: Oliver and Boyd
Beattie, J. H. M. (1980). On Understanding Sacrifice. In *Sacrifice*, ed. M. F. C. Bourdillon and M. Fortes, pp. 29–44. London: Academic Press
Buchanan, C., *et al.* (1984). *Essays on Eucharistic Sacrifice in the Early Church*. Bramcote: Grove Books

Daly, R. J. (1978a). *The Origins of the Christian Doctrine of Sacrifice*. London: Darton, Longman and Todd

　(1978b). *Christian Sacrifice: The Judaeo-Christian Background before Origen*, Studies in Christian Antiquity, 18. Washington: Catholic University of America Press

Evans, C. F. (1970). *Resurrection and the New Testament*. London: SCM Press

Fernandez, J. (1974). The Mission of Metaphor in Expressive Culture. *Current Anthropology* 15, 119–45

Frankovich, L. F. (1976). Augustine's Theory of Eucharistic Sacrifice. Unpublished Ph.D. thesis, Marquette University

Hanson, R. P. C. (1979). *Eucharistic Offering in the Early Church*. Bramcote: Grove Books

Hardy, D. W. and D. F. Ford (1984). *Jubilate, Theology in Praise*. London: Darton, Longman and Todd

Hermisson, H.-J. (1965). *Sprache und Ritus im altisraelitischen Kult: Zur 'Spiritualisierung' der Kultbegriffe im Alten Testament*. Neukirchen-Vluyn: Neukirchener Verlag

Jeremias, J. (1963). *Der Opfertod Jesu Christi*. Stüttgart: Calwer Verlag

Leach, E. R. (1968). Ritual. In *International Encyclopaedia of Social Sciences*. New York: Macmillan

　(1976). *Culture and Communication*. Cambridge: Cambridge University Press

Newman, J. H. (1877). *The Via Media* (3rd edn). London: Pickering

Riches, J. (1980). *Jesus and the Transformation of Judaism*. London: Darton, Longman and Todd

Smart, N. (1971). *The Phenomenon of Religion*. London: Collins

　(1972). *The Concept of Worship*. London: Macmillan

Sykes, S. W. (1980). Sacrifice in the New Testament and Christian Theology. In *Sacrifice*, ed. M. F. C. Bourdillon and M. Fortes, pp. 61–83. London: Academic Press

　(1983). Story and Eucharist. *Interpretation* 37 (October), 365–76

　(1984). *The Identity of Christianity, Theologians and the Essence of Christianity from Schleiermacher to Barth*. London: SPCK

Wainwright, G. (1980). *Doxology*. London: Epworth Press

Williams, R. (1982). *Eucharistic Sacrifice – The Roots of a Metaphor*. Bramcote: Grove Books

17

CHRIST DIED FOR US: REFLECTIONS ON THE SACRIFICIAL LANGUAGE OF SALVATION

I. U. DALFERTH

Jesus Christ, the Apostles' Creed states, 'suffered under Pontius Pilate, was crucified, dead and buried'. The account of his death could hardly be more sober. The events leading to his death and burial are carefully listed. But nothing is said to bring out the vital importance which Christians attach to his death. The events as such seem not to point beyond themselves. Only the wider context of the whole Creed and the contextualization of these events in a narrative sequence that comprises not only Jesus' life and death but also the acts of God in his conception, resurrection and ascension give a clue as to their saving significance. To express the latter, it is not sufficient to mention these events; one has to rehearse the whole story told by the Creed.

The Nicene Creed, in contrast, does not content itself with these indirect pointers. It expressly mentions that Christ '*for us men*, and *for our salvation* came down from heaven' and that he 'was crucified *for us* under Pontius Pilate, suffered and was buried' (my italics). The saving significance of the whole sequence of events in general and of Christ's crucifixion in particular is explicitly stated – it was for us, for our salvation, that all this happened. Jesus Christ not only died, he died for us. The sober rehearsal of his story is thus emphasized to be more than a biographical sketch of the history of this particular person long since past. In speaking of his crucifixion for us the Creed speaks of a total soteriological event in which this person no less than the confessing believer himself and every other human being participate. It tells not just the story of Jesus Christ; in doing so it tells our story as well as his.

Both the Apostles' Creed and the Nicene Creed are classic summary expressions of the Christian experience of salvation: Christ has died for us – in order that we may live. But both are marked by a remarkable sobriety in their soteriological emphasis. They state the fact, but they refrain from its interpretation.

Yet the fact cannot be appropriated without interpretation nor can it be intelligibly communicated to others. In reflecting upon the story, summarized by the Creeds and told at length by the scriptures, the Christian faith, by its very nature, attempts to penetrate the mystery of salvation and to arrive at a fuller understanding of it; and because the reflection, communication and every other activity of the faith are essentially localized, concrete and performed in a particular context, it has arrived at a variety of interpretations and, based on these, theological theories of salvation which in turn in many cases have found their way into the wording of our Creeds and confessions.

This is most conspicuously so in the confessional statements of the reformation. Article 2 of the Thirty-Nine Articles of the Church of England[1] states that Jesus Christ 'truely suffered, was crucified, dead and buried, to reconcile His Father to us, and to be a sacrifice, not only for original guilt, but also for all actual sins of men'. This is a verbatim quotation from Article 3 of the Augsburg Confession and exemplifies clearly the Lutheran or, rather, Melanchthonian influence on the beginnings of Anglican theology (Meyer 1967). Yet in talking of reconciliation and sacrifice both Lutherans and Anglicans quite clearly move beyond what is stated in the Creeds. Are they justified in doing so? Are we as Christians committed to believe not only in our salvation but also in a certain understanding and interpretation of our salvation? Is it, in particular, essential to understand Christ's atoning death for us in terms of sacrifice?

In the wake of the Tractarian Movement within the Church of England and under the impact of the suffering in the First World War, Anglican theology seems to have been inclined to answer this question, even emphatically, in the affirmative. In 1920, for example, L. W. Grensted published *A Short History of the Doctrine of the Atonement* which testifies from the first to the last page to his conviction of the 'supreme mystical value' of the 'conception of sacrifice' (p. 189). On the one hand he observes that in Roman Catholic theology 'the idea of sacrifice ... has tended, since the Council of Trent, to displace the language of the Satisfaction theory' (p. 182); and he welcomes this because 'it has the great advantage that it is far less liable to inadequate transactional misinterpretations' (p. 189). On the other hand he points out that not only Calvin but also Luther and especially Melanchthon 'constantly use [...] sacrificial language of Christ, the one true Victim for sin' (p. 208). 'This retention of sacrificial language in Protestant theology', he goes on to emphasize, 'is interesting ... it forms a certain common Catholic basis for doctrinal statement, the value of which for mutual understanding has been very great, and may perhaps become greater still' (p. 209).[2]

This observation is truly Anglican in spirit. It discerns a possible doctrinal *via media* between Protestantism and Catholicism precisely in the sacrificial language used by both sides. Doctrinal reconciliation in disputed areas like the atonement, eucharistic theology or the Christian ministry may become possible if only we would learn to appreciate the fullness of sacrifice. Sacrifice may turn out to be the long-searched-for common denominator of doctrine, liturgy and Christian life in and between the Churches. It is this spirit which is exhibited in such books as S. C. Gayford's *Sacrifice and Priesthood* (1924), F. C. N. Hicks' *The Fullness of Sacrifice. An Essay in Reconciliation* (1930), which attempts to show 'the bearing of a true idea of sacrifice upon eucharistic controversy' (p. v), and O. C. Quick's *Doctrines of the Creed* ([1938] 1963), in which Quick concludes his discussion of the theories of atonement by stressing that he 'found the most satisfactory to be that which most clearly bases itself on sacrificial ideas' (p. 240). Anglican theology, it seems – and more examples could be cited – has shown an obvious and remarkable doctrinal interest in sacrifice in this century. But are the hopes which it associates with sacrificial language justified?

Some believe this to be self-evidently so. They argue thus: Christian doctrine has to reflect Christian worship; and Christian worship which precedes and underlies all credal and doctrinal formulation is essentially to be understood in terms of sacrifice. For the first Christians 'sacrifice was the only way of worship known, and so, even though they no longer practised it literally, the Christians spoke of their worship as the offering of spiritual sacrifices. The result is that sacrificial language is embedded in the liturgies used by all the major Christian denominations' (Young 1975, 10). Yet although it is true that worship has priority over doctrinal formulation, it is by no means clear that it has to be understood in terms of sacrifice. 'Sacrifice' and 'worship' are not synonymous and Christian worship is not to be equated with the offering of spiritual sacrifices (Hahn 1970, 86–7). To do this is either to reduce the mystery and richness of meaning of Christian worship to just one aspect of its much more comprehensive significance or to empty sacrificial language of its specific content. And even if it were true that at the beginnings of Christianity sacrifice was the only way of worship known, it would still be the case that to make a true historical observation about religious practices and their understanding at a certain time is not by itself to make a compelling conceptual point about worship. Christian worship, being centred upon Jesus Christ, has moved in more than one respect beyond the contemporary practice and understanding of worship. Its meaning is essentially determined by the significance given to Jesus Christ. The sacrificial understanding of worship, therefore, is not grounded in a general conceptual or factual link between 'worship' and 'sacrifice', but is itself derived from and dependent on the sacrificial understanding of Christ's atoning death. But then Christian worship does not provide independent grounds for doctrinal hopes in sacrificial language.

The case to be examined, therefore, is the sacrificial understanding of Christ's atoning death. On it depends, in the last resort, all other sacrificial language in Christian theology. This is acknowledged by the title of Hicks' book which, although its immediate concern is to achieve reconciliation between the 'Evangelical' and the 'Anglo-Catholic' groups in the Church of England and their differing views of sacrifice in the eucharistic controversy, clearly echoes the wording of Article 2 of the Thirty-Nine Articles quoted above. The question, therefore, arises: *Is it essential or preferable or at least justifiable to understand Christ's atoning death for us in terms of sacrifice?*

The first part of this essay seeks to explore this question. I shall argue that the doctrinal hopes of Anglican theology in sacrificial language are misplaced. The evidence is much too diverse to support exclusively or essentially this narrow interpretative option. Although sacrificial language is and may be used, there is much more to the total soteriological event of the atonement than can be expressed in terms of sacrifice. Yet if it is a possible though not essential understanding of atonement, is it then preferable to or more adequate than others? Not in any generally justifiable way, as I try to show in the second part by way of a tentative reconsideration of the Christian experience of salvation and, especially, its ontological implications. These conflict, I shall argue, with the ontological presuppositions of the sacrificial framework of thought and its language of vicarious substitution. This provides further reasons for not expecting too much from sacrificial language in doctrinal matters.

I

THE NEW TESTAMENT EVIDENCE

According to the rule, stated in Article 6, that nothing 'should be believed or an Article of the Faith, or be thought requisite or necessary to salvation' that is not contained in the holy scriptures because 'whatsoever is not read therein, nor may be proved thereby, is not to be required of any man', there can be no doubt that the Thirty-Nine Articles are justified in using the language of sacrifice with reference to the atoning death of Christ. Although sacrificial language is neither frequent nor prominent in most of the New Testament writings (Hahn 1967), the whole of the New Testament is permeated by sacrificial thought and symbolism. All traditions, from Paul to the Johannine corpus, can interpret Christ's atoning death for us, not all that often but unmistakably and in constantly changing ways, as a sacrifice, or rather self-sacrifice, and our salvation as redemption through his blood. To this effect a great variety of terms and images are used which are related in various ways, in various degrees, to various forms of the sacrificial cult of the temple.[3]

The most obvious example is the Epistle to the Hebrews which understands Christ's death as 'the perfect sacrifice' (9:14), the 'single offering which brings to perfection those whom he has sanctified' (10:14). Christ the high priest has accomplished 'once and for all' (9:12) and in a perfect way the priestly work willed by God thus replacing the cultic sacrifices of the temple. This perfection is brought out by the author of Hebrews in a twofold way. On the one hand the different parts of the donor, the victim and the priest in the sacrificial act coincide in Christ: he is donor (though he does not perform, as in the Old Testament ritual, the slaying) and victim at the cross, and he performs the priestly act of presenting his self-sacrifice to God by entering into the heavenly presence of his Father at the ascension (9:7, 21–4); and while the self-sacrifice has taken place once and for all (9:15–17, 25–8), he continually offers it to God for us in the heavenly tabernacle (8:1–5; 9:11, 24). On the other hand he is the perfection not just of one but of all types of sacrifices. In Heb. 9–10 his death is presented as both the perfect sin-offering of the Day of Atonement and the fulfilment of the covenant-offering of Exod. 24 and the red heifer of Num. 19. This combines traditions which in the Old Testament were sharply distinguished and which in other places of the New Testament can be applied separately or together to the crucifixion seen as a sin-offering (Matt. 26:28b) or as a covenant sacrifice (1 Cor. 11:25; Mark 14:24; Luke 22:20a; Matt. 26:28a). Similarly Eph. 5:2 uses the imagery of the burnt-offering to express Christ's self-sacrificing love; and sacrificial thought is also implied in the many texts that speak of the 'blood' of Christ (Hebrews *passim*; Rom. 5:9; Col. 1:20; Eph. 1:7 and 2:13; 1 John 1:7; Rev. 5:9) or regard him as the Lamb of sacrifice (John 1:29; 1 Pet. 1:19; Eph. 5:2; Rev. 5:6–10) or explicitly as the Passover Lamb (1 Cor. 5:6–8). Again in texts like Rom. 3:25; Heb. 2:17 or 1 John 2:2 and 4:10 phrases made of the Greek root *hilask-* together with *peri* which in the LXX serve as translations of the Hebrew *kipper 'al* are used to explain the saving efficacy of Christ's death in analogy to the temple cult. Sacrificial thought is most likely also implied in the constant New Testament identification of Christ with the suffering Servant of Isa. 52–3 (cf. Isa. 53:10). The same is true of the tradition of the Lord's Supper which talks about his blood shed 'for many' (Mark 14:24) or 'for you' (Luke 22:20), although it is by no means self-evident or universally agreed that Jesus himself understood and interpreted his atoning death as a representative or even vicarious sacrifice.[4] Moreover, according to the tradition cited by Paul the Lord's Supper is the 'proclamation of the Lord's death until he comes' (1 Cor. 11:26) but it is not necessarily for this reason the proclamation of his sacrificial death or even a sacrifice itself. And similarly the surrender-terminology of Mark 10:45; 1 Tim. 2:5–6 may or may not have sacrificial overtones.

Yet although there may be dispute over the interpretation of individual texts, there is abundant evidence that the New Testament uses sacrificial language with reference to the atoning death of Christ. To this extent the Reformation confessions are not without justification for their choice of expression. However, it does not follow that for this reason the soteriological event of Christ's death for us has to be understood in terms of sacrifice. The unquestionable fact of sacrificial terminology in the New Testament is one thing, but to take it to be essential or more adequate than other language used is another. And even when we acknowledge it to be essential to the world of meaning of, say, Hebrews because it is its principal way of communicating the fact that Christ's death has indeed achieved the atonement, this does not by itself justify us ln taking it to be essential for a proper Christian understanding of salvation. Not only what constitutes a scriptural 'proof' but also what is read or not read in the scriptures is, and always has been, more complex than to list appropriate quotations from the Old and New Testaments. The scriptural evidence has to be assessed before it can be used in theological argument; and in our particular case this involves paying attention to at least three features of the New Testament use of sacrificial language: its devaluation of the sacrificial cult, its spiritualizing use of the theme of sacrifice, and the limited function of the sacrificial symbolism in the Christian language of salvation.

DEVALUATION OF SACRIFICE

Firstly, even where sacrificial language is employed, there is a clear and unmistakable tendency in the New Testament to focus attention away from the sacrificial cult: 'A most obvious feature of the New Testament communities is the way in which the language of the Jewish cult – sacrifice, offering, temple and priesthood – rapidly came to be redeployed . . . and the reason for this astonishing fact lies not in any direct attack by Jesus on the sacrificial system but in the refocussing of religious attention' (Sykes 1980, 68). Christians stopped sacrificing and instead proclaimed Jesus to be the Christ. The significance given to Jesus and his atoning death led to the rapid devaluation of the language of the sacrificial cult in the Christian world of meaning. It was still, to some extent, employed to communicate the Christian experience of salvation and the atonement achieved by Christ. But the activities of the sacrificial cult very soon ceased to be part of the fabric of the new Christian faith. Being centred upon Christ, it was outside the ritual and transcended the sacrificial framework of the temple cult and of the religious orientation of its cultural environment. Thus when Christ's death was understood as a sacrifice by Christians this was not because it was misunderstood as a ritual act of slaying (which it was not) but because this supreme act of human existence governed by love was thought to be best expressed and communicable in terms of sacrifice. Sacrifice was the universal religious rite of late antiquity and everybody in the Graeco-Roman world could be expected to discern a sacrificial allusion (Young 1975, 9–12). Yet it was precisely this hermeneutical and communicative appropriateness that caused difficulties in conveying the uniqueness and distinctiveness of Christ's atoning death. Thus in the very use of sacrificial language the sacrificial framework of the cult had to be transcended. The difficulties are obvious, and only partially resolved when Christ's death is spoken of as the 'supreme sacrifice', the 'fulfillment of sacrifice' or the 'end of sacrifice': it is still the ritual framework of Old Testament cult and thought which is used typologically as a hermeneutical means to bring out the significance of this event. Yet for Christians, this is essentially a backward-looking perspective which views Christ exclusively in the light of the history past. Sacrificial language thus

> furthered the misunderstanding that in fact the death of Jesus was only as important as Temple worship, and stood alongside it; it could not represent the eschatological superseding and abolition of it. In the last resort this is the reason for the astonishing predominance of the Greek preposition *huper* as an expression of the saving efficacy of the death of Jesus in the New Testament texts, as opposed to *peri* made more familiar through the LXX as a translation of the Hebrew *'al*. (Hengel 1981, 52)

The use of sacrificial language in the New Testament, therefore, has to be seen as part of its overall tendency of focussing religious attention away from the sacrificial and cultic world of meaning by focussing it exclusively on Jesus Christ.

This refocussing of attention is also characteristic of the Lord's Supper, the memorial of the 'new covenant in my blood' (1 Cor. 11:25). It focusses attention away from the older covenants, indeed from all covenants, not by suspending them or by adding a new one to them as the Mosaic covenant was an addition to the Abrahamic, but by focussing on the *person of Christ himself*. Christ is not a second Moses, a founder or bringer of a new covenant, he *is* the new covenant. By the blood which he shed he did not establish a new covenant relationship with God which is now valid for us although he has passed away. The new covenant is Christ himself, his very person and not a work he has achieved. Consequently we cannot partake in it without partaking in the person of Christ himself (Wenz 1982). But then it is not enough to understand his death as the foundational covenant sacrifice accomplished on the cross. It rather has to be seen as the supreme act of this new covenant, God's being at one with us even in death. This at-one-ment is reality in his person and not only realized by what he did; and it is, as his death and resurrection show, valid not only for those alive. We do not pass out of this new relationship with God when we die, for being in Christ means that Christ is with us even in death. The Lord's Supper thus is the memorial not of a new covenant instituted by Christ but of Christ himself; and this is shown by participating in his body and blood and not simply by remembering in ritual and symbol the foundational sacrifice of a new cult. In eating the bread and drinking the cup we remember him (1 Cor. 11:24–5) by reminding ourselves that only by focussing exclusively on him we shall be at one with God even in death. Christ's death for us, his body broken for us and his blood shed for us, Christians proclaim as the sole focus of life by eating and drinking together in the name of their Lord (1 Cor. 11:26).

SPIRITUALIZATION OF SACRIFICE

The second feature, a corollary of the first, is the obviously *spiritualizing* way in which the New Testament employs the theme of sacrifice. By this I do not mean primarily the 'spiritual sacrifices' of which the New Testament sometimes speaks (1 Pet. 2: 5; Heb. 13: 15; Rom. 12: 1–2) or its occasional stress on Christian suffering on behalf of or in loyalty to Christ (Phil. 1: 29). These instances of sacrificial language applied to Christian life and worship clearly depend on its prior application to Christ himself: only because they understood his death in terms of sacrifice could Christians speak of their worship as the offering of spiritual sacrifices. Yet it was not in the latter context but in the former that the Christian spiritualization of the theme of sacrifice has its roots. For in speaking of Christ's death for us in terms of sacrifice, the New Testament does not refer to a ritual act of killing but uses sacrifice as an interpretative symbol to communicate the soteriological meaning of his death to its audience. It is not the act of killing at the crucifixion (which was a judicial execution, not a ritual slaying) but Christ's self-offering culminating in his acceptance of death which it is at pains to emphasize. The sacrificial symbolism, therefore, illuminates Christ's life and death as a story of self-sacrifice; and because his story is part of the story of each of us, it presents his self-sacrifice as exemplary for our own life: Christ is the exemplum not only of Christian but of human life and death.

It would be quite wrong to conclude from the symbolical usage of sacrifice by the New Testament writers that they were spiritualizing Christ's atoning death or no longer referred to a real event. On the contrary, by speaking of it in terms of sacrifice they underlined the reality of this event – the Christian message of the crucified Messiah must have sounded scandalous and aggressive to a Jewish audience and aesthetically and ethically repulsive to the Gentile world (Hengel 1981, 31–40; Moule 1980, 150–1). But as the soteriological event of his atoning death is a very specific eschatological reality in our sinful world, they had to use sacrificial language symbolically in order to bring out and to communicate intelligibly the meaning of this extraordinary event. What they spiritualized, therefore, was not this event but sacrifice; and because it was done by focussing on Christ's extraordinary story, they started a hermeneutical process which led to a christological transformation of the sacrificial thought and language which was first used to interpret this event. To understand Christ's death in terms of sacrifice was possible only by understanding true sacrifice, because of the uniqueness and fundamentally eschatological character of this event, in terms of Christ's death for us: it came to be seen as the central, final and universal sacrifice, the fulfilment and archetype of all other sacrifices. By focussing exclusively on Christ, his life and death became the focus of all sacrificial thinking. The Christian spiritualizing of the theme of sacrifice, therefore, resulted in its christologizing; but it started with the symbolical usage of sacrifice to convey the meaning of the story of Jesus Christ.

In using sacrifice symbolically the New Testament writers were in line with the general and widespread process of spiritualization which the religious world of the Roman Empire underwent at the time of the emergence of the Christian faith (Wenschkewitz 1932; McKelvey 1969). Christians did not inaugurate this process, they participated in it; and they used it to communicate their specific message. For spiritualization, I should like to suggest, is a process of symbolization by which things or actions (or descriptions of things, events and actions) become used as interpretative symbols, that is, by which the meaning which things, events or actions have acquired in one context is used to discover, to elucidate, to articulate or to represent the meaning of things or events in some other context. The spiritualization of the theme of sacrifice is thus the concentration on the *notion* of sacrifice rather than on sacrifices themselves by relating it to meaning, understanding and communication rather than to certain ritual acts and performances. With its designating or referential import thus reduced, it becomes possible to apply it beyond the limits of the cultic framework, using its primary meaning to bring out a secondary meaning in some other, non-cultic context. By the very nature of this process this involves a shift from the purely cultic to the wider religious and ethical implications of this notion. For to use it symbolically is to invest it with the structure of symbols, that is, the distinction between symbol and symbolized: something meaningful in itself stands for (the meaning of) something else.

This is most clearly so in the case of sacrifice itself which is, as has frequently been pointed out, essentially of symbolic structure. Sacrifices presuppose consecration, that is, the making of something into a symbol (Beattie 1980, 30).[5] Thus the thing sacrificed, in blood sacrifices usually another living creature and most often a domestic animal, is made to stand for or to symbolize something else, namely 'the person or persons who are making the sacrifice or upon whose behalf the sacrifice is being made' (*ibid.*); and in the sacrificial act man is symbolically giving (part of) himself by killing the consecrated animal and offering its life to God as a vicarious sacrifice of himself. But this essentially vicarious function of sacrifice depends wholly on the consecration; and consecration involves and presupposes a whole system of religious rules and ritual conventions which specify not only the (possible) effects of sacrifice but also what, in a given situation, is to be sacrificed, how it is to be made into a symbol of man, what exactly it stands for and how the sacrificial act is properly conducted. In brief, sacrifice presupposes a regulated relationship between God and man, a cultic framework of thought and action that assigns certain roles and functions to the participants and invests their actions with a power to achieve effects which they do not possess in themselves. Only in a context like this the idea of a sacrificial, vicarious death begins to make sense.

Now it is not sacrifice itself but the notion of sacrifice that is used symbolically in Christian language; and it is not the term (or cluster of terms) but its meaning which is used to stand for or to elucidate something else; and again this symbolic usage is dependent on a system of rules which allow this notion to be used beyond its primary referential import. As the notion of sacrifice, as opposed to sacrifices themselves, is a conceptual entity, this system of rules consists precisely in the semantic, or generally linguistic, rules that govern the use of this cluster of terms. These rules do not incorporate and specify the sacrificial act but the meaning of this act; and its meaning is constituted not by the ritual killing but by the attitude of the participants and the rules and conventions that regulate their actions. It is, therefore, quite natural that the spiritualization of the theme of sacrifice should involve a shift towards its religious and ethical implications: it is not the ritual killing but the total meaning of this act, constituted by the attitudes of the participants and the religious system that regulates their actions, which is being used symbolically.[6]

It follows that to speak of Christ's atoning death in terms of self-sacrifice is to imply something about the attitudes of all participants involved in this saving event and about the system of rules that relates them and shapes their common story; and the adequacy of this interpretation is to be checked against the evidence which we have on these matters. Thus without presupposing the Law that regulates the relationship between God and man the sacrificial symbolism would lose most of its point; it could hardly be used meaningfully to bring out the saving significance of Christ's death. Similarly if the evidence of the life and death of Jesus of Nazareth would show no marks of selfless self-dedication, to interpret it in terms of self-sacrifice would be grossly inadequate. Again if it would be impossible to illuminate God's story and his part in this event in terms of sacrifice, the sacrificial symbolism would clearly be inadequate. And, finally, if it does not help to interpret our individual story to us, it would fail to do the job it is supposed to do: to communicate the soteriological meaning and eschatological import of Christ's death to each of us. This last point, above all, needs emphasizing. If our individual stories are part of Christ's story, his story is the essential framework for understanding our own story; but then any interpretation of his story that fails to illuminate ours is not fully adequate and true in the sense relevant here: it fails to convey the *for us*.

LIMITED FUNCTION OF SACRIFICIAL SYMBOLISM

However – and this is the third feature of the New Testament use of sacrificial language to be mentioned – are we, therefore, to jump to sadomasochistic conclusions in order to make our story correspond to his story interpreted in terms of the sacrificial symbolism if our own life is not (or not sufficiently) illuminated by this interpretation? Some have, not without justification, accused the Christian tradition of having encouraged this (Soelle 1975). Yet it is important to remember here that sacrificial language is only one and not the most prominent strand in a plurality of terms and symbols used in the New Testament to express the Christian experience of salvation. In his extensive but by no means exhaustive study *Christ. The Christian Experience in the Modern World* (1980) E. Schillebeeckx has helpfully examined some of the main features of the New Testament terminology of salvation. In particular, he has outlined the semantic structure and the historical background of 'sixteen key concepts, which occur repeatedly in all parts of the New Testament' (p. 477). Together they provide a good idea of the astonishing multiplicity of ways, not always and in every respect compatible with each other, in which the New Testament writers express and communicate their understanding of salvation.

This very diversity and multiplicity is significant, for it resists all attempts at reduction. There is, first of all, no single concept comprehensive enough to include all or most of the New Testament views of salvation. We need, as John Knox (1959, 146ff.) has shown, at least the two categories of 'victory' and 'sacrifice' to do justice to the material (see also Sweet 1981). But even then we have to include such diverse views in those categories that the concept of 'sacrifice' is stretched into unintelligibility: it is in danger of losing all specific and informative content. This is well illustrated by Young (1975, 135ff.) in whose work 'sacrifice' virtually dissolves into 'worship' and 'prayer'.[7]

Secondly, there are not just one or two interpretations of Christ's atoning death for us which are authentic while all the others are not. To claim otherwise is not only contrary to the New Testament evidence, it is to commit the hermeneutical fallacy of the 'absolute interpretation' of which the quest for the 'original understanding' is a familiar version: even if we knew that Jesus interpreted his death in terms of sacrifice, we should still have to ask the question whether he was right and whether this understanding is the only or most appropriate one (cf. Lash 1981). The historically prior is not necessarily for this reason also the more true; and the fact that the sacrificial understanding of Christ's death can be traced back to the beginning of Christianity does not exclude other understandings as equally or even more adequate.

Thus attempts at reduction are bound to fail on both factual and hermeneutical grounds. But there is an even deeper theological reason for the irreducibility of the multiplicity of ways in which the New Testament writers talk of salvation. We cannot reduce it to some general underlying uniformity of experience or stereotype of interpretation without losing sight of the soteriological event which they, each in his own way, seek to express. For it is precisely the specific detail, not some vague generalities, that gives content and substance to the Christian experience of salvation. Nowhere is the soteriological event experienced there set out without interpretation. But in the very nature of the case – it is, after all, part of your story and my story as well as of Jesus Christ's and God's own story and therefore bound to be presented in different autobiographical perspectives, that is, from the inside and not, as it were, 'objectively' and authoritatively from the outside – this event is only given and accessible to theological reflection in an irreducible variety of interpretations. It follows that we are not justified in concentrating on just one or two of these to the exclusion of the others. For by what criteria could we do so? Statistical frequency of occurrence in the New Testament texts neither proves nor disproves a given cluster of terms or symbols to be an adequate interpretation of Christ's atoning death. But neither does its prominence or lack of prominence at the beginnings of the Christian faith or in its later historical developments. There have been many attempts in the twenty centuries of theological reflection to elevate one or other strand of the New Testament language of salvation to doctrinal prominence. One has been to interpret the Christian experience of salvation in a legal or penitential framework in terms of compensation, meritorious satisfaction or vicarious punishment; another to interpret it in a framework of power struggle in terms of captivity, ransom, victory and liberation; a third to interpret it in a (spiritualized) cultic framework in terms of sacrifice, suffering and self-offering. But the Church has been well advised not to propound any of these as a definite doctrinal interpretation of the atoning death of Christ. The Christian world of meaning, as the New Testament kept reminding the Church, is characterized by an irreducible variety of interpretations of this event, because what is at stake here is your story and my story in all their specific detail, their hopes and disappointments, failures and successes, joys and fears shared and unsharable which make them the unmistakable stories they are. It would be wrong to assume that each of these stories could or should be told in the same uniform way or that each of them would allow for only one appropriate way of telling it: the stories of our lives are complex and many-faceted enough to allow for a multitude of perspectives on them, each of which brings out, to a varying degree, one or some of the many points or features they have. That this is no less true of the story of Christ has in fact been acknowledged by the theological tradition when it spoke of him in terms of his prophetic, kingly and priestly office: to do justice to him we have to tell his story in at least these three mutually irreducible ways.

The adequacy of sacrificial language, therefore, to interpret the total soteriological event meaningfully to a given person or community cannot in general be assumed. It has to be checked by the other ways Christ's story is and can be told and it has to prove itself to be true to and illuminating of both our individual and our common story. Christ's atoning death for us is not bound to be understood, and not necessarily understood better, in terms of sacrifice. The Christian world of meaning knows of many other ways to interpret and communicate it intelligibly. But sacrificial language and symbolism are one of the powerful interpretative resources of the Christian tradition of which we can avail ourselves, at some times more appropriately than at others, to interpret Christ's and our own story meaningfully to ourselves and to others.

CONCLUSION AND CONSEQUENCES

Thus although it is possible and justifiable, it is neither essential nor necessarily always and everywhere preferable to understand Christ's atoning death in terms of sacrifice. Christ has died *for us*, but this is not to say that his death was a sacrifice. Christians are committed by their faith to believe in the atonement, not in its sacrificial interpretation. The Anglican hope in sacrificial language as a common basis for doctrinal statement, therefore, is misplaced: it concentrates upon an interpretation where it should insist on that which this among others seeks to interpret. Doctrinal unity is not a matter of assimilating or reducing the various traditions to one particular interpretation or understanding of salvation. It is a matter of integrating the irreducible diversity of interpretations by pointing, as unmistakably as possible, to the common experience which they reflect and attempt to communicate in their different ways. In this respect, however, the sobriety of the Creeds is more promising ecumenically than the interpretative stand of the Reformation confessions. They allow for unity without requiring uniformity. They allow every Christian, however he interprets his faith to himself in his particular community, to join in the common experience of the universal Church. To be sure it is not enough simply to repeat the text of the Creeds. This has to be accompanied by constant theological reflection which penetrates the Christian experience of salvation expressed there in order to find the means most appropriate for a given time and place to communicate what they say meaningfully and intelligibly. But this must not blur the vital distinction between our salvation and how we conceive of our salvation. For our conceptions of it are at best faint approximations to the fullness of its mystery.

If my argument so far carries any conviction at all it has consequences *inter alia* for a proper understanding of the eucharist and the Christian ministry. Given the devaluation of the sacrificial cult, the spiritualization of sacrifice and the limited function of the sacrificial symbolism in the New Testament, it is hardly appropriate to understand the eucharist exclusively or essentially in terms of sacrifice whether it is thought to be a sacrificial act in its own right or a memorial of Christ's sacrifice. At each Lord's Supper the first Christians proclaimed 'the Lord's death until he comes' (1 Cor. 11:26), and much as this may 'cry out to be thought of as a sacrifice' (Baker 1981, 269), it in fact cries out and asks to be understood at least as much in all the other ways in which the saving significance of this event has been and may be expressed and interpreted.[8] It is the Lord's saving death, not his sacrifice, which we are to proclaim at the eucharist. To work out the meaning of his death and its eucharistic proclamation exclusively in terms of sacrifice is at best a narrow and one-sided approach to the eucharist and at worst a misrepresentation of and blindness to the richness of its meaning. There is more to Christ's death than sacrifice; and there is more to the eucharist than the model of sacrifice allows us to bring out.

But then to understand the Christian ministry as a 'priesthood', the office of the Christian *sacerdos* (Tertullian) which is a natural development of the emphasis on the eucharist as a sacrifice instituted by Christ, the true high priest – to say nothing of its corollary of excluding both women and non-episcopally ordained men from it – is as unfounded as the presupposed view of the eucharist. The meaning and saving significance of Christ's atoning death cannot be reduced to one of our interpretations of it to the exclusion of others. This is by no means to say that every doctrinal stand is as acceptable as any other or that it does not matter how we understand and interpret the atonement. To acknowledge the irreducible diversity of Christian life and thought is not to plead for a total doctrinal relativism or subjectivism. There is a definite though notoriously difficult and by no means self-evident standard by which all doctrinal interpretations are to be judged: they have to be true to the common Christian experience as expressed, above all, in the scriptures and summarized in the Creeds. This does not mean that they have to be true to the scriptural and credal formulations in the sense that we can never move beyond these forms of words. Seriously as those have to be taken as primal data for determining what the Christian experience of salvation is, they do not save us the trouble of theological judgement or the labour of distinguishing between the experience experienced and its form of expression. The Bible is not a phrase-book of religious jargon; it is the source-book of the Christian story. Nothing can pass as Christian experience, therefore, that cannot show itself to participate in the experience of redemption normatively expressed in this story. And there is only one way to show this participation: by participating in the rehearsal of this common story within the Church as the rehearsal of one's own individual story, that is by joining into the common confession, worship, *homologia* and *diakonia* of the Church. Being true to the Christian experience, therefore, involves not uniformity but unity based on participation in worship. It follows that a proper understanding of the Christian experience of salvation is never a merely individual matter but a process of corporate insight through mutual self-correction and help within the Christian community.

But what exactly is the Christian experience of salvation, interpreted and understood in the Church in so many different ways? It is this question to which I shall turn in the remainder of this essay.

II

THE CHRISTIAN EXPERIENCE OF SALVATION

The Christian experience of salvation is the experience of the saving significance of the death of Jesus Christ. In the light of his resurrection and through the working of the Spirit Christians discern the true eschatological nature of this death as a death for us, that is, for all mankind; and they bear witness to this by reciting the atoning death of their living Lord as the central article of their faith. From the beginning the heart of the Christian Gospel has been the proclamation that Christ has died for us. In 1 Cor. 15: 3–4, for example, one of the oldest statements of the Christian *kerygma* we have, Paul reminds the Corinthians of the *'paradosis'* which he himself had received and handed on to them in fixed form: 'Christ died for our sins according to the Scriptures and ... was buried and ... was raised on the third day according to the Scriptures.'

There are good reasons to believe, as M. Hengel (1981) has shown, that this pre-Pauline soteriological formula is most likely to be traced back to the Hellenists in Jerusalem and their original translation of the primitive Christian message in the Greek language. The new message was to be proclaimed not only to the Aramaic-speaking Jews of Palestine but also to all those in the Diaspora who only spoke Greek. 'What is more likely than to suppose that the formula *Christos apethanen huper (tōn hamartiōn) hēmōn ...* was formed in connection with this creative translation of the new kerygma into Greek?' (Hengel 1981, 50).

This, of course, is only an historical hypothesis and has to be assessed on the basis of the evidence adduced. But there can be no doubt that the saving significance of the death of the Messiah expressed in this formula is part of the very essence of the original Christian experience of salvation. This does not mean that the Christian faith is interested exclusively in Christ's death, for his death cannot be divorced or understood apart from the total story of his life. This story is an essential part of the meaning of his death. But although it is essential, it is not the only context within which his death has to be understood. If it were his death would be of individual and perhaps historical but hardly of universal significance. It would be the death of this particular individual who, no doubt, has left his decisive mark on history by becoming the exemplum (1 Pet. 2: 21), remembered and imitated in a multitude of ways, of a life of self-devotion to others. But it would mark the end of his story and could serve as an exemplar only for those who are later in time and know of him. It would be a closed story with historical effects but without universal saving significance. Yet it is precisely the latter which for Christians is the reason for taking a more than merely historical interest in the story of the life and death of this particular individual. Christ's story, they claim, is not closed and exclusive but open and inclusive: it includes my story and yours and our stories presuppose and continue in his. To tell his story properly, then, is to tell it as part of the story of every human being; without it our individual stories lack their full significance. This inclusiveness and not some vague generality specifiable in moral, religious or whatever terms is the universality of Christ's story: it is the pre-history and post-history of every human story whether we, from our autobiographical and therefore necessarily incomplete view on our own story, accept this as true or not. This is not to blur the difference between his story and ours but to stress their intimate relationship and irreversible order: his story includes ours, our story is included in his; his story provides the framework to bring out the ultimate significance of each of our individual stories, none of our human stories is told in full without being told as part of Christ's story. This is what Christians mean when they speak of the soteriological significance of Christ's story. But then his death is part of our stories as much as it is part of his story and our stories are no less important for the meaning of his death than is his own. The Christian *kerygma*, therefore, is most characteristically the message of our salvation achieved through the death of Jesus Christ and vindicated by his resurrection. Even the hymn in Philippians, the Lucan passion narrative or the Acts which associate the death of Jesus Christ with the vindication of God's design rather than with the redemption of others neither deny nor neglect a soteriological understanding of his death and resurrection nor do they present us with a pure, non-soteriological *kerygma* (Hofius 1976; Beck 1981). Such a *kerygma* would be a contradiction in terms; and even though those relatively late texts do not state it explicitly, a soteriological understanding of Christ's death is both presupposed and taken for granted (Hengel 1981, 34, 71): our salvation cannot be divorced from Christ's death nor Christ's death from our salvation – he has died *for us* as the New Testament writers, each in his own way, proclaim.

SOTERIOLOGY AND HISTORY

It follows that Christian faith and Christian theology are concerned not just with Jesus Christ's death but with his *death for us*. What does this difference amount to? It is the difference between an historical event and a soteriological event, between the totality of his life and death as it is in principle accessible to historical research and the total soteriological event of which his life and death as much as ours are essential constituents; and the two are to be distinguished because they not only have a different structure but also different consequences and implications. Thus the death of Jesus Christ is the last of a series of events that constitute the biography of this particular person in space and time. As such it is a historical fact susceptible to historical research and corroboration. From all we know it was a judicial execution following a trial when Pontius Pilate was prefect of Judaea; and on the basis of the evidence available nobody reasonably can deny that this could be objectively established, at any rate in principle. Yet when Christians confess their salvation through the death of Christ they do not simply refer to this public event of the crucifixion of Jesus. They refer to a soteriological event, not just to a historical fact, to a complex interlocking of their own stories with his, not simply to the end of his particular story; and they mark this in the most elementary way by speaking of Christ's *death for us*. This is not just a different description of the same event, a mere manner of speaking. For while the death of Jesus Christ was the result of a public execution this is not true of the death of Jesus Christ for us. Similarly it is the death of Jesus Christ for us, not the judicial slaying of Jesus Christ, which has atoning significance. And while his death is an event that belongs exclusively to the particular story of Jesus Christ, his death for us is an event that belongs to the story of each and every one of us.

This obviously raises the question of the relationship between Christ's death and his death for us, between the historical fact and the soteriological event. Should we say that Christians refer to a historical event *as* a soteriological event, that is, that they interpret his death *as* a death for us? Soteriology would then be an interpretative dimension of history, history and soteriology would be related as fact and interpretation.

Many theologians seem to operate with such a model of 'fact plus interpretation'. Hengel, for example, characterizes his study of the atonement as an investigation into the 'Origin of the Soteriological Interpretation of the Death of Jesus' (chapter 2). Similarly C. F. D. Moule (1980), speaking of 'the interpretation of historical events in terms of what transcends history' (p. 163), explores the scope of the death of Christ by asking 'how is that death to be interpreted and estimated?' and then distinguishing 'at least three ways of estimating the death of Christ', all of which 'have to be reckoned with' (p. 108). Yet to start from the methodological assumption that to speak of Christ's death for us is one possible interpretation of this death among others – even if it 'cannot be historically verified, and is not accepted by all alike' (p. 163) – is to misconstrue both the basis and the origin of the Christian faith. The Christian experience of salvation is neither an individual nor a corporate theological interpretation of the public death of Jesus Christ, it is the enthusiastic experience of his atoning death for us; and what Christians have theologically interpreted in a multitude of different ways is not the historical fact of his death but the soteriological event of his (living and) dying for us.

The simple model of 'fact plus interpretation', therefore, proves to be hermeneutically inadequate on at least three accounts. First, to oppose fact and interpretation in this way is quite misleading: there are no uninterpreted facts, only different and differently related interpretations of states and events. The crude fact/interpretation dichotomy has to be replaced by a distinction of different levels of interpretation or a series of interpretations and reinterpretations. Secondly, however, even with a model modified in this way the Christian message of the atoning death of Christ cannot be conceived as the result of a two-stage interpretative process: historical event – soteriological interpretation. The soteriological understanding of Christ's death is not a secondary soteriological interpretation of a primary unsoteriological understanding of Jesus' death and resurrection; it is a primary and primitive understanding of a soteriological event: his dying for us. Christians do not transform a historical event into a soteriological event by theological reflection upon it; they discern and experience a soteriological event,[9] they express their experience in a great variety of ways, and they reflect theologically upon this variety of symbolic expressions to bring out their coherence and inner unity. But at no stage in this complex and multifaceted process do they transform a non-soteriological event or experience into a soteriological one. The saving significance of Christ's death is in no sense the result of what Christians do or think; it is the fundamental presupposition and origin of everything they think, do and, indeed, are.

But then, thirdly, we cannot say that Christians interpret the historically given death of Christ in one possible way among others. In speaking of the saving significance of his death they do not impose their subjective theological interpretation on an objective historical event. The objective/subjective dichotomy implied by the above model is highly misleading. If interpretation is understood as giving meaning to his death rather than as discerning or discovering, appropriating and penetrating the given meaning of it, we would do better to drop the terminology altogether.[10] It would strictly contradict the universality of the Christian message if the saving efficacy of Christ's death were to depend on our soteriological interpretation of a particular historical event. The saving significance of his death is not restricted to those who understand and interpret it soteriologically, it is not a subjective (individual or corporate) interpretation of a historical event. For to be saved is not the result of giving saving significance to the death of Christ any more than it is the result of our believing ourselves to be saved. The saving significance of Christ's death does not follow, it precedes everything we believe, think or do.

Christian faith, then, is not creative in the sense that it invests a plainly historical event with soteriological significance. Rather than producing a soteriological interpretation of Christ's death, it is produced by the soteriological event of Christ's atoning death for us; and in its epistemic dimension it is the discernment and penetration of its own origin and foundation. This discernment of faith Christians express in both linguistic and non-linguistic actions in a multitude of situationally and culturally determined ways thus interpreting and communicating their particular perspective on the soteriological event under the conditions of a given time and place. The language of faith, therefore, is not only essentially expressive and symbolic. Since it seeks to communicate an *event* in which Christians know everyone to be involved, it is of narrative and sequential structure and of self-involving character. Christians symbolize the soteriological event in terms of a becoming and happening whose participants are God, Jesus Christ and we ourselves; and the various soteriological symbols, metaphors and forms of narratives which we find in the New Testament, for example, present and stress the roles which these participants play in different ways.

For Christians, then, the primary and basic given is not the historical fact but the soteriological event. To speak, historically, of Christ's death is in effect a partial abstraction from the full event of his dying for us. Soteriology is not an interpretative dimension of history, rather history is a perspectival narrowing of soteriology. It is the unavoidable perspective of sinful man on Christ's atoning death for us. Conversely we can characterize the soteriological event as the eschatological truth of the historical event. It is the full significance of what has happened in the public slaying of Jesus Christ *sub specie dei*; and we participate in this divine perspective by being brought to experience and discern the saving significance of his death through the agency of the Holy Spirit. To spell out the full significance of this event, we cannot restrict ourselves to the telling of the story of Jesus Christ or even of the stories of Jesus Christ and God; we have to go on to tell the story of every human being. Because this is impossible and, if done in a generalizing way as the story of 'man', at best uninteresting and at worst highly misleading, soteriology in no way is a theory of salvation but an application of Christ's story to our individual stories and the exploration of their significance in the light of his. It thus necessarily leads to proclamation, confession, and I-statements. For not by generalizing about men but by provoking I-confessions it shows the universality of Christ's story as the pre-history and post-history of the story of every human being.

SOTERIOLOGY AND ONTOLOGY

If the primary given for Christian faith and theology is the total soteriological event of Christ's atoning death for us, we shall fail to understand it if we do not pay attention to its ontological implications. From the start theological reflection is faced with an irreducibly *relational eschatological reality*.[11] It is a *reality* because the soteriological event is not the result of the interpretative activity of the Christian faith but the foundation of the very existence of it; it is an *eschatological* reality because, as the Christian faith conceives and communicates it, it is an action of God constituted by the Father, realized in the Son, experienced through the Spirit and, accordingly, understood properly only in a trinitarian context; and it is irreducibly *relational* because it cannot be reduced to isolated sets of more basic, non-relational facts, events or things. We cannot analyse Christ's atoning death for us into a set of facts about Jesus, about God, about ourselves and about the relations which hold between these sets of facts. Attempts to do this inevitably distort the event which we seek to understand. That Christ has died for us is not, as we have seen, a matter of an intentional (interpretative) relation between us and his death; but neither is it a certain (that is, soteriological) kind of external relation between these two poles or *relata*. Both interpretations would hold good only for those who live *post Christum natum* and are thus tantamount to a denial of the universality of its saving significance. The relational structure of the soteriological event is rather that of a real relation in the sense of constituting not only a particular kind of relationship between Jesus Christ and all of us that cannot be analysed either in terms of logical or in terms of spatio-temporal relations but at the same time the *relata* of this relation. Because it would be as impossible for him to be and for us not to be related to him as it would be for us to be without his being related to us, this relationship is essential to the very being of Jesus Christ and of ourselves at whatever time and place we may live. It is primarily not a matter of what we do but of who we are, of our being human persons and not just human agents (Dalferth and Jüngel 1981). For by incorporating us into Christ so that we exist in Christ (whether as agents we acknowledge and live that or not) this relationship constitutes us as persons in communion with God and Christ as a corporate person (Moule 1980) in and through whom we have personal being. Christologically this requires the distinction between humanity and divinity with respect to the person of Christ, anthropologically the distinction between person and agent with respect to human beings. And because as human agents we may or may not exist in accordance with our personal being and christological relationship to God, sin and righteousness are our human modes of existence. The ontological import of soteriology, therefore, is an ontology of persons and personal relations constituted by God's relationship to them in and through Christ.

The total soteriological event can thus be described as a complex reality of personal relations which involves God, Jesus Christ and us in such a way that it is most appropriately specified as God's saving action in and through Jesus Christ towards and for us. As God's saving action it is a dynamic eschatological reality which not only implies a distinction between our world as it is (nature) and as it should and will be (creation) but also introduces a polar tension in our understanding of God, Jesus Christ and ourselves. It aims at transforming us from sinful men, who as agents exist in conflict with our personal being, into members of the body of Christ, who as agents and persons live together in and through Christ as children in communion with their father. The Christian doctrine of man, therefore, both in the sense of the individual human being and in the sense of the whole (history) of mankind requires two stories to be told of man, the story of the sinner and the story of the saved. Similarly it shows Jesus in the totality of his life and death to be not only a particularly gifted individual human being but the Christ, that is, God's saving word addressed to us. Accordingly it requires two stories to be told about him, a story of a human life of aspiration, suffering and death and a story of divine passion, humiliation, rejection and resurrection. Again it reveals God to be primarily not the wrathful judge whom we have to fear but our saviour whose nature is love; and again we have to tell two stories about God: 'a story of power, transcendence and judgement – and a story of weakness, immanence and forgiveness' (Sykes 1980, 79). But even in these twofold ways we can speak about God, Jesus Christ and ourselves separately only by concentrating on one or the other dimension of the total soteriological event, thus relatively, though never totally, abstracting from its other constitutive dimensions. Christian theology (that is, talk of God), christology and anthropology (including cosmology) are relative abstractions from the total soteriological event from different points of view. Each of them can lay claim to truth only insofar as it does not restrict itself to its own specific dimension to the exclusion of all the others but includes and repeats from its particular perspective the total soteriological event and the twofold story it requires to be told of God, Jesus Christ and us in our world.

A methodological consequence of this is that on the one hand *story* figures so prominently in Christian thought and that on the other hand Christian doctrines form a *system*, that is, they are so closely interlocked that you cannot change one without affecting all the others. We cannot, not even from a single perspective, say everything at once but are bound by the discursive nature of our thinking, speaking and writing to express ourselves in sequential order. The most appropriate way to express the totality of the soteriological event, therefore, is to express it by means of the narrative totality of a story. But although a story does not have to say everything in order to say all, that is, to present the whole truth, it will not be a narrative presentation of the soteriological event unless it comprises a story about God, about Jesus Christ and about ourselves in such a way that it is told as my story and your story. But then Christian doctrines which are the results, accepted to a varying degree by the Christian community, of theological reflection upon these stories are not statements of (metaphysical) facts but shorthand formulae which sum up (aspects of) these stories. They have, as it were, not a predicative but a narrative deep structure. To understand them correctly, we have to re-translate them into the narrative sequential form of a story. Doctrinal statements like 'God is love' or 'Jesus Christ is both wholly God and wholly man' are neither factual nor metaphysical assertions nor are they narrative in themselves. They are conceptual summaries of narratives, statements which require to be unfolded in stories (Dalferth 1981, 664ff.).

Similarly, and more importantly in the present context, the relational ontological structure of the total soteriological event calls for interpretations of the credal statement that Christ has died for us which do justice to the irreducible relationality of the reality expressed. Our interpretative symbols and forms of expression must not suggest separations and divisions untrue to this eschatological reality. It is not enough, for example, to say that he has died *instead of* us or *in the place of* us (in the sense of the Greek preposition *anti*) as we could say of a lifeboat crew that gave its life in a successful attempt to rescue our lives; nor is it enough to interpret it as his death *for the sake of* us (in one sense of the Greek preposition *huper*) as we would say of a lifeboat crew that gave its life in a (perhaps unsuccessful) rescue operation or that by its action, although ill-fated, set an inspiring example of self-sacrifice and selfless devotion for the benefit of others. All these interpretations imply the idea of a *vicarious* action or death which, when worked out within a legal (penal) or sacrificial (cultic) framework of thought, involves *substitution* of one party (thing or person) for the other, the offender or the victim; and these ideas in turn presuppose both an ontological individualism with respect to the parties involved in the substitutionary or vicarious action (they must exist and be identifiable in themselves, that is, independently of this action or event and of each other) and the analysis of this action in terms of a merely external relationship between them. But to interpret the saving event of Christ's death for us along these lines is to conceive it as an action or event, predicable of this particular individual and through its effects somehow related to us who are also conceived as separate individuals. Yet this is to miss completely the essentially personal character of this event. Personhood cannot be reduced to individuals or subjects and their actions and relations; and the ontological relation that constitutes persons as persons is to be distinguished from the relations in which persons engage (Dalferth and Jüngel 1981). The ontological individualism and ontology of external relations presupposed above, however, fails on both accounts. It is unable to give an acceptable account of what constitutes persons and of personal relations and thus is not in a position to communicate meaningfully the relational structure of the soteriological reality. The latter is not the outcome of a secondary relating of the already constituted and separately identifiable entities God, Jesus Christ and man, but their dynamic constitution or, rather, re-constitution – their 'rebirth' (John) or 'new creation' (Paul) – in and through these relations. The ontological result of this is that in each case two stories are to be told: a story of the creator and the creation and a story of the saviour and the redemption, a story of Jesus Christ the man and of humanity and a story of Jesus Christ the Word of God addressed to us and of divinity, a story of the sinner and of sin and a story of the righteous and of salvation; and although these two stories are irreducible and of equal importance they do require a definite order of telling because in each case the second story has eschatological priority over the first. The specific relational reality of the total soteriological event, therefore, implies an ontology and personal relations in terms of Law and Gospel which in each case allows us to make sense of both stories, their irreversible order, and the impossibility of telling one set of these stories without in fact including all the others from this particular point of view.[12]

Because Christ is constitutive of our personal being he is not just externally related to us. As Christ (that is, the Word of God addressed to us) he cannot be identified apart from his atoning death for who he is and what he is is constituted by God's relationship of paternal love to him and by his saving relationship of the obedient Son to us. But neither are we ourselves identifiable in the full sense of who and what we are apart from this event and Christ's relation to us which mediates and reveals God's parental love to all of us by showing him to be the firstborn son of many brothers and sisters. He, therefore, is not just an extraordinary individual whose selfless life and death is an inspiring example for others. It does not affect us in the way a noble idea does. But neither do we have to postulate an inscrutable metaphysical causality to explain the universality of its effects or the absolute validity of a given legal or cultic framework of thought which allows for vicarious substitution. It affects us because as persons we participate in him, are part of him by being incorporated into his person or, as C. F. D. Moule has put it, because it is 'the effect of the death or sufferings of the one on the many in terms of a corporate structure of relationship' (1980, 115). This corporate relationship, however, is not a spatio-temporal but an eschatological reality. It is an action of God the Father, Son and Spirit which constitutes and maintains Jesus Christ as an inclusive person who by incorporating us into him brings us into personal communion with God. Christ's relationship to us is thus not that of a vicarious substitution for us in a fictional (legal or cultic) transaction between humanity and God. Rather he is to be conceived as the *representative* or *mediator* who in his very person presents or mediates God to us and us to God, thus showing the vital differences between the creator and the creation not to be a lethal separation: in and through him we, though mortal beings, live in the eternal community with the immortal God.

The saving efficacy of his death for us is thus not to be conceived in terms of a work from the merits of which we profit. Not in what he has done (his work) but in who he is (his person) rests our salvation. He is not merely the *exemplum* but the *sacramentum* of our salvation: in him salvation *is achieved*, and it is achieved *for every one of us*. By being incorporated into his person we participate in this *sacramentum*; and because this participation is not the result of any activity on our part, it is not bound to end with our death as human agents. As an inclusive person Christ became not only one of us but one with each of us and because of our mortality this at-one-ment with us inevitably involved death. Yet if he is one with us even in death, we are not even in death separated from him and thus from God's paternal love. By incorporating the life and death of each of us into himself, he integrates our individual stories in his own story and thus provides them with a pre-history and post-history that stretches far beyond the beginning and end of our individual stories and common human story. We thus acquire a past and a future which transcends our individual past and future not by dissolving the individuality and particularity of our story but by providing it with the context that brings out its real significance: we are part of a larger story, the story of God's dealings with his creation.

Christians, who by the Holy Spirit are brought to experience their sacramental existence in Christ, know that because of Christ's at-one-ment with us our lives conform beyond the individual narrative structure of our particular stories to the pattern of Christ's own story. They therefore hope that they participate not only in his past but also in his future. Thus in confessing that Christ has died for us they affirm that he wanted to be one with us even in death and thus proclaim the hope that we shall be one with him in his resurrection. His story provides the pattern of our stories so that what is true of him is and will be true of each and every one of us: 'apethanen – etaphē – egēgerta'. He died – he was buried – he rose again.

NOTES

1 As to the problem of its confessional status, see Wright (1981), pp. 123–5.
2 A somewhat similar view seems to have been adopted by Young (1975, 12), who states with respect to the sacrificial imagery of the traditional language of the Church that 'to open up again a wider perspective on the subject could enhance mutual understanding among Christians of different traditions'. This I do not wish to dispute. But while it is one thing to hold the view, highly debatable in itself, that 'sacrifice is integral to a religious outlook' (p. 136), it is quite another to draw the conclusion that it forms a certain common Catholic basis for *doctrinal* statement. I do not agree with the former, but in what follows I shall concentrate only on the latter.
3 The New Testament evidence is reviewed by Wendland (1960), Brown (1978) and Sykes (1980) and summarized and related to later developments by Young (1975, Part 1) and Gubler (1977).
4 That Jesus himself understood his death as a representative sacrifice is argued or

CHRIST DIED FOR US

presupposed by, for example, Jeremias (1966; 1972, 277ff., 288ff.); Patsch (1972); Goppelt (1975, 234ff., 241ff., 261ff.); Pesch (1978); Schürmann (1979; 1980); Hengel (1980; 1981, 72–3); Stuhlmacher (1980); O'Neill (1981); Janowski (1982). It has been criticized by Gray (1925, 397); Kümmel (1974, 90ff.; 1978; 1980); and Roloff (1977, 211ff.).

5 Beattie follows Evans-Pritchard 'in excluding from consideration in the context of sacrifice such practices . . . as the pouring of libations, the offering of food and drink at shrines, and so on' (1980, 31). Of course, the concept may be used in a much more comprehensive way. But this involves the danger of its being emptied of its specific content: the more practices it comprehends, the less informative it is. For the sake of conceptual clarity we should not try to reduce all religious practices to kinds of sacrifice but rather understand sacrifice as one distinctive religious practice among others. Sacrifices, though not all religious activities, are of *symbolic structure*: they are *for* something, *to* someone and usually (though not invariably) substitutionary in character.

6 The process of spiritualization is in constant danger of turning into a process of secularization. The former takes place within the religious system and involves a shift in the understanding of 'sacrifice' from its cultic to its wider religious and ethical implications. The latter is the transposition of the notion into a different system altogether with the progressive loss of its symbolic structure. In the end any death that takes place within the context of some larger cause (e.g. war) may qualify as sacrifice.

7 This may be due to a hermeneutical confusion. The variety 'in the interpretation of Christ's sacrificial death' (Young 1975, 123) is one thing; the variety of interpretations of Christ's atoning death for us, one of which is the sacrificial understanding, is quite another. Not the interpretations of Christ's sacrificial death, but the sacrificial interpretation of Christ's death for us is the problem of the sacrificial language of salvation.

8 For example, as in Ignatius and Gregory Nazianzen, as 'medicine of immortality, the antidote against death' (Ignatius, *Epistle to the Ephesians* xx, 2), when Christ is understood as the 'one physician, fleshly and spiritual, begotten and unbegotten' (*ibid.*, VII, 2).

9 Moule (1980, 53–4) makes a similar point by speaking of 'some sort of spiritual *contact*', the 'contact of the many with the one'.

10 See Moule's distinction between 'evolution' and 'development' (1980, 1ff.).

11 For what follows, see Dalferth 1984, ch. 3.

12 See Luther's ontology of *coram*-relations: Joest (1967); Ebeling (1979, 346–55).

Baker, J. (1981). 'Carried about by Every Wind?': The Development of Doctrine. In *Believing in the Church. The Corporate Nature of Faith*, The Doctrine Commission of the Church of England, pp. 262–85. London: SPCK

Beattie, J.H.M. (1980). On Understanding Sacrifice. In *Sacrifice*, ed. M.F.C. Bourdillon and M. Fortes, pp. 29–44. London: Academic Press

Beck, B.E. (1981). *Imitatio Christi* and the Lucan Passion Narrative. In *Suffering and Martyrdom in the New Testament*, ed. W. Horbury and B. McNeil, pp. 28–47. Cambridge: Cambridge University Press

Brown, C. (1978). Sacrifice. In *The New International Dictionary of New Testament Theology*, pp. 415–36. Exeter: Paternoster Press

Dalferth, I. U. (1981). *Religiöse Rede von Gott*. Munich: Kaiser
 (1984). *Existenz Gottes und christlicher Glaube. Skizzen zu einer eschatologischen Ontologie*. Munich: Kaiser

Dalferth, I. U. and E. Jüngel (1981). Person und Gottebenbildlichkeit. In *Christlicher Glaube in Moderner Gesellschaft*, ed. F. Böckler *et al.*, vol.xxiv, pp. 57–99. Freiburg: Herder

Ebeling, G. (1979). *Dogmatik des Christlichen Glaubens*, vol. i. Tübingen: Mohr

Gayford, S. C. (1924). *Sacrifice and Priesthood, Jewish and Christian*. London: Methuen

Goppelt, L. (1975). *Theologie des Neuen Testaments*, vol. i: *Jesu Wirken In seiner theologischen Bedeutung*, ed. J. Roloff. Göttingen: Vandenhoek & Ruprecht

Gray, G. B. (1925). *Sacrifice in the Old Testament. Its Theory and Practice*. Repr. New York 1971 (The Library of Biblical Studies), ed. H. M. Orbinsky

Grensted, L. W. (1920). *A Short History of the Doctrine of the Atonement*. Manchester: Manchester University Press (rep. 1962)

Gubler, M.-L. (1977). *Die Frühesten Deutungen des Todes Jesu*. Freiburg: Vandenhoek & Ruprecht

Hahn, F. (1967). Die altestamentlichen Motive in der urchristlichen Abendmahlsüberlieferung. *Evangelische Theologie* 27 (1967) 337–74
 (1970). *Der urchristliche Gottesdienst*. Stuttgart: Katholisches Bibelwerk

Hengel, M. (1980). Der stellvertretende Sühnetod Jesu, *Internationale Katholische Zeitscrift* 9, 1–25, 135–47
 (1981). *The Atonement. A Study of the Origins of the Doctrine in the New Testament*. London: SCM Press

Hicks, F. C. N. (1930). *The Fullness of Sacrifice. An Essay in Reconciliation*. London: Macmillan

Hofius, O. (1976). *Der Christushymnus Philipper 2, 6–11: Untersuchungen zu Gestalt und Aussage eines Urchristlichen Psalms*. Tübingen: Mohr

Janowski, B. (1982). Auslösung des verwirkten Lebens. Zur Geschichte und Struktur der biblischen Lösegeldvorstellung. *Zeitschrift für Theologie und Kirche* 79, 25–59

Jeremias, J. (1966). *The Eucharistic Words of Jesus* (2nd edn). London: SCM Press
 (1972). *New Testament Theology*, vol. i: *The Proclamation of Jesus*. London: SCM Press

Joest, W. (1967). *Ontologie der Person bei Luther*. Göttingen: Vandenhoeck & Ruprecht

Knox, J. (1959). *The Death of Christ. The Cross in New Testament History and Faith*. London: Collins

Kümmel, W. G. (1974). *The Theology of the New Testament*. London: SCM Press
 (1978). Jesusforschung seit 1965. iv. *Theologische Rundschau* 43, 233–65
 (1980). Jesusforschung seit 1965, vi. *Theologische Rundschau* 45, 293–337

Lash, N. (1981). What might martyrdom mean? In *Suffering and Martyrdom in the New Testament*, ed. W. Horbury and B. McNeil, pp. 183–98. Cambridge: Cambridge University Press

McKelvey, R. J. (1969). *The New Temple*. London: Oxford University Press

Meyer, C. S. (1967). Melanchthon's Influence on English Thought in the Sixteenth Century. *Miscellanea Historiae Ecclesiasticae* (Louvain) 2, 163–85

Moule, C.F.D. (1980). *The Origin of Christology*. Cambridge: Cambridge University Press

O'Neill, J.C. (1981). Did Jesus Teach that his Death would be Vicarious as well as Typical? In *Suffering and Martyrdom in the New Testament*, ed. W. Horbury and B. McNeil, pp. 9–27. Cambridge: Cambridge University Press

Patsch, H. (1972). *Abendmahl und historischer Jesus*. Stuttgart: Calwer Verlag

Pesch, R. (1978). Das Abendmahl und Jesu Todesverständnis. *Quaestiones Disputatae* (Freiburg: Herder)

Quick, O.C. ([1938] 1963). *Doctrines of the Creed. Their Basis in Scripture and their Meaning Today*. London: Collins (Fontana Library)

Roloff, J. (1977). *Neues Testament*. Neukirchen: Neukirchner Verlag

Schillebeeckx, E. (1980). *Christ. The Christian Experience in the Modern World*. London: SCM Press

Schürmann, H. (1979). Jesu ureigenes Todesverständnis. In *Begegnung mit dem Wort. Festschrift für H. Zimmermann*, ed. J. Zmijewski and E. Nellessen, pp. 273–309. Bonn: Hanstein

  (1980). Jesu Todesverständnis im Verstehenshorizont seiner Umwelt. *Theologie und Glaube* 70, 141–60

Soelle, D. (1975). *Suffering*. London: Darton, Longman and Todd

Stuhlmacher, P. (1980). Existenzstellvertretung für die Vielen: Mk 10, 45 (Mt 20, 28). In *Werden und Wirken des Alten Testaments. Festschrift für C. Westermann*, ed. R. Albertz *et al.*, pp. 412–27. Göttingen: Vandenhoek & Ruprecht

Sweet, J.P.M. (1981). Maintaining the Testimony of Jesus: the Suffering of Christians in the Revelation of John. In *Suffering and Martyrdom in the New Testament*, ed. W. Horbury and B. McNeil, pp. 101–17. Cambridge: Cambridge University Press

Sykes, S.W. (1980). Sacrifice in the New Testament and Christian Theology. In *Sacrifice*, ed. M.F.C. Bourdillon and M. Fortes, pp. 61–83. London: Academic Press

Wendland, H.D. (1960). Opfer (III. 'Im NT'). In *Die Religion in Geschichte und Gegenwart*, vol. IV (3rd edn), cols. 1647–51. Tübingen: Mohr

Wenschkewitz, H. (1932). *Die Spiritualisierung der Kultusbegriffe Tempel, Priester und Opfer im Neuen Testament*, Angelos-Beiheft 4 (Leipzig)

Wenz, G. (1982). Die Lehre vom Opfer Christi im Herrenmahl als Problem ökumenischer Theologie. *Kerygma und Dogma* 28 (1982), 7–41

Wright, T. (1981). Doctrine Declared. In *Believing in the Church. The Corporate Nature of Faith*, The Doctrine Commission of the Church of England. London: SPCK, 108–41

Young, F.M. (1975). *Sacrifice and the Death of Christ*. London: SPCK

INDEX OF BIBLICAL AND ANCIENT REFERENCES

Compiled by the Reverend Peter Eaton, The Fellows' Chaplain of Magdalen College, Oxford

326

4. OTHER ANCIENT SOURCES

INDEX OF PERSONS

Compiled by the Reverend Peter Eaton, The Fellows' Chaplain of Magdalen College, Oxford